OUTDOOR LIFE GUN DATA BOOK

BY
F. Philip Rice

Drawings by Miki

Published by Outdoor Life Books
Distributed to trade by Stackpole Books

Published by
  Outdoor Life Books
  Grolier Book Clubs, Inc.
  380 Madison Avenue
  New York, NY 10017

Distributed to the trade by
  Stackpole Books
  Cameron and Kelker Streets
  Harrisburg, PA 17105

Library of Congress Cataloging-in-Publication Data

Rice, F. Philip.
  Outdoor life gun data book.

  Includes index.
  1. Hunting guns. 2. Pistols. I. Title
II. Title: Gun data book.
SK274.R52 1986   799.2'0283   86-12709
ISBN 0-943822-75-0

Second Edition, Revised and Updated, 1986

Second Printing, 1987

Manufactured in the United States of America

Contents

Ballistics

Caliber, Cartridge, and Bullet Recommendations

Iron Sights

Telescope Sights

Sighting and Aiming

Handloading Rifle Cartridges

PART IV. MISCELLANEOUS

PART ONE

Rifles and Ammunition

Types of Rifles

Semiautomatic, or autoloader. This rifle fires each time the trigger is pulled. The empty case is ejected and a new cartridge chambered by the action of the gun's recoil or spent gases. The advantage of the semiautomatic is firepower. The disadvantages are danger, below-average accuracy and proneness to malfunction.

Bolt action. This action depends on a manually operated steel bolt assembly to chamber and seal a cartridge, and then to eject the spent case. The advantages are ease of disassembly and cleaning, and superior accuracy. The disadvantage is slowness in repeated firing.

Lever Action. When the finger lever is moved downward and forward, the empty case is ejected, allowing another cartridge to be pushed onto the carrier. When the lever is returned, the bolt pushes the cartridge into the changer ready for firing. The advantages are lightness, speed of operation. Disadvantages, not as accurate or as strong as the bolt action.

Slide, or pump action. A backward and forward movement of the forend ejects the spent case, rechambers a fresh cartridge, and recocks the rifle. Advantages are speed of reloading and firing; disadvantage is less accuracy.

Single-shot. This rifle comes in either a breakopen or bolt action. It is most often a beginner's gun, used for plinking or target shooting, where speed in refiring is not needed.

U. S. Centerfire Rifles: Military Style Autoloading

Model	Action	Caliber	Capacity	Weight
Auto-Ordnance 27A-1	Semiauto	.45ACP	30-shot mag.	11½ lbs.
Auto-Ordnance 1927A-3	Semiauto	.22	10-, 30-, 50-shot mag.	7 lbs.
Bush-master Auto Rifle	Auto	.223	30-shot mag.	6½ lbs.
Colt AR-15 Sporter	Semiauto	.223	5-shot mag.	7½ lbs. 5.8 lbs. with collapsible stock
Commando Arms Carbine	Semiauto	9mm or .45ACP	5-, 15-, 30-, or 90-shot mag.	8 lbs.
Demro Tac-1M Carbine	Auto	9mm or .45ACP	32-shot (9mm), 30-shot (.45ACP)	7¾ lbs.
Demro XF-7 Wasp Carbine	Auto	9mm or .45ACP	32-shot (9mm), 30-shot (.45 ACP)	7¾ lbs.
Iver Johnson M-1 Carbines PM30G, PM 5.7	Semiauto, gas operated	.30U.S. 5.7MMJ	15- or 30-shot mag.	6½ lbs.

Barrel	Length Overall	Sights	Features
16″	39½″	Blade front, open rear, adj.	Also in Deluxe, Lightwt., and Pistol Models
16″	39½″	Blade front, open rear, adj.	Like 27A-1 except .22 caliber
18½″	37½″	Post front, adj., quick-flip rear peep, adj.	Maple or nylon-coated folding stock
20″ 16″ (with collapsible stock)	38⅜″ 32″ with collapsible stock	Post front, quick-flip, rear, adj., or with 3x scope	Polycarbonate stock or collapsible stock
16½″	37″	Blade front, peep rear	Walnut stock, also comes blued or nickle-plated
16⅞″	35¾″	Blade front, open rear, adj.	Walnut stock
16⅞″	35¾″	Blade front, open rear, adj.	Like Tac 1M except collapsible stock
12″ or 18″	29½″ 35½″	Click adj. peep rear	Hardwood stock, also blue (PM30P), stainless steel (PM30PS), and PM30s (Sporter)

Auto Ordnance 27 A-1

U. S. Centerfire Rifles: Military Style Autoloading

Model	Action	Caliber	Capacity	Weight
Iver Johnson PP30 Super Enforcer	Semiauto, gas operated	.30	15- or 30-shot mag.	4 lbs
Ruger Mini-14 .223 Carbine	Auto	.223	5-shot mag.	6.4 lbs
Springfield Armory M-1 Garand Rifle	Semiauto, gas operated	.30/06	8-shot mag.	9½ lbs
Springfield Armory MIA Rifle	Semiauto, gas operated	7.62mm Nato (.308)	5-, 10-, or 20-shot mag.	8¾ lbs
Springfield Armory BM-59	Semiauto, gas operated or selective fire	7.62mm Nato (.308)	20-shot mag.	9½ lbs
Universal 1003 Autoloading Carbine	Auto	.30M1	5-shot mag.	5½ lbs
Universal 1256 "Ferret"	Auto	.256	5-shot mag.	5½ lbs
Universal 2566 "Ferret"	Auto	.256	5-shot mag.	5½ lbs
Universal Model 1006	Auto	.30M1	5-shot mag.	6 lbs
Universal 1005 SB Carbine	Auto	.30M1	5-shot mag.	6 lbs
Universal 5000 PT Carbine	Auto	.30M1	5-shot mag.	5½ lbs
Universal Commemorative 1981 Carbine	Auto	.30M1	5-, 15-, or 30-shot mag.	5½ lbs
Weaver Arms Nighthawk	Semiauto	9mm Para.	25-shot mag.	8½ lbs
Wilkinson "Terry" Carbine	Semiauto	9mm Para.	30-shot mag.	7 lbs 2 oz

Barrel	Length Overall	Sights	Features
9½″		Adj.	Also comes PPS (stainless steel)
18½″	37½″	Ramp front, adj. rear	Hardwood stock, also in stainless steel
24″	43½″	Blade front, click adj. peep rear	Walnut stock, also comes National Match, Ultra Match
25¹/₁₆″	44¼″	Blade front, click adj. peep rear, also 3–9X 2ART scope	Walnut or birch, also comes Match Grade, Super Match, or MIA-A1 assault rifle. Equivalent to M-14 rifle
17½″	38½″	Blade front, click adj. peep rear	Std. Italian model, or Ital-Alpine, or Alpine Paratrooper, or Nigerian Mark IV Model
16″ or 18″	35½″	Blade front with wings, adj. rear	Hardwood stock
18″	35½″	Blade front with wings, adj. rear	Same as 1003 Auto
18″	35½″	Blade front with wings, adj. rear	Stainless steel
16″ or 18″	35½″	Blade front with wings, adj. rear	Same as 1003 except stainless steel
16″ or 18″	35½″	Blade front with wings, adj. rear	Same as 1003 except super-mirrored Blue finish, also Nickel (1010N), 18K Gold (1015G), Black Teflon (1020TB), or Camouflage Olive Teflon (1025TCO)
18″	36″	Blade front with wings, adj. rear	Same as 1003 except folding stock
16″ or 18″	35½″	Weaver scope	Black walnut stock, like 1003
16.1″	26½″ (stock retracted)	Hooded bead front, adj. open V rear	Retractable metal frame stock
16³/₁₆″	28½″	Williams adj.	Maple stock

U. S. Centerfire Rifles: Sporting Autoloading

Model	Action	Caliber	Capacity	Weight
Browning High-Power Auto Rifle	Semiauto, gas operated	.243, .270, .30/06, .308	4-shot mag.	7⅜ lbs
Browning Magnum Auto	Semiauto, gas operated	7mm Mag., .300 Win. Mag.	3-shot mag.	8⅜ lbs
Remington Model Four Auto	Semiauto, gas operated	.243, 6mm, .270, 7mm Exp., .308, .30/06	4-shot mag.	7½ lbs
Ruger .44 Autoloading Carbine	Piston, gas operated	.44	4-shot mag.	5¾ lbs

Remington Model Four Centerfire Autoloader

U. S. Centerfire Rifles: Bolt Action

Model	Action	Caliber	Capacity	Weight
Alpha 1 Bolt Action Rifle		.243, 7mm/08, .308	4-shot mag.	6–6½ lbs
Bighorn Bolt Action Rifle		Custom .22/250 through all std. Mag.		6¾ lbs
Browning BBR Bolt Action Rifle		.25/06, .270, .30/06, 7mm Mag., .300 Mag., .338 Mag.	4-shot (std.) 3-shot (Mag.)	8 lbs
Browning BBR Short Action		.22/250, .243, .257, 7mm/08, .308	4-shot mag.	7½ or 9½ lbs

Barrel	Length Overall	Sights	Features
22"	43"	Adj. folding leaf rear, ramp front/gold bead. Tapped for scope	5 grades
24"	45"	Same as std.	Same as std. except cal.
22"	42"	Gold bead front on ramp, step rear, adj.	Model 7400 does not have Monte Carlo stock, Collector's edit. has 24K gold inlays, .30/06 only, only 1500 made
18½"	36¾"	1⁄16" front, folding leaf rear, adj. Tapped for scope	Walnut stock

Barrel	Length Overall	Sights	Features
20"	39½"	Tapped for scope	Side safety, walnut Monte Carlo stock
To customer specs. 2 bbls. supplied		Tapped for scope	Mauser action, several grades
22"	44½"	Tapped for scope	Walnut Monte Carlo stock, adj. trig., from Japan by Browning
22" or 24"		Tapped for scope	Same as BBR Bolt Action

U. S. Centerfire Rifles: Bolt Action (*cont.*)

Model	Action	Caliber	Capacity	Weight
Colt Sauer Rifle		.25/06, .270, .30/06, 7mm Mag., .300 Weath. Mag., .300 Win. Mag.	3- and 4-shot mag.	8 lbs (std.)
Colt Short Action Rifle		.22/250, .243, .308	3-shot mag.	7½ lbs
Colt Sauer Grand African		.458 Win. Mag.	3-shot mag.	10½ lbs
Harrington & Richardson 340 Rifle		.243, .7 × 57, .270, .308, .30/06	5-shot mag.	7¼ lbs
Kimber 82 Hornet Sporter		.22 Hornet	3-shot mag.	6½ lbs
Kimber 82 Super America		.22LR, Mag., Hornet	3-shot mag.	6½ lbs
Remington Seven Bolt Action Rifle		.222, .243, 7mm/08, 6mm, .308	5-shot (.222), others 4-shot	6¼ lbs
Remington 700ADL Bolt Action Rifle		.222, .22/250, 6mm, .243, .25/06, .270, .308, .30/06		7 lbs
Remington 700BDL Bolt Action Rifle		.222, .223, .22/250, 6mm, .243, .25/06, .270, 7mm/08, .308, .30/06		7 lbs
Remington 700 BDL Bolt Action Rifle		.17 Rem., 7mm Rem. Mag., .300 Win. Mag., 8mm Rem. Mag.		7½ lbs
Remington 700C Custom				
Remington 700BLL Varmint		.222, .223, .22/250, 6mm, .243, .25/06, 7mm/08, .308		9 lbs
Remington 700 Safari		.375 H&H, .458 Win. Mag.		

Barrel	Length Overall	Sights	Features
24"	43¾"	Tapped for scope	Tang-type safety, also comes in Grand Alaskan (.375 H&H)
24"	43"	Tapped for scope	Same as Colt Sauer
24"	44½"	Ivory bead hooded ramp front, sliding rear, adj.	Monte Carlo stock, tang-type safety
22"	43"	Tapped for scope	Mauser action, adj. trig., walnut stock
22½"	41"	Blade front on ramp, open rear, adj.	Walnut stock, all steel construction
22½"	41"	With or without scope	Classic stock, similar to 82 Hornet
18½"	37½"	Ramp front, open rear, adj.	Walnut scope
22" or 24"	41½"–43½"	Gold bead ramp front, step adj. rear/windage screw	Also comes in left hand (700 BDL left), slide safety, Monte Carlo stock
22" or 24"	41½"–43½"	Same as 700ADL	Also in Peerless and Premier Grade
	44½"	Same as 700 ADL	Mag. model
Choice of 20", 22", or 24"		With or without sights	Same as 700BDL
24"	43½"	None	Same as 700BDL
			Same as 700 BDL

U. S. Centerfire Rifles: Bolt Action (*cont.*)

Model	Action	Caliber	Capacity	Weight
Remington 700 Classic Rifle		.22/250, 6mm, .243, .270, .30/06, 7mm Rem. Mag., 300 H&H Mag.		7 lbs
Remington 788 Bolt Action Rifle		.22/250, .222, .223, 7mm/08, .243, .308	4-shot mag.	7–7½ lbs
Ruger 77 Bolt Action Rifle		.22/250, .220 Swift, .243, 6mm, .308, .358 Win., .458 Win. Mag.	5-shot mag.	6¾ lbs
Ruger 77 Ultra Light		.243, .308		6 lbs
Ruger 77 Magnum		.25/06, .270, .280, 7 × 57, .30/06, 7mm Rem. Mag., .300 Win., .338 Win. Mag., .458 Win. Mag.	5-shot (.30/06) 3-shot (.458 Win. Mag.)	
Ruger 77 Magnum Round Top		.25/06, .270, .30/06, 7mm Rem. Mag.		
Ruger International 77 Rifle		.243, .308		6 lbs
Ruger 77 Varmint		.22/250, .220 Swift, .243, 6mm, .25/06, .280, .308		9 lbs
Savage 110C Bolt Action Rifle		.22/250, .243, .270, .308, .30/06, .300 Win. Mag., 7mm Rem. Mag.	4-shot 3-shot (Mag.)	7 lbs
Savage 110S Silhouette Rifle		.308, 7mm/08	5-shot mag.	8 lbs
Savage 110V Varmint Rifle		.22/250 only		
Smith & Wesson M1500 Bolt Action Rifle		.222, .223, .243, .25/06, .270, .30/06, .308, 7mm Rem. Mag., .300 Win. Mag.		7½–7¾ lbs
Smith & Wesson 1500 Mountaineer Rifle		.223, .243, .270, .30/06, 7mm Rem. Mag.		
Smith & Wesson 1500 Varmint Deluxe Rifle		.222, .22/250, .223		9 lbs 5 oz

Barrel	Length Overall	Sights	Features
22" (6mm, .243, .270, .30/06), 24" (.22/250, 7mm, .300 H&H)	43½"	Tapped for scope	Classic version of M700 ADL with straight stock
18½" 24" (.223 and .22/250)	41⅝"	Blade ramp front, open rear, adj.	Also with 4X scope
22" 24" (Swift)	42"	Optional gold bead ramp front, folding leaf rear, adj.	Tang safety, scope optional
20"			Similar to std. Model 77
22" (7 × 57, .280, .30/06), 24" (all other calibers)	Varies with cal.		Similar to std. 77 except Mag. action
		Open sights std. equipment	Same as Mag. 77 except rd. top receiver
18½"	38½"		Similar to std. 77, Mannlicher-style stock
24"	44"	Tapped for scope	Adj. trig.
22" 24""" (Mag.)	43"	Ramp front, open rear, adj. Tapped for scope	Walnut Monte Carlo stock, Model 110 CL left hand in .243, .270, .30/06, .308, and 7mm Rem. Mag.
22"	43"	None. Tapped for scope	Top tang safety
26"			Similar to Model 110C
22" 24" (7mm Rem. Mag.)	42" 42½" (.270, .30/06, 7mm)	Hooded ramp gold bead front, open notch rear, adj. Tapped for scope	Walnut Monte Carlo stock, also in Deluxe without sights
22" 24" (7mm)		None. Tapped for scope	Similar to M1500 except satin-finished stock
22" heavy bbl.			Adj. trig., similar to std. 1500

Weatherby Mark V Deluxe

U. S. Centerfire Rifles: Bolt Action (*cont.*)

Model	Action	Caliber	Capacity	Weight
Smith & Wesson 1700 LS "Classic Hunter"		.243, .270, .30/06	5-shot mag.	
Stevens 110E Bolt Action		.270, .308, .30/06, .243	4-shot mag.	6¾ lbs
Weatherby Mark V. Bolt Action Rifle, also Lazer Mark V. (with laser carving)		All Weath. cal., .22/250, .30/06		6½–10½ lbs
Weatherby Fibermark Rifle		.240 Weath. Mag. thru .340 Weath. Mag.		
Weatherby Mark V. Rifle Left Hand		All Weath. cal. except .224, .22/250 (and 26″ No. 2 contour .300 WM)		
Weatherby Vanguard Bolt Action Rifle		.25/06, .243, .270, .30/06, 7mm, .300 Win. Mag.	5-shot 3-shot (7mm and .300 Win. Mag.)	7⅞ lbs
Winchester 70 XTR Sporter Magnum		.264 Win. Mag., 7mm Rem. Mag., .300 Win. Mag., .338 Win. Mag.	3-shot mag.	7¾ lbs
Winchester 70 XTR Sporter		.270, .30/06	5-shot mag.	
Winchester 70 XTR Sporter Varmint Rifle		.223, .22/250, .243 only		9¾ lbs
Winchester 70 Westerner		.223, .243, .270, .308, .30/06, 7mm Rem. Mag., .300 Win. Mag.		
Winchester 70 XTR Super Express Magnum		.375 H&H, .458 Win. Mag.	3-shot mag.	8½ lbs

Barrel	Length Overall	Sights	Features
			Similar to std. 1500 except classic-style stock
22″	43″	Gold bead ramp front, step adj. rear. Tapped for scope	Walnut Monte Carlo stock
24″ or 26″	43¼″–46½″	Optional	Adj. trig., thumb safety, walnut Monte Carlo stock
24″ or 26″			Same as std. except fiberglass stock
24″	44½″	Optional	Walnut stock, adj. trig.
24″	44½″	Hooded ramp front, adj. folding leaf rear	Walnut Monte Carlo stock, 3-position safety
			Same as Sporter Mag.
24″	44½″		Walnut Monte Carlo stock
22″ 24″ (Mag.)		Iron sights and/or 4X scope	
24″ (.375) 22″ (.458)		Hooded ramp front, open rear	Walnut Monte Carlo stock

U. S. Centerfire Rifles: Bolt Action (*cont.*)

Model	Action	Caliber	Capacity	Weight
Winchester 70 XTR Featherweight		.243, .257, .270, 7 × 57, .30/06, .308		6¾ lbs
Winslow Basic Rifle		.22/250, .243, .244, .257, .308, .30/06, .280, .270, .25/06, .284, .358, 7mm plus following Mag.: .300 Weath., .300 Win., .338 Win., .358 Norma, .375 H&H, .458 Win., .257 Weath., .264 Win., .270 Weath., 7mm Weath., 7mm Rem., .300 H&H, .308 Norma	4-shot mag.	7–9 lbs
Winslow Varmint		17 cal. available incl. .17/222, .17/222 Mag., .17/233, .222 Rem., .223		

U. S. Centerfire Rifles: Lever Action

Model	Action	Caliber	Capacity	Weight
Browning B-92 Lever Action		.357 Mag., .44 Rem. Mag.	11-shot mag.	5 lbs 8 oz
Browning BLR Lever Action Rifle		.22/250, .257 Roberts, 7mm/08, .308, .358	4-shot mag.	6 lbs 15 oz
Marlin 1894 Lever Action Carbine		.44 Mag.	10-shot mag.	6 lbs
Marlin 1894CS Carbine		.38 Spec., .357 Mag.	9-shot mag.	6 lbs
Marlin 1894C Carbine 357		.357 Mag.	9-shot mag.	6 lbs
Marlin 1895S Lever Action Rifle		.45/70	4-shot mag.	7½ lbs

Barrel	Length Overall	Sights	Features
22″		Ramped blade front sight	Walnut stock, classic
24″ or 26″	43″ (std.) 45″ (Mag.)	Tapped for scope	Two different stocks, also in Grade Crown (carving and inlays) and 3 other grades: Royal, Imperial, Emperor with different carving, engraving
			With 2 stocks

Barrel	Length Overall	Sights	Features
20″	37½″	Post front, cloverleaf rear with notched elev. ramp	From Japan by Browning
20″	39¾″	Gold bead hooded front ramp, square notch adj. rear	Walnut stock, half-cock hammer safety, from Japan by Browning
20″	37½″	Hooded ramp front, semi-buckhorn adj. Tapped for scope	Walnut stock, Model 1894S has hammer safety
18½″	35½″	Like 1894	Similar to 1894S except chambering
18½″	35½″	Bead front, adj. semi-buckhorn folding rear	Walnut stock, tapped for scope
22″	40½″	Bead front, semi-buckhorn folding rear	Walnut stock, tapped for scope

U. S. Centerfire Rifles: Lever Action (*cont.*)

Model	Action	Caliber	Capacity	Weight
Marlin 336C Lever Action Carbine		.30/30 or .35 Rem.	6-shot mag.	7 lbs
Marlin 336 Extra-Range Carbine		.307 or .356	5-shot mag.	
Marlin 336 T Lever Action Carbine		.30/30		6¾ lbs
Marlin 30A Lever Action Carbine		.30/30	6-shot mag.	7 lbs
Marlin 444S Lever Action Sporter		.444	4-shot mag.	7½ lbs
Marlin 375 Rifle		.375	5-shot mag.	6¾ lbs
Mossberg Roy Rogers 479RR		.30/30	5-shot mag.	6¾ lbs
Mossberg 479PCA Lever Action Rifle		.30/30	6-shot mag.	7 lbs
Savage 99E		.250, .300, .243, .308	5-shot mag.	7 lbs
Savage 99C		.243, .308, 7mm/08	5-shot mag.	6¾ lbs
Winchester 94XTR Angle Eject		.307 Win., .356, .375	6-shot mag.	7 lbs
Winchester 94 Lever Action Carbine		.30/30	6-shot mag.	6½ lbs

Winchester 94 Lever Action Carbine

Barrel	Length Overall	Sights	Features
20"	38½"	Ramp front, semi-buckhorn folding rear, adj.	Walnut stock, Model 336CS has hammer safety
		Same as 336C	Similar to 336CS except cal., has hammer safety
18½"	37"	Same as 336C	Same as 336C except straight stock
20"	38½"	Ramp front, adj. semi-buckhorn folding rear	Same as 336C except checkered walnut, Model 30AS has hammer safety
22"	40½"	Hooded ramp front, folding semi-buckhorn rear, adj.	Walnut stock, Model 444SS has hammer safety
20"	38½"	Same as 444S	Same as 444S
18"	36½"	Gold bead ramp front, semi-buckhorn adj. rear	Ltd. edition
20"	38½"	Bead on ramp front, open rear, adj.	Blue finish, hammer block safety
22"	39¾"	Ramp front, adj. ramp, rear sight	Slide safety
22"	41¾"	Hooded ramp front, adj. rear	Walnut Monte Carlo stock
20"	38⅝"	Hooded ramp front, semi-buckhorn rear, adj.	Walnut Monte Carlo stock
16" or 20"	37¾"	Bead front sight on ramp, open rear	Walnut straight stock, half-cock hammer safety

U. S. Centerfire Rifles: Lever Action (*cont.*)

Model	Action	Caliber	Capacity	Weight
Winchester 94 Wrangler		.32 Spec.	5-shot mag.	6⅛ lbs
Winchester 94 Std.		.30/30	6-shot mag.	6½ lbs
Winchester 94XTR		.30/30	6-shot mag.	6½ lbs
Winchester 94 Trapper		.30/30	5-shot mag.	6⅛ lbs
Winchester 94 Antique		.30/30	6-shot mag.	6½ lbs
Winchester Chief Crazy Horse Commemorative		.38/55	7-shot mag.	

U. S. Centerfire Rifles: Pump Action

Model	Action	Caliber	Capacity	Weight
Remington Six Slide Action		6mm, .243, .270, .308, .30/06	4-shot mag.	7½ lbs
Remington 7600		Same as Model Six	Same as Six	Same as Six

Remington Model Six Centerfire Pump Action Rifle

Barrel	Length Overall	Sights	Features
16"	33¾"	Hooded blade front sight, semi-buckhorn rear	Roll-engraved
20"	37¾"	Same as 94 Wrangler	Economical version
20"	37¾"	Same as Std.	Same as 94 Std. except finish
16"	33¾"	Same as Std.	
20"	37¾"	Same as Std.	Special "vintage" appearance
24"	41¾"	Dovetailed blade front, buckhorn rear, adj.	Ltd. edition

Barrel	Length Overall	Sights	Features
22"	42"	Gold bead front on ramp, open step rear, adj.	Walnut Monte Carlo stock
Same as Six	Same as Six	Same as Six	Same as Model Six except Monte Carlo stock

U. S. Centerfire Rifles: Single Shot

Model	Action	Caliber	Capacity	Weight
Browning '78 Single-Shot Rifle		.22/250		7¾ lbs (oct. bbl.), 8½ lbs (rd. bbl.)
Harrington & Richardson 171 Calvary		.45/70		7 lbs
Harrington & Richardson 174 Little Big Horn Commemorative Carbine		.45/70		7 lbs 4 oz
Harrington & Richardson 158 Topper Rifle		.30/30, .22 Hornet, .357 Mag., .44 Mag.		6 lbs
Ljutic Recoiless Space Rifle		.22/250, .30/30, .30/06, .308		8¾ lbs
Navy Arms Rolling Block Rifle		.45/70		
Ruger No. 1 Single Shot		.220 Swift, .22/250, .243, 6mm Rem., .25/06, .270, 7 × 57mm, .30/06, 7mm Rem. Mag., .300 Win., .338 Win. Mag., .45/70, .458 Win. Mag., .375 H&H Mag.		8 lbs
Ruger No. 3 Carbine Single Shot		.22 Hornet, .223, .375 Win., .45/70		6 lbs
Thompson/Center Single Shot Rifle		.223 Rem., .22/250, .243 Win., 7mm Rem. Mag., .30/06		6¾ lbs

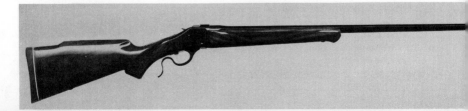

Barrel	Length Overall	Sights	Features
26"	42"	None. Scope mount and rings	Auto ejector, adj. trig., half-cock safety, from Japan by Browning
22"	41"	Blade front, leaf rear, adj.	Replica of 1873 Springfield Carbine
22"	41"	Blade front, tang-mounted aperture rear, adj.	Replica of 1873 Springfield Carbine, Little Big Horn Com.
22"	37"	Blade front, folding rear, adj.	Side lever break-open action
24"	44"	Iron or scope mounts	Anti-recoil mechanism
26½", also in 18", 26", 30" oct. bbl. and 26", 30" half-rd. bbl.		Fixed front, rear, adj.	Available in Buffalo Rife (oct. bbl.) and Creedmore (half-rd., half-oct. bbl.)
22", 24", 26"	42"	3 models have open sights, scope rings	Top tang safety, also Light Sporter, Med. Sporter, Varminter, Tropical Rifle, International
22"	38½"	Gold bead front, adj. folding rear	Top tang safety, adj. trig.
23"	39½"	Blade on ramp front, open rear, adj.	Break-open, dbl. or single set trig., cross-bolt safety

Browning Model B-78 Single-Shot Rifle

U. S. Rimfire Rifles: Military Style Autoloading

Model	Action	Caliber	Capacity	Weight
Auto-Ordnance 1927A-3	Auto	.22LR	10-, 30-, 50-shot mag.	7 lbs
Charter AR-7 Explorer Carbine	Auto	.22LR	8-shot mag.	2½ lbs
U.S. Arms PMAI "Assault" 22	Auto	.22LR	25-shot mag.	5½ lbs
Universal 2200 Leatherneck Carbine	Auto	.22LR	10- or 30-shot mag.	5½ lbs

U. S. Rimfire Rifles: Sporting Autoloading

Model	Action	Caliber	Capacity	Weight
Browning Autoloading Rifle		.22LR or .22S (in Grade I)	11-shot mag.	4¾ lbs
Browning BAR-22		.22LR	15-shot mag.	6½ lbs
Harrington & Richardson 700 Auto		.22 Mag.	5- or 10-shot mag.	6½ lbs
Marlin 990 Semi-Auto Rifle		.22LR	18-shot mag.	5½ lbs
Marlin 995 Semi-Auto Rifle		.22LR	7-shot mag.	5½ lbs
Marlin 60 Semi-Auto Rifle		.22LR	18-shot mag.	5½ lbs
Marlin 70 Auto		.22LR	7-shot mag.	5½ lbs
Marlin 75C Semi-Auto Rifle		.22LR	14-shot mag.	5 lbs
Mossberg 353 Autoloading Rifle		.22LR	7-shot mag.	5 lbs
Mossberg 380 Auto Rifle		.22LR	15-shot mag.	5½ lbs
Mossberg 377 Plinkster Auto Rifle		.22LRD	15-shot mag.	6½ lbs

Barrel	Length Overall	Sights	Features
16″		Blade front, open rear, adj.	Like Model 1927 Thompson
16″	34½″	Square blade front, aperture rear, adj.	Take-down design, Black or Satin Chrome
18″	38½″	Blade front on ramp, open rear, adj.	Stained black stock, made by Mossberg
18″	35¾″	Blade front, peep rear, adj.	Like GI carbine except rimfire

Barrel	Length Overall	Sights	Features
19½″	37″	Gold bead front, folding leaf rear	From Japan by Browning, Grades I, II, III
20¼″	38½″	Gold bead front, folding leaf rear	Cross-bolt safety, from Japan by Browning, Grades I, II
22″	43½″	Blade front, folding leaf rear, Deluxe has scope	Walnut Monte Carlo stock, also in Deluxe
22″	40¾″	Ramp bead front, semi-buckhorn rear, adj.	Walnut Monte Carlo stock
18″	36¾″	Ramp bead front, folding semi-buckhorn rear	Walnut Monte Carlo stock
22″	41″	Ramp front, open adj. rear	Walnut Monte Carlo stock
22″	41″	Ramp front, open rear, adj.	Walnut Monte Carlo stock
18″	36¾″	Ramp front, open rear, adj.	Walnut Monte Carlo stock
18″	38″	Bead on front ramp, U-notch rear, adj.	
20″		Bead front, open rear, adj., 4X scope optional	Walnut stock
20″	40″	Comes with 4X scope	Walnut stock

U. S. Rimfire Rifles: Sporting Autoloading (*cont.*)

Model	Action	Caliber	Capacity	Weight
Remington Nylon 66MB Auto Rifle		.22LR	14-shot mag.	4 lbs
Remington 552A Autoloading Rifle		.22S, .22L, .22LR	S—20-shot; L—17-shot; LR—15-shot	5¾ lbs
Ruger 10/22 Autoloading Carbine		.22LR	10-shot mag.	5 lbs 12 oz
Ruger 10/22 Auto Sporter		.22LR	10-shot mag.	5 lbs
Weatherby Mark XXII Auto Rifle, Clip Model		.22LR	5- or 10-shot clip, 15-shot mag.	6 lbs

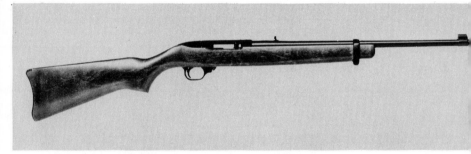

Ruger 10/22 Autoloading Carbine

U. S. Rimfire Rifles: Bolt Action

Model	Action	Caliber	Capacity	Weight
Harrington & Richardson 865 Rifle		.22S, .22L, .22LR	5-shot mag.	5 lbs
Harrington & Richardson 5200 Sporter		.22LR	5-shot mag.	6½ lbs
Kimber 82 Bolt Action Rifle		.22LR, .22 Mag.	5- or 10-shot mag.	6½ lbs
Kimber 82 Super America		.22LR, .22 Mag., .22 Hornet		

Barrel	Length Overall	Sights	Features
19⅝"	38½"	Blade ramp front, open rear, adj.	Nylon stock, top tang safety, Model 66BD has black stock; Model 66AB has black stock, chrome receiver
21"	40"	Bead front, step open rear, adj., Model 552 BDL has blade ramp front	Cross-bolt safety, Model 552 BDL has DuPont finished walnut stock
18½"	36¾"	Gold bead front, folding leaf rear, adj.	Cross-bolt safety, birch stock
18½"	36¾"	Gold bead front, folding leaf rear, adj.	Same as Carbine except walnut stock
24"	42¼"	Gold bead ramp front, 3-leaf folding rear	Single shot selector, Mark XXII Tubular Model has tubular mag.

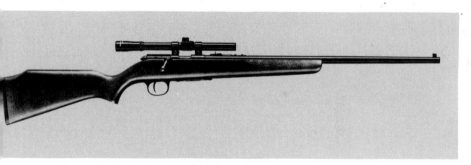

Harrington & Richardson Model 865

Barrel	Length Overall	Sights	Features
22"	39"	Blade front, open rear, step adj.	Walnut Monte Carlo stock, sliding side safety
24"	42"	Hooded ramp front, Lyman rear peep, adj.	Walnut Classic stock
22½"	41"	Blade front on ramp, open rear, adj.	Classic or Cascade stock with or without sights
		With or without scope	Walnut Classic stock

U. S. Rimfire Rifles: Bolt Action (*cont.*)

Model	Action	Caliber	Capacity	Weight
Marlin 780 Bolt Action Rifle		.22S, .22L, .22LR	7-shot mag.	5½ lbs
Marlin 781 Bolt Action Rifle		.22S, .22L .22LR		6 lbs
Marlin 782 Bolt Action Rifle		.22 Mag. only		6 lbs
Marlin 783 Bolt Action Rifle		.22 Mag.	12-shot mag.	
Marlin 25 Bolt Action Repeater				
Marlin 25M Bolt Action Rifle		.22 Mag.	7-shot mag.	
Mossberg 341 Bolt Action Rifle		.22S, .22L, .22LR	7-shot mag.	6½ lbs
Mossberg 640K Chuckster		.22 Mag.	5-shot	6½ lbs
Remington 541-S		.22S, .22L, .22LR	5- or 10-shot mag.	5½ lbs
Remington 581 Rifle		.22S, .22L, .22LR	5-shot mag., also comes with single shot adapter.	4¾ lbs
Remington 582 Rifle		.22S, .22L, .22LR	S—20-shot; L—15-shot; LR—14-shot	5½ lbs
Ruger 22 Rimfire Bolt Action Rifle		.22LR	10-shot mag.	5 lbs

U. S. Rimfire Rifles: Lever Action

Model	Action	Caliber	Capacity	Weight
Browning BL-22 Lever Action Rifle		.22S, .22L, .22LR	S—22-shot; L—17-shot; LR—15-shot mag.	5 lbs
Marlin 1894M Carbine		.22 Mag.	11-shot mag.	6 lbs

Barrel	Length Overall	Sights	Features
22"	41"	Ramp front, folding semi-buckhorn rear, adj.	Gold-plated trig.
			Same as 780 except mag.
			Same as 780 except cal.
			Same as 780
		Ramp front, open rear, adj.	Same as 780 except walnut stock
22"			Same as Model 25
24"	43½"	Bead front, U-notch rear, adj.	Sliding side safety
24"	44¾"	Ramp front with bead, leaf rear, adj.	Monte Carlo stock
24"	42⅝"	None. Tapped for scope	Thumb safety, walnut stock
24"	42⅜"	Bead post front, open rear, screw adj.	Walnut Monte Carlo stock
			Same as 581 except mag.
20"	39¼"	Gold bead front, folding leaf rear, adj.	3-position safety

Barrel	Length Overall	Sights	Features
20"	36¾"	Bead post front, folding leaf rear	Walnut stock, half-cock safety from Japan by Browning
20"	37½"	Ramp front with brass bead, semi-buckhorn folding rear	Straight grip stock, hammer block safety

U. S. Rimfire Rifles: Lever Action (*cont.*)

Model	Action	Caliber	Capacity	Weight
Marlin Golden 39A Lever Action Rifle		.22S, .22L, .22LR	S—26-shot; L—21-shot; LR—19-shot	6½ lbs
Marlin Golden 39M Carbine		.22S, .22L, .22LR	S—21-shot; L—16-shot; LR—15-shot	6 lbs
Winchester 9422 XTR Lever Action Rifle		.22S, .22L, .22LR	S-21-shot, L-17-shot, LR-15-shot	6¼ lbs
Wincester 9422 Annie Oakley Commemorative				

Marlin Golden 39A Lever Action Rifle

U. S. Rimfire Rifles: Pump Action

Model	Action	Caliber	Capacity	Weight
Remington 572 Fieldmaster Pump Rifle		.22S, .22L, .22LR	20-shot (S) 17-shot (L) 14-shot (LR)	5½ lbs

Barrel	Length Overall	Sights	Features
24″	40″	Bead ramp front, folding, semi-buckhorn rear, adj.	Walnut stock
20″	36″	Ramp front with hood, folding rear semi-buckhorn, adj.	Walnut stock
20½″	37⅛″	Hooded ramp front, semi-buckhorn rear, adj.	Walnut stock
			Same as 9422 except gold plating

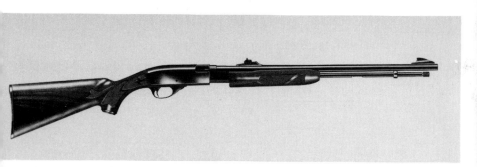

Remington Model 572 BDL Deluxe .22 Rimfire Pump Action Rifle

Barrel	Length Overall	Sights	Features
21″	42″	Blade ramp front, sliding ramp rear	Cross-bolt safety, also comes in Deluxe

U. S. Rimfire Rifles: Single Shot

Model	Action	Caliber	Capacity	Weight
Chipmunk Single Shot Rifle		.22S, .22L, .22LR		2½ lbs
Harrington & Richardson 750		.22S, .22L, .22LR		5 lbs
Marlin 15 Bolt Action Rifle		.22S, .22L, .22LR		5½ lbs
Savage-Stevens 72 Crackshot		.22S, .22L, .22LR		4½ lbs
Savage-Stevens 89		.22LR		5 lbs

U. S. Target Rifles: Centerfire and Rimfire

Model	Action	Caliber	Capacity	Weight
Harrington & Richardson 5200 Rifle		.22LR	Single shot	11 lbs
M-S Safari Arms Silhouette Rifle		.22LR	Single shot	10 lbs 2 oz
M-S Safari Arms 1000 Yd. Match Rifle		.30/338, .300 Win. Mag.	Single shot	18½ lbs
Mossberg 144 Target Rifle		.22LR	7-shot mag.	8 lbs
Remington 540-XR Rimfire Position Rifle		.22LR	Single shot	8 lbs 13 oz
Remington 540-XR JR Junior Rimfire Position Rifle				
Remington 40-XC Nat'l Match Course Rifle		7.62 Nato	5-shot	10 lbs

Barrel	Length Overall	Sights	Features
16⅛"	30"	Post on ramp front, peep rear, adj.	Also comes in fully engraved model
22"	39"	Blade front, open rear, step adj.	Side safety
22"	41"	Ramp front, open rear, adj.	Thumb safety
22"	37"	Blade front, step adj. rear	Falling block action
18½"	35"	Blade front, step adj. rear	Hammer must be cocked by hand

Barrel	Length Overall	Sights	Features
28"	46"	None	Adj. trig., walnut stock, target style
23" (rimfire) 24" (centerfire)		Tapped for scope	Fiberglass stock, electronic trig.
28"		Tapped for scope	Fiberglass stock, adj. electronic trig.
27"	43"	Lyman 17A hooded front/inserts, Mossberg S331 receiver peep	Walnut, target-style stock, adj. trig.
26"	43½"–46¾", adj.	Tapped for scope	Adj. trig.
	Adj. length		Same as 540-XR except shorter stock
23½"	42½"	None	Meets all match specifications

U. S. Target Rifles: Centerfire and Rimfire (*cont.*)

Model	Action	Caliber	Capacity	Weight
Remington 40-XB Rangemaster Target Centerfire	.22/250, 6mm, .243, .25/06, 7mm Rem. Mag., .30/338, .300 Win. Mag., .308, .30/06	Single shot or repeating model	9¼ or 11¼ lbs	
Remington 40-XR Rimfire Position Rifle		.22LR	Single shot	10 lbs
Remington Model 40XB-BR		.222, .223, 6mm × 47, 6mm BR Rem., .308 Win.	Single shot	7¼ or 12 lbs
Wichita Silhouette Rifle		All std. cal. with max. cartridge length of 2.8″	Single shot	9 lbs

FN-LAR Competition Auto

Imported Centerfire Rifles: Military Style Autoloading

Model	Action	Caliber	Capacity	Weight
AKM Auto Rifle	Semiauto	7.62 × 39	30-shot mag.	6.4 lbs
AUG (Steyr)	Semiauto, gas operated	.223 Rem.	30- or 40-shot mag.	7.2 lbs 7.9 lbs 8.6 lbs
F.N.-LAR Competition	Semiauto, gas operated	.308 Win.	20-shot mag.	9 lbs 7 oz

Barrel	Length Overall	Sights	Features
	47"	Scope blocks installed	Adj. trig.
24"	43"	Tapped for scope	Meets all ISU specs adj. trig.
20" or 26"	38" or 44"	Supplied with scope blocks	Adj. trig.
24"		Tapped for scope	Legal for all NRA competitions

Barrel	Length Overall	Sights	Features
16.33"	34.65"	Post front, U-notch rear, adj.	From Egypt
16" 20" 24"	27" 31" 35"	1.5X optical, adj.	Interchangeable bbls.
21"	44½"	Post front, aperture rear, adj.	Synthetic stock

Imported Centerfire Rifles: Military Style Autoloading (*cont.*)

Model	Action	Caliber	Capacity	Weight
F.N.-H.B.	Like LAR	Like LAR	Like LAR	
F.N.-LAR Paratrooper	Like LAR	Like LAR	Like LAR	
FN 308 Model 44	Like LAR	Like LAR	Like LAR	
FNC Auto Rifle	Semiauto, gas operated	.223 Rem.	30-shot mag.	9.61 lbs
FNC 11, 22, 23 Auto Rifle	Semiauto, gas operated	.223 Rem.		
Galil 38	Semiauto, gas operated	.308 Win.	25-shot mag.	8.7 lbs
Heckler & Koch HK-91	Auto	.308	5- or 20-shot mag.	9½ lbs
Heckler & Koch HK-93	Auto	.223	25- or 40-shot mag.	7¾ lbs
Heckler & Koch HK-94	Auto carbine	9mm	15- or 30-shot mag.	6½ lbs
SIG-STG 57	Auto, gas assisted	.308	20-shot mag.	9½ lbs
Sterling Mark 6 Carbine	Semiauto	9mm	34-shot mag.	7½ lbs
Steyr AUG	Semiauto, gas operated	.223	30- or 40-shot mag.	7.2 lbs
UZI Carbine	Semiauto	9mm	25- or 32-shot mag.	8½ lbs
Valmet M76 Std. or M82 Bullpup Carbine	Semiauto	.223	15- or 30-shot mag.	7¾ lbs
Valmet M78 Rifle	Semiauto	.308	20-shot mag.	10.5 lbs
Valmet M78 Standard Rifle	Semiauto	7.62mm × 39	20-shot mag.	10.5 lbs

Barrel	Length Overall	Sights	Features
			Same as LAR except heavy bbl. and tripod
Shorter than 21″		Modified rear sight	Folding skeleton stock
18″			Skeleton-type folding stock, folding cocking handle, from Belgium
18″		Post front, flip-over aperture rear, adj.	Std.—synthetic stock; Paratrooper–folding stock
16⅛″			Similar to FNC Auto Rifle. Model 11–folding metal stock; 22—full synthetic stock; 33—wood stock
21″	41.3″	Post front, flip-type "L" rear	Tube type, metal folding stock, operated right or left hand, from Israel
19″	40¼″	Post front, aperture rear, adj., or H&K scope	Black plastic stock, or plastic (A-2), or retractable metal (A-3)
16.13″	35½″	Like HK-91	Like HK-91, from West Germany
16″	34¾″	Hooded post front, aperture rear, adj.	Plastic stock, or fixed (A-2), or retractable metal (A-3)
18¾″	39″	Adj. post front, adj. aperture rear	Walnut stock
16.1″	35″	Post front, flip-type peep rear	Walnut stock
16″, 20″, 24″	27″	1.5X scope only	Right or left hand, from Austria
16.1″	24.2″	Post front, "L" flip-type rear, adj.	From Israel, folding metal stock
16½″	28″	Post front, peep rear	Wooden or folding steel stock
24″	43″	Hooded post front, open adj. rear	Folding carrying handle
24″	43″	Hooded post front, open adj. rear	Birch butt stock

Imported Centerfire Rifles: Sporting Autoloading

Model	Action	Caliber	Capacity	Weight
Heckler & Koch SL7 Auto Rifle	Roller-locked action	.308	3- or 10-shot mag.	8 lbs
Heckler & Koch HK770 Auto Rifle	Roller-locked bolt system	.308, .223 Rem., .30/06	3-shot mag.	7½ lbs

Heckler & Koch SL7 Auto Rifle

Imported Centerfire Rifles: Bolt Action

Model	Action	Caliber	Capacity	Weight
Alpine Bolt Action Rifle		.22/250, .243, .264, .270, .30/06, .308, .308 Norma Mag., 7mm Rem. Mag., 8mm, .300 Win. Mag.	5-shot 3-shot (Mag.)	7½ lbs
Anschutz 1432D, 1532D Classic Rifles		.22 Hornet (1432D), .222 Rem. (1532D)	5-shot clip (.22 Hornet), 2-shot clip (.222 Rem.)	7¾ lbs
Anschutz 1432D, 1532D Custom Rifles				

Barrel	Length Overall	Sights	Features
17″	39¾″	Hooded post front, aperture rear, adj.	From West Germany
19.6″	42.8″	Adj. blade front, open, folddown rear, adj.	Walnut stock, from West Germany

Barrel	Length Overall	Sights	Features
23″ 24″ (Mag.)		Ramp front, open rear, adj.	Std. or Custom, from England
23½″	42½″	None. Tapped for scope	Adj. trig., from Germany
			Same as Classic models except has Monte Carlo stock

Imported Centerfire Rifles: Bolt Action (*cont.*)

Model	Action	Caliber	Capacity	Weight
BSA CF-2 Bolt Action Rifle		.222 Rem., .22/250, .243, 6.5 × 55, 7mm Mauser, 7 × 64, .270, .308, .30/06, 7mm Rem. Mag., .300 Win. Mag.		7¾ lbs
BSA CF-2 Stutzen Stock Rifle		.222, 6.5 × 55, .308, .30/06, .270, 7 × 64		7½ lbs
Champlin Rifle		All std. cal. except .458 Win. and .460 Wea.		8 lbs
Heym Model SR-20 Bolt Action Rifles		5.6 × 57, .243, 6.5 × 57, .270, 7 × 57, 7 × 64, .308, .30/06, 9.3 × 62, 6.5 × 68, 7mm Rem. Mag., .300 Win. Mag., 8 × 68X, .375 H&H		7–8 lbs
Kassnar/Parker-Hale Super		.22/250, .243, 6mm, .25/06, .270, .30/06, .308, 7mm Mag., .300 Mag.	5-shot 4-shot (Mag.)	
Kassnar/Parker-Hale Varmint		.22/250, .243, 6mm, .25/06	5-shot	
Kassnar/Parker-Hale Midland Rifle		.243, .270, .30/06, .308	4-shot	
Klein-Guenther K-15 Insta-Fire Rifle		.243, .25/06, .270, .30/06, .308, 7 × 57, .308 Norma Mag., 7mm Rem. Mag., .375 H&H; .257, .270, .300 Weath. Mag.		7 lbs 12 oz
Krico 400D Bolt Action Rifle		.22 Hornet	5-shot mag.	6½ lbs
Krico 600/700 E Bolt Action		.17 Rem., .222, .222 Rem. Mag., .223, .243, .308, 7 × 57, 7 × 64, .270, .30/06, 7mm Rem. Mag., .300 Win. Mag.	3-shot mag.	7.2 lbs

Barrel	Length Overall	Sights	Features
24"	45"	Hooded ramp front, open rear, adj.	Single or dbl. trig. (optional), side safety
20½"	41.3"		Similar to CF-2
Up to 26", rd. or oct.	45"	Bead on ramp front, 3-leaf folding rear	Right or left, tang safety
20½" 24" 26"		Silver bead ramp front, folding leaf rear, adj.	3-position safety, from West Germany, also in left hand
24"	45"	Hooded bead front, folding adj. rear	Walnut Monte Carlo stock, slide thumb safety
24"	45"	Tapped for scope	High comb, walnut stock
24"	45"	Bead front sight, folding adj. rear	Tang safety, walnut stock
24" 26" (Mag.)	43½"	Tapped for scope	Right or left hand, from West Germany
24"	43"	Hooded post front, open rear, adj.	Walnut stock, single or dbl. set trig., from West Germany
24" 26" (Mag.)	44" (24" bbl.)	Hooded ramp front, fixed rear	Adj. single or dbl. trig., from West Germany

Imported Centerfire Rifles: Bolt Action (*cont.*)

Model	Action	Caliber	Capacity	Weight
Krico 600/700 EAC Bolt Action		.17 Rem., .222, .223, .22/250, .243, .308, 7 × 57, 7 × 64, .270, .30/06, 9.3 × 62		7.5 lbs
Krico 600/700 L Deluxe Bolt Action		.17 Rem., .222, .223, .22/250, .243, .308, 7 × 57, 7 × 64, .270, .30/06, 9.3 × 62, 8 × 68S, 7mm Rem. Mag., .300 Win. Mag., 9.3 × 64		
Krico 620L/720L		Varmint and Std. cal.		6.8 lbs
Mark X Marquis Mann-Licher-Style Carbine		.270, 7 × 57, .30/06, .308		7½ lbs
Mark X Classic Rifle		.22/250, .243, .270, .308, .30/06, .25/06, 7 × 57, 7mm Rem. Mag., .300 Win. Mag.		7½ lbs
Mark X Alaskan Magnum Rifle		.375 H&H, .458 Win. Mag.	3-shot mag.	8¼ lbs
Mauser 66 Bolt Action		5.6 × 61, .243, 6.5 × 57, .270, 7 × 64, .308, .30/06, 9.3 × 62		7½ lbs
Mauser 77 Bolt Action Rifle		.243, .6.5 × 57, .270, 7 × 64, .308, .30/06	3-shot mag.	7½ lbs
O&L Wolverine Bolt Action Rifle		.308, .270, .30/06, .300 Win. Mag., 9.3 × 62		7 lbs
Sako Std. Sporter		.17 Rem., .222, .223, .22/250, .220 Swift, .243, .308, .25/06, .270, .30/06, 7mm Rem. Mag., .300 Win. Mag., .375 H&H Mag.		6¾ lbs (short and med. action), 8 lbs (long action)
Sako Classic Sporter		.243, .270, .30/06, 7mm Rem. Mag.		

Barrel	Length Overall	Sights	Features
			Similar to 600/700E
			Similar to 600/700E
21"			Similar to 600/700E
20"	40"	Ramp front with hood, open rear, adj.	Adj. trig., from Czechoslovakia
24"	44"	Ramp front with hood, open rear, adj.	Walnut Monte Carlo stock, sliding safety, from Czechoslovakia
24"	44¾"	Hooded ramp front, open rear, adj.	Walnut Monte Carlo stock, adj. trig., from Czechoslovakia
24"	41"	Hooded ramp front, open rear, adj.	Interchangeable bbls., dbl. or single trig., Model 66S is ultralight (7 lbs, 21" bbl.)
24"	44"	Ramp front, open rear, adj.	Single or dbl. set trig.
20"	39½"	Hooded ramp front, fixed rear	Fiberglass stock, from West Germany
23" (.222, .223, .243), 24" (other cal.)		None	Adj. trig., from Finland, also comes in Deluxe and Super Deluxe
			Similar to Std./Classic stock

Imported Centerfire Rifles: Bolt Action (*cont.*)

Model	Action	Caliber	Capacity	Weight
Sako Safari Grade Bolt Action		.300 Win. Mag., .338 Win. Mag., .375 Win. Mag.		
Sako Carbine		.222 Rem., .243, .270, .30/06		7½ lbs
Sako Finnsport 2700 Sporter		Same cal., actions as std.		6½–8 lbs
Sako Heavy Barrel		.222, .223, .220 Swift, .22/250, .243, .308	5-shot mag.	8¼–8½ lbs
Shilen DGA Rifles		All cal.		7½ lbs (Sporter) 9 lbs (Varminter)
Steyr-Mannlicher S & S/T		.300 Win. Mag., .338 Win. Mag., 7mm Rem. Mag., 300 H&H Mag., .375 H&H Mag., 6.5 × 68, 8 × 68S, 9.3 × 64; S/T (.375 H&H Mag., .458 Win. Mag., 9.3 × 64)		
Steyr-Mannlicher		*7 × 64, 7 × 57, *.25/06, *.270, *.30/06, 6.5 × 57, 8 × 57JS, 9.3 × 62, 6.5 × 55, 7.5 × 55 (*These cal. also in left hand)	5-shot mag.	6.8–7.5 lbs
Steyr-Mannlicher ML79 "Luxus"		Same cal. as M	3- or 6-shot mag.	
Steyr-Mannlicher SL & L		SL (.222, .222 Rem. Mag., .223), L (.22/250, 6mm, .243, .308, 5.6 × 57)	5-shot mag.	6 lbs
Steyr-Mannlicher Varmint SL & L		SL (.222 Rem.), L (.22/250, .243, .308, 5.6 × 57)	5-shot	
Tikka 55 Deluxe Rifle		.17 Rem., .222, .22/250, 6mm Rem., .243, .308	3-, 5-, or 10-shot mag.	6½ lbs

Barrel	Length Overall	Sights	Features
			Similar to Std., but with long action
20″			Similar to Std.
		Scope mounts	Monte Carlo stock
			Same as Super Sporter except has Monte Carlo stock
24″ (Sporter) 25″ (Varminter)		Tapped for scope	Adj. trig., side safety
25½″	45″	Ramp front, U-notch rear	Single or dbl. set trig.
20″ (full stock) 23½″ (half stock)	39″ (full stock) 43″ (half stock)	Ramp front, open U-notch rear	Single or dbl. set trig., also in Professional Model/synthetic stock
			Same as M except single set trig.
20″ (full stock) 23½″ (half stock)	38¼″ (full stock)	Ramp front, open U-notch rear	Single or dbl. set trig.
26″ heavy bbl.		Tapped for scope	Single or dbl. set trig.
23″	41½″	Bead on front ramp, rear, adj.	Adj. trig., from Finland

Imported Centerfire Rifles: Bolt Action (*cont.*)

Model	Action	Caliber	Capacity	Weight
Tikka 4601–4607		.30/06, .308, .270, .243, 7mm Mag., .300 Win. Mag., .222 Rem.		
Tradewinds Husky Model 5000 Bolt Rifle		.270, .30/06, .308, .243, .22/250		6 lbs 11 oz
Whitworth Express Rifle		.22/250, .243, .25/06, .270, 7 × 57, .308, .30/06, .300 Win. Mag., 7mm Rem. Mag., .375 H&H, .458 Win. Mag.		7½–8 lbs

Imported Centerfire Rifles: Lever Action

Model	Action	Caliber	Capacity	Weight
Dixie Engraved 1873 Rifle		.44/40	11-shot mag.	7¾ lbs
Rossi Saddle-Ring Carbine		.38 Spec., .357 Mag., .44/40, .44 Mag.	10-shot mag.	5¾ lbs

Imported Centerfire Rifles: Single Shot

Model	Action	Caliber	Capacity	Weight
Heckler & Koch HK877 Single Shot Rifle		.30/06 with interchangeable .22/250 bbl.		6 lbs
Heym-Ruger Model HR 30/38 Rifle		.243, 6.5 × 57R, 7 × 64, 7 × 65R, .308, .30/06, 6.5 × 68R, .300 Win. Mag., 8 × 68S, 9.3 × 74R (Mag.)		6½–7 lbs
Sharps "Old Reliable" Rifle		.45/70, .45/120/3¼" Sharps		9½ lbs

Barrel	Length Overall	Sights	Features
			Adj. trig.
23¾"		Fixed hood front, rear, adj.	Walnut Monte Carlo stock
24"	44"	Ramp front with hood, 3-leaf open-sight rear, adj. (.375 and .458 only), other cal. have std. open sights	Adj. trig., Classic English, walnut stock

Barrel	Length Overall	Sights	Features
20"	39"	Blade front, rear, adj.	Duplicate of Win. 1873, from Italy
20"	37"	Blade front, buckhorn rear	Re-creation of famous carbine

Barrel	Length Overall	Sights	Features
24"	41"	Bead front, U-notch rear	Sliding safety, adj. trig., from West Germany
24" (std. cal.) 26" (Mag.)		Bead on ramp front, leaf rear	From West Germany, 4 grades, also oct. bbl.
28"	45"	Blade front, folding leaf rear	Lever action, also in Sporter Rifle and Carbine, and Military Carbine

Imported Rimfire Rifles: Military Style Autoloading

Model	Action	Caliber	Capacity	Weight
AP-74 Auto Rifle		.22LR	15-shot mag.	6½ lbs
AM-180 Auto Carbine	Semiauto or auto	.22LR	177-rd. mag.	5¾ lbs (empty)

Ap-74 Auto Rifle

Imported Rimfire Rifles: Sporting Autoloading

Model	Action	Caliber	Capacity	Weight
Anschutz Deluxe 520/61 Auto		.22LR	10-shot mag.	6½ lbs
Erma ESG22 Gas-Operated Carbine		.22 Mag., .22LR	12-shot 15-shot (LR)	6 lbs
Heckler & Koch HK270 Auto Rifle		.22LR	5- and 20-shot mag.	5½ lbs
Heckler & Koch 300 Auto Rifle		.22 Mag.	5-shot clip	5¾ lbs
Kassnar-Squires Bingham M-16		.22LR	15-shot mag.	6 lbs
Kassnar-Squires Bingham 20 Rifle		.22LR	15-shot mag.	6 lbs
Tradewinds 260-A Auto Rifle		.22LR	5- and 10-shot mag.	5¾ lbs

Barrel	Length Overall	Sights	Features
20"	38½"	Ramp front, peep rear, adj.	AR-15 look-alike
16½"	36"	Blade front, peep rear, adj., also with Laser sight system	Plastic stock, from Austria

Barrel	Length Overall	Sights	Features
24"	43"	Hooded ramp front, folding leaf rear	Monte Carlo stock, single stage trig., rotary safety, from West Germany
18"	35½"	Military post front, peep rear, adj.	Styled after M-1 Carbine
19¾"	38.2"	Post front adj., diopter rear, adj.	3½ lb trig. pull, from West Germany
19¾"	39½"	Post front adj., V-notch rear, adj.	Single stage trig., from West Germany
19½"	38"	Post front, adj., peep rear, adj.	Replica of AR-15, from Philippines
20"	41"	Blade on ramp front, V-notch rear, adj., comes with 4X scope	Mahogany stock
22½"	41½"	Ramp front with hood, 3-leaf folding rear	Walnut stock

Imported Rimfire Rifles: Bolt Action

Model	Action	Caliber	Capacity	Weight
Anschutz Deluxe 1416/1516 Rifles		.22LR (1416D), .22 Mag. (1516D)	5-shot clip (LR) 4-shot mag. (Mag.)	6 lbs
Anschutz 1418D, 1518D		.22LR (1418D), .22 Mag. (1518D)		5½ lbs
Anschutz 1422D/1522D		.22LR (1422D), .22 Mag. (1522D)	5-shot (1422D) 4-shot (1522D)	7¼ lbs
Clayco 4 Bolt Action Rifle		.22LR	5-shot mag.	5¾ lbs
Kassnar-Squires Bingham 1400 Rifle		.22LR	5-shot mag.	7 lbs
Krico 302 Bolt Action		.22LR	5- or 10-shot mag.	6½ lbs
Krico 302 DR C Bolt Action		.22LR Mag.	5- or 10-shot mag.	6½ lbs
Krico 304 Bolt Action Rifle		.22LR or Mag.		6.2 lbs
Tradewinds 311-A Bolt Action Rifle		.22LR	5- or 10-shot mag.	6 lbs

Imported Rimfire Rifles: Lever Action

Model	Action	Caliber	Capacity	Weight
Erma EG73 Lever Action Carbine		.22 Mag.	12-shot mag.	6 lbs
Erma Lever Action Carbine		.22S, .22L, .22LR	21-shot (S) 17-shot (L) 15-shot (LR)	5½ lbs

Imported Rimfire Rifles: Pump Action

Model	Action	Caliber	Capacity	Weight
Rossi 62SA Pump Rifle		.22S, .22L, .22LR	20-shot (S) 16-shot (L) 14-shot (LR)	5¾ lbs
Rossi 62 SAC Carbine			Fewer cartridges than rifle	

Barrel	Length Overall	Sights	Features
22½"	41"	Hooded ramp front, folding leaf rear	Walnut Monte Carlo stock, adj. trig., from West Germany
19¾"			Same as 1416D/1516D except Mannlicher-style stock, from West Germany
24"	43"	Hooded ramp front, folding leaf rear	Adj. single-stage trig., from West Germany, also comes in Custom
24"	42"	Ramp front with bead, open rear, adj.	Wing-type safety
23"	41½"	Blade on ramp front, open rear, adj.	Philippine mahogany stock, Model 1500 has .22 Mag.
24"		Post front, rear, adj.	Model 352 is .22 Mag., from West Germany
24"	43"	Post front, rear, adj.	Single or dbl. set trig.
20"			Like 302 except Mannlicher-style stock
22½"	41¼"	Ramp front, folding leaf rear	Sliding safety, walnut Monte Carlo stock

Barrel	Length Overall	Sights	Features
19¼"	37⅜"	Hooded ramp front, buckhorn rear	Side ejection, beech stock
18½"			Similar to EG73 except cal.; EG12L same as EG73 except walnut stock, engraved receiver, oct. bbl.

Barrel	Length Overall	Sights	Features
23"	39¼"	Fixed front, adj. rear	Straight walnut stock, from Brazil
14½"			Similar to std. model

Imported Target Rifles: Centerfire and Rimfire

Model	Action	Caliber	Capacity	Weight
Anschutz Mark 2000 Target Rifle		.22LR	Single shot	8 lbs
Anschutz 1811 Match Rifle		.22LR	Single shot	11 lbs
Anschutz 1813 Super Match Rifle				15½ lbs
Anschutz 1807 Match Rifle				10 lbs
Anschutz 1810 Super Match II				
Anschutz 54.18 MS Silhouette Rifle				
Anschutz 1827B Biathlon Rifle		.22LR	5-shot mag.	9 lbs
Anschutz 1808ED Super Running Target		.22LR	Single shot	9¼ lbs
Anschutz Model 1403D Match Rifle		.22LR	Single shot	7¾ lbs
Anschutz Model 64-MS		.22LR	Single shot	8 lbs
BSA Martini ISU Match Rifle		.22LR	Single shot	10¾ lbs
Beeman/Feinwerk-Bau 2000 Target Rifle		.22LR		9 lbs 12 oz
Beeman/Feinwerk-Bau Ultra Match 22 Free Rifle		.22LR		17 lbs
Beeman/Weihrauch HW60 Target Rifle		.22LR	Single shot	10.8 lbs
Finnish Lion Std. Target Rifle		.22LR	Single shot	10½ lbs
Krico Model 640S Match Sporter		.17 Rem., .222, .223, .22/250, .243, .308	5-shot mag.	7.5 lbs
Krico 340S (MS) Silhouette Rifle		.22LR	5-shot	8.1 lbs

Barrel	Length Overall	Sights	Features
26″	43″	Globe front, microclick, peep rear	Walnut stock
27½″	46″	None	Single stage adj. trig., right or left hand
	46″		Like 1811 except adj. stock
26″	44½″	Int'l sight, or Match sight	Like 1811
			Like Super Match 1813 Rifle except hardwood stock
			Same as Anschutz 1813 Super Match but with metallic stock
21½″	42½″	Globe front, micrometer rear	Adj. trig.
23½″	42″	Tapped for scope	Adj. trig., hardwood stock
26″	44″	None	Walnut stock, sliding side safety, adj. single-stage trig.
21¾″	39½″	Tapped for scope	2-stage adj. trig., designed for metallic silhouette competition
28″ Mark V. has heavier bbl.	43″–44″	Modified PH-1 tunnel front, PH-25 aperture rear	Meets ISU specs, adj. trig.
26¼″ 22″ (Mini-Match)	43¾″	Globe front with inserts, micrometer match aperture rear	Meets ISU std. rifle specs, adj. trig., Std. or Mini-Match models
26.4″		Globe front with inserts, micrometer match aperture rear	Adj. mechanical or electronic trig., adj. cheekpiece right or left hand
26.8″	45.7″	Hooded ramp front, match-type aperture rear	Adj. match trig., right or left hand
27⅝″	44⁹⁄₁₆″	Globe front, int'nl micrometer rear available, inserts for both available	Adj. trig.
20″		None	Single or dbl. set trig., also comes in .22 Hornet
21″	39.5″	Receiver grooved for tip-off mounts	Adj. 2-stage match trig. or dbl. set trig., meets NRA MS rules

Imported Target Rifles: Centerfire and Rimfire (*cont.*)

Model	Action	Caliber	Capacity	Weight
Krico 630S Target Match Rifle		.17 Rem., .222, .223, .22/250, .243, .308, .22LR (Model 360S), .22 Hornet (Model 430S)	Single shot	9.5 lbs
Krico Model 430S Target Match Rifle		.22 Hornet	Single shot or repeater	8.8 lbs
Krico 330S Match Rifle		.22LR	Single shot	9.9 lbs
Krico 650SS Sniper Rifle		.222, .223, .243, .308		10.6 lbs
Mauser 66SP Match Rifle		.308	3-shot mag.	12 lbs
Shilen DGA Benchrest Single Shot Rifle		.22, .22/250, 6 × 47, .308	Single shot	To customer specs
Steyr-Mannlicher SSG Marksman		.308	5- or 10-shot mag.	8.6 lbs
Steyr-Mannlicher SSG Match				11 lbs
Swiss K-31 Target Rifle		.308	6-shot mag.	9½ lbs
Tikka 65 Wild Boar Rifle		7 × 64, .308, .30/06, 7mm Rem. Mag., .300 Win. Mag.	5-shot mag.	7½ lbs
Walther U.I.T. Super		.22LR	Single shot	10 lbs 3 oz
Walther U.I.T. Match				
Walther GX-1 Match Rifle				15½ lbs
Walther Running Boar Match Rifle		.22LR	Single shot	8 lbs 5 oz

Barrel	Length Overall	Sights	Features
23.5″	43.3″	Tapped for scope	Choice of match trig. or dbl. set trig.
24″		Tapped for scope	Dbl. set or match trig.
25.6″		Hooded front/inserts, diopter match rear	Match trig.
26″	46″	Tapped for scope	Match trig.
27½″		Tapped for scope	Match trig., adj.
Choice		Choice	Fiberglass stock, benchrest trig., custom-made rifle
25.6″	44.5″	Hooded blade front, folding leaf rear	Single or dbl. set trig.
Heavy bbl.		Walther target peep sights	Like SSG Marksman, synthetic or walnut stock
26″	44″	Blade front, ladder-type adj. rear	Walnut stock
20½″	41″	Bead on post front, ramp-type open rear	Adj. trig.
25½″	44¾″	Globe-type front, adj. aperture rear, bases for scope	Adj. trig., meets NRA and U.I.T. specs
			Similar to Super except scope
25½″	44½″		Same gen. specs as U.I.T.
23.6″	42″	Tapped for scope	Right or left hand

Rifle Stock and Fit

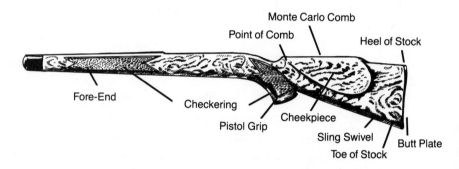

Nomenclature of a rifle stock.

The fit of a rifle is determined primarily by the shape and design of the rifle stock. Specifically, five parts are important:

1. Drop at heel and length of pull
2. Comb
3. Cheekpiece
4. Forend
5. Pistol grip

Drop at Heel
The drop at heel is determined by the slope of the comb from front to rear and is measured by an imaginary line running from the line of sight down to the heel of the stock. The drop at heel for an average man using open sights is usually 2½ " to 2¾ ". If the drop is too great, the felt recoil is excessive. When scope sights are used, the drop is less, usually 2" to 2½ ", since the eye must be on a higher plane to see through the scope.

The target rifle has straight stock to minimize the effects of recoil. The smaller the difference in drop between comb and heel, the less a rifle kicks. When a stock slopes downward toward the butt, the comb rises when the gun is fired, striking the shooter on the cheekbone. But when the stock is straight, with little or no drop at heel, the recoil brings the stock straight back against the shoulder, minimizing the kick. As long as the butt of the stock is wide and flat, the recoil will be distributed over a large area of the shoulder.

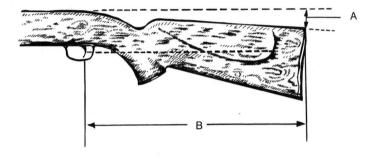

How to measure drop at heel (A) and length of pull (B).

Length of Pull

The length of pull is the distance between the trigger and the butt. The length of pull varies, since different men and women have different arm lengths, but the shooter should be able to put his gun comfortably to his shoulder with his finger on the trigger. If the pull is too great, the butt will catch on his shoulder, or he will be unable to reach the trigger comfortably. If it is too short, it will be more difficult to hold the butt firmly to the shoulder while sighting. For the average man, a pull of 13¼" to 13½" is about right. For the average woman, 13" is good. The table shows the recommended length of pull for different persons.

Length of Pull

Size	Recommended Length of Pull
Tall men (6' 1"–6' 3"	13¾"–14"
Average men (5' 8"–6'	13¼"–13½"
Short men, average women	13"–13¼"
Short women, boys	12¾"

Comb

A Monte Carlo stock has a comb that is raised to support the shooter's cheek, in order to bring the eye in line with a telescopic sight. (The telescopic sight is higher than an open sight.) The Monte Carlo has little value when an open sight is used, since it forces the shooter to squeeze his cheek down uncomfortably on the comb to align his eye with the sights, causing an unnecessary blow on the cheek from the recoil. The comb should be of the proper height and thickness to insure that the shooter is able to put his eye quickly in line with the sights and to maintain a steady pressure on his cheek.

Cheekpiece

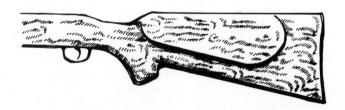

Poor cheekpiece design. Cheekpiece has forward edge to strike shooter's cheek. View from butt also shows it is excessively rounded into comb, not giving full support to face.

Good cheekpiece design. Note forward portion blends into comb, leaving no edge to hit cheek. Butt view also shows it is flat, which gives maximum support to face.

The cheekpiece should be so designed that the cheek rests comfortably on it. Ordinarily, this requires a flat surface. Also, the forward portion should merge smoothly into the comb, and the bottom should not extend out from the stock more than ½" to ⅝".

Sometimes the comb of the Monte Carlo slopes upward toward the butt. This is a good design because the comb will recoil away from the face. If the shooter places his cheek up to the forward part of the comb, however, he does not receive much support and would do better to use a standard comb.

Forend

A well-designed forend is large enough to fill the hand. Circular or oval shapes are comfortable to hold and allow the shooter to grip them tightly, giving maximum control. Triangular or square forends are harder to hold, but the flat bottoms are useful for bench shooting, where a secure rest is desired.

FOREND DESIGN

Round or oval-shaped forends are best for hunting rifles. Either type fill hand, give good control and keep fingers from barrel.

Triangular-shaped or square slab-sided forends are poor for hunting rifles, though their flat bottoms may prove of some use in benchrest shooting.

Pistol Grip

The pistol grip should be of proper circumference so the shooter can hold the stock firmly and comfortably without undue strain, or without cramping the fingers. Generally, this means a round grip of about 4½″ in diameter. Men with large hands may need about 5″; women and boys may find 4″ comfortable.

Well-designed, functional stock for a hunting rifle.

A target stock is very straight with full pistol grip and wide, heavy forend. These features make more body-to-stock contact for steadier holding.

Designed for International Match Shooting, this specialized stock has no place in the field but excels on the target range.

Barrels

Length and Bullet Velocity

Does a rifle with a longer barrel produce a greater bullet velocity than one with a shorter barrel? Not necessarily; it depends on the amount and kind of powder used, the pressure achieved, and other factors. Regardless of barrel length, a bullet driven by slow-burning powder loses much more velocity than one using a small amount of fast-burning powder. For example, a .220 Swift loaded with No. 4350, a fairly slow-burning powder, loses more velocity in a 22″ barrel than the same cartridge loaded with No. 3031, a medium-burning powder.

On high-powered rifles, which use one kind of powder, cutting barrel length usually decreases bullet velocity. For instance, velocities for the .243 Winchester are usually measured in a 26″ barrel. With a 100-grain factory load, the velocity is 3,050, but in the popular Winchester Model 70 Featherweight with a 22″ barrel, velocity is 2,925.

In other instances, a long barrel is a handicap. The .22 rimfire achieves its maximum velocity in about an 18″ barrel and in some cases in a 16″ barrel. If a 28″ barrel is used, bullet velocity will actually be less.

Therefore, the relationship between bullet velocity and barrel length is variable, depending on the powder used, pressure achieved, and other factors. Generally, however, cutting off the barrel of a high-powered rifle does decrease bullet velocity, because the barrel is cut shorter than originally designed.

Rifling

Rifling is a system of spiral grooves cut into the rifle bore. They spin the bullet so that it will move steadily, nose forward, with a minimum of wobble toward the target. The grooves are the spiral cuts running the length of the barrel. Groove diameter is the measurement from the bottom of one groove to the bottom of the opposite groove. The raised portions of the bore between the grooves are lands, and the measurement between lands is the bore diameter.

The most common type of rifling today, so-called Enfield rifling, uses square lands and grooves. The number of grooves varies from two (found in Model 1903-A3 Springfields and in replacements made during World War II for Model 1917 Enfields), to sixteen shallow grooves such as those found in the Marlin Micro-Groove system. The original Model 1903 Springfield with the .30/06 cartridge had four narrow lands and four

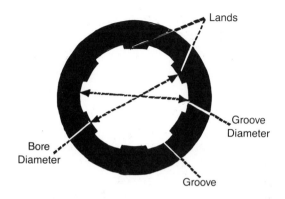

Rifling with square lands and grooves.

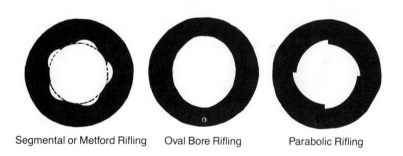

Segmental or Metford Rifling   Oval Bore Rifling   Parabolic Rifling

wide grooves. Most factory-made high-powered rifle barrels have either four or six grooves. Neither has a particular advantage over the other.

Other forms of rifling were used in the past. These were the segmented or Medford, with lands and grooves with rounded-off edges, the oval-bore rifling with the oval turning as it moved down the barrel so the bullet would spin, and the parabolic rifling, which was similar to a rotating pinwheel when one looked down the barrel. Parabolic rifling was used around 1920. Oval-bore rifling was used at one time in both England and the United States. Metford rifling was used in Europe for blackpowder guns, because the black powder was not so likely to foul the barrel, since there were no sharp edges in the rifling.

Caliber

Some confusion exists as to how caliber is determined. In the United States, a common practice has been to use the bore diameter of the barrel as the first numerals in the name of a cartridge. The .30 Remington, the .270 Winchester, and the .219 Zipper are named in this way. But in recent years, the diameter of the barrel grooves has been used. The .243, the new .246 and .338 Winchester Magnums, and the .308 were named in this way. In other instances, neither bore nor groove diameter corresponds to caliber. The .280 Remington, for example, has a bore diameter of .276 and a groove diameter of .284. The accompanying table shows some rifling specifications for other calibers.

Rifling Specifications for Different Calibers

Caliber	Bore Diameter	Groove Diameter	Width Grooves	Number Grooves	Twist
.22 Short	.219	.224	.0688	6	24
.22 L. R.	.217	.222	.0681	6	16
.218 Bee	.219	.224	.074	6	16
.22 Hornet	.217	.222	.0681	6	16
.220 Swift	.2191	.224	.074	6	14
.250/3000	.250	.256	.0785	6	14
.257 Roberts	.250	.256	.095	6	10
.270	.270	.277	.160	4	10
.30/30	.300	.308	.0942	6	12
.30/06	.300	.308	.176	4	10
.32 Special	.305	.311	.099	6	16
.375 Magnum	.366	.376	.115	6	12

There is some difference also between American and European practices. When bore diameter is .300", Americans cut the groove diameter to .308", with each groove cut to a depth of .004". They used bullets with a diameter equal to groove diameter. Europeans usually cut deeper grooves and use bullets somewhat smaller than groove diameter. Americans claim better accuracy; Europeans claim higher velocities and longer barrel life.

Twist

Twist is the rate at which the rifled grooves turn inside the barrel. It is always stated as one full turn in a given number of inches. For example, a twist of 1–10 means one full turn in 10″ of rifle barrel. Twist is used to keep the bullet from wobbling as it leaves the barrel. Without the proper amount of twist, the bullet would wobble much like a top. Spin a top too fast, and it wobbles before settling down to a smooth spin. Spin it too slowly, and it also wobbles.

What is the correct amount of spin for rifle bullets? This depends upon the bullet length, weight, shape, and velocity. The longer the bullet and the faster it moves, the sharper must be the twist. The .22 short bullet can be stabilized with a 1–24 twist, but a .22 Long Rifle bullet needs a 1–16 twist. The long high-velocity .30/06 needs a twist of 1–10.

The amount of twist needed will also depend on the weight of the bullet. For example, a 150-grain bullet may shoot well in a particular gun, but any bullet heavier than 150 grains will wobble or keyhole (enter the target sideways). When this happens, the shooter should not use the heavier-weight bullet if he wants the greatest accuracy. The most accurate twist is usually the one that will stabilize the heaviest bullet to be shot through the barrel at the longest ranges at which the rifle will be used.

The shape of the bullet also affects the ease or difficulty of keeping a bullet point on and accurate. Round-nosed bullets are easier to stabilize than those with sharp points, because their center of gravity is nearer the center of the bullet. A bullet with a long, sharp point is inherently unstable and requires a sharp twist to keep it accurate.

Twist in Popular Calibers

Caliber	Twist
17 Remington	1–9
.22/250 Remington	1–14
.222 Remington	1–14
.25/06 Remington	1–10
.243 Winchester	1–9
.270 Winchester	1–10
.30/06	1–10
.308 Winchester	1–10
7mm Remington Magnum	1–9
.264 Winchester Magnum	1–9
.350 Remington Magnum	1–16
.300 Winchester Magnum	1–10
.375 H&H Magnum	1–12
.458 Winchester Magnum	1–14

Sometimes a rifle will be accurate when it is new but inaccurate as it grows older. This usually happens because the twist has been minimal to start with, and it is not great enough to hold up as the barrel begins to wear. This is a special problem with the .32 Special. The rifling in this gun is barely adequate when new, so when the rifling starts to go the bullet starts to wobble and you cannot hit the broad side of a barn.

Generally, the shooter does not have to worry about twist, since most rifles are manufactured with a suitable amount. The table shows the amount of twist for barrels of some popular calibers.

Bullets

The jacket of the bullet is the envelope of metal surrounding the soft lead core. Sometimes bullets are full-jacketed, as in military projectiles. At other times they are half-jacketed, meaning that the thin metal envelope extends only partially up the length of the bearing surface. Some bullets, of course, have no jacket at all. The cannelure of the bullet is a relatively shallow groove rolled into the bullet's surface to serve as a seat into which the case mouth may be crimped to secure the bullet tightly.

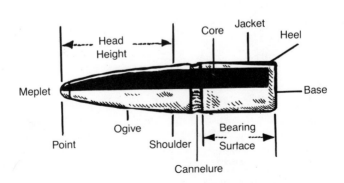

Parts of a typical bullet.

Cannelures on lead bullets are also used to provide reservoirs for lubricant. The ogive is all the bullet forward of the bearing surface, regardless of shape.

Bullet Designations and Designs

Bullets are designated in a number of ways. They are designated by weight in grains, ranging from 15 grains for a special .22 short-gallery load to 500 grains for the .460 Weatherby, 510 grains for the largest .458 Winchester Magnum, and 900 grains for the British .600 Nitro Express. (One ounce = 480 grains.) Bullets may be designated by the material of the jacket (steel-jacketed or copper-jacketed) or by the material of the nose (silvertip—really tin—bronze-point, or lead). Bullets are also commonly designated by shape, such as pointed, round, hollow-point, flat-nosed, tapered-heel, boat-tail (also a tapered-heel bullet), hollow-base, Spitzer (a very sharply pointed nose), and so on. Bullets are also designated by the trade name of the manufacturer. Thus, the Partition bullet is a trade name used by the Nosler Bullet Company to designate a bullet that is partitioned by a ring swaged into the jacket. The partition is solid, with only a very small hole in the center. A lead core is inserted into the nose and another into the base. (Such a design is intended to give optimum expansion and maximum penetration. The front half expands radically, and the back half penetrates deeply before expanding. Such a bullet is considered one of the best big-game designs.) Similarly, Weatherby, Norma, and DWM are designations of manufacturers.

One of the most important ways of designating bullets is by their expansion qualities. Some bullets practically shatter on impact, so are designated disintegration (D). Others, particularly the fully steel-jacketed bullets, hardly expand at all. In between are various types of expanding bullets and controlled-expansion bullets. Generally speaking, the softer, rounder, flatter, or more hollow points expand the fastest; those with more pointed, harder, jacketed points expand more slowly. The amount of expansion is determined by a combination of jacket thickness and strength, core hardness and amount of core exposed, the shape of the bullet core and point, striking velocity, and other variables. Expansion is controlled by a large number of different designs. The DWM strong-jacket bullet has an abnormally thick portion on the rear of the jacket, which penetrates but does not expand as fast as the softer front portion. The Nosler solidbase Zipido bullet has a completely solid base, which is too hard to be deformed by impact, allowing for maximum penetration of the base and conventional expansion of the forward part.

MODERN BULLET DESIGNS

Full-jacketed or non-expanding solid bullet. Only opening in jacket is at base of bullet.

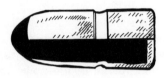

Expanding bullet with round nose and soft point. Large area of lead exposed at tip with one-piece jacket covering sides and base of bullet. Cannelure aids in crimping cartridge case neck into the bullet.

Expanding bullet with round nose and soft point. One-piece jacket has slits in forward portion to weaken nose and bring on quick-controlled expansion.

Hollow-point expanding bullet. Jacket encloses sides and base but is weakened by knurling near tip to promote quick expansion.

Nosler Partition bullet has metal jacket open at both ends to expose lead. Partition strengthens base of bullet and jacket decreases in thickness toward tip. One of the best expanding bullet designs.

Boattail bullet is tapered at base to reduce air drag. A top bullet design for long-range shooting.

Winchester Silvertip has copper jacket that covers side and base of bullet. Tip is covered with soft aluminum case that extends back and under copper jacket. The Silvertip has good "expanding" qualities.

Remington Bronze-Point has a bronze wedge in tip that produces good expansion when it is driven to the rear of the bullet on impact.

Remington Core-Lokt is a soft-point, round-nose bullet. Forward edge of jacket has scalloped edge to insure uniform mushrooming. Bullet is strengthened by increased jacket thickness near base.

Hornady pointed soft-point expanding bullet has lead core exposed at the tip. One-piece jacket covers base and side of bullet. Note pronounced thinning of jacket in nose section.

RWS H-Mantle bullet is a semi-fragmenting bullet design. Outer jacket is steel, covered with cupro-nickle alloy. Tip cap enclosing internal cavity is copper. Jacket is indented at halfway point to separate frangible forward section from base.

Remington hollow-point Core-Lokt has shallow tip cavity to lessen quick expansion. Jacket is purposely thin at nose to weaken it.

Remington's Core-Lokt bullets have scalloped edges on the jackets to insure uniform mushrooming, along with thicker jackets at the base to cut down the rate of expansion.

Bullet Abbreviations

The list shows some common abbreviations of bullet designations:

BP—Bronze point	NP—Nosler Partition
BT—Boat-tail	OPE—Open-point expanding
C—Copper-plated	P—Pointed
CL—Core-lokt	PCL—Pointed core-lokt
D—Disintegrating	PE—Pointed expanding
DC—Dual-core	PEP—Positive expanded point
E—Expanding	PL—Power-lokt
FJ—Full-jacket	PP—Power-point
FMC—Full-metal-core	PSP—Pointed soft-point
FMJ—Full-metal-jacket	Prem.—Premium
FN—Flat-nosed	R—Round
FP—Flat-point	RN—Round-nosed
HP—Hollow-point	S—Spitzer
HS—Hi-shok	SJHP—Semi-Jacketed Hollow Point
HSP—Hollow soft-point	SJMP—Semi-Jacketed Metal Point
JHP—Jacketed hollow-point	SP—Soft-point
K—Kopperklad	SPE—Semipointed expanding
L—Lead	SPS—Semipointed soft-point
LU—Lubaloy	SS—Semi-Spitzer
MAT—Match	ST—Silvertip
MC—Metal case	SX—Super Explosive
NOSLER—Nosler	TH—Tapered heel

Frequently, of course, these abbreviations are used in combination, for example, PSPCL (pointed soft-point core-lokt), PP(SP) (power-point, soft-point), or CLSP (core-lokt, soft-point).

Sectional Densities

The sectional density of a bullet is a three-place decimal figure representing the ratio of bullet weight (in pounds) to a cross-sectional area (the square of the diameter in square inches). On the one hand, the higher

Sectional Densities of Bullets

Bullet	Sectional Density	Bullet	Sectional Density
.22 Caliber (.222")		6.5mm (.264")	
40 Gr.	.114	100 Gr.	.206
.22 Caliber (.223")		129 Gr.	.266
45 Gr.	.128	140 Gr.	.288
.22 Caliber (.224")		160 Gr.	.330
45 Gr.	.128	.270 Caliber (.277")	
50 Gr.	.143	100 Gr.	.186
53 Gr.	.151	130 Gr.	.242
55 Gr.	.157	150 Gr.	.279
60 Gr.	.171	7mm (.284")	
6mm (.243")		120 Gr.	.212
70 Gr.	.169	139 Gr.	.246
75 Gr.	.181	154 Gr.	.273
87 Gr.	.210	175 Gr.	.310
100 Gr.	.241	7.35mm (.300")	
.25 Caliber (.257")		128 Gr.	.202
60 Gr.	.130	.30 Caliber (.308")	
75 Gr.	.162	100 Gr.	.151
87 Gr.	.188	110 Gr.	.166
100 Gr.	.216	130 Gr.	.196
117 Gr.	.253	150 Gr.	.227
165 Gr.	.247	158 Gr.	.177
168 Gr.	.253	.35 Caliber (.358")	
170 Gr.	.257	200 Gr.	.224
180 Gr.	.272	250 Gr.	.280
190 Gr.	.286	275 Gr.	.308
220 Gr.	.332	.375 Caliber (.375")	
.303 Caliber (.312")		270 Gr.	.275
150 Gr.	.218	300 Gr.	.306
174 Gr.	.252	.44 Caliber (.429")	
.32 Caliber (.321")		240 Gr.	.186
170 Gr.	.234	.44 Caliber (.430")	
8mm (.323")		265 Gr.	.204
150 Gr.	.206	.45 Caliber (.452")	
170 Gr.	.233	185 Gr.	.127
.338 Caliber (.338")		.45 Caliber (.454")	
200 Gr.	.250	250 Gr.	.173
225 Gr.	.281	.45 Caliber (.458")	
250 Gr.	.312	300 Gr.	.206
.348 Caliber (.348")		350 Gr.	.243
200 Gr.	.236	500 Gr.	.347
.35 Caliber (.357")			

the sectional density of a bullet, the less velocity loss over a long range and the deeper will be its penetration into a target. If a bullet has too high a sectional density, however, excessive chamber pressures prohibit loading the cartridge enough to produce high velocities within safety limitations. Therefore, unusually long, heavy bullets with sectional densities above .300 are seldom used. On the other hand, chunky, light bullets with low sectional densities lose velocity rapidly over long ranges, but they are satisfactory for short ranges, for example, in wooded areas. The table on page 71 gives some sectional densities of bullets of popular weights in standard calibers.

Cartridges and Cartridge Cases

Types of Cartridges
A cartridge is not the same as a bullet. A bullet is the projectile shot from a gun. The term "cartridge" refers to the case, powder, primer, and bullet together. It is incorrect to go into a store and ask for .22 bullets or .308 bullets, because they are really cartridges. In England, even shotgun shells are called shotgun cartridges.

The centerfire cartridge.

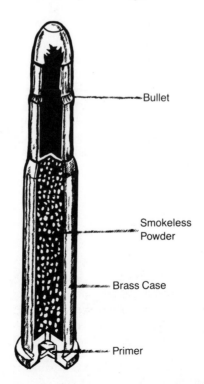

Bullet

Smokeless
Powder

Brass Case

Primer

The rimfire cartridge.

Basically, there are three types of cartridges: rimfire, centerfire, and shotshells. Rimfires include all those cartridges in which the primer is sealed in the rim rather than the center of the base. The majority of "high-powered" cartridges today are centerfire, since their case heads can be made stronger to stand higher pressures. Rimfire cartridges are primarily of .22 caliber (except for the new 5mm Remington Rimfire Magnum). The cartridge cases of these small calibers do not have to be very strong, since the firing of the cartridge depends on the rim's being crushed by the firing pin.

Cartridges are also sometimes classified according to the game on which they are used. Thus the .17 Remington, .22 Hornet, .218 Bee, or .222 Remington are known as varmint cartridges, since they are used on game like crows and woodchucks. Others, like the .30/30, the .32 Special, and the .303 Savage are primarily deer cartridges, while other bigger ones such as the .338 Winchester Magnum, .340 Weatherby Magnum, or .375 H&H Magnum are big-game cartridges. Such terms are relative, however, since cartridges such as the .30/06 are often used for big game, such as elk or moose, as well as for smaller game such as deer.

Cartridge Cases

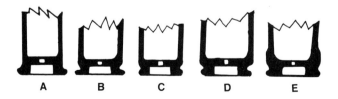

Types of cartridge cases. A. Rimmed Case B. Semi-rimmed Case C. Rimless Case D. Rebated Case E. Belted Case

Basically there are five types of cartridge cases: rimmed, semirimmed, rimless, rebated, and belted. The rimless case is the most commonly used design today, until you get into the magnum calibers, which more commonly use the belted case (the strongest design available). The rimmed cases were commonly used in many of the older types of cartridges, such as the .30/30 Winchester and the .32 Winchester Special. The .225 is a good example of a semirimmed cartridge.

Headspace

Headspace in a cartridge is the distance between the rear face of the case head and the forward face of the surface that arrests movement of the cartridge into the chamber. The rimmed cartridge is prevented from going farther foward into the chamber by the rim of the cartridge. The belted cartridge is held by the forward portion of the belt. The rimless

POINTS OF HEADSPACE

Rimmed cartridge is held by forward part of rim.

Belted cartridge is held by forward portion of belt.

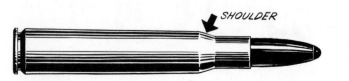

Rimless cartridge is held by shoulder.

cartridge is held by the shoulder. Correct headspace is extremely important. When the headspace in the gun is greater than that of the cartridge, the cartridge case may rupture on firing, conceivably allowing blowback toward the shooter. What usually happens, however, is that the ruptured case expands to fill the chamber, preventing the hot gases from escaping to the rear.

Cartridge Numbers

There are basically three types of numbering systems used to designate cartridges: American, British, and European or metric. The original American system utilized three numerical indicators, such as .44/40/220 or .45/70/500. The first numeral indicated the bullet diameter in hundredths (or thousandths) of an inch, the second was the number of grains of black powder, and the third was the weight of the bullet in grains. When this system is used today, the bullet weight is dropped, so that we have designations like the .25/20, the .30/30, the .30/40, the .32/20, the .32/40, the .38/40, the .38/55, the .44/40, or the .45/70. The first numeral is the bullet diameter; the second is the powder weight. From looking at these numerals, one can tell immediately that a cartridge with 40 grains of powder is going to be considerably longer than one with 20 grains of powder. Generally, the name of the company that designed the cartridge is added, so that we have the .44/40 Winchester, for example. The .45/70 now comes in the .45/70 Government 1873 Springfield and the .45/70 Government 1886 Winchester.

The most common American practice today is to designate the cartridge by the approximate diameter of the bullet, which in the United States is similar in diameter to the groove diameter of the rifle barrel. The .243, .246, and .308 are examples of this type of designation. But as we have seen in the section on rifle barrels, sometimes the cartridge number corresponds to the bore diameter of the barrel (as in the .219 Zipper or .270 Winchester). At other times it is only approximate and does not correspond to either bore or groove diameter (as in the .218 Bee, which has a bore diameter of .219 and a groove diameter of .224).

Occasionally the second numeral designates something other than powder weight or diameter. For example, the "06" in the .30/06 means the cartridge was adopted in 1906. The "3000" in the .250/3000 Savage indicates that the original velocity of the 87-grain bullet was 3,000 feet per second.

The British system designates case diameter (and bullet diameter when different from case diameter) and case length. The .577/3" has a cartridge case of .577 and a length of 3". The .577-.500/2¾" has a cartridge case diameter of .577, a bullet diameter of .500, and a cartridge case 2¾" long.

The third system of cartridge numbering is the metric system, which is used throughout most of the rest of the world, and occasionally in the United States. This system uses three, four, or five designations. The first numeral indicates bore diameter in millimeters; the second indicates case length in millimeters. Thus, a cartridge designated 7.92 × 57 has a bore diameter of 7.92mm and a case length of 57mm. If an R is added, it indicates a rimmed case (e.g., 7.92 × 57R). In this particular caliber, two different bullet diameters have been used. J indicates a smaller diameter (.318") and S, the larger diameter (.323"). Thus, we might have a 7.92 × 57JR. In this example, the third and fourth designations indicate case type. The maker's name is sometimes added, for example, the 7 × 61mm

Interchangeability Chart for Centerfire Rifle Ammunition

Caliber	Centerfire Rifle
.22 Savage	5.6 × 52R
.22 Hornet	5.6 × 35R
.223 Remington	5.56mm U.S.; 5.56 × 45mm; .223/5.56mm Military
.25 Remington	6.5 × 52
.243 Winchester	6 × 51mm Winchester
.25/35 Winchester	.25/35 WCF; 6.5 × 52R
6.5mm Italian	6.5mm Mannlicher-Carcano; 6.5 × 52mm Italian M1891
6.5mm Japanese	6.5mm Arisaka; 6.5 × 50mm Japanese Arisaka
6.5mm Swedish	6.5 × 55mm; 6.5 × 55mm Mauser; 6.5mm Swedish Mauser; 6.5 × 55 Norwegian Krag
.270 Winchester	.270 WCF
7mm Mauser	7 × 57mm; 7 × 57mm Mauser
7mm Remington Magnum	7mm Magnum
7.35mm Italian	7.35mm Carcano; 7.35mm Terni; 7.35mm M38
.30/30 Winchester	.30/30; .30/30 WCF; .30 WCF; 7.62 × 51R
.308 Winchester	7.62mm NATO; 7.62mm U.S.; 7.62 × 51mm; 7.62mm M59
.30/06	.30/1906 U.S.; .300 U.S.; Cartridge .30.M2; Cartridge .30.M1; 7.62 × 63mm; .30 U.S. Gov't.
.300 H&H Magnum	Holland's Super .300; .300 H&H; .30 Super; .300 Belted Rimless Magnum
7.7mm Japanese	7.7 × 58mm; 7.7mm Arisaka
.303 British	.303 Enfield; 7.7 × 57R
7.65mm Mauser	.30 Mauser; 7.65 × 53mm; 7.65mm Argentine Mauser; 7.65mm M1889
8mm Mannlicher-Schoenauer (M/1960)	8 × 56
8mm Mauser	8.57mm Mauser; 7.92 × 57mm
.358 Winchester	8.8mm Winchester; .358 (8.8mm) Winchester
.375 Magnum	.375 Holland & Holland; .375 Belted Rimless Magnum Nitro Express; .375 H&H Magnum

Sharpe and Hart, or some flowery adjective, such as Magnum Bombe, to indicate high performance. American manufacturers have designated some cartridges with the metric system. The 6mm Remington and the 6.5 or 7mm Remington Magnums are good examples.

Cartridge Equivalents

The chart shows interchangeability of centerfire rifle ammunition. There are no American cartridges made or recommended for the 6.5mm Italian service rifles or the .5- or .30-caliber (6.5 or 7.7mm) Japanese rifles.

Centerfire Rifle Cartridges

.17 Remington. The lightest of the high-velocity (4,020 fps), flat-trajectory varmint cartridges. But the extremely light bullet (only 25 grains) is not as hard hitting as the .22s and is more susceptible to wind influence over long ranges. Limited usefulness.

.22 Hornet. The first high-speed .22 especially for varmint hunting, introduced in 1930. Flat trajectory and effective killing power out to 175 yards.

.218 Bee. A slightly greater velocity and flatter trajectory than the .22 Hornet. Introduced in 1968, but rifles for it are not sold today.

.222 Remington. Has largely replaced the old Hornet and Bee where a greater velocity and longer range is desired (effective range for varmints is 225 yards). A fine benchrest and varmint cartridge. Available in a number of bolt-action rifles.

.222 Remington Magnum. Although rifles are no longer made for this caliber, Remington ammunition is still available for rifles already in use. Along with the .223, it is one of the best varmint cartridges in use. Hard-hitting and flat trajectory out to about 250 yards.

.22/250 Remington. The most powerful, highest-velocity, flattest trajectory of any .22-caliber cartridge for guns on the market. Made in 55-grain bullets. The favorite of those shooters who want the flattest trajectory at long ranges coupled with maximum striking power.

.220 Swift. The highest-velocity, flattest trajectory of any standard rifle cartridge ever produced commercially in the United States. Muzzle velocity for the 50-grain modern cartridge offered by Norma is 4,111 fps. The midrange trajectory at 300 yards is an unbelievable 3″. Case life and barrel life are short, because of high velocities, but no other cartridge of this caliber has ever surpassed it for long-range varmint shooting. Unfortunately, new guns are no longer offered in this caliber.

.22 Savage Hi-Power. The 71-grain bullet is slower-moving than any of the other long-range .22 caliber bullets, except the .22 Hornet, but the foot-pounds of energy delivered at 300 yards is 383, compared to 127–130 foot-pounds in the .22 Hornet, 321–610 in the .222 Remington, and 453–608 in the .223 Remington. When sighted in at 200 yards, the drop is only 4.5″ at 250 yards. A good cartridge for those wanting a heavy .22 cartridge for large varmints at distances up to 250 yards.

.223 Remington. Slightly greater velocity and flatter trajectory than the .222. Similar ballistically to the .222 Magnum, but the case capacity of the .223 is slightly less and the neck is shorter. The .223 should not be used in .222, since excessive headspace may result in case rupture. Used by the military as the 5.56mm.

.224 Weatherby Magnum (Varmintmaster). Slightly greater velocity and energy than the .225 Winchester, with the same weight (55-grain ullet).

.225 Winchester. A semirimmed cartridge, which along with the .225 Weatherby Magnum has gained the reputation of ranking second only to the .22/250 Remington as the most powerful .22 centerfire. (Rifles for the .220 Swift are no longer made.) Available only in 55-grain bullets, it is an exceptionally accurate, long-range varmint or target cartridge.

.240 Weatherby Magnum. The highest-velocity and flattest trajectory of any of the .24 calibers, except for the .244 H&H Magnum. It has superior ballistics to both the .243 and 6mm, and comes in 70-, 87-, and 100-grain bullets. A versatile, long-range, accurate, hard-hitting choice for varmints, antelope, and deer.

.243 Winchester. One of the best for long-range varmint, antelope, and deer hunting. When sighted in at 250 yards and using a 100-grain bullet, the drop at 300 yards is only 3.5″. The drop at 400 yards is 16.5″, which is still acceptable for antelope and deer hunting if the hunter holds high. Use 80-grain bullets for varmints and 100-grain for deer. With 100-grain bullets, provides greater killing power than the same weight bullets in the .270 at ranges of 400 yards and over. Excellent choice for open, long-range shooting for game no larger than deer.

6mm Remington and .244 Remington. The 6mm and .244 Remington cartridges can be used interchangeably, except bullets over 90 grains will not remain stabilized when shot out of the .244. Because the hunters wanted at least a 100-grain bullet, Remington ceased production of the .244 guns and ammunition and came out instead with the 6mm. Cartridges of this caliber may be obtained in 80- or 100-grains, so they are useful for larger varmints or deer. Ballistics are comparable to the .243, so this is an excellent choice for long-range, open shooting.

.25/06 Remington. The finest .25 caliber made: hard-hitting, flat trajectory, with five different size bullets (87-, 90-, 100-, 117-, and 120-grain) to choose from. Thus, this is one of the best all-around cartridges for open-range hunting of both varmints and medium-size game (antelope, deer, sheep, goats). It is slightly superior ballistically to the 6.5mm Remington Magnum and only slightly inferior to the .270 Winchester. Use the 90-grain bullet for very long-range antelope and deer shooting, since this weight has the flattest trajectory.

.25/20 Winchester. An old-timer, originating in 1893, now made only in 86-grain bullets, which move at a slow velocity and are accurate only out to about 125 yards. There are better pest loads than this one, but it has killed its share of wild turkeys, rabbits, and varmints.

.25/35 Winchester. Its origin goes back to the 1890s. The 117-grain bullet can be used on deer at modest ranges out to about 200 yards (sight in at 150 yards), but the energy at that range is only 620 foot-pounds. Other .25 calibers (the .25/06 Remington, .250 Savage, and .257 Roberts) are far better choices.

.250/3000 Savage. A fine cartridge for varmints or deer, available in either 87- or 100-grain bullets. When sighted in at 200 yards, the drop at 250 yards is only 3.5". The ballistics are comparable to the .257 Roberts but quite inferior to the .243 Winchester, 6mm Remington, .240 Weatherby Magnum, and .25/06 Remington. Popular for more than forty years, it is still used a lot today, but better cartridges of similar caliber have been developed.

.256 Winchester. This short cartridge was developed both as a high-speed, flat-trajectory handgun cartridge and as a rifle cartridge. In comparison with other cartridges, this one is very powerful handgun ammunition but quite modest rifle ammunition. It cannot compare ballistically with other .25-caliber rifle cartridges, which are made with much greater powder charges. (Compare with .25/06, .250 Savage, or .257 Roberts.) It has a trajectory similar to the .25/35 Winchester and is quite accurate up to 200 yards, but at that range hits with about half the striking power of the .25/35. About the only .25 caliber to which it is superior is the .25/20 Winchester.

.257 Roberts. Rifles of standard make are no longer chambered for this cartridge, but 100- and 117-grain commercial loads can still be obtained, so guns still available are quite versatile. Ballistics are comparable but slightly superior to the .250 Savage. Use 100-grain bullets for open-country deer shooting, and 117-grain for woods hunting.

.257 Weatherby Magnum. Has the flattest trajectory and highest striking energy of any .25-caliber cartridge, so may be used at extremely long ranges for varmints or smaller big game such as antelope.

6.5 Japanese. A .25-caliber cartridge with slightly less velocity and striking power than the 6.5 × 54 MS. Norma offers both 139-grain and 156-grain bullets, but the 139 is far superior, since both muzzle velocity and striking power of the 139 are far greater than on the 156. With 139-grain bullets, it is useful at modest ranges up to 200 yards but is inferior to the 6.5 × 55 Swedish (which is quite popular) or to the 6.5mm Remington Magnum.

6.5 Italian (Carcano). This cartridge, made by Norma in a 139- and 156-grain bullet, has the slowest muzzle velocity and weakest striking power of any of the 6.5mm imports, so is not as popular as its Japanese, German, or Swedish counterparts.

6.5 × 55mm (Swedish). The most popular of the 6.5mm imports, with the fastest muzzle velocity and hardest striking power. It has little recoil, is resistant to deflection by the wind, and quite accurate. Made in 77-, 139-, and 156-grain bullets the 139-grain bullet is the most popular. When sighted in at 200 yards, the bullet drops only 5″ at 250 yards and 13″ at 300 yards.

6.5 Remington Magnum. When using a 120-grain bullet, the trajectory compares favorably to the 6.5 × 55 (with 139-grain bullet), but the striking power is slightly less. The 100-grain bullet is excellent for larger varmints and antelope, and the 120-grain bullet useful on medium-size game such as deer. Not quite as powerful as the .25/06 when using the same 120-grain bullet weight.

.264 Winchester Magnum. Gives magnum power and velocity from a medium-short belted case. Has very flat trajectory and high energy at long ranges, and uses controlled expansion bullets in 100 or 140 grains. Best used for long-range shooting in flat country for antelope (100 grains), mule deer (140 grains), or long-range mountain shooting for sheep or goats (either weight bullet).

.270 Winchester. One of the best long-range cartridges for a variety of game. Obtained in 100-, 130-, or 150-grain loads. The 100 grain is useful on larger varmints, deer, and antelope; the 130 grain is useful on sheep, goats, and mule deer; the Winchester 150 grain with power-point bullet can be used on caribou, elk, or moose, while the somewhat slower 150-grain core-lokt is better designed for woods hunting. When sighted in at 250 yards, the drop at 300 yards is only 3.5″ and 4″ respectively with the 100- and 130-grain bullets; at 400 yards, it is 14.5″ and 16″.

.270 Weatherby Magnum. Bullets are available in 100-, 130-, or 150-grain weights. While all are delivered at higher speeds and with greater energy than from the standard .270, the superiority of this magnum is best seen in the 150-grain loads. The premium .270 delivers a maximum of 1,830 foot-pounds of energy at 300 yards, but the Magnum delivers

2,259. Thus, the magnum is most useful for those who hunt big game at long ranges but, in the 100-grain bullets, can still be used for medium game.

.280 Remington. Interchangeable with the 7mm Express Remington. Slightly more powerful than the .270, with as fine or a little better ballistics. However, it is now available in only the 165-grain bullet, so its use must be limited to game like sheep, goats, deer, elk, and moose.

7mm–08 Remington. Available only in 140-grain bullet for those needing high velocity and energy at long ranges.

7mm Express Remington. Interchangeable with .280 Remington but with 150-grain bullet, has a flatter trajectory, much higher velocity, and greater energy delivered than the .280. Not quite as powerful as the 7mm Remington Magnum. Very close to the 7mm–08 Remington in ballistics.

.284 Winchester. A short, fat, rimless case offering maximum power and ballistics almost identical to the .270. Available in 150-grain bullets.

7mm Mauser. This is the 7 × 57, which originated in 1893 as a Spanish military cartridge. It is still very popular because of high velocities, flat trajectories, and a variety of loads available. Medium loads are good for deer; heavy loads are good for brush shooting and big game such as elk and moose. An excellent, versatile choice for a variety of game.

7mm Remington Magnum. Tremendous striking power combined with a flat trajectory at long ranges have made this cartridge very popular for medium and medium-large game. Five cartridge weights (125, 150, 160, 165, and 175 grains) make this a flexible choice for antelope, deer, sheep, goats, elk, caribou, and moose. The 125-grain bullet has a slightly flatter trajectory and striking power comparable to the 130-grain .270. The 150-grain bullet has a flatter trajectory and much greater striking power than the same weight bullet in either the .270 or .30/06 calibers. In fact, it is equal to the .300 Winchester Magnum in both trajectory and energy delivered. Similarly, the 175-grain bullet is much superior to the 180-grain .30/06 in both trajectory and striking power and about equal to the .300 Winchester Magnum in both categories. Therefore, do not neglect this choice for all medium-large American game, except larger bear and buffalo.

7mm Weatherby Magnum. Almost identical to the 7mm Remington Magnum in trajectory and energy delivered. Loaded with 139-, 140-, 154-, 160-, and 175-grain bullets, this is an excellent choice for medium and large game.

.30 M-1 Carbine. A weak, slow-velocity cartridge loaded with 110-grain bullets. Even at 100 yards, it develops only 600 foot-pounds of energy, so is obviously too weak for deer and larger game. Might have limited usefulness for pests, but it is really not recommended for any use. The centerfire .22s, except the Hornet, all develop much more energy with a flatter trajectory, so they are preferred for varmints.

7.5 × 55mm Swiss. This cartridge with 180-grain bullets compares favorably with the 6.5 × 55mm (Swedish). It has ample striking power and a flat trajectory. When sighted in at 200 yards it drops only 8.9″ at 300 yards.

.30/30 Accelerator. The accelerator cartridges are designed for those needing a light bullet (55 grains), greater velocity, longer ranges, and a flatter trajectory than is possible with the old .30/30. This cartridge accomplishes this nicely. The light bullet is suitable for varmints, rabbits, and other small game.

.30/30 Winchester. A favorite of old-time deer hunters, who fire them in light carbines. However, this should be considered only as a relatively short-range weapon. The 1,356 foot-pounds of energy (with a 150-grain load) is fine at 100 yards, but at 200 yards it has dropped to 944. To avoid crippling game, however, ranges of 150 yards and less are recommended.

.30 Remington. Rimless version of the .30/30 for autoloaders and slide-action guns, with only slightly less killing power and a not-quite-so-flat trajectory. Available in 170-grain bullets, so is best used as a brush gun at limited ranges not much over 100 yards. Has less killing power at 100 yards than the .30/06 at 300 yards.

.300 Savage. A short cartridge developed for use in lever action rifles, it is loaded with either 150-grain or 180-grain bullets. It is far superior ballistically to the .303 Savage but has never equaled the .30/06. When sighted in at 200 yards, using the 150-grain bullet, the drop at 250 yards is only 3.5″ but increases to about 11″ at 300 yards. With the 180-grain bullet, the drop at 300 yards is about 15″. Thus, the 180-grain is better used at shorter distances and in brush, and is adequate for game larger than deer, such as small bear, elk, moose, and caribou. Do not use it on dangerous bear, however.

.30/40 Krag. Rifles are no longer chambered with this caliber, but cartridges are still available in 180- and 220-grain bullets. A little more striking power and a flatter trajectory than the .300 Savage. Best used at modest ranges and as a brush gun for medium American game.

.30/06. The most popular big-game cartridge in the United States. A flat trajectory and bullet weights of 110, 125, 150, 165, 180, 200, and 220 make this a versatile, powerful weapon, useful on smaller game in open country and heavy game in the woods and brush. The 220-grain bullet has enough power for all large American game except grizzlies and Alaskan brown bear.

.30/06 Accelerator. With a 55-grain bullet, this cartridge delivers a muzzle velocity of 4,080 fps, second only to the .220 Swift. It also ranks second to the .220 Swift in trajectory, dropping only 5″ at 300 yards when sighted in at 200. This makes this a superior weapon for varmint shooting at long ranges. The small bullet weight and low energy delivered at long ranges precludes use on larger game.

.300 Winchester Magnum. This cartridge is powerful at long ranges and has a very flat trajectory. With the 180-grain bullet, it delivers 2,196 foot-pounds of energy at 300 yards, or 460 more than the .30/06. When sighted in at 250 yards, the drop at 400 yards is only 14.5″. Ballistics are similar to the 7mm Remington Magnum, so this cartridge is also suitable for all larger American game except larger bear.

.300 H&H Magnum. This cartridge has more power than the .30/06, moving faster and developing more foot-pounds of energy, with a flatter trajectory. It does not come up to the superb performance of either the 7mm Remington Magnum or the .300 Winchester Magnum. It is a fine cartridge, however, and the 150-, 180-, and 220-grain bullet weights are definitely medium-large game cartridges: sheep, goats, deer, elk, caribou, and moose.

.300 Weatherby Magnum. One of the finest all-around big-game cartridges. Bullet weights of 110, 150, 180, and 220 grains allow a versatile usage for all American game the size of antelope and larger. The 150-grain load has a much flatter trajectory than the .270 and even flatter than the .308 Magnum, 7mm Remington Magnum, and the .300 Winchester Magnum, so this is an excellent choice for very long-range shooting. The 220-grain bullet is heavy enough to be a fine black bear, grizzly, polar bear, elk, caribou, and moose cartridge, and just big enough for Alaskan brown bear.

.303 Savage. Not quite as good ballistically as the .30/30. The heavy bullets (with high sectional densities) of 190 grains are best used in brush and wooded country at limited ranges. They have somewhat more penetrating power than the lighter bullets used in the .30/30.

.303 British. This cartridge is available in a bullet weight of 180 grains. The 180-grain loads are only a little better ballistically than the .30/40 Krag. In summary, this is an adequate deer cartridge, especially at short ranges, but it will never break any records for performance.

.308 Accelerator. With its 55-grain bullet, this cartridge delivers a fast, low-energy, flat trajectory at long ranges, making it a fine varmint load with slightly less power than the .30/06 accelerator.

.308 Winchester. The commercial equivalent of the 7.62mm Nato cartridge, designed with a short case for use in short actions. A powerful cartridge for its size, its ballistics with the 125-grain bullet almost equal those of the .30/06 but begin to fall behind in the 150- and 180-grain bullets. The wide choice of bullet size (110, 125, 150, 180, and 200 grains) makes this a versatile weapon, adequate for varmints, deer, elk, caribou, moose, and smaller bear. It is not quite heavy enough for dangerous game but may be used both in open country or in brush for other game. One advantage is that rifles of this caliber are much lighter to carry than the .30/06, especially in autoloaders.

.308 Norma Magnum. With the 180-grain bullet, the only load available, this delivers a little more power, with an even flatter trajectory, than the 7mm Remington Magnum and .300 Winchester Magnum. The case is the same length as the .30/06, so by rechambering the barrel and opening up the bolt face, .30/06 rifles can be converted to shoot the .308 Norma Magnum. A high-performance cartridge that will handle all larger game, except more dangerous bear.

7.62 × 39 Short Russian. With its 125-grain bullet and short cartridge this delivers less velocity and power than the standard Russian.

7.62 Russian. Loaded with 180-grain bullets, this cartridge does not have as much power as the .30/06, even though the trajectory is as flat. No real advantages for large game, but it is still a fine deer load, about equivalent to the 180-grain .308 Winchester.

7.65 Argentine Mauser. Loaded with the 150-grain bullet, the ballistics are similar to the .308 Winchester, so it is a fine deer load.

7.7 Japanese. Norma loads this with either 130- or 180-grain bullets. The 130 grain performs about like Norma's load for the .308. The 180 grain closely matches the 180-grain .308 Winchester in performance.

.32/20 Winchester. An old, outmoded cartridge that is the weakest of all centerfire cartridges discussed in this book (including the .17 Remington). Should not be used beyond 125 yards, and then only on small game like rabbits and turkeys.

.32 Winchester Special. An old favorite of many brush-country deer hunters, with modest power (about 1,000 foot-pounds of energy) at 200 yards. Almost identical ballistically to the .30/30 Winchester and, like it, is best used for short ranges not much over 100 yards.

8mm Mauser. There are several different cartridges of this approximate size that it is easy to become confused. The following is a list of available cartridges.

The 8mm cartridge is rimless. The letter J designates a smaller-size bullet (.318″); the letter S designates .323″; J and S together indicate a diameter of .323, with the bullet usable in both the smaller and larger bores. The shooter must be careful to match the bullet with the markings on the barrel. The Federal, Remington-Peters, and Winchester-Western car-

8mm Mauser (Federal, Remington-Peters, and Winchester-Western) (.322")	170 grain
8 × 57J (Norma)	159 grain
	196 grain
8 × 57JS (Norma)	196 grain

tridges are loaded lightly because of the danger of being used in poor-quality rifles, so this 170-grain bullet develops slightly more power than the .32 Winchester Special. The Norma loads are more powerful, however, developing power equivalent to the .300 Savage.

8mm Remington Magnum. This is a powerful cartridge delivering large amounts of energy with a flat trajectory at all ranges out to 300 yards. The 185- or 220-grain bullets are designed to use with medium and large game and pack considerably more wallop than comparable size .30/06s.

9.3 × 57mm. This is a heavy load (286-grain bullet) moving at medium speeds designed for use with medium to large game at up to 200-yard ranges. It is still far weaker, however, than the larger magnum cartridges so is not as good for dangerous game as the magnums.

9.3 × 62mm. This is also loaded with a 286-grain bullet by Norma, but packs a greater punch at faster velocities than does the 9.3 × 57mm.

.338 Winchester Magnum. A high-powered, flat-trajectory cartridge for all American big game the size of deer and larger. Standard loads are with 200-, or 250-grain bullets. Trajectory with the 200-grain bullet is similar to the 7mm Remington Magnum and .300 Winchester Magnum, but it is flatter than the .270 Winchester with 150 grains and flatter than .30/06 with 180 grains, and is thus an excellent choice for open-country deer hunting. The 250-grain load is heavy enough to down black bear or to crash through brush in woods while hunting for elk, moose, or deer.

.340 Weatherby Magnum. Packs more punch and has a flatter trajectory than the .338 Winchester Magnum. Choice of 200-, 210-, or 250-grain bullets allows use for all American big game the size of deer and up. Recoil is heavy so this caliber should not be selected if the hunter only wants to use it as a deer rifle.

.348 Winchester. A short cartridge designed for use in lever-action rifles, although no guns are made for it today. Only the 200-grain cartridge is available. With the silvertip bullet, it packs about ¾ the wallop of the .348 Winchester Magnum. Still used in Alaska, primarily for deer and moose.

.35 Remington. A fine, but close-range woods rifle for deer and moose, especially with the 200-grain load, which is more destructive than the smaller 150-grain bullet, or the .30 or .32 calibers with which it can be compared.

.350 Remington Magnum. A short magnum for use in standard or short-action rifles at 100 yards. The 200-grain bullet delivers about the same foot-pounds of energy as does the 200-grain .30/06, but the wallop is less than the .30/06 at 200–300 yard ranges. Nevertheless, this is a fine choice for a medium-size big-game rifle that is big enough, without being so big that it develops excessive recoil.

.351 Winchester, Self-Loading. A very short, fat cartridge loaded only with 180-grain bullets without as much power as the .30/30 Winchester. Only the Winchester '07 autoloader is chambered for it. It is used more by police than as a hunting rifle, since it is good only as a close-range woods rifle (less than 100 yards).

.358 Winchester. Has the same length case as the .308 and is a larger-caliber version of it. The 200-grain bullet gives a similar trajectory to the 200-grain .308 out to 300 yards and delivers a similar punch out to 100 yards. After 100 yards, however, the foot-pounds decline considerably below the .308.

.375 H&H Magnum. A "medium"-caliber big-game cartridge used worldwide as an all-around choice for big and dangerous game. It is a safe choice on North American grizzlies or Alaskan brown bear and is useful on many large African species. (It cannot be used on elephant, rhino, or buffalo, since African law requires a .40 caliber.) The 270-grain load delivers about 200 more foot-pounds of energy, with a flatter trajectory, than does the 250-grain .338 Winchester Magnum. Also available in 300-grain bullets. Delivers a heavy recoil to the shooter.

.378 Weatherby Magnum. Uses the same 270- and 300-grain bullets (not cartridges) as the .375 H&H Magnum but delivers over 1,100 more foot-pounds of energy at 100 yards, and about 460–740 more foot-pounds at 300 yards, and with a much flatter trajectory than the .375 H&H Magnum. Weatherby advertises this cartridge as "designed for the purpose of killing thick-skinned animals where extremely deep penetration is needed." Thus, this cartridge is adequate for the largest game but cannot be used on elephant, rhino, and buffalo in Africa because of game laws requiring .40 caliber or over for those species. The recoil is so great that it is too much for many hunters not used to handling truly magnum loads.

.38/40 Winchester. This is an even weaker cartridge than the .38/55, with only 399 foot-pounds of energy at 100 yards with the 180-grain bullet. Even if your deer is standing a foot away, the foot-pounds of energy delivered is only 538. When sighted in at 100 yards, the drop at 200 yards is 34". The only large-caliber cartridges weaker than this are the .32/20 Winchester and the .25/20 Winchester. The principal reason it has killed so many deer is that it makes a large hole and lets out a lot of blood.

.38/55 Winchester. This is a short-range, low-power load for woods hunting for deer or moose. The 255-grain, large-caliber bullet generates 802 foot-pounds of energy at 100 yards. When sighted in at 100 yards, the drop at 200 is 23.4", so don't try any long, open-country shooting with this old-timer.

.44/40 Winchester. Loaded with a 200-grain bullet, this very short cartridge generates only a fraction more energy than the .38/40 Winchester and will drop a full 33" at 200 yards if sighted in at 100. So don't try to kill anything with it at ranges over 100 yards.

.44 Remington Magnum. This was originally designed as a powerful revolver cartridge but is now used primarily as a carbine cartridge for short-range woods shooting for deer. This cartridge has proved its merit in its 240-grain load, which generates about the same power at 100 yards as the .38/55 Winchester, but not quite as much as the .30/30.

.444 Marlin. The 240- and 260-grain bullets with which this cartridge is equipped develop over 2,600 foot-pounds of muzzle energy, but the large caliber slows the bullet so rapidly that it has decreased to 1,760 foot-pounds at 100 yards, about equivalent to the 150-grain .300 Savage or the 175-grain 7mm Mauser. Obviously, this is a short-range cartridge but will down almost all American game at close ranges. It is not a good brush gun or big-game cartridge, however, because the soft-point bullet smashes too easily.

.45/70 Government, 1873 Springfield and 1886 Winchester. This huge cartridge loaded with a 300- or 405-grain bullet is an extremely slow-moving, low-powered weapon (developing only 1,227–1,619 foot-pounds of energy at 100 yards). But at ranges of 125 yards or less, it tears up a lot of flesh and can be counted on for a quick kill.

.458 Winchester Magnum. This cartridge, loaded with either 500- or 510-grain bullets, ranks next to the .460 Weatherby Magnum as the most powerful U.S. cartridge. It is designed to stop the heaviest game: Alaskan brown bear, Indian tiger, or African elephant, buffalo, or rhino. The 510-grain steel-point is designed for elephants, the 500-grain soft-point for other game. The recoil is tremendous, however, second only to the .460 Weatherby Magnum.

.460 Weatherby Magnum. The most powerful American cartridge, using the same 500-grain bullets as the .458 Winchester Magnum but developing 2,800 more foot-pounds of energy at 100 yards. The trajectory is also flatter than the .458 Winchester, with a drop of only 10" at 300 yards when sighted at 300 yards. This cartridge should only be used for the largest, most dangerous game like elephant, rhino, and buffalo.

CENTERFIRE RIFLE CARTRIDGES

(R) = REMINGTON; (W) = WINCHESTER-WESTERN; (F) = FEDERAL; (H) = HORNADY-FRONTIER; (PMC) = Patton & Morgan Corp.

Cartridge	Wt. Grs.	Type	Bbl. (In.)	VELOCITY (fps) Muzzle	100 yds.	200 yds.	300 yds.	ENERGY (ft. lbs.) Muzzle	100 yds.	200 yds.	300 yds.	BULLET PATH† 100 yds.	200 yds.	300 yds.
17 Remington (R)	25	HPPL	24	4040	3284	2644	2086	906	599	388	242	+0.5	-1.5	-8.5
22 Hornet (R) (W)	45	PSP, HP, OPE	24	2690	2042	1502	1128	723	417	225	127	0.0	-7.7	-31.3
218 Bee (W)	46	OPE	24	2760	2102	1550	1155	778	451	245	136	0.0	-7.2	-29.4
222 Remington (R) (W) (F) (H)	50	PSP, SX	24	3140	2602	2123	1700	1094	752	500	321	+2.2	0.0	-10.0
222 Remington (R) (PMC)	50	HPPL	24	3140	2635	2182	1777	1094	771	529	351	+2.1	0.0	-9.5
222 Remington (W) (R) (PMC)	55	FMC	24	3020	2675	2355	2057	1114	874	677	517	+2.0	0.0	-8.3
222 Remington (F)	55	MC BT	24	3240	2740	2480	2230	1115	915	750	610	+1.9	0.0	-7.7
222 Remington Magnum (R)	55	PSP	24	3240	2748	2305	1906	1282	922	649	444	+1.9	0.0	-8.5
222 Remington Magnum (R)	55	HPPL	24	3240	2773	2352	1969	1282	939	675	473	+1.8	0.0	-8.5
223 Remington (R) (W) (F) (H) (PMC)	55	PSP	24	3240	2747	2304	1905	1282	921	648	473	+1.9	0.0	-8.5
223 Remington (R)	55	HPPL	24	3240	2773	2352	1969	1282	939	675	473	+1.8	0.0	-8.2
223 Remington (W) (F) (PMC)	55	MC	24	3240	2759	2326	1933	1282	929	660	456	+1.9	0.0	-8.4
223 Remington (H)	55	FMC, MC BT	24	3240	2877	2543	2232	1282	1011	790	608	+1.7	0.0	-7.1
225 Winchester (W)	55	PSP	24	3570	3066	2616	2208	1556	1148	836	595	+1.2	0.0	-6.2
22-250 Remington (R) (W) (H) (PMC)	55	PSP	24	3730	3180	2695	2257	1699	1235	887	622	+1.0	0.0	-5.7
22-250 Remington (R)	55	HPPL	24	3730	3253	2826	2436	1699	1292	975	725	+0.9	0.0	-5.2
22-250 Remington (F) — Premium	55	BTHP	24	3730	3330	2960	2630	1700	1350	1070	840	+0.8	0.0	-4.8
220 Swift (H)	55	SP	24	3630	3176	2763	2370	1609	1229	927	686	+1.0	0.0	-5.6
220 Swift (H)	60	HP	24	3530	3134	2755	2420	1657	1305	1016	780	+1.1	0.0	-5.7
243 (W) (R) (F) (H) (PMC)	80	PSP, HPPL, FMJ	24	3350	2955	2593	2259	1993	1551	1194	906	+1.1	0.0	-7.0
243 Winchester (F) — Premium	85	BTHP	24	3320	3070	2830	2600	2080	1770	1510	1280	+1.6	0.0	-6.8
243 Winchester (W) (R) (F) (H) (PMC)	100	PPSP, PSPCL, SP	24	2960	2697	2449	2215	1945	1615	1332	1089	+1.5	0.0	-7.8
243 Winchester (F) — Premium	100	BTSP	24	2960	2760	2570	2380	1950	1690	1460	1260	+1.4	0.0	-5.8
6mm Remington (W) (Also, 244 Rem.)	80	PSP, HPPL	24	3470	3064	2694	2352	2139	1667	1289	982	+1.2	0.0	-6.0
6mm Remington (R) (W) (R)	100	PSPCL, PPSP	24	3130	2857	2600	2357	2175	1812	1501	1233	+1.7	0.0	-6.8
25-20 Winchester (W) (R)	86	SP	24	1460	1194	1030	931	407	272	203	165	0.0	-23.5	-79.6
256 Winchester (W)	60	OPE	24	2760	2097	1542	1149	1015	586	317	176	0.0	-7.3	-29.6
25-35 Winchester (W)	117	SP	24	2230	1866	1545	1282	1292	904	620	427	0.0	-9.2	-33.1
250 Savage (W)	87	PSP	24	3030	2673	2342	2036	1773	1380	1059	801	+2.0	0.0	-8.4
250 Savage (W)	100	ST	24	2820	2504	2210	1936	1765	1351	1017	751	+2.4	0.0	-10.1
250 Savage (R)	100	PSP	24	2820	2467	2140	1839	1765	1392	1084	832	+2.3	0.0	-9.5
257 Roberts (W) (R)	100	ST	24	2900	2541	2210	1904	1867	1433	1084	805	+2.3	0.0	-9.4
257 Roberts (W) (R)	117	SP	24	2650	2291	1961	1663	1824	1363	999	718	+2.9	0.0	-12.0
25-06 Remington (R)	87	HPPL	24	3440	3043	2680	2344	2286	1733	1363	1098	+1.2	0.0	-6.3
25-06 Remington (R) (F)	90	PEP, HP	24	3440	2995	2580	2287	2364	1850	1478	1161	+1.2	0.0	-6.1
25-06 Remington (R)	100	PSPCL	24	3230	2893	2580	2287	2316	1858	1478	1161	+1.6	0.0	-6.9
25-06 Remington (R)	117	PSPCL, PEP	24	3060	2790	2502	2269	2430	2013	1668	1372	+1.8	0.0	-7.4
25-06 Remington (R) (W)	120	PSPCL	24	3010	2749	2502	2269	2414	2020	1660	1360	+1.9	0.0	-7.3
6.5mm Remington Magnum (R)	120	PSPCL	24	3210	2905	2621	2353	2745	2248	1830	1475	+1.3	0.0	-6.6
264 Winchester Magnum (W) (R)	140	PSP	24	3030	2782	2548	2326	2854	2406	2018	1682	+1.8	0.0	-6.7
270 Winchester (W) (R)	100	PSP	24	3480	3067	2690	2343	2689	2088	1606	1219	+1.3	0.0	-6.2
270 Winchester (W) (R)	130	PPSP, BP, SP	24	3110	2849	2604	2371	2791	2343	1957	1622	+1.2	0.0	-6.8
270 Winchester (W) (R) (F)	130	ST, PSPCL	24	(row continues onto next page)										

Ballistics table (continued). Columns: Cartridge | Bullet Wt. (grs.) | Bullet Type | Bbl. (in.) | Velocity (fps): Muzzle / 100 / 200 / 300 yd | Energy (ft-lbs): Muzzle / 100 / 200 / 300 yd | Trajectory (in.)

Cartridge	Wt.	Bullet Type	Bbl.	V₀	V₁₀₀	V₂₀₀	V₃₀₀	E₀	E₁₀₀	E₂₀₀	E₃₀₀	T1	T2	T3
270 Winchester (R) (F)	150	SPCL, SP	24	—	—	—	—	—	—	—	—	0.0	0.0	7.0
270 Winchester (F) — Premium	150	NP	24	2900	2550	2225	1926	2801	2165	1649	1235	+2.2	0.0	9.3
7mm Mauser (F) (R)	175	SP	24	2440	2137	1857	1603	2313	1774	1340	998	+2.1	6.8	8.2
7mm Mauser (F) (R)	140	SP	24	2660	2450	2260	2070	2200	1865	1585	1330	—	—	23.7
7mm-08 Remington (R)	140	PSPCL	24	2860	2625	2402	2189	2542	2142	1793	1490	+2.4	0.0	3.2
280 Remington (R)	150	SPCL	24	2970	2699	2444	2203	2937	2426	1989	1616	+2.1	0.0	8.1
280 Remington (R)	165	PPSP	24	2820	2510	2220	1950	2913	2308	1805	1393	+1.9	0.0	7.8
284 Winchester (W)	150	PSPCL, PPSP, SP	24	2860	2595	2344	2108	2724	2243	1830	1480	+2.3	0.0	9.4
7mm Remington Magnum (R) (W) (F)	150	PSPCL, PPSP, SP	24	3110	2830	2568	2320	3221	2667	2196	1792	—	0.0	8.5
7mm Remington Magnum (F)—Premium	150	BTSP	24	3110	2920	2750	2580	3220	2850	2510	2210	+2.1	0.0	7.0
7mm Remington Magnum (F)—Premium	165	BTSP	24	2860	2710	2560	2420	3000	2690	2410	2150	+1.7	0.0	6.2
7mm Remington Magnum (R) (W) (F) (H)	175	PSPCL, PPSP	24	2860	2645	2440	2244	3178	2718	2313	1956	+1.6	0.0	6.9
7mm Remington Magnum (F)—Premium	160	NP	24	2950	2730	2520	2320	3090	2650	2250	1910	+1.6	0.0	7.9
30 Carbine (R) (W) (F) (H)	110	FMC, MC, FMJ, FMC	20	1990	1567	1236	1035	967	600	373	262	+2.0	-13.5	49.9
30 Carbine (W) (F) (H) (PMC)	110	SPCL, ST	20	1990	1596	1278	1070	967	622	399	280	+1.8	-13.0	47.4
30 Remington (R)	170	SP, HSP, SP, RN	24	2120	1822	1555	1328	1696	1253	913	666	0.0	9.7	33.8
30-30 Accelerator (R)	55	SP	24	3400	2693	2085	1570	1412	886	521	301	0.0	0.0	10.2
30-30 Winchester (F)	125	HP	24	2570	2090	1660	1320	1830	1210	770	480	+2.0	0.0	28.1
30-30 Winchester (W) (F) (PMC)	150	OPE, PPSP, ST, SP	24	2390	2018	1684	1398	1902	1356	944	651	0.0	7.3	27.9
30-30 Winchester (R) (H)	170	SPCL	24	2390	1973	1605	1303	1902	1296	858	565	0.0	7.7	30.0
30-30 Winchester (W) (R) (F) (PMC)	150	PPSP, ST, SPCL, SP, HPCL	24	2200	1895	1619	1381	1827	1355	989	720	0.0	8.2	31.1
300 Savage (W)	150	PPSP	24	2630	2311	2015	1743	2303	1779	1352	1012	+2.8	8.9	11.5
300 Savage (W) (F) (R)	150	ST, SP, PSPCL	24	2630	2354	2095	1853	2303	1845	1462	1143	+2.7	0.0	10.7
300 Savage (R) (W) (F)	180	SPCL, PPSP	24	2350	2025	1728	1467	2207	1639	1193	860	0.0	7.7	27.1
30-40 Krag (R) (W)	180	SPCL, PPSP	24	2430	2098	1795	1525	2360	1761	1288	929	0.0	7.1	25.0
303 Savage (W)	190	ST	24	1940	1657	1410	1211	1588	1158	839	619	+1.0	-11.9	41.4
308 Accelerator (R)	55	PSP	24	3770	3215	2726	2286	1735	1262	907	638	+2.0	0.0	5.6
308 Winchester (W)	125	PSP	24	3050	2697	2370	2067	2582	2019	1559	1186	+2.4	0.0	8.2
308 Winchester (W)	150	PPSP	24	2820	2488	2179	1893	2648	2061	1581	1193	+2.3	0.0	9.8
308 Winchester (W) (R) (F) (H) (PMC)	150	ST, PSPCL, SP	24	2820	2533	2263	2009	2648	2137	1705	1344	+2.3	0.0	9.1
308 Winchester (PMC)	147	FMC-BT	24	2750	2473	2257	2052	2428	2037	1697	1403	+2.9	0.0	9.1
308 Winchester (H)	165	BTSP	24	2700	2520	2330	2160	2670	2310	1990	1700	+2.6	0.0	8.4
308 Winchester (W) (R) (F) (PMC)	180	PPSP, SPCL	24	2620	2274	1955	1666	2743	2086	1527	1109	+1.8	0.0	12.1
308 Winchester (W) (R) (F)	180	ST, PSPCL, SP	24	3140	2780	2447	2138	2839	2288	1896	1557	+2.2	0.0	9.9
30-06 Springfield (W) (R) (F)	125	PSP, PSP, SP	24	2920	2617	2265	1972	2820	2217	1662	1269	+2.1	0.0	7.7
30-06 Springfield (W)	150	PPSP	24	2910	2656	2416	2189	2820	2281	1708	1295	+2.0	0.0	9.0
30-06 Springfield (W) (R) (F) (H) (PMC)	150	ST, PSPCL, SP, SP	24	2910	2555	2310	2080	2630	2349	1827	1445	+2.0	0.0	8.5
30-06 Springfield (PMC)	150	BP	24	2810	2534	2283	2047	2033	2170	1944	1596	+2.2	0.0	8.8
30-06 Springfield (R)	150	FMC (M-2)	24	4080	3485	2965	2502	2872	2352	1780	1440	+1.0	0.0	8.0
30-06 Accelerator (R)	55	PSP	24	2800	2610	2420	2240	2870	2490	2150	764	+2.3	0.0	9.0
30-06 Springfield (W)	165	PSPCL	24	2800	2348	2023	1727	2913	2203	1635	1534	+2.1	0.0	9.0
30-06 Springfield (F) (H)	165	BTSP	24	2700	2469	2250	2042	2913	2436	2023	1840	+2.7	0.0	11.3
30-06 Springfield (R) (W)	180	SPCL, PPSP	24	2700	2485	2280	2084	2913	2468	2077	1192	+2.4	0.0	9.3
30-06 Springfield (W) (PMC)	180	PSPCL, ST	24	2410	2130	1870	1632	2837	2216	1708	1666	0.0	0.0	9.1
30-06 Springfield (R) (W) (F) (H) (PMC)	180	BP	24	2410	2192	1985	1791	3315	2785	2325	1736	+2.1	0.0	23.6
30-06 Springfield (W) (R) (F)	220	PPSP, SPCL	24	2880	2640	2412	2196	3605	2900	2314	1301	+1.3	0.0	21.6
30-06 Springfield (W)	220	ST	24	3290	2951	2636	2342	3501	3011	2578	1927	+1.9	0.0	8.0
300 H & H Magnum (W) (R)	150	ST, PSPCL	24	2960	2745	2540	2344	3560	3180	2830	1827	+1.7	0.0	6.6
300 Winchester Magnum (W) (R)	180	PPSP, PSPCL	24	2830	2680	2530	2380	—	—	—	2196	0.0	0.0	7.3
300 Winchester Magnum (W) (R) (F) (H)	180	PPSP, PSPCL, SP	24	2460	2124	1817	1542	2418	1803	1319	2520	0.0	-6.9	7.1
300 Winchester Magnum (F) Premium	180	BTSP	24	2460	2233	2018	1816	2418	1803	1319	950	+1.7	-6.1	24.4
303 British (R)	180	SPCL	24	1210	1021	913	—	325	231	185	1318	0.0	-32.3	20.8
303 British (R)	180	PPSP	24	1210	1021	913	834	325	231	185	154	0.0	-32.3	-106.3
32-20 Winchester (W) (R)	100	SP	24	—	—	—	834	—	—	—	154	0.0	0.0	-106.3
32-20 Winchester (W) (R)	100	L	24	—	—	—	—	—	—	—	—	—	—	—

(cont.)

CENTERFIRE RIFLE CARTRIDGES (continued)

Cartridge	BULLET Wt. Grs.	BULLET Type	Bbl. (in.)	VELOCITY (fps) Muzzle	100 yds.	200 yds.	300 yds.	ENERGY (ft. lbs.) Muzzle	100 yds.	200 yds.	300 yds.	BULLET PATH† 100 yds.	200 yds.	300 yds.
32 Winchester Special (F) (R)	170	SP	24	2250	1920	1630	1370	1911	1390	1000	710	0.0	- 8.6	- 30.5
8mm Mauser (R) (W)	170	SPCL, PPSP	24	2360	1969	1622	1333	2102	1463	993	671	0.0	- 8.2	- 29.8
8mm Mauser (F)	170	SP	24	2510	2110	1740	1430	2380	1670	1140	770	0.0	- 7.0	- 25.7
8mm Remington Magnum (R)	185	PSPCL	24	3080	2761	2464	2186	3896	3131	2494	1963	+1.8	0.0	- 7.6
8mm Remington Magnum (R)	220	PSPCL	24	2830	2581	2346	2123	3912	3254	2688	2201	+2.2	0.0	- 8.5
338 Winchester Magnum (W)	200	PPSP	24	2960	2658	2375	2110	3890	3137	2505	1977	+2.0	0.0	- 8.2
338 Winchester Magnum (W)	250	ST	24	2660	2395	2145	1910	3927	3184	2554	2025	+2.6	0.0	- 10.2
348 Winchester (W)	200	ST	20	2520	2215	1931	1672	2820	2178	1656	1241	0.0	- 6.2	- 21.9
351 Winchester S.L. (W)	180	SP	20	1850	1556	1310	1128	1368	968	686	508	0.0	- 13.6	- 47.5
35 Remington (R)	150	PSPCL	24	2300	1874	1506	1218	1762	1169	755	494	0.0	- 9.2	- 33.0
35 Remington (R) (F)	200	SPCL, SP	24	2080	1698	1376	1140	1921	1280	841	577	0.0	- 11.3	- 41.2
35 Remington (W)	200	PPSP, ST	24	2020	1646	1335	1114	1812	1203	791	551	0.0	- 12.1	- 43.9
358 Winchester (W)	200	ST	24	2490	2171	1876	1610	2753	2093	1563	1151	0.0	- 6.5	- 23.0
350 Remington Magnum (R)	200	PSPCL	20	2710	2410	2130	1870	3261	2579	2014	1553	+2.6	0.0	- 10.3
375 Winchester (W)	200	PPSP	24	2200	1841	1526	1268	2150	1506	1034	714	0.0	- 9.5	- 33.8
375 Winchester (W)	250	PPSP	24	1900	1647	1424	1239	2005	1506	1126	852	0.0	- 12.0	- 40.9
38-55 Winchester (W)	255	SP	24	1320	1190	1091	1018	987	802	674	587	0.0	- 23.4	- 75.2
375 H & H Magnum (R) (W)	270	SP, PPSP	24	2690	2420	2166	1928	4337	3510	2812	2228	+2.5	0.0	- 10.0
375 H & H Magnum (W)	300	ST	24	2530	2268	2022	1793	4263	3426	2723	2141	+2.9	0.0	- 11.5
375 H & H Magnum (R) (W)	300	FMC, MC	24	2530	2171	1843	1551	4263	3139	2262	1602	0.0	- 6.5	- 23.4
38-40 Winchester (W)	180	SP	24	1160	999	901	822	538	399	324	273	0.0	- 33.9	- 110.6
44-40 Winchester (W) (R)	200	SP, SP	24	1190	1006	900	822	629	449	360	300	0.0	- 33.3	- 109.5
44 Remington Magnum (R)	240	SP, SJHP	20	1760	1380	1114	970	1650	1015	661	501	0.0	- 17.6	- 63.1
44 Remington Magnum (F) (W)	240	HSP	20	1760	1380	1090	950	1650	1015	640	485	0.0	- 18.1	- 65.1
444 Marlin (R)	240	SP	24	2350	1815	1377	1087	2942	1755	1010	630	0.0	- 9.9	- 38.5
444 Marlin (R)	265	SP	24	2120	1733	1405	1160	2644	1768	1162	791	0.0	- 10.8	- 39.5
45-70 Government (F)	300	HSP	24	1810	1410	1120	970	2180	1320	840	630	0.0	- 17.0	- 61.4
45-70 Government (W)	300	JHP	24	1880	1559	1294	1105	2355	1619	1116	814	0.0	- 13.5	- 47.1
45-70 Government (R)	405	SP	24	1330	1168	1055	977	1590	1227	1001	858	0.0	- 24.6	- 80.3
458 Winchester Magnum (W) (R)	500	FMC, MC	24	2040	1823	1623	1442	4620	3689	2924	2308	0.0	- 9.6	- 32.5
458 Winchester Magnum (W) (R)	510	SP, SP	24	2040	1770	1527	1319	4712	3547	2640	1970	0.0	- 10.3	- 35.6

*Price for 50. †Bullet Path based on line-of-sight 0.9" above center of bore. Bullet type abbreviations: BP—Bronze Point; BT—Boat Tail; CL—Core Lokt; FN—Flat Nose; FMC—Full Metal Case; FMJ—Full Metal Jacket; HP—Hollow Point; HSP—Hollow Soft Point; JHP—Jacketed Hollow Point; L—Lead; Lu—Lubaloy; MAT—Match; MC—Metal Case; NP—Nosler Partition; OPE—Open Point Expanding; PCL—Pointed Core Lokt; PEP—Pointed Expanding Point; PL—Power-Lokt; PP—Power-Lokt; Prem.—Premium; PSP—Pointed Soft Point; SJHP—Semi-Jacketed Hollow Point; SJMP—Semi-Jacketed Metal Point; SP—Soft Point; ST—Silvertip; SX—Super Explosive. PMC prices slightly less.

WEATHERBY MAGNUM CARTRIDGES

Cartridge	Wt. Grs.	Bullet Type	Bbl. (in.)	Velocity (fps) Muzzle	100 Yds.	200 Yds.	300 Yds.	Energy (ft. lbs.) Muzzle	100 Yds.	200 Yds.	300 Yds.	Bullet Path† 100 Yds.	200 Yds.	300 Yds.
224 Weatherby Magnum	55	PE	26	3650	3214	2808	2433	1627	1262	963	723	+2.8	+3.6	0.0
240 Weatherby Magnum	87	PE	26	3500	3165	2848	2550	2367	1935	1567	1256	+2.8	+3.6	0.0
240 Weatherby Magnum	100	PE	26	3395	3115	2848	2594	2560	2155	1802	1495	+2.8	+3.5	0.0
240 Weatherby Magnum	100	NP	26	3395	3068	2758	2468	2560	2090	1690	1353	+1.1	0.0	−5.7
257 Weatherby Magnum	87	PE	26	3825	3470	3135	2818	2827	2327	1900	1535	+2.1	+2.9	0.0
257 Weatherby Magnum	100	PE	26	3555	3256	2971	2700	2807	2355	1960	1619	+2.5	+3.2	0.0
257 Weatherby Magnum	100	NP	26	3555	3242	2945	2663	2807	2335	1926	1575	+0.9	0.0	−4.7
257 Weatherby Magnum	117	SPE	26	3300	2853	2443	2074	2830	2115	1551	1118	+3.8	+4.9	0.0
270 Weatherby Magnum	100	PE	26	3760	3341	2949	2585	3140	2479	1932	1484	+1.2	0.0	−5.9
270 Weatherby Magnum	130	PE	26	3375	3110	2856	2615	3289	2793	2355	1974	+2.4	+3.2	0.0
270 Weatherby Magnum	130	NP	26	3375	3113	2862	2624	3289	2798	2365	1988	+2.8	+3.5	0.0
270 Weatherby Magnum	150	PE	26	3245	3012	2789	2575	3508	3022	2592	2209	+1.0	0.0	−5.2
270 Weatherby Magnum	150	NP	26	3245	3022	2809	2604	3508	3043	2629	2259	+3.1	+3.8	0.0
7mm Weatherby Magnum	139	PE	26	3300	3037	2786	2546	3362	2848	2396	2001	+1.2	0.0	−5.4
7mm Weatherby Magnum	140	NP	26	3300	3047	2806	2575	3386	2887	2448	2062	+3.0	+3.7	0.0
7mm Weatherby Magnum	154	PE	26	3160	2928	2706	2494	3415	2932	2504	2127	+1.1	0.0	−5.4
7mm Weatherby Magnum	160	NP	26	3150	2935	2727	2528	3526	3061	2643	2271	+3.3	+4.1	0.0
7mm Weatherby Magnum	175	RN	26	3070	2714	2383	2082	3663	2863	2207	1685	+1.3	0.0	−5.8
300 Weatherby Magnum	110	PE	26	3900	3465	3057	2677	3716	2933	2283	1750	+1.6	0.0	−7.5
300 Weatherby Magnum	150	PE	26	3545	3248	2965	2696	4187	3515	2929	2422	+2.2	+3.0	0.0
300 Weatherby Magnum	150	NP	26	3545	3191	2857	2544	4187	3392	2719	2156	+2.5	+3.2	0.0
300 Weatherby Magnum	180	PE	26	3245	3010	2785	2569	4210	3622	3100	2639	+1.0	0.0	−5.3
300 Weatherby Magnum	180	NP	26	3245	2964	2696	2444	4210	3512	2906	2388	+3.1	+3.8	0.0
300 Weatherby Magnum	220	SPE	26	2905	2578	2276	2000	4123	3248	2531	1955	+1.3	0.0	−6.0
340 Weatherby Magnum	200	PE	26	3210	2947	2696	2458	4577	3857	3228	2683	+1.9	0.0	−8.6
340 Weatherby Magnum	210	NP	26	3180	2927	2686	2457	4717	3996	3365	2816	+3.2	+4.0	0.0
340 Weatherby Magnum	250	SPE	26	2850	2516	2209	1929	4510	3515	2710	2066	+1.3	0.0	−6.2
340 Weatherby Magnum	250	NP	26	2850	2563	2296	2049	4510	3648	2927	2331	+2.0	0.0	−9.2
378 Weatherby Magnum	270	SPE	26	3180	2796	2440	2117	6064	4688	3570	2688	+1.8	0.0	−8.2
378 Weatherby Magnum	300	SPE	26	2925	2564	2234	1935	5700	4380	3325	2495	+1.5	0.0	−7.3
378 Weatherby Magnum	300	FMJ	26	2925	2620	2340	2080	5700	4574	3648	2883	+1.9	0.0	−9.0
460 Weatherby Magnum	500	RN	26	2700	2395	2115	1858	8095	6370	4968	3834	+4.9	0.0	−10.3
460 Weatherby Magnum	500	FMJ	26	2700	2416	2154	1912	8095	6482	5153	4060	+2.3	0.0	−9.8

†Bullet Path based on line of sight 1.5" above center of bore. Bullet type abbreviations: FMJ—Full Metal Jacket; NP—Nosler Partition; PE—Pointed Expanding; RN—Round Nose; SPE— Semi-Pointed Expanding.

NORMA C.F. RIFLE CARTRIDGES

Cartridge	Wt. Grs.	Bullet Type	Velocity (fps) Muzzle	100 Yds.	200 Yds.	300 Yds.	Energy (ft. lbs.) Muzzle	100 Yds.	200 Yds.	300 Yds.	Bullet Path† 100 Yds.	200 Yds.	300 Yds.
22 Hornet	45	HP	2430	1895	1355	985	590	360	185	95	0.0	-7.7	-31.3
222 Remington	50	SP	3200	2650	2180	1760	1135	780	475	310	+2.2	0.0	-10.0
222 Remington	50	FMJ	3200	2610	2130	1710	1135	755	454	292	+2.2	0.0	-9.6
222 Remington	53	SP	3115	2670	2190	1770	1140	840	480	313	+2.1	0.0	-9.4
22-250 Remington	53	SP	3710	3190	2740	2250	1615	1200	751	506	+1.0	0.0	-5.7
220 Swift	50	SP	4110	3610	3135	2680	1875	1450	1090	800	+0.6	0.0	-4.1
22 Savage Hi-Power	71	SP, FMJ	2790	2295	1885	1560	1225	830	560	385	+1.4	0.0	-11.4
243 Winchester	100	SP, FMJ	3070	2790	2540	2320	2090	1730	1430	1190	+1.4	0.0	-6.3
6.5 × 50 Jap.	139	SBT	2360	2185	2035	1900	1720	1475	1243	1083	+2.8	0.0	-11.1
6.5 × 50 Jap.	156	SP	2065	1870	1690	1530	1480	1215	990	810	+4.3	0.0	-16.4
6.5 × 52 Carcano	156	SP	2430	2210	2000	1800	2045	1690	1385	1125	+2.9	0.0	-11.7
6.5 × 55 Swedish	139	PPC	2855	2660	2500	2350	2512	2181	1875	1657	+1.7	0.0	-7.6
6.5 × 55 Swedish	140	Nosler	2855	2665	2505	2350	2530	2210	1930	1677	+1.7	0.0	-7.6
6.5 × 55 Swedish	156	SP	2645	2415	2205	2010	2425	2015	1701	1414	+2.5	0.0	-10.6
270 Winchester	130	SP	3140	2885	2640	2405	2845	2400	2010	1670	+1.4	0.0	-6.6
270 Winchester	150	SP	2800	2615	2435	2260	2615	2280	1975	1705	+1.8	0.0	-7.7
7 × 57 R	150	SP, FMJ	2690	2475	2285	2080	2410	2040	1830	1515	+2.0	0.0	-8.4
7 × 57 Mauser	150	SP	2755	2540	2330	2135	2530	2150	1810	1515	+2.0	0.0	-8.4
280 Remington	150	PPC	2870	2640	2400	2200	2740	2320	2015	1695	+1.9	0.0	-7.9
280 Remington	170	SP	2710	2460	2220	1945	2765	2280	1910	1510	+2.3	0.0	-9.2
7 × 64 Brenneke	150	SP	2890	2600	2330	2115	2780	2250	1810	1490	+1.7	0.0	-7.5
7 × 64 Brenneke	170	PPC	2750	2455	2200	1915	2865	2365	1694	1466	+2.8	0.0	-10.0
7mm Remington Magnum	150	FMJ	3250	2960	2640	2440	3520	2920	2320	1985	+1.2	0.0	-5.8
7mm Remington Magnum	150	PPC	2995	2780	2460	2260	2985	2575	2118	1788	+1.4	0.0	-6.0
7mm Remington Magnum	170	PPC	3020	2750	2510	2410	3440	2860	2520	2323	+2.0	0.0	-8.7
30 Carbine	110	SP	1970	1595	1260	1055	950	620	400	280	0.0	-4.0	-12.5
7.62 × 39 Soviet	125	SP	2340	1860	1430	1100	1470	1037	614	363	+2.5	0.0	-8.6
30-30 Winchester	150	SP	2330	2000	1660	1380	1805	1330	966	666	0.0	-7.7	-27.9
30-30 Winchester	170	SP	2135	1810	1530	1180	1715	1235	936	557	0.0	-8.9	-31.1
308 Winchester	130	SP	2900	2595	2390	2060	2430	1935	1545	1273	+1.8	0.0	-7.9
308 Winchester	146	FMJBT	2810	2595	2390	2180	2560	2180	1760	1426	+1.8	0.0	-7.4
308 Winchester	150	SP	2860	2570	2300	2050	2725	2200	1954	1400	+1.9	0.0	-8.5
308 Winchester	168	HPBT	2550	2370	2180	2010	2276	1966	1663	1414	+2.3	0.0	-8.7
308 Winchester	180	DC	2610	2400	2210	2020	2725	2305	1954	1632	+2.4	0.0	-9.3
308 Winchester	180	Nosler	2610	2400	2210	2020	2725	2305	1954	1369	+2.4	0.0	-9.3
308 Winchester	180	A	2610	2400	2170	1870	2725	2305	1884	1399	+2.4	0.0	-9.3
308 Winchester	180	PPC	2460	2395	2180	1850	2690	2185	1800	1285	+2.7	0.0	-9.6
308 Winchester	200	PPC	2460	2220	2000	1690	2965	2390	1901	1480	+1.4	0.0	-10.3
30-06 Springfield	130	SP	3205	2875	2560	2263	2945	2395	2115	1335	+1.4	0.0	-6.7
30-06 Springfield	146	FMJBT	2770	2555	2340	2140	2490	2485	1920	1525	+1.7	0.0	-7.3
30-06 Springfield	150	SP	2970	2680	2400	2140	2915	2485	2105	1775	+1.7	0.0	-7.8
30-06 Springfield	180	DC	2700	2495	2295	2110	2915	2485	2105	1775	+2.0	0.0	-8.6
30-06 Springfield	180	Nosler	2700	2495	2295	2110	2915	2485	2105	1505	+2.0	0.0	-8.6
30-06 Springfield	180	A	2700	2490	2270	1940	2915	2480	2061	1521	+2.0	0.0	-8.5
30-06 Springfield	180	PPC	2700	2490	2280	1950	2915	2480	2079		+2.0	0.0	-8.5

Cartridge	Wt. Grs.	Bullet Type		Velocity (fps)				Energy (ft.-lbs.)			Bullet Path†		
7.5 × 55 Swiss	180	SBT	2650	2460	2250	2060	2800	2380	2020	1690	+2.1	0.0	−8.9
7.62 × 54R Russian	180	SBT	2575	2360	2165	1975	2650	2270	1875	1560	+2.3	0.0	−9.5
7.65 × 53 Argentine	150	SP	2660	2390	2120	1870	2355	1895	1573	1224	+2.1	0.0	−8.8
300 Winchester Magnum	180	SBT	3020	2780	2590	2400	3645	3095	2683	2304	+1.4	0.0	−7.4
308 Norma Magnum	180	DC	3020	2780	2580	2385	3645	3095	2670	2270	+1.3	0.0	−8.0
303 British	150	SP	2720	2440	2170	1930	2465	1985	1570	1240	+2.2	0.0	−9.7
7.7 × 58 Jap.	130	SP	2950	2635	2340	2065	2513	2005	1581	1230	+1.8	0.0	−8.2
7.7 × 58 Jap.	180	SBT	2495	2290	2100	1920	2485	2100	1765	1475	+2.6	0.0	−10.4
8 × 57 Mauser JS	165	PPC	2855	2525	2225	1955	2985	2335	1733	1338	+2.0	0.0	−8.0
8 × 57 Mauser JS	196	A	2525	2195	1895	1625	2780	2100	1560	1150	+2.9	0.0	−12.7
9.3 × 57 Mauser	286	A	2065	1820	1580	1400	2715	2100	1622	1274	+3.4	0.0	−21.7
9.3 × 62 Mauser	286	A	2360	2090	1830	1580	3545	2770	2177	1622	+3.0	0.0	−20.2

†Bullet Path based on line of sight 1.5" above center of bore. Bullet type abbreviations: HP—Hollow Point; SP—Soft Point; FMJ—Full Metal Jacket; PPC—Protected Power Cavity: Nosler— Nosler Partition; FMJBT—Full Metal Jacket Boat Tail; SBT—Spitzer Boat Tail; A—Alaska (Round Nose Soft Point); DC—Dual Core. *50 Rounds Per Box

Courtesy Gun Digest

CIL Range Table

RANGE TABLE—Values shown in this table are based on a sight height 1½″ above line of
bore. **RECOMMENDED SIGHTING:** ⊕ Indicates the most favorable sighting range in

Description	First Crosses Line of Sight (app. yds.)	50 yds.	75 yds.	100 yds.	125 yds.
22 Hornet	29.0	—	+1.5	—	—
22 Savage	25.0	—	—	+2.0	—
222 Remington	30.0	—	—	+2.0	—
243 Winchester	30.0	—	—	—	+2.5
243 Winchester	27.5	—	—	—	+3.0
244 Remington	30.0	—	—	—	+2.5
6.5 × 53mm Man.-Sch.	25.5	—	+1.5	—	—
6.5 × 55mm	21.0	—	—	+3.5	—
25-20 Winchester	16.0	+2.0	—	⊕	−4.0
25-35 Winchester	23.0	—	+1.5	—	—
250 Savage	27.5	—	—	+2.0	—
257 Roberts	24.0	—	—	+2.5	—
270 Winchester	31.5	—	—	—	+2.5
270 Winchester	27.5	—	—	—	+3.0
270 Winchester	28.5	—	—	+2.0	—
7 × 57mm Mauser	27.0	—	—	—	+4.0
7 × 57mm Mauser	29.0	—	—	+2.5	—
7mm Remington Magnum	25.0	—	—	—	+3.5
30-30 Winchester	27.0	—	+1.5	—	—
30-30 Winchester	23.0	—	+1.5	—	—
30-30 Winchester	23.0	—	+1.5	—	—
30-30 Winchester	23.0	—	+1.5	—	—
30-30 Winchester	27.0	—	+1.5	—	—
30 Remington	20.0	—	+2.0	—	—
30-30 Krag	21.0	—	—	+3.0	—
30-06 Springfield	27.0	—	—	—	+3.0
30-06 Springfield	25.0	—	—	—	+3.5
30-06 Springfield	25.0	—	—	—	+3.5
30-06 Springfield	24.0	—	—	+2.5	—
30-06 Springfield	21.0	—	—	—	+4.0
30-06 Springfield	20.0	—	—	—	+4.0
30-06 Springfield	21.0	—	—	+3.0	—
300 Winchester Magnum	27.5	—	—	—	+3.0
300 Holland & Holland Magnum	25.0	—	—	—	+3.5
300 Savage	26.0	—	—	+2.5	—
300 Savage	26.0	—	—	+2.5	—
300 Savage	20.0	—	—	+3.5	—
300 Savage	21.5	—	—	+3.0	—
303 Savage	17.5	—	—	+3.0	—
303 British	22.0	—	—	—	+4.5
303 British	22.0	—	—	—	+4.5
303 British	23.0	—	—	+3.0	—
303 British	19.0	—	—	—	+4.5
303 British	17.5	—	—	—	+5.0
303 British	16.0	—	—	+4.5	—
308 Winchester	23.5	—	—	—	+3.5
308 Winchester	25.0	—	—	—	+3.5

order to minimize the sighting problem at shorter and longer ranges. + Indicates inches high; — Indicates inches low.

150 yds.	200 yds.	250 yds.	300 yds.	400 yds.	500 yds.	Bullet Wt. Grs.	Type
⊕	−4.0	—	—	—	—	45	PSP
—	⊕	−4.5	—	—	—	70	PSP
—	⊕	−3.5	—	—	—	50	PSP
—	—	⊕	−3.0	−15.5	−36.5	75	PSP
—	—	⊕	−3.5	−16.5	−35.5	100	PSP
—	—	⊕	−3.0	−15.5	−36.5	75	PSP
⊕	−4.0	—	—	—	—	160	SP
—	⊕	−5.0	−13.0	−39.0	—	160	SP
—	—	—	—	—	—	86	SP
⊕	−4.5	—	—	—	—	117	SP
—	⊕	−3.5	—	—	—	100	PSP
—	⊕	−4.5	—	—	—	117	PSP
—	—	⊕	−3.5	−14.5	−33.5	100	PSP
—	—	⊕	−4.0	−16.0	−35.5	130	PSP
—	⊕	−4.0	—	−25.0	—	160	KKSP
—	—	⊕	−4.5	−18.5	−41.0	139	PSP
—	⊕	−4.0	—	−28.5	—	160	KKSP
—	—	⊕	−4.0	−18.0	−43.0	175	SP
⊕	−4.0	—	—	—	—	150	PNEU
⊕	−4.5	—	—	—	—	170	KKSP
⊕	−4.5	—	—	—	—	170	ST
⊕	−4.5	—	—	—	—	170	MC
⊕	−4.0	—	—	—	—	150	ST
⊕	−5.0	—	—	—	—	170	KKSP
—	⊕	−5.5	—	−41.0	—	180	KKSP
—	—	⊕	−4.0	−19.5	−47.0	130	HP
—	—	⊕	−4.0	−17.5	−41.0	150	PSP
—	—	⊕	−4.0	−17.5	−41.0	150	ST
—	⊕	−4.0	—	−32.5	—	180	KKSP
—	—	⊕	−4.5	−20.5	−46.0	180	CPE
—	—	⊕	−4.5	−21.0	−48.5	180	ST
—	⊕	−5.5	—	−41.0	—	220	KKSP
—	—	⊕	−3.5	−14.5	−32.5	180	ST
—	—	⊕	−4.0	−17.5	−39.0	180	PSP
—	⊕	−3.5	—	−29.0	—	150	PSP
—	⊕	−3.5	—	−29.0	—	150	ST
—	⊕	−5.5	—	−43.0	—	180	KKSP
—	⊕	−5.5	—	−35.0	—	180	ST
—	⊕	−5.5	—	—	—	190	KKSP
—	—	⊕	−5.0	−23.0	−53.5	150	PSP
—	—	⊕	−5.0	−23.0	−53.5	150	ST
—	⊕	−5.0	—	−41.0	—	180	KKSP
—	—	⊕	−5.0	−23.0	−52.5	180	CPE
—	—	⊕	−5.5	−26.5	−71.0	180	ST
—	⊕	−7.0	—	−54.0	—	215	KKSP
—	—	⊕	−4.5	−23.5	−59.0	130	HP
—	—	⊕	−4.5	−20.0	−47.5	150	PSP

(cont.)

CIL Range Table (*cont.*)

Description	First Crosses Line of Sight (app. yds.)	50 yds.	75 yds.	100 yds.	125 yds.
308 Winchester	25.0	—	—	—	+3.5
308 Winchester	23.0	—	—	+3.0	—
308 Winchester	22.0	—	—	—	+4.5
308 Winchester	22.0	—	—	+3.0	—
8mm Mauser	22.5	—	—	+3.5	—
32-20 Winchester	16.5	+2.0	—	⊕	−3.5
32 Winchester Special	23.0	—	+2.0	—	—
32 Winchester Special	23.0	—	+2.0	—	—
32 Remington	20.0	—	+2.0	—	—
32-40 Winchester	21.0	+1.0	—	⊕	−2.5
35 Remington	19.5	—	+2.5	—	—
351 Winchester Self-Loading	16.0	—	+3.0	—	—
358 (8.8mm) Winchester	20.5	—	—	+3.0	—
38-40 Winchester	14.5	+2.5	—	⊕	−4.0
38-55 Winchester	13.5	—	+4.0	—	—
43 (11mm) Mauser	16.0	+2.0	—	⊕	−3.5
44-40 Winchester	12.5	+3.0	—	⊕	−4.5
44 Remington Magnum	13.0	—	+4.5	—	—

Short Range Sighting-in—It is preferable to sight-in a rifle at the "recommended sighting" range. However, it is sometimes necessary to sight-in a rifle at a distance shorter than the "recommended sighting" range because you don't have the necessary yardage available. To do this, find from the range table at what distance the bullet will first cross the line of sight. Put up a target at this distance and from a firm rest fire a three-shot group. The center point of the group is the "cen-

150 yds.	200 yds.	250 yds.	300 yds.	400 yds.	500 yds.	Bullet Wt. Grs.	Type
—	—	⊕	−4.5	−20.0	−47.5	150	ST
—	⊕	−5.5	—	−38.0	—	180	KKSP
—	—	⊕	−5.0	−21.5	−51.5	180	ST
—	⊕	−5.0	−12.0	−35.0	−48.5	200	KKSP
—	⊕	−5.5	—	−33.5	—	170	PSP
—	—	—	—	—	—	115	SP
⊕	−4.5	—	—	—	—	170	KKSP
⊕	−4.5	—	—	—	—	170	ST
⊕	−5.0	—	—	—	—	170	KKSP
—	—	—	—	—	—	170	KKSP
⊕	−6.0	—	—	—	—	200	SP
⊕	−7.5	—	—	—	—	180	SP
—	⊕	−5.0	—	−38.5	—	200	KKSP
—	—	—	—	—	—	180	SP
⊕	−8.5	—	—	—	—	255	SP
—	—	—	—	—	—	385	LEAD
—	—	—	—	—	—	200	SP
⊕	−8.0	—	—	—	—	240	SP

ter of impact"—the average spot where the bullets strike. Adjust sights to bring the center of impact to the center of the target then fire another group. If the center of impact is on target the rifle will be sighted in at the range recommended in the range table. It is, however, desirable to fire a target at that range as soon as possible as a double check.

Rimfire Cartridges

Cartridge Type	Wt. Grs.	Bullet Type	Muzzle	Velocity (fps) 18½″ Barrel 50 yds.
22 CB Short (CCI & Win. only)	29	Solid	727	667
22 CB Long (CCI only)	29	Solid	727	667
22 Short Standard Velocity	29	Solid	1045	—
22 Short High Velocity (Fed., Rem., Win.)	29	Solid	1095	—
22 Short High Velocity (CCI only)	29	Solid	1132	1004
22 Short High Velocity HP (Fed., Rem., Win.)	27	Hollow Point	1120	—
22 Short High Vel. HP (CCI only)	27	Hollow Point	1164	1013
22 Long Standard Vel. (CCI only)	29	Solid	1180	1038
22 Long High Velocity (Fed., Rem., Win.)	29	Solid	1240	—
22 Long Rifle Stand. Velocity (CCI only)	40	Solid	1138	1046
22 Long Rifle Stand. Velocity (Fed., Rem., Win.)	40	Solid	1150	—
22 Long Rifle High Vel. (CCI only)	40	Solid	1341	1150
22 Long Rifle High Velocity (Fed., Rem., Win.)	40	Solid	1255	—
22 Long Rifle High Velocity HP (CCI only)	37	Hollow Point	1370	1165
22 Long Rifle High Velocity HP (Fed., Rem., Win.)	36–38	Hollow Point	1280	—
22 Long Rifle Yellow Jacket (Rem. only)	33	Hollow Point	1500	1240
22 Long Rifle Spitfire (Fed. only)	33	Hollow Point	1500	1240
22 Long Rifle Viper (Rem. only)	36	Solid	1410	1187
22 Stinger (CCI only)	32	Hollow Point	1687	1300
22 Winchester Magnum Rimfire (Win. only)	40	FMC or HP	1910	—
22 Winchester Magnum Rimfire (CCI only)	40	FMC or HP	2025	1688
22 Long Rifle Pistol Match (Win., Fed.)	40	Solid	—	—
22 Long Rifle Match (Rifle) (CCI, Fed.)	40	Solid	1138	1047
22 Long Rifle Shot (CCI, Fed., Win.)	—	#11 or #12 shot	1047	—
22 Winchester Magnum Rimfire Shot (CCI only)	—	#11 shot	1126	—
22 Short Match (CCI only)	29	Solid	830	752

Please note that the actual ballistics obtained in your gun can vary considerably from the advertised ballistics.

100 yds.	Energy (ft. lbs.) Muzzle	50 yds.	100 yds.	Velocity (fps) 6" Barrel Muzzle	50 yds.	Energy (ft. lbs.) Muzzle	50 yds.
610	34	29	24	706	—	32	—
610	34	29	24	706	—	32	—
810	70	—	42	865	—	48	—
903	77	—	53	—	—	—	—
920	83	65	55	1065	—	73	—
904	75	—	49	—	—	—	—
920	81	62	51	1077	—	69	—
946	90	69	58	1031	—	68	—
962	99	—	60	—	—	—	—
975	115	97	84	1027	925	93	76
976	117	—	85	—	—	—	—
1045	160	117	97	1150	1010	117	90
1017	140	—	92	—	—	—	—
1040	154	111	89	1190	1040	116	88
1010	131	—	82	—	—	—	—
1075	165	110	85	—	—	—	—
1075	165	110	85	—	—	—	—
1056	159	113	89	—	—	—	—
1158	202	120	95	1430	1100	145	86
1326	324	—	156	—	—	—	—
1407	364	253	176	1339	1110	159	109
—	—	—	—	1060	950	100	80
975	116	97	84	1027	925	93	76
—	—	—	—	950	—	—	—
—	—	—	—	1000	—	—	—
695	44	36	31	786	—	39	—

.22 Caliber Rimfire Cartridges (Federal)

	Federal Load Number	Cartridges Per Box	Cartridge	Bullet Type	Bullet Wt. in Grains	Velocity in Ft. Per Sec.	
						Muzzle	100 yds
	701	50	22 Short	Solid	29	1095	905
	703	50	22 Short	Hollow Point	29	1120	905
	706	50	22 Long	Solid	29	1240	960
HI Power	710	50	22 Long Rifle	Solid	40	1255	1015
	712	50	22 Long Rifle	Hollow Point	38	1280	1020
	716	50	22 Long Rifle	No. 12 Shot	25	—	—
100 Pack	810	100	22 Long Rifle	Solid	40	1255	1015
	812	100	22 Long Rifle	Hollow Point	38	1280	1020
Champion Standard Velocity	711	50	22 Long Rifle	Solid	40	1150	975
	811	100	22 Long Rifle	Solid	40	1150	975

Unless otherwise noted, these ballistic specifications were derived from test barrels 24 inches in

Energy in foot/lbs.		Bullet Drop In inches at	Drift In 10 mph cross-wind		Height of Trajectory Inches above line of sight if sighted in at ⊕ yardage. Sight .9″ above bore.				
100		100	100		100	150	50	100	150
Muzzle	yds	yds	yds	50 yds	yds	yds	yds	yds	yds
77	53	16.8	5.3″	⊕	−8.0	−26.8	+4.0	⊕	−14.7
81	53	16.4	5.9″	⊕	−7.9	−26.4	+3.9	⊕	−14.6
99	60	14.1	6.9″	⊕	−6.8	−23.0	+3.4	⊕	−12.8
140	92	13.2	5.5″	⊕	−6.2	−20.8	+3.1	⊕	−11.5
138	88	12.9	5.9″	⊕	−6.1	−20.6	+3.1	⊕	−11.4
—	—	—	—	—	—	—	—	—	—
140	92	13.2	5.5″	⊕	−6.2	−20.8	+3.1	⊕	−11.5
138	88	12.9	5.9″	⊕	−6.1	−20.6	+3.1	⊕	−11.4
117	85	15.0	4.4″	⊕	−7.0	−23.2	+3.5	⊕	−12.6
117	85	15.0	4.4″	⊕	−7.0	−23.2	+3.5	⊕	−12.6

length. All specifications are nominal; individual guns may vary from test barrel figures.

Table of Bullet Energies

This table of energies has been worked out by application of the existing formula for computing energy and gives the foot-pounds of striking energy for one grain of bullet weight. The formula for using this table is simple: multiply the foot-pounds opposite the desired velocity by the weight of your bullet. Velocities have been carefully worked out for each increasing ten foot-seconds. For example, to obtain the energy of a 145-grain bullet

Velocity in fps	Energy	Velocity in fps	Energy	Velocity in fps	Energy
600	.80	840	1.56	1080	2.59
610	.82	850	1.60	1090	2.63
620	.85	860	1.64	1100	2.68
630	.88	870	1.68	1110	2.73
640	.91	880	1.72	1120	2.78
650	.94	890	1.76	1130	2.83
660	.96	900	1.79	1140	2.88
670	.99	910	1.83	1150	2.93
680	1.02	920	1.87	1160	2.99
690	1.05	930	1.92	1170	3.04
700	1.08	940	1.96	1180	3.09
710	1.11	950	2.00	1190	3.14
720	1.15	960	2.04	1200	3.19
730	1.18	970	2.08	1210	3.25
740	1.21	980	2.13	1220	3.30
750	1.24	990	2.17	1230	3.36
760	1.28	1000	2.22	1240	3.41
770	1.31	1010	2.26	1250	3.47
780	1.34	1020	2.31	1260	3.52
790	1.38	1030	2.35	1270	3.58
800	1.42	1040	2.40	1280	3.63
810	1.45	1050	2.45	1290	3.69
820	1.49	1060	2.49	1300	3.75
830	1.53	1070	2.54	1310	3.81
1320	3.86	1720	6.57	2120	9.98
1330	3.92	1730	6.64	2130	10.07
1340	3.98	1740	6.72	2140	10.17
1350	4.04	1750	6.80	2150	10.26
1360	4.10	1760	6.88	2160	10.36
1370	4.16	1770	6.95	2170	10.45
1380	4.22	1780	7.03	2180	10.55
1390	4.29	1790	7.11	2190	10.65
1400	4.35	1800	7.19	2200	10.74
1410	4.41	1810	7.27	2210	10.84
1420	4.47	1820	7.35	2220	10.94
1430	4.54	1830	7.43	2230	11.04
1440	4.60	1840	7.51	2240	11.14
1450	4.66	1850	7.60	2250	11.24
1460	4.73	1860	7.68	2260	11.34
1470	4.79	1870	7.76	2270	11.44
1480	4.86	1880	7.84	2280	11.54
1490	4.93	1890	7.94	2290	11.64
1500	5.00	1900	8.01	2300	11.74
1510	5.06	1910	8.10	2310	11.83
1520	5.13	1920	8.18	2320	11.95
1530	5.19	1930	8.37	2330	12.05
1540	5.26	1940	8.35	2340	12.16
1550	5.33	1950	8.44	2350	12.26

at 2835 f.s. locate 2830 f.s. in the proper column and you find the energy to be 17.78 foot-pounds. The next figure is for 2480 f.s. and runs 17.91. Difference, .13 foot-pounds. Halve this and get .06, which, added to 17.78, gives 17.84. To get bullet energy, multiply 17.84 by 145 grains, and the figure is 2586.8 or 2587 foot-pounds. Use of this table saves much time in figuring muzzle or remaining energy of bullets.

Velocity in fps	Energy	Velocity in fps	Energy	Velocity in fps	Energy
1560	5.40	1960	8.53	2360	12.37
1570	5.47	1970	8.61	2370	12.47
1580	5.54	1980	8.70	2380	12.58
1590	5.61	1990	8.79	2390	12.68
1600	5.68	2000	8.88	2400	12.78
1610	5.75	2010	8.97	2410	12.90
1620	5.82	2020	9.06	2420	13.00
1630	5.90	2030	9.15	2430	13.11
1640	5.97	2040	9.24	2440	13.22
1650	6.04	2050	9.33	2450	13.33
1660	6.12	2060	9.42	2460	13.44
1670	6.19	2070	9.50	2470	13.55
1680	6.26	2080	9.60	2480	13.66
1690	6.34	2090	9.70	2490	13.77
1700	6.41	2100	9.80	2500	13.88
1710	6.49	2110	9.90	2510	13.99
2520	14.10	2920	18.93	3320	24.43
2530	14.20	2930	19.06	3330	24.58
2540	14.32	2940	19.19	3340	24.73
2550	14.44	2950	19.32	3350	24.87
2560	14.55	2960	19.45	3360	25.02
2570	14.67	2970	19.59	3370	25.17
2580	14.78	2980	19.72	3380	25.32
2590	14.89	2990	19.85	3390	25.47
2600	15.01	3000	20.00	3400	25.62
2610	15.13	3010	20.12	3410	25.77
2620	15.24	3020	20.25	3420	25.93
2630	15.36	3030	20.39	3430	26.08
2640	15.48	3040	20.52	3440	26.23
2650	15.59	3050	20.66	3450	26.38
2660	15.71	3060	20.79	3460	26.54
2670	15.83	3070	20.93	3470	26.69
2680	15.96	3080	21.07	3480	26.85
2690	16.07	3090	21.16	3490	27.00
2700	16.19	3100	21.29	3500	27.16
2710	16.31	3110	21.43	3510	27.31
2720	16.43	3120	21.57	3520	27.47
2730	16.55	3130	21.71	3530	27.62
2740	16.67	3140	21.85	3540	27.78
2750	16.79	3150	21.99	3550	27.94
2760	16.91	3160	22.12	3560	28.10
2770	17.04	3170	22.26	3570	28.25
2780	17.16	3180	22.41	3580	28.41
2790	17.28	3190	22.55	3590	28.57
2800	17.41	3200	22.69	3600	28.73
2810	17.53	3210	22.83	3610	28.94
2820	17.66	3220	22.97	3620	29.10
2830	17.78	3230	23.12	3630	29.26

Table of Bullet Energies

Velocity in fps	Energy	Velocity in fps	Energy	Velocity in fps	Energy
2840	17.91	3240	23.26	3640	29.42
2850	18.04	3250	23.41	3650	29.58
2860	18.16	3260	23.55	3660	29.75
2870	18.29	3270	23.70	3670	29.91
2880	18.42	3280	23.84	3680	30.07
2890	18.55	3290	23.99	3690	30.24
2900	18.67	3300	24.14	3700	30.40
2910	18.80	3310	24.28	3710	30.56
3720	30.73	4020	35.89	4320	41.45
3730	30.90	4030	36.07	4330	41.64
3740	31.06	4040	36.25	4340	41.83
3750	31.23	4050	36.43	4350	42.02
3760	31.40	4060	36.61	4360	42.22
3770	31.56	4070	36.79	4370	42.41
3780	31.73	4080	36.97	4380	42.61
3790	31.90	4090	37.15	4390	42.80
3800	32.07	4100	37.33	4400	43.00
3810	32.24	4110	37.51	4410	43.19
3820	32.41	4120	37.70	4420	43.39
3830	32.58	4130	37.88	4430	43.58
3840	32.75	4140	38.06	4440	43.78
3850	32.92	4150	38.25	4450	43.98
3860	33.09	4160	38.43	4460	44.18
3870	33.26	4170	38.62	4470	44.38
3880	33.45	4180	38.80	4480	44.58
3890	33.62	4190	38.99	4490	44.77
3900	33.78	4200	39.18	4500	44.97
3910	33.95	4210	39.36	4510	45.17
3920	34.12	4220	39.55	4520	45.37
3930	34.30	4230	39.74	4530	45.58
3940	34.48	4240	39.92	4540	45.78
3950	34.65	4250	40.11	4550	45.98
3960	34.82	4260	40.30	4560	46.18
3970	35.00	4270	40.49	4570	46.38
3980	35.18	4280	40.68	4580	46.59
3990	35.36	4290	40.87	4590	46.79
4000	35.53	4300	41.06		
4010	35.71	4310	41.25		

Caliber, Cartridge, and Bullet Recommendations

Small Game, Pests—Short-Range Shooting
.22 Short High-Velocity. 29 grains. Up to 50 yards. Only for snakes, rats, smallest pests.

　.22 Short High-Velocity Hollow Point. 27 grains. Up to 50 yards for smallest pests. Recommended over rounded-nose bullets for hunting.

　.22 Long High-Velocity. 29 grains. Up to about 60 yards, only for smallest pests.

.22 Long-Rifle. 40 grains. Up to about 75 yards. For smallest game and pests such as squirrels, crows, and rats.

.22 Long Rifle High-Velocity. 40 grains. Up to about 75 yards for smallest game and pests, such as squirrels, crows, and rats.

.22 Long Rifle High-Velocity Hollow Point. 36 or 37 grains. Up to about 75 yards for small game such as squirrels, rabbits, and raccoon, and for game birds like ruffed grouse. Also for pests like crows, snapping turtles, and so on.

.22 Winchester Automatic. 45 grains. Up to about 75 yards for smallest game and pests such as squirrels, crows, and rats.

.22 WRF (Remington Special). 45 grains. Excellent for small game, such as squirrels and rabbits, and for various small pests. Good up to 100 yards.

.22 WMR. 40 grains with jacket hollow point best for hunting. Excellent up to 125 yards for rabbits, jackrabbits, ground squirrels, chucks, and other small game and varmints.

5mm Remington Rimfire Magnum. 38 grains. Excellent up to 150 yards for rabbits, jackrabbits, ground squirrels, chucks, and other small and medium game and varmints.

Varmints—Long-Range Shooting

.17 Remington. 25 grains. A light load for use up to 250 yards. Poor performance in wind.

5mm Remington Rimfire Magnum. See description under Short Range.

.22 WMR. See description under Short Range.

.218 Bee. 46 grains. Useful up to 200 yards.

.22 Hornet. 45 or 46 grains. Hollow point best. Use up to 175 yards.

.222 Remington. 50 grains. Up to 225 yards.

.222 Remington Magnum. 55 grains. Up to 250 yards. One of the best.

.22/250 Remington. 55 grains. Up to 300 yards. The most powerful, flattest-trajectory .22 caliber for which guns are made.

.220 Swift. 55 or 60 grains. Up to 350 yards.

.22 Savage Hi-Power. 70 grains. Up to 250 yards for large varmints.

.223 Remington. 55 grains. Up to 250 yards. Similar to .222 Remington Magnum.

.224 Weatherby Magnum (Varmintmaster). 55-grain bullet only recommended because of flatter trajectory. Up to 300 yards.

.225 Winchester. 55-grain bullet. Up to 300 yards. Comparable to .224 Weatherby Magnum.

.240 Weatherby Magnum. 70 grains for smaller varmints at longest distance. Up to 350 yards. 90 grains for larger varmints, up to 300 yards.

.243 Winchester. 80 grains. Up to 300 yards.

.244 Remington or 6mm Remington. Use 80 grains. Up to 300 yards. For larger varmints.

.25/06 Remington. Use 87 grains. Up to 300 yards.

.250 Savage. Use 87 grains. Up to 250 yards.

.257 Roberts. Use 87 grains. Up to 250 yards.

.257 Weatherby Magnum. Use 87 grains. Up to 300 yards. Most powerful .25 caliber.

.30/30 Accelerator. Up to 225 yards.

.30/06 Accelerator. Up to 300 yards.

.308 Accelerator. Up to 300 yards.

Obviously, larger calibers with flat trajectories, such as the 6.5 Remington Magnum (with 120 grains), the .264 Winchester Magnum (100 grains), the .270 Winchester (with 100 grains), the .270 Weatherby Magnum (with 100 grains), and even the 7mm Mauser (with 150 grains) are more than adequate for larger varmints and predators. This is more fire-power than is needed for varmints, however, so these calibers have not been recommended here. However, owners of such guns can use them on larger varmints and predators with telling effect.

Antelope, Mountain Sheep, and Goats
Since these animals are hard to reach and are usually shot at the longest ranges, the best cartridges are those shooting bullets 100–150 grains with the flattest trajectories and the greatest accuracy. These include the following:

.240 Weatherby Magnum. 100 grains. Up to 350 yards.

.243 Winchester. 100 grains. Up to 310 yards.

6mm Remington. 100 grains. Up to 325 yards.

.25/06. 100 or 120 grains. Up to 300 yards.

.257 Weatherby. 100 or 117 grains. 117 grains up to 300 yards, and 100 grains up to 350 yards.

6.5 Remington Magnum. 100 or 120 grains. Up to 300 yards.

.264 Winchester Magnum. 100 or 140 grains. Up to 350 yards.

.270 Winchester. 100, 130, or 150 grains. Up to 325 yards.

.270 Weatherby Magnum. 130 or 150 grains. Up to 350 yards.

.280 Remington. 165 grains. Up to 300 yards.

7mm Express Remington. 150 grains. Up to 300 yards.

7mm-08 Remington. 140 grains. Up to 300 yards.

.284 Winchester. 150 grains. Up to 325 yards.

7mm Remington Magnum. 125 or 150 grains. Up to 350 yards.

7mm Weatherby Magnum. 139 or 154 grains. Up to 350 yards.

.30/06 Springfield. 125 or 150 grains. Up to 325 yards.
.300 Winchester Magnum. 150 grains. Up to 350 yards.
.300 H&H Magnum. 150 grains. Up to 400 yards.
.300 Weatherby Magnum. 150 grains. Up to 400 yards.
.308 Winchester. 125 or 150 grains. Up to 300 yards.

Deer, Black Bear—Brush and Woods Shooting
The ideal woods cartridge has a fairly slow-moving, heavy bullet (150 grains or over), which will plow through brush with a minimum of deflection and a maximum of energy. Ranges are usually short, so the hunter does not need to be concerned about trajectory at long distances. There are some cartridges that are adequate for these purposes for deer but may be slightly on the light side for maximum stopping power for black bear, even though they may have been used many times to kill bear. These somewhat weaker loads are listed separately as brush-shooting deer loads. In addition, some cartridges will serve adequately as brush guns (the heavier-weight bullets should be used in the brush) but will also reach out to distances of 200 yards or better when the occasion demands (for this purpose, the lighter bullets should be selected). Those that can be used for these farther distances, as well as short, are marked with an asterisk(*).

Deer Only—not quite heavy enough for black bear
.30 Remington. 170 grains.
.30/30. 150, 170 grains.
.303 Savage. 190 grains.
.303 British. 180 grains.
.32 Remington. 170 grains.
.32 Winchester Special. 170 grains.
.38/55 Winchester. 255 grains.
Deer and Bear
***.270 Winchester.** 150 grains.
***.280 Remington.** 165 grains.
7mm Mauser. 150, 175 grains.
***.300 Savage.** 150, 180 grains.
***.30/40 Krag.** 180 grains.
***.30/06.** 150, 165, 180, 200, 220 grains.
***.308.** 150, 165, 180, 200 grains.
8mm Mauser. 170 grains.
***.348 Winchester.** 200 grains.
***.358 Winchester.** 200 grains.
9.3 × 57. 286 grains.
9.3 × 62. 286 grains.

Deer—Open Country, Long-Range Shooting
This type of hunting is common in the West, especially for mule deer.
It involves long ranges, flat trajectories, and sufficient power to down
large deer. Bullets selected should expand rapidly, since deer are a thin-
skinned animal. The foot-pounds of energy delivered at 300 yards are
listed to give a comparison.

	Foot-Pounds at 300 Yards
.240 Weatherby. 100 grains	1495
.243 Winchester. 100 grains	1260
6mm Remington. 100 grains	1233
.25/06. 120 grains	1372
.257 Weatherby. 100 or 117 grains	1619, 1650
6.5 Remington Magnum. 120 grains	1475
.270 Winchester. 130 grains	1527, 1622, 1740
.280 Remington. 165 grains	1393
.284 Winchester. 150 grains	1480
.30/06 Springfield. 125, 150 grains	1269, 1295, 1445, 1596
.303 Savage. 190 grains	619
.308 Winchester. 125, 150, 165 grains	1186, 1193, 1344, 1700
7mm Express Remington. 150 grains	1616
7mm.-08 Remington. 140 grains	1490

In addition, for those hunters who do not mind a rifle that delivers a
hefty recoil and who want maximum power with the flattest trajectory
at the longest ranges, the following magnums are also highly recommended. These should not be used if the hunter is bothered significantly
by the recoil.

	Foot-Pounds at 300 Yards
.264 Winchester Magnum. 140 grains	1682
.270 Weatherby Magnum. 150 grains	2209, 2259
7mm Remington Magnum. 150 grains	1792, 2210
7mm Weatherby Magnum. 154 grains	2127
.300 H&H Magnum. 180 grains	1927
.300 Winchester Magnum. 150 grains	1827

Caribou
The caribou is a large animal, with bulls weighing over 600 pounds, and
is usually shot at long ranges. Therefore, suggested calibers range from
the .264 Winchester Magnum up to the .340 Weatherby Magnum, using

medium- and large-size bullets. Since grizzly bears are often encountered in caribou country, calibers that are also suitable for grizzlies are marked with an asterisk(*). Only bullets as large as 180, 200 grains should be used on these dangerous bears.

.264 Winchester Magnum. 140 grains.
.270 Winchester. 130, 150 grains.
.270 Weatherby Magnum. 150 grains.
.280 Remington. 165 grains.
.284 Winchester. 150 grains.
7mm Remington Magnum. 150, 165, 175 grains.
7mm Weatherby Magnum. 154, 175 grains.
.30/06 Springfield. 150, 180, 200 grains.
*.300 H&H Magnum. 150, 180 grains.
*.300 Winchester Magnum. 150, 180 grains.
*.300 Weatherby Magnum. 150, 180 grains.
.308 Winchester. 150, 165, 180, 200 grains.
*.308 Norma Magnum. 180 grains.
*.338 Winchester Magnum. 200 grains.
*.340 Weatherby Magnum. 200 grains.

Moose and Elk
Moose and elk are big animals, some weighing over 1,000 pounds. In addition, they have heavy bone and muscle structures, which require powerful cartridges, capable of deep penetration to reach vital organs. Bullets that are too light or that expand too rapidly break up prematurely, leaving wounded animals. Of the two animals, moose are easier to bring down, especially since shots are usually at closer range than on elk. Many an Alaskan moose has been killed with a .30/30, but this does not mean it is a heavy enough load, especially for big bulls, which require as powerful a cartridge as elk. Elk are often killed at over 300 yards, many with rear quartering shots. In addition, elk are ranked as the third most difficult North American animal to kill. Thus, the best loads are 180 grains or more, of heavily constructed bullets, with the .30/06 considered minimum for both moose and elk. The more powerful magnums are even better. The following are recommended:

*Varies with weight and bullet type, thus more than one figure for designated bullet weights.

	Foot-Pounds of Energy at 300 Yards
*.30/06. 180, 220 grains	1567, 1666
.300 Winchester Magnum. 180, 220 grains	2196, 2520
.300 H&H Magnum. 180, 220 grains	1765, 1927
8mm Remington Magnum. 185, 220 grains	1963, 2201
.300 Weatherby Magnum. 180, 220 grains	1955, 2639
*.303 British. 180 grains	1544
*.308 Winchester. 180 grains	1527, 1896
.308 Norma Magnum. 180 grains	2268
.338 Winchester Magnum. 200, 250 grains	1977, 2025
.340 Weatherby Magnum. 200, 250 grains	2331, 2683
.350 Remington Magnum. 200 grains	1553
.375 H&H Magnum. 270 grains	2228
**.378 Weatherby Magnum. 270 grains	2688

Grizzly, Polar Bear, Alaskan Brown Bear

The best rifle for these dangerous bears is the most powerful the hunter can aim and shoot well. Not only must the hunter be able to kill the bear, he must stop it as well. These bears are seldom stopped with the first shot, even a shot in the heart-lung area. Once hit, a bear not downed will either: (1) run away or (2) charge toward the hunter, both with incredible speed. This means that sufficient fire power is necessary to prevent the wounded animal from escaping or from killing the hunter. For this reason, calibers like the .300 Weatherby Magnum should be considered minimum, with bullets 200 grains or heavier. In general, loads for brown bear should be heavier than for either grizzlies or polar bear. The following are recommended:

.300 Weatherby Magnum. 220 grains.

.338 Winchester Magnum. 250 grains.

.340 Weatherby Magnum. 250 grains.

.375 H&H Magnum. 270, 300 grains.

.378 Weatherby Magnum. 270, 300 grains.

Elephant, Rhino, Buffalo

By law, .40 calibers or over must be used to hunt these species in Africa. Solid bullets are used to penetrate the tough hide and bone of these animals. The following calibers are recommended:

*Minimum size for this game.
**Generally, more power than needed.

.458 Winchester Magnum. 500-grain, metal-case bullet.
.460 Weatherby Magnum. 500-grain, full-metal jacket.

Iron Sights

Types of Rear Sights
There are basically two types of iron rear sights: the *open sight* and the *aperture or peep sight*. Open sights will be discussed here, and peep sights in a later section.

Types of Open Rear Sights

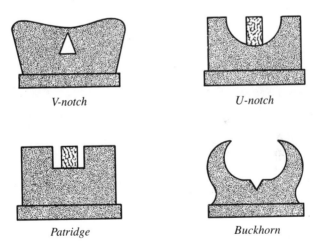

| V-notch | U-notch |

| Patridge | Buckhorn |

Open rear sights may be subdivided into types according to design. One common type has a *V-notch*. Some Vs are cut shallow, others fairly deeply. Another type of open rear sight has a *U-notch*. Still a third type, the so-called *"Patridge" sight,* employs a square notch.

A fourth type of sight may utilize a V or U notch, but the sides of the leaf curl upward and inward over the sighting notch. This type is called the *buckhorn sight.*

Selection and Aiming of Open Rear Sights

Of the four types of open rear sights discussed, the Patridge is the most accurate. Thus it is the best for target shooting, but is hard to use for hunting. The figure illustrates proper sighting with a Patridge sight. In order to be accurate, the shooter must center the front square blade directly in the square notch, and just at the bottom of the target. This means focusing on the rear sight, front sight, and target at the same time. This is possible for a young man with good eyesight, who has time to aim, as in target shooting, but it is hard to do speedily in hunting by everyone, especially an older shooter with poor eyesight. If the shooter is far-sighted, he may have trouble focusing on the rear sight; if he is near-sighted, he may have trouble focusing on the front sight and the target.

Sighting with basic rear sights.

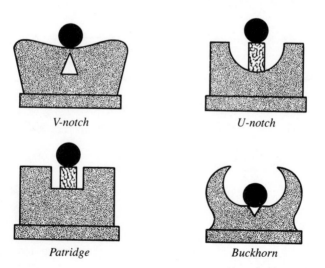

V-notch   U-notch

Patridge   Buckhorn

The buckhorn type sight is still sometimes standard equipment on new rifles. It is popular with inexperienced shooters but is actually the worst type of sight for hunting because the extended wings obscure part of the target and block out part of the light. In addition, most shooters have trouble getting the front bead or blade well down into the notch of the buckhorn sight.

Both the V- and U-notch open sights are better choices for hunting, provided a shallow, wide V or U is used. A shallow V allows the hunter to see more of his game. The light diamond enables the shooter to center the front bead right over the center of the V.

The U-shaped sight is somewhat harder to line up on game than the shallow V, primarily because it is hard for the average hunter to remember to get the front post down into the U at the same place each time a hurried sighting is made. The natural tendency is to look at the target through the U, without getting the post down into the U. The result is to fire high.

Of course, all types of open rear sights have the optical disadvantages already mentioned. It is hard to focus on the front and rear sights and the target at the same time. The rear sight fuzzes up, and the shooter cannot tell how he is holding the front bead in relation to the rear notch. It is easy for the shooter to fail to pull the front bead down into the notch, particularly if the notch is deep and the bottom has less access to light and is darker than the rest.

Types of Mounts and Adjustments of Open Rear Sights

There are variations of the basic types of open rear sights, depending on the system of mounting and adjustment. The oldest type, and the least adjustable, is an extension strap of thin steel upturned at one end to form the sight, and dovetailed into the gun at the other end. Elevation adjustment is accomplished by spring-lifting the rear of the sight into a series of elevated notches. Each notch, depending upon the length of the rifle barrel and the gradations of the notches, represents several inches' change. Windage adjustment is obtained by moving the entire sight sideways with a punch and hammer.

There have been some refinements made to this basic spring-steel design, allowing for easier adjustment. Williams offers a dovetail open sight with a locking and unlocking screw, which allows the whole sight to be moved for windage adjustment. Elevation variation is obtained by selecting leafs of various heights, plus an elevation set screw that can be turned a full $\frac{1}{16}''$.

Another system is to provide an adjustable notch. Lyman offers a leaf sight, available in various heights, which is also adjustable by unlocking two screws that hold the elevation blade firmly in place. Thus, the folding leaf sight is available as an auxiliary sight on scope-mounted rifles.

Another type of mount and adjustment for an open rear sight is offered by Williams—the guide open sight. It can be obtained in various types and heights of blades, and it offers positive locking adjustments for both windage and elevation.

Adjusting the Open Rear Sight

In making adjustments to a rear sight, the shooter must remember that *the adjustment must be made in the direction of the needed correction.*

If a gun is shooting high, the elevation of the rear sight must be adjusted downward; if a gun is shooting to the left, the windage adjustment must be made to the right.

Suppose a gun is shooting high, and the open notch cannot be adjusted downward as needed. In such a case, either a lower blade should be installed or the notch should be filed down to the desired depth to lower the line of sight. If a gun is shooting too low, and putting the sight on the next step upward makes it shoot too high, leave the adjustment on the higher step and file down the notch as necessary, or install a lower blade.

Adjusting windage is sometimes difficult. Dovetail-mounted rear sights without screw adjustments have to be tapped with a punch and hammer in the direction the correction is needed.

The Rear Aperture or Peep Sight

The aperture or peep sight is essentially a hole through which the shooter looks, lining up the front bead in the center of the hole. This type of sight is the most accurate of all the iron sights, whether for target shooting or hunting. One advantage is that the eye does not focus on the rear aperture but looks through it to the front sight and target. This eliminates the necessity of focusing on front and rear sights at the same time, and is a real help to the far-sighted shooter. As the eye looks through the aperture, it tends to center the front sight in the aperture automatically, without conscious effort. In practice, the shooter can almost ignore the rear sight, concentrating on getting the front sight lined up with the target.

Peep sights can also be subclassified into three types according to the position of mounting: (1) *tang sight,* which is mounted on the tang, (2) *cocking-piece sight,* which is mounted on the cocking piece, and (3)

Lyman 57 SML micrometer sight.

receiver sight, which is mounted on the receiver, and is now the most common. Both the tang and cocking-piece sights are mounted close to the eye, and are thus easy and fast to sight through. For this reason, however, the shooter has to be careful not to be hit in the eye when such sights are mounted on a rifle with a short stock. The tang sight is mounted on a long stem, so is easily bent.

The cocking-piece sight always seems to have some wobble in it and is not particularly accurate.

The receiver sight is by far the most popular today. It is strong, accurate, and easy to adjust, particularly with micrometer click adjustments, and it has practically replaced all other types of rear aperture sights.

Most sights can be adjusted in ¼-minute adjustments, others in ½-minute adjustments. More precise target sights have ⅛-minute adjustments. Adjusting the elevation 1 minute raises or lowers the elevation 1″ at 100 yards, 2″ at 200 yards, and so on. So a ¼-minute click would equal ¼″ at 100 yards or 1″ at 400 yards.

Sight Discs and Aperture Sizes for Rear Sights
All aperture receiver sights can be obtained with different size sight discs and different types and sizes of apertures. One sight manufacturer recommends an aperture diameter of .040″ (the smallest) for target shooting,

and .093″ (the largest) for hunting. Another company makes an aperture (the inner hole) with a diameter of .125″.

Some receiver sights come with insert discs for target shooting. These decrease the size of the aperture. They may be fine for the most accurate shooting on a range but should never be used for hunting, since they decrease the field of vision. The best aperture for hunting is one with the largest hole, since it lets in more light and enables the shooter to see through the aperture easily to locate the game.

Advantages of a Peep Sight

A peep sight with an adequate size hole is the fastest of all sights and far more accurate than an open sight. The hunter can focus on a running deer faster than with an open sight or a low-powered scope. The peep sight is the best choice for brush hunting at short ranges. For distance shooting, the scope is preferred, of course, because of its powers of magnification. However, a rifle that is equipped with both scope and iron sights is quite useful, particularly when the scope fogs up in the rain or snow. The Lyman 48 Receiver Sight has a slide that can be taken in or out instantly, without changing the setting of the sight, so is quite useful when used as an auxiliary sight along with a scope with a quick-detachable side mount.

Types of Front Sights

Front sights can be divided into two basic types: (1) the *open front sight* and (2) the *hooded front sight.* Generally, the open sight is used for hunting and the hooded sight for target shooting. The hooded front sight is often referred to as a *target front sight.* Each of these basic types has subcategories of design, which are discussed in detail in succeeding sections.

Open Front Sights

The simplest type of open front sight is a blade, usually with a colored bead at the top front, dovetailed or pinned to the front of the barrel. There are two basic designs of Lyman open front sights. Numbers 3 and 28 are dovetailed to the barrel directly. The two are identical except for bead size. Either may be obtained in heights of .290″, .330″, .345″, .360″, .390″, .410″, .445″, .500″, or .560″. Numbers 26 and 32 open sights are identical also except for bead size and are pinned between sight lugs at the muzzle. Each of the four sights mentioned here is offered with a choice of ivory, silver, gold, or red bead. Under most hunting conditions, the 3/32" bead is preferred.

More commonly, especially on rifles that have high receiver sights, open front sights are mounted on a ramp. The well-known Williams front sights are mounted on low-base and high-base ramps. The methods of attaching the ramp to the barrel and the sight to the ramp are simple. These sighting blades come in two different widths and a variety of heights.

There are a variety of methods of attaching ramps to the barrel: they may be screwed on, sweated on, or slid on with a band.

The question arises as to the best color of bead for hunting and target work. Under poor light conditions, such as in thick woods, the ivory bead is the most visible. In bright sunlight, the red plastic bead is best, but for all-around hunting conditions, the gold bead is preferred, especially one that is flat on the forward face. A flat face is best because it does not reflect the sunlight as easily as a round bead. When the bead is round, the side on which the sun is shining looks the brightest. Under these conditions, there is a tendency for the hunter to see only the bright side of the bead and pull his aim off to the right or left, depending on which way the sun is shining. If the light is coming from the hunter's right, he sees the right side of the bead, moves the muzzle left, and shoots to the left. The flat-faced bead tends to minimize this tendency to shoot away from the light.

For target shooting, a plain, flat-topped, iron blade sight, smoked black enough with camphor or a match, is the most accurate of open front sights. Such a blade is hard to use on game, however.

Hooded Front Sights

Hooded front sights are just what the name implies: front sights with a round, tubular hood over them. Such a sight is really a front aperture sight. The shooter takes aim by centering the bull in the front aperture. When this is used along with a receiver aperture sight, the combination is considered by every expert to be the most accurate iron sight for target shooting. The front aperture is centered over the bullseye, and these together placed in the center of the rear aperture. Such a sight alignment is the most precise that can be accomplished with iron sights.

Most hooded front sights come equipped with steel or plastic inserts to change the size and shape of the aperture, to take advantage of various lighting, distance, and target conditions.

Amount of Adjustment Necessary to Correct Front Sight Error

				Distance Between Front and Rear Sights						
Ins.	**14″**	**15″**	**16″**	**17″**	**18″**	**19″**	**20″**	**21″**	**22″**	**23″**
1	.0038	.0041	.0044	.0047	.0050	.0053	.0055	.0058	.0061	.0064
2	.0078	.0083	.0089	.0094	.0100	.0105	.0111	.0115	.0122	.0127
3	.0117	.0125	.0133	.0142	.0150	.0159	.0167	.0175	.0184	.0192
4	.0155	.0167	.0178	.0189	.0200	.0211	.0222	.0234	.0244	.0255
5	.0194	.0208	.0222	.0236	.0250	.0264	.0278	.0292	.0306	.0319
6	.0233	.0250	.0267	.0283	.0300	.0317	.0333	.0350	.0367	.0384

The table above shows the increase in front sight height that's required to compensate for a given error at 100 yards. Suppose your rifle has a 27″ sight radius, and shoots 4″ high at 100 yards, with the receiver sight adjusted as low as possible. The 27″ column shows that the correction for

Correcting Front Sight Error

Since a front sight is not adjustable, a method must be found to correct for front sight error if a much higher sight, such as a micrometer receiver sight, is mounted on the rear. Sometimes errors can be adjusted in the rear sight alone. However, if the rear sight is too high but has already been adjusted as low as possible, some method must be found for raising the front sight. This is the principal reason different height blades and ramps are sold. But how does the shooter know how high to raise the front sight? The table gives the amount of adjustment necessary to correct front sight error.

Telescope Sights

Types of Scopes: Magnification and Selection

There are two general types of scopes: *fixed-power scopes* and *variable-power scopes.* Fixed-power scopes are found in different magnifications from 1X up through 36X, with 2X through 6X the most popular for big-game hunting.

Variable-power scope ranges are:

1X–4X	2½X–8X
1½X–4X	2½X–9X
1½X–4½X	3X–6X
1½X–5X	3X–7X
1½X–6X	3X–8X
1¾X–5X	3X–9X
2X–5X	3X–10X
2X–7X	4X–12X
2½X–5X	5X–13X
2½X–7X	6X–18X

Distance Between Front and Rear Sights

24″	25″	26″	27″	28″	29″	30″	31″	32″	33″	34″
.0066	.0069	.0072	.0074	.0077	.0080	.0082	.0085	.0088	.0091	.0093
.0133	.0138	.0144	.0149	.0155	.0160	.0156	.0171	.0177	.0182	.0188
.0201	.0209	.0217	.0226	.0234	.0243	.0251	.0259	.0268	.0276	.0285
.0266	.0278	.0289	.0300	.0311	.0322	.0333	.0344	.0355	.0366	.0377
.0333	.0347	.0361	.0375	.0389	.0403	.0417	.0431	.0445	.0458	.0472
.0400	.0417	.0434	.0450	.0467	.0484	.0500	.0517	.0534	.0551	.0567

a 4″ error is .0300″. This correction is added to the overall height of the front sight (including dovetail). Use a micrometer or similar accurate device to measure sight height. Thus, if your original sight measured .360″, it should be replaced with a sight .390″ high, such as a J height sight.

The 3X–9X is the most popular choice for all-around hunting purposes.

Scopes are also classified according to use. The four most usual divisions are: (1) big-game scopes, (2) varmint scopes, (3) target scopes, and (4) scopes for .22s. Big-game scopes are usually of low magnification, the exact amount depending on the type of hunting. For brush and woods shooting, a 2½X–3X scope is best, since it lest in a lot of light and gives a wide field of view. A 2½X scope gives a field of view of approximately 40′ at 100 yards. For the hunter who does a lot of hunting in mountain terrain and in flat, open country at long ranges, a 4X scope is a popular choice, but is difficult to use in the woods. About 6X is the maximum upper limit of magnification for a hunter who wants to combine long-range deer, antelope, sheep, or goat hunting with occasional varmint plinking. Such a choice is also a good one for the long-range trophy hunter who needs this much power to pick out good racks or horns from herds of animals, and who is able to get standing shots. However, the field of view is only 20′ at 100 yards, so this is a difficult scope to use on running whitetails and is not recommended for most hunting purposes.

The varmint scopes are designed to take birds, small animals, and predators at long distances, so the magnification may run from 6X to 15X. For serious, very long-range shooting with rifles with super-flat trajectories, 8X to 15X scopes are used.

Target scopes usually have the highest magnification. Small-bore shooters usually select scopes as high as 20X or even 30X. Those using .30 caliber rifles are often annoyed by mirage when scope powers are too high, so 10X–12X is usually the upper limit.

Scopes for .22s are relatively inexpensive, since the optical requirements are not as great as on big-game rifles and the .22 scopes do not have to be constructed to take the heavy recoil of centerfire cartridges. Usually, powers of 4X–6X are most popular.

Leupold Vari-X II 3×9 scope with adjustable objective.

It should be obvious that the hunter who shoots a variety of game under different conditions is best off with a variable power scope that is adjustable from about 2½X–9X. The 2½X is small enough for big-game woods hunting and the 9X powerful enough for varmint plinking. If the hunter wants only big-game hunting, a scope 2X–7X is certainly adequate.

The variable-power scope is the most versatile choice, but it does have some disadvantages. It is long and heavy. The Leupold Vari-X II AO Scope, adjustable from 3X to 9X, weights 14.5 ounces and is 12.3″ long. This is in contrast to Leupold's M8–4X scope, which weighs 8.8 ounces and is only 11.4″ long.

Also, variable-power scopes are not as sturdy as the fixed-power models, even though they are now made stronger than they once were. They must utilize a larger objective lens to let in light. Even then, the field of view is smaller at each setting than on the fixed-power models. In spite of these objections, however, the variable-power scopes are still a wise choice for the average hunter.

Magnification, Eyepiece, and Field of View
The reason scopes with too high a magnification cannot be used is that the larger the magnification the smaller the field of view. Field of view

Field of View of Lyman Scopes

Magnification	2½	3	4	6	8	10	12	15	20	25	30
Field of View (in feet)	43	35	30	20	14	12	9.3	8.9	5.6	4.3	4

is measured in feet, as the horizontal area viewed at 100 yards distance when looking through a scope. The table shows the field of view at 100 yards of various Lyman scopes of different power.

It is obvious that very high-powered scopes can be used only on stationary targets, or for standing game such as in varmint shooting. However, when game is running, especially at closer ranges, a low-powered scope with a much wider field of view is necessary to pick up the running game. Of course, a high-powered scope, because of its superior magnification, will enable one to look more clearly and deeply into dark woods than a low-powered scope, but if the shooter cannot locate the game because of a narrow field of view, there is no point in using the higher-powered scope.

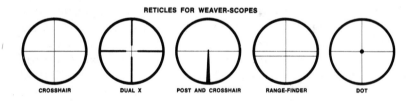

RETICLES FOR WEAVER-SCOPES

CROSSHAIR   DUAL X   POST AND CROSSHAIR   RANGE-FINDER   DOT

Weaver K4 scope and views.

In an effort to widen the field of view, some manufacturers have widened the eyepiece. Weaver now offers scopes in their regular round eyepieces and in a new W, or wider-view, model. The latter has a flattened but horizontally wider eyepiece to widen the horizontal field of view. The accompanying table, by Weaver, compares the field of view of the regular and wider-view models.

Comparison of Field of View on Regular and Wider-View Models of Weaver Scopes

Regular Model	K3	K4	K6	V4.5	V7	V9
Field of View (in feet)	37	30	20	54-21	40-15	33-12
Wider View Model	K3-W	K4-W	K6-W	V4.5-W	V7-W	V9-W
Field of View (in feet)	55	37½	25	70-26	53-20	41-16

Redfield also manufacturers scopes with this type of eyepiece. Some shooters may have trouble sighting with the flattened eyepiece. If so, they should continue to use the regular round models.

Objective Lens Diameter, Exit Pupil Diameter, and Brightness
One of the considerations in selecting a scope is its *relative brightness*, that is, the amount of illumination allowed in the field of view, which in turn affects the viewer's ability to see the target. The relative brightness of a scope of any kind, including binoculars, is a standard specification used by every manufacturer of optical instruments. A scope with a relative brightness of 25 will be bright and suitable for use in hunting in the dim light of dawn and dusk when game is roaming about. One with a relative brightness of 2.5 will not transmit enough light to see clearly on dark and cloudy days when aiming at game; it is only bright enough for target shooting in broad daylight on a bright sunny day. It is important, therefore, that the hunter have a scope that he can really see through under poor light conditions.

It is not necessary, however, to have a scope with a relative brightness of much more than 25, because 25 is all the light that the pupil of an eye can utilize. The relative brightness of a scope is determined by squaring the diameter of the *exit pupil*. Thus, relative brightness = (exit pupil diameter)^2. The exit pupil diameter, in turn, is calculated by dividing the *objective lens diameter* of the scope (in millimeters) by the scope's *magnification* according to the formula that follows.

$$\text{Exit pupil diameter (in mm)} = \frac{\text{Objective lens diameter (in mm)}}{\text{Magnification}}$$

Thus, if a 4X scope has an objective lens diameter of 20mm, the exit pupil diameter is 5mm and the relative brightness is 25. (Since the objective lens diameter is usually stated in inches, conversion to millimeters involves multiplying inches by 25.4, the number of millimeters per inch.)

The maximum relative brightness needed for a scope is 25 because this is all the light the human eye can accommodate. Under dim light conditions, the pupil of the human eye enlarges to a maximum not to exceed 5mm, the identical maximum dimension needed for the exit pupil diameter. A scope can be made with an exit pupil diameter much larger than 5mm, but the 5mm diameter of the pupil of the eye cannot see more. The only thing a larger exit pupil diameter does is allow the shooter to see through the scope at different angles to the eye lense without having to align the eye precisely to the scope axis. If the pupil is aligned anywhere within the exit pupil, a satisfactory view will be obtained through the scope. This allows the hunter to quickly throw his rifle to his shoulder with cheek pressed against the stock. If the eye comes anywhere within the exit pupil, aim is achieved.

Reticules and Their Selection

One of the shooter's decisions concerns the type of reticule he wants in his scope, since most manufacturers offer a choice. The chart illustrates the wide variety of reticules available. No one scope is available in all these different types, so the shooter must investigate the types each manufacturer offers. Alternate names are given as listed by different manufacturers.

In deciding on a reticule, the shooter needs to consider a number of things.

1. Coarse reticules are easier to see in poor light than fine ones, but they cover up more of a target, particularly at long distances.

2. The shorter the range, the coarser the reticule can be and still not cover up too much target. Long-range targets require fine reticules to keep from being blocked out. One of the most popular reticules at all ranges is the plain crosshair (see No. 4).

3. The purpose of the horizontal crosshair (see reticule No. 5) is to keep the shooter from canting his rifle as well as to indicate the intersection point.

4. Thick post-type reticules (see Nos. 5, 9, and 13) are picked up easily in poor light and aimed quickly, but block out the target when the hunter has to aim high at long distances. Incidentally, the correct aiming point for a post is at the top of the post.

5. The intersection of crosshairs gives a clearly defined aiming point. Thick ones are easy to see, but do not define the aiming point well and cover up part of the target; thin ones give a clearly defined aiming point and do not cover up game, but they are harder to see in poor light.

6. Dots come in various sizes (see Nos. 3 and 6). The larger the dot, the more target it covers. A 2-minute dot covers 2" at 100 yards; a 4-minute dot covers 4" at 100 yards, 8" at 200 yards, and 16" at 400 yards. It is easy to see why finer dots are needed at longer ranges.

7. Range-finder reticules (Nos. 8, 11, 14) are designed to enable the hunter to estimate ranges of animals he is sighting. Obviously, the animal must be standing still before an accurate determination can be made. In reticule No. 11, the hunter turns the range ring on the scope, which moves the top stadia wire until the vital target area is bracketed between the wires. This simultaneously rotates a trajectory cam, tilting the scope to create an automatic elevation correction, so all the hunter has to do is hold the crosshairs on the target.

8. Sometimes a combination reticule is the best answer. Thus, a post and crosshair (see reticule No. 5 or No. 13) provides an easily seen, thick post in poor light as well as a horizontal crosshair to prevent the shooter from canting the rifle. The thick post may obscure part of the target if the hunter must hold high at long ranges, however. The tapered cross-hairs (No. 10—the writer's favorite), or the 4-PCCH (No. 1), or the dualine (No. 2—one of the most popular) offer thick crosshairs for easy sighting in poor light but fine intersection lines so that very little of the target is obscured. The crosshairs and dot in No. 12 is also a fine sight for a variety of conditions.

9. A dot alone is one of the fastest of all sights under adequate light conditions (see No. 7). It is not appropriate for target shooting at long ranges, since it obscures too much bullseye, but it is a fine sight for hunting, especially at short ranges, if the dot is not so big that it obscures too much target (No. 3 is too large). If it is fairly small, as it should be, it may be hard to locate in poor light, so under these conditions a crosshair and dot is superior to the dot alone (No. 12).

Weaver Quik-Point Sight.

10. One of the most interesting types of scopes is Weaver's Quik-Point, which is made for shotguns, centerfire rifles, and .22 rifles. It utilizes a blaze-orange dot, focused to infinity, which is simply put on the target for aiming, with one or both eyes open. It is especially useful for woods or brush shooting. At long ranges it becomes inaccurate, since the dot begins to obscure too much of the target.

11. To aid under poor light conditions, some scopes come equipped with a lighted aiming point. Bushnell's Lite-Site has a lighted aiming point powered by a compact battery, which is clicked on at dawn or dusk. When off under normal light conditions, only the crosshairs remain in view.

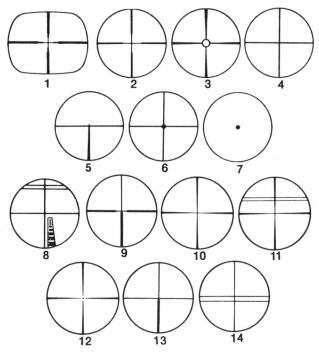

Types of reticules.

Eye Relief and Its Adjustment

Eye relief is the distance the eye must be held back of the rear end of the scope to see a full field through it. With target scopes, the range is about 1⅞" to 2½". With hunting scopes, the range is from about 3" to

5", with 3+ being the most common. For scopes for .22s, the range varies from 2" to 4", with the usual distance somewhat shorter than on high-powered rifles, since the shooter does not have to worry about recoil. The manufacturer of each scope specifies the correct eye relief or eye relief range for it, in inches. Of course, most scopes offer a satisfactory field of view over a range of distances, so the shooter does not have to place his eye at the exact distance away from the scope. But if his eye is closer or farther than the range, he will get only a partial field of view or will black out his field of view entirely. Therefore, it is necessary to mount the scope so that the correct eye relief is obtained with the shooter's cheek correctly and comfortably placed on the cheekpiece. Also, if the shooter gets his eye too close to the scope of a high-powered rifle, the kickback caused by the recoil may severely injure his eye.

In order to mount the hunting scope on the rifle to give the correct eye relief, the scope and mount must be selected in relation to each other so the scope can be positioned properly. The scope mounting is secured to the scope tube by two rings. The rings can be located to encircle the scope tube anywhere between the enlarged eyepiece and the enlarged objective, except where the housing of the adjusting dials comes. Therefore, the mount must be screwed on the rifle in such a fore-and-aft position that there is no trouble in locating the eyepiece of the scope at the correct distance from the eye, and the rings must encircle the scope tube at places where it is possible for them to do so. A mount that can be secured only in a fixed place may not allow the scope tube to be positioned correctly and at a place where the rings can encircle the tube. With most combinations of scopes, mounts, and rifles there is no trouble, but with others, correct eye-relief adjustment is impossible. Before buying, if the shooter is not sure, he should hold the scope on the rifle temporarily in correct eye-relief position, and similarly hold the mount where it has to be, and see if the rings will encircle the scope tube at a possible location.

Scope Mounts with Adjustments

The first consideration in selecting a scope mount is whether or not the scope the shooter is using has internal adjustments for windage and elevation or whether the adjustments must be made in the mount. Most scopes today have internal adjustments, although some mounts have windage adjustments even when this adjustment is also in the scope. This makes it easier to get the scope lined up.

If the shooter wants to use one scope on several rifles, he can use

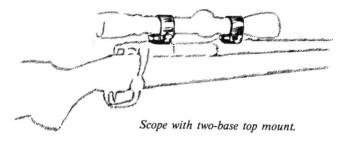

Scope with two-base top mount.

Typical side mount (top) and quick-detachable side mount (bottom).

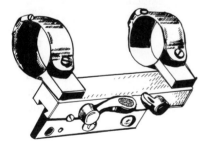

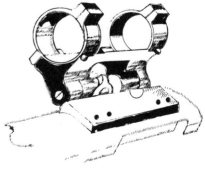

Basic design of swing or pivot mount.

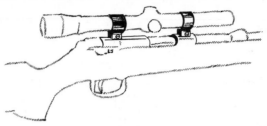

This scope is mounted on a .22 rifle with a typical tip-off mount. Note bases of rings are fastened to grooved receiver of rifle.

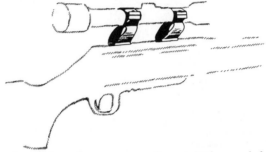

Basic design of a see-through scope mount. Scope is high enough for hunter to use iron sights through openings in mount.

adjustable scope mounts on each rifle. Thus, he can move the scope from one rifle to the other and always be in adjustment. Or, if the shooter wants to use two scopes on one rifle, for example, a 2X and a 6X scope, he can sight in one scope by adjusting for windage and elevation in the base and in the other by adjustments within the tube. Two mounts with external adjustments are the B-Square and Beeman. Buehler also makes a Micro Dial Universal Mount, which is advertised as appropriate primarily for scopes with internal adjustments. By using it, the shooter can keep the reticule of the scope perfectly centered (assuming the reticule is the type that moves as the scope is adjusted), and do only the fine adjustments internally.

Of course, the scope mounts of some target scopes have the adjustments in the mounts. Included in this group are Unertl's Target Mounts or Varmint Mounts.

Types of Mounts for Scopes with Internal Adjustments
Mounts for scopes with internal adjustments in the tube can be grouped into seven categories: (1) *two-base top mount*, (2) *bridge mount*, (3) *see-through bridge mount*, (4) *side-bracket mount*, (5) *swing or pivot mount*, (6) *offset mount*, and (7) *tip-off mount*.

The *two-base top mount* has two separate bases with detachable or integral rings for encircling and holding the scope. The bases are screwed into the receiver, and the rings that hold the scope are in turn screwed into the bases, with the scope forming a connecting bridge. This type of mount is designed primarily for the shooter who wants to put his scope on his rifle and leave it there. If the scope does not work, or fogs up, the shooter can remove it from the rings (some even have detachable mounts), but the bases still prevent the use of iron sights. However, the shooter can install another scope, already sighted in, if this happens.

The *bridge mount* is also a top mount, but has a metal piece connecting the bases and an integral part of them. This type of mount is strong and solid and quite appropriate for heavy calibers with a lot of recoil. The metal base has rings for holding the scope, as do other mounts. Bases are usually screwed to the rifle. Some have a dovetail or other arrangement so the rings and scope can be removed together from the scope base. Some of these mounts can be used with auxiliary iron sights, unless the bases get in the way.

The *see-through bridge mount* is designed to allow the shooter to see under the scope if he wants to use iron sights. Since the scope is never removed, it is also readily available for long-range shots, giving the hunter a choice of two different sights at any time. The idea is fine, but such a mount should be used only on rifles with Monte Carlo combs or fairly high roll-over cheekpieces. Otherwise, the scope is mounted so much higher than the comb that the shooter will have to strain to get

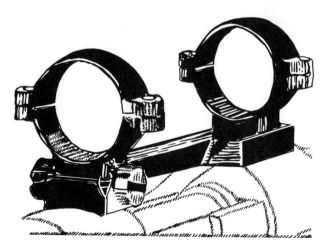

Leupold bridge mount.

his eye high enough to get a good sight through the tube. Since it is mounted high, the scope is ungainly looking and more vulnerable to damage and jarring.

The *side-bracket mount* is designed so the shooter can use either a scope or an iron receiver sight, depending on conditions. But usually the scope must be quickly detachable and the iron receiver sight mounted on a slide, which can be quickly slipped in place. The base portion of the scope mount is screwed and pinned to the side of the receiver, so when the scope and rings are removed there are no obstructions along the top of the barrel that prevent the use of iron sights. This is one of the best choices for the hunter whose scope becomes damaged or fogged and who wants a receiver sight inserted. The excellent Jaeger Quick Detachable Side Mount is a notable example. The rings of this mount can be obtained high enough to use iron sights beneath without removing the scope, if desired.

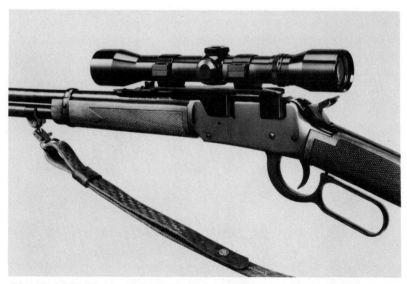

This Model 94 Winchester is equipped with a Williams dovetail open sight, a Q.C. top mount, and a 4X Twilight Scope.

The Williams QC Side Mount also allows both the scope and the receiver sight to be available for instant use.

The *swing or pivot mount* is basically a hinged bracket screwed to the side or top of the receiver, allowing the shooter to swing the scope out of the way to use the iron sights. Pachmayr makes both a top mount and a side mount. Weaver also makes an excellent model. The writer has used a Weaver Pivot Mount for years and has never found that the scope gets out of adjustment.

The *offset mount* is really a side mount, with the scope offset to one side so that either the scope or iron sight is available for instant use. This type has really only one practical use, and that is for rifles that have top ejectors. The shooter has to cock his head over to the side of the stock to see through the scope, a somewhat awkward way to sight.

The *tip-off mount* is used only on .22 caliber rifles, since it is not as rugged as other mounts. The scope rings are attached directly to dovetail

Williams side mount with standard rings (left) and with HCO rings (right).

grooves in the receiver rather than first to bases. Such a mount is inexpensive, and it works well for the low-caliber rifle for which it is designed.

Focusing the Scope

All scopes have at least one type of focusing: *eye-piece focusing* (sometimes called *ocular focusing* or *reticule focusing*). This type of focusing means that the eyepiece is adjustable for clearness of reticule. In making this adjustment, loosen the ring or collar that secures the eyepiece and, while looking through the scope, turn the eyepiece sleeve one way then the other until the reticule appears distinct and black. Then screw the locking collar up tight.

While the adjustment is to focus the reticule, it will also affect the clarity of the target at both extremes of adjustment. While looking through the eyepiece, the shooter will notice that if the eyepiece is turned clockwise far enough, not only will the reticule get out of focus, but the image of the target as well. As the eyepiece is turned clockwise, the image of the target becomes smaller. Similarly, if the eyepiece is turned counterclockwise, the reticule gets out of focus, and eventually the image of the target, except in this instance the target gets larger. In focusing on the reticule, it is also helpful to look at the target occasionally to see if the clearest image is also obtained.

More powerful scopes, generally 8X or 9X power and above, and some makes of variable scopes also have a *range or distance adjustment,* which is accomplished by moving the objective lens back or forward. Scopes that have this adjustment have two knurled sleeves at the front end. The rear sleeve has a micrometer graduation for distances, with the yardage marked on it. To focus, the front sleeve is unscrewed several turns, and the rear sleeve is set on the proper distance. Then the front sleeve is screwed up tight. Since the focus is not changed until the front sleeve is tight, it is vital to be certain this is done.

Unless scopes of 8X or 9X and above are focused for distance to give a clear image, parallax will result. Parallax appears as a movement of the reticule on the target when the eye is moved up and down. To check to see if it is present, move the eye up, down, and sideways while aiming at a target. If the reticule moves on the target, the scope contains parallax and will be inaccurate, since the aim will move as the reticule moves. Also, the center of the reticule will not be the actual point of impact of the bullet. Focusing for distance removes the parallax. On lower-power scopes that do not have a range adjustment on the objective lens, the scope is usually factory adjusted to be parallax-free at 100 yards. This insures minimal parallax at all ranges.

Fogging of the Scope

Fogging is caused by the condensation of moisture on the inside of the lenses of the scope. Quality scopes are filled with the dry gas nitrogen and properly sealed against leakage, so ought never to fog up. The parts to be sealed are threaded together, and an "O" ring is compressed between them. This is the same kind of seal used in the windows of airplanes and should hold for the life of the scope. To insure this seal, the shooter should never try to take his scope apart. If he does, he will let out the nitrogen, let in moisture, and fogging will result. If a scope begins to fog up, the best thing to do is send it back to the manufacturer.

There are some things the shooter can do to minimize the possibility of fogging. Keep the scope protected from the rain by carrying a thin plastic cover for gun and scope in case of inclement weather, or use scope caps over the lenses. Also, in cold weather, do not take the scope into a heated room, since moisture may condense in it when it is taken back out in the cold. Therefore, leave the scope in the cold overnight if going hunting the next morning. This will prevent fogging on the outside of the lens also.

Adjusting for Windage and Elevation

The method of adjusting the scope for windage and elevation will depend upon whether the scope has internal adjustments or whether the adjustments are in the scope mount. Sometimes the mount has an adjustment for windage but not for elevation. In this case, the mount adjustment is used to get a rough adjustment for windage, with the fine adjustment accomplished internally.

Let us assume first that the scope can be internally adjusted. This means it has two adjusting dials, one on the top of the scope, for elevation, and one on the side of the scope, for windage. Some dials have clicks and/or gradations of ¼ minute, others of ½ minute, and still others for 1 minute. The table below shows the theoretical change in impact for different minutes of angle at various distances.

Thus, if a shooter has a scope with adjustment and gradations of ¼ minute and wants to change the point of impact of the bullet 1″ at 25 yards, he must move the dial 16 clicks or graduations. If he wants to

Theoretical change in point of impact at different distances with various graduations of scope dial adjustments

Graduations of Adjustment	25	50	75	100	150 (yards)	200	250	300	400
				Changes in Impact at Each Distance (inches)					
¼ Minute	1/16″	1/8″	3/16″	¼″	3/8″	½″	5/8″	¾″	1″
½ Minute	1/3″	¼″	3/8″	½″	¾″	1″	1¼″	1½″	2″
1 Minute	¼″	½″	¾″	1″	1½″	2″	2½″	3″	4″

change the point of impact 4″ at 200 yards, he must move the dial 8 clicks or graduations. In practice, the graduations on the scope dials will not be this precise, nor do all cartridges have the same ballistics at different distances, so the only way the shooter can determine the actual change in point of impact of his bullet is by firing groups of shots. (See the following section on sighting in a rifle.)

If the scope does not have internal adjustments, the adjustments must be made in the mount. Usually, mount adjustments for hunting scopes are not as precise or accurate as are internal adjustments, but most target mounts click in ¼″ adjustments and are very accurate. Unertl's varmint and target scopes use mounting bases 7.2″ apart, which allows for a true ¼-minute click adjustments in the rear mount.

Incidentally, for scopes with externally adjusted mounts, the actual change in point of impact for a certain number of gradations or clicks on the dial will depend partially on how widely the front and rear mounting bases are separated. The farther apart the mounting bases, the

Relationship of distance between mounting bases and changes in point of impact (in inches) at 100 yards for scopes with ¼-minute click adjustments

Center to Center of Telescope Bases	Changes in Impact in Inches Per 100 Yds.
6″	.300
7.2″	.250 (¼-minute adjustment)
8″	.225
9″	.200
9.6″	.1875
10″	.180
10.585″	.170
10.905″	.165
11.25″	.160
11.612″	.155
12″	.150

more the scope must be moved by the rear base adjustment to achieve a particular change in point of impact. The table shows the relationship between the distance between the mounting bases and the change in impact in inches per 100 yards for scopes with ¼-minute click adjustments.

Only those scope bases with ¼-minute adjustments that have been mounted 7.2″ apart provide a true ¼-minute click adjustment. The others are actually adjusted with each click at the number of minutes of angle as there are inches per 100 yards in the table. Thus, scope bases 12″ apart allow for a .15-minute adjustment per click at 100 yards.

Sighting and Aiming

Sighting in a Rifle
Before getting into the details of how to sight in a rifle, some principles should be kept in mind.

The best distance to begin sighting in is 25 yards. The reasons for this range are several. First, it is close enough so that the bullets will generally hit on the target, and one can shoot accurately enough to get a good grouping on one's shots. Second, the scope-sighted big-game rifle that is zeroed in at 25 yards will generally be sighted in at ranges just over 200 yards, depending on the ballistics of the ammunition used.

The reason for this last statement has to do with the trajectory path of a bullet. Bullets do not travel in a straight line, but in a downward curve called a *trajectory.* The bullet begins falling slowly the moment it leaves the muzzle. To compensate for this so the bullet will hit the line

Trajectory, or path of the bullet, never rises above line of bore but crosses the line of sight. To compensate for bullet drop, the bore must be pointed upward; this is done by adjusting the rear sight so it is higher than the front sight.

of sight, the rear sight is moved upward, and the muzzle must be raised to be on target. Thus, with the muzzle pointed at an angle crossing the line of sight, the bullet crosses the line of sight twice: once near the muzzle as it rises above the line of sight and again at some distance from the muzzle, as it falls below the line of sight.

In other words, if a rifle is sighted in at 25 yards, the trajectory is such that for most high-powered rifles the bullet will again cross the line of sight at ranges just over 200 yards and is therefore sighted in for that range also. Of course, since each caliber has its own ballistical characteristics, there are some variations. The table shows how high or low a bullet will strike at ranges up to 350 yards when the rifle is set at 0 (for most calibers) or at $-\frac{1}{2}$", $-\frac{1}{4}$", $+\frac{1}{4}$", $+\frac{1}{2}$" (for a few other calibers) at 25 yards.

From the table, it is clear that there are some calibers (.250 Savage, .300 H&H Magnum, .338 Winchester Magnum, .358 Winchester) that are zeroed in perfectly at 200 yards when sighted in at 25 yards. Most calibers, such as the .30/06 or .308, are zeroed in slightly beyond 200 yards when zeroed at 25 yards. A few calibers, such as the lower-power .22's, because of their low power, fall rapidly and are zeroed in at ranges of 50 to 150 yards when zeroed at 25 yards. Some other calibers, such as the 6mm Remington, are zeroed in at 250 yards when sighted in at 25 yards. Because of their flat trajectory, many of the calibers shown are still accurate out to 300 yards and beyond, even when zeroed at 25 yards. Thus, for all-round purposes, 25 yards is the best range for sighting in. If a hunter wants his rifle zeroed in at much longer ranges, he will have to sight in at 25 yards so that the point of impact at 100 yards is slightly above the inches shown in the chart just discussed. For example, referring to the previous table for a moment, the .30/06 shooting 150-grain bullets is $2\frac{1}{4}$" high at 100 yards, but 6" low at 300 yards. How can the shooter zero it in to shoot right on the target at 300 yards? Let us suppose he has a telescopic sight with $\frac{1}{4}$-minute graduations. Moving the elevation one graduation will raise the sight $\frac{1}{4}$" at 100 yards and $\frac{3}{4}$" at 300 yards. (See page 134, "Theoretical Change in Point of Impact at Different Distances with Various Graduations of Scope Dial Adjustments.") But the sight must be raised 6". 6" $\div$ $\frac{3}{4}$" = 8 graduations the sight must be raised to put the point of impact on the target at 300 yards. Eight graduations will raise the point of impact 8 $\times$ $\frac{1}{4}$" or 2" at 100 yards (for a total of 2" + $2\frac{1}{4}$" or $4\frac{1}{4}$" high at 100 yards) and 8 $\times$ $\frac{1}{16}$" or $\frac{1}{2}$" at 25 yards (for a total of $\frac{1}{2}$" high at 25 yards). The shooter can check this by sighting in at 25 yards (he should be shooting $\frac{1}{2}$" high)

Bullet Impact in Inches at Various Distances When Rifle Is Sighted in at 25 Yards

Caliber	Bullet Wt.	25 yds.	50 yds.	100 yds.	150 yds.	200 yds.	250 yds.	300 yds.	350 yds.
.22 Long Rifle Hi-Speed	40	0	+ ½	−4	−16	......	......	......	......
.22 Winchester Mag.	40	0	+ ¾	0	− 1½	− 6¼	......	......	......
.22 Hornet	45	0	+1	+1¾	+ ½	− 3½	− 9	......	......
.220 Swift	45	−½	+ ¼	+1½	− 1¾	+ 1½	+ ½	− 3	− 7½
.222 Remington	50	0	+ ¾	+2¼	+ 2	+ ½	− 2½	− 8	−14
.222 Remington Mag.	55	−¼	+ ½	+1½	+ 2	+ 1½	− ½	− 5	−10
.223 Remington	55	−¼	+ ½	+1½	+ 2	+ 1½	− ½	− 5	−10
.22/250 Remington	55	−¼	+ ½	−1¾	+ 2	+ 1½	0	− 3	− 7¼
.225 Winchester	55	−¼	+ ½	+2	+ 2¼	+ 1½	− 1	− 4	− 8¼
.243 Winchester	80	−¼	+ ½	+1¾	+ 2	+ 1¼	− ½	− 2¾	− 7
.243 Winchester	100	0	+ ¾	+2	+ 2¼	+ 1¾	− ½	− 4	− 9¾
6mm Remington	100	0	+ ¾	+1¾	+ 2¾	+ 2	0	− 4	− 8¾
.244 Remington	75	−¼	+ ½	+1¾	+ 2	+ 1¾	− ½	− 2¾	− 7
.244 Remington	90	0	+ ¾	+2	+ 2¼	+ 1¾	− ½	− 4¼	− 9
.250 Savage	87	0	+ ¾	+2¼	+ 2	0	− 3½	− 8½	−16
.250 Savage	100	0	+1	+2¼	+ 2¼	+ 1½	− 2	− 7	−15
.25/06 Remington	87	−¼	+ ½	+1¾	+ 2	+ 1¾	− ½	− 2¾	− 7
.256 Winchester Mag.	60	0	+ ¾	+1¼	+ 1¼	− 3	− 8½	......	......
.257 Roberts	100	0	+1	+2¼	+ 2¼	+ 1½	− 2	− 7	−15
.257 Roberts	117	0	+1¼	+2¼	+ 1½	− 1	− 6½	−14	......
6.5mm Remington Mag.	120	0	+ ¾	+2	+ 1¾	+ ½	− 2¼	− 6½	−12¼
.264 Winchester Mag.	100	−¼	+ ¼	+2	+ 2¼	+ 2	+ ½	− 2	− 6¼
.264 Winchester Mag.	140	0	+ ¾	+2½	+ 2¾	+ 2	0	− 3	− 8
.270 Winchester	100	−¼	+ ¾	+1¾	+ 2½	+ 1¼	0	− 4	− 8¾
.270 Winchester	130	0	+ ¾	+2½	+ 2¾	+ 2	0	− 4¼	− 9¾
.270 Winchester	150	0	+1	+1¾	+ 1¾	− ½	− 4	− 8¾	−15
.280 Remington	100	−¼	+ ¾	+1¾	+ 2¼	+ 1½	0	− 3	− 7½
.280 Remington	125	0	+ ¾	+2½	+ 2½	+ 1½	− ¼	− 4½	− 9¼
.280 Remington	150	0	+1	+2¼	+ 2¼	+ 1¼	− 2	− 6	−12
.230 Remington	165	0	+1	+2½	+ 2¼	+ 1	− 2¼	− 7½	−15
.284 Winchester	125	0	+1	+2¾	+ 2½	+ 1¾	− ¼	− 4	− 9½
.284 Winchester	150	0	+1	+2½	+ 2½	+ 1¼	− 1	− 5½	−11¾
7mm Remington Mag.	125	−¼	+ ¾	+2	+ 2	+ 1½	0	− 2	− 6
7mm Remington Mag.	150	−¼	+ ¾	+1¾	+ 2	+ 1¼	− ½	− 3	− 7
7mm Remington Mag.	175	0	+1	−2¼	+ 2¼	+ 1¼	− 1½	− 5¾	−13¼
.30/30 Winchester	150	0	+1	+2¾	+ 2¼	− ¾	− 5	−12	......
.30/30 Winchester	170	+¼	+1¼	+2¾	+ 2	− 2½	−10	......	......
.30/06	110	0	+1	+2¼	+ 2¼	+ 1	− 2	− 6½	−14
.30/06	125	0	+ ¾	+2	+ 1¾	+ ½	− 2¼	− 6½	−12¾
.30/06	150	0	+1	+2¼	+ 2¼	+ 1¼	− 1½	− 6	−13
.30/06	180	0	+1	+2¼	+ 2¼	+ ¾	− 2½	− 8	−16¼
.30/06	180	0	+1	+2¼	+ 2¼	+ ¾	− 2½	− 8	−16¼
.30/06	220	0	+1	+1¾	+ ½	− 2	− 7	−15	......
.300 Winchester Mag.	150	0	+ ¾	+2¼	+ 2½	+ 1¾	0	− 3	− 7¾
.300 Winchester Mag.	180	0	+ ¾	+2	+ 2¼	+ 1¼	− 1	− 4½	−10
.300 H&H Magnum	150	0	+1	+2½	+ 3	+ 2	0	− 5	−10
.300 H&H Magnum	180	0	+1	+2	+ 2	+ ½	− 3	− 7½	−14
.300 H&H Magnum	220	0	+ ¾	+2	+ 1¾	0	− 2¼	− 8	−16¾
.300 Savage	150	0	+1	+1¾	+ 1¾	− ½	− 4	−10¼	......
.300 Savage	180	0	+1¼	+2¾	+ 2	− ½	− 5½	−13½	......
.308 Winchester	110	0	+1	+2¼	+ 2¼	+ 1	− 2	− 6½	−14

Bullet Impact in Inches at Various Distances When Rifle is Sighted in at 25 Yards (*cont.*)

Caliber	Bullet Wt.	25 yds.	50 yds.	100 yds.	150 yds.	200 yds.	250 yds.	300 yds.	350 yds.
.308 Winchester	125	0	+ ¾	+2	+ 2	+ ½	− 2¼	− 6¾	−13¾
.308 Winchester	150	0	+1	+2¼	+ 2	+ ½	− 2½	− 7¼	−13¾
.308 Winchester	180	0	+1	+1¾	+ 1¾	− ½	− 4	− 8¾	−16½
.308 Winchester	200	0	+1	+2	+ 1	− 1	− 7	−14½	......
.338 Winchester Mag.	200	0	+ ¾	+2½	+ 2½	+ 1½	− 2	− 5¾	−11¾
.338 Winchester Mag.	250	0	+ ¾	+2	+ 2	0	− 3¼	− 9	−18½
.338 Winchester Mag.	300	+¼	+1¼	+3	+ 2¾	0	− 5	−12½	−22
.35 Remington	150	0	+1	+2	+ 1	− 2¾	−10	−19	......
.35 Remington	200	+¼	+1½	+3	+ 1¾	− 3	−13	−23½	......
.350 Remington Mag.	200	+¼	+1¼	+2¾	+ 2¾	0	− 4¾	−11½	−19¼
.350 Remington Mag.	250	0	+1	+1¾	+ ½	− 2	− 7	−15	......
.358 Winchester	250	0	+1¼	+2½	+ 2	0	− 4½	−13¾	......
.375 H&H Magnum	270	0	+1	+2¼	+ 2¼	+ 1	− 2	− 8½	−18½
.375 H&H Magnum	300	+¼	+1½	+3	+ 1¾	0	− 4¼	−12½	......
.44 Remington Mag.	240	+½	+2	+2¾	0	−10½	......	......	......
.444 Marlin	240	+¼	+1½	+2½	+ 1¾	− 2	− 9½	−20¼	......
.458 Winchester Mag.	510	+½	+1¼	+2½	+ 1¼	− 2¾	−14	−27½	......

Equipment for sighting in a rifle: a steady benchrest; padded rests for stock and forend; notepad and pencil; good supply of cartridges.

This shooter is using one padded rest on a concrete platform to sight in his rifle. Shooting glasses should be worn for safety, ear muffs to protect against muzzle blast and to prevent flinching.

and also at 100 yards (he should be shooting 4½″ high). If he zeroes in at 300 yards, the point of impact will never be over 4½″ high and will only be 6″ low at 350 yards.

The shooter should do his sighting in with the same ammunition he intends to use if he is doing target shooting or if his hunting targets are small. Only in this way will his sighting in be most accurate. For example, the 110-grain .30/06 has a point of impact 1″ high at 200 yards, but the 220-grain bullet has a point of impact 2″ low, a difference of 3″. This difference does not matter too much for large game such as deer, but it is significant for target shooting, or it would be significant for small varmint shooting. For the most precise shooting, you should resight every time you change bullet weights or bullet characteristics. Since big-game hunting is not that precise, resighting is not necessary for this type of hunting. For example, if you are shooting a .30/30, and sight it in at 25 yards, the point of impact with 150-grain bullets is 2½ " high at 150 yards and 2" high with 170-grain bullets, not enough to make any difference. Or if you are shooting a .308 sighted in at 25 yards, the point of impact is 2" low at 250 yards with 110-grain bullets and 7" low with 200-grain bullets, still not enough to make a big difference in big-game hunting, but a significant difference in varmint shooting. Therefore, whether you sight in every time you change bullets and/or cartridges will depend upon the precision you need.

Try to do your sighting in under calm wind conditions. This is especially true if the shooter is sighting in not at 25 yards but at long ranges, or if he needs maximum precision, as in target shooting. Actually, wind does not make too much difference at 25-yard ranges for hunting purposes, but since errors at 25 yards are multiplied as one reaches out to farther and farther ranges, it is better not to have errors to multiply. Obviously, the stronger the wind, the greater the problem. And winds crossing at a 90° angle cause more problems than winds quartering from either side. (See a succeeding section on wind allowance.)

A benchrest provides the best support for sighting in, but if one is not available, *sight in in a prone position, using a padded rest for the forend of the rifle.* It is necessary that the gun rest on a padded surface, since recoil tends to push the barrel away from a hard surface.

With these general considerations in mind, what is the procedure in sighting in?

1. Place a target at 25 yards, and fire three test shots.

2. Draw lines between the three bullet holes and mark the center of the group. Measure the exact horizontal and vertical distance (in inches) the group center is off from the center of the bullseye. The windage correction needed is the horizontal distance, the elevation correction needed is the vertical distance.

3. Change the sight settings to make the needed windage and elevation corrections. With a telescope sight with ¼-minute graduations on the dial, moving the dial one graduation will correct the line of sight ¹⁄₁₆" at 25 yards. (See the previous section under telescope sights on adjusting for windage and elevation.) The same principle applies to micrometer receiver sights. Find out how much adjusting the sight one graduation moves the point of impact at 25 yards, and adjust elevation and windage accordingly. For iron sights without micrometer adjustments, move the rear sight in the direction needed by whatever means are provided for that sight, or with a punch and hammer if necessary. It may take some time to adjust iron sights correctly. (See the previous sections on adjust-

ing open rear sights under the general subject of iron sights.) With iron sights, you may have to shoot several groups of three shots, until the necessary adjustments are made.

4. With all types of sights, check the adjustments by firing a group of three shots once more. If the group is still off, adjust accordingly.

Correction for Wind
All wind has some effect on the flight path of the bullet, but whether or not the effect is significant will depend upon the type of shooting (whether target or hunting), the range (wind effects are greater at long ranges), the shape of the bullet and its ballistics, and the direction the wind is blowing. If a horizontal clock face is used in describing the direction of the wind, with the shooter at the center of the face and the target at 12 o'clock, a 3-o'clock wind would come directly from the right, a 6-o'clock wind would come directly from the rear, and a 9-o'clock wind would come directly from the left.

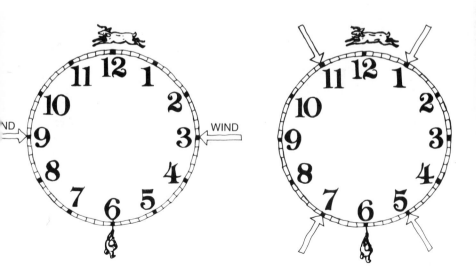

Crosswinds blowing at right angles (9 and 3 o'clock) with your line of aim (left) cause more bullet drift than winds coming from 1, 5, 7 or 11 o'clock.

For the man with a rifle, when the wind is from 3 o'clock or 9 o'clock its effect is greatest. As the angle diminishes, the effect of the wind is less pronounced. Winds from 1, 5, 7, or 11 o'clock require about half the correction needed for a wind of the same speed blowing from 9 or 3 o'clock. Winds from 2, 4, 8, and 10 o'clock have about ⅞ of the sideward force of 3- or 9-o'clock winds of the same velocity.

The first task in making wind corrections is to judge the velocity of the wind. The table helps make estimations of wind velocity.

Judging Wind Velocity

1 mph	Hardly appreciable; cannot be felt.
2–5 mph	Very light breeze. At 3 mph, there is very little drift to smoke, and you may be able to feel a slight breeze on your cheek. At 5 mph, breeze on your cheek is definitely apparent.
10–12 mph	A rather strong breeze. Leaves are blowing along ground, lightweight flags are beginning to be extended from poles.
14–18 mph	Quite a strong breeze. At 15 mph, dirt and loose paper are raised into the air; small loose branches are moved along the ground.
20–25 mph.	A hard, strong wind. We pull our hats and lean against it. At 20 mph, the wind sways small bushes and trees. Experienced shooters cease firing.
Over 30 mph	A gale too strong for successful rifle shooting.

How much effect does the wind have on the trajectory of a bullet? This depends upon many factors, but the following table gives some drift figures for wind traveling at 6.8 mph at 90° angles across of line of sight.

Drift Effect of Wind Blowing 6.8 mph at 90° Across Line of Sight

			Wind Drift in Inches			
Caliber	Bullet	Muzzle Vol.	100 yds.	200 yds.	300 yds.	400 yds.
.220 Swift	48 gr.	4.40 fps	.66″	2.65″	5.95″	10.6″
.250 Sav.	87 gr.	3000 fps	.62″	2.47″	5.50″	
.270	100 gr.	3540 fps	.50″	2.00″	2.00″	8.00″
.270	130 gr.	3120 fps	.45″	1.80″	4.05″	7.20″
.30/06	110 gr.	3380 fps	1.04″	4.18″	9.40″	

Here are some other figures on what wind will do. A .22LR bullet with a muzzle velocity of 1,100 fps will be blown off the aiming point 3.6″ at 100 yards and 14.4″ at 200 yards by a 100 mph crosswind (see the table). A similar wind will blow a .30/06 180-grain Silvertip bullet off its course approximately 8″ at 400 yards. A 30 mph wind will blow it off its course 12″ at 200 yards and 24″ at 400 yards. This means considerable correction for high winds at long ranges.

Table of Wind Allowance
.22 Long Rifle Cartridge, 40-Grain Bullet M.V. 1100 f.s.

Distance	Miles per Hour	Inches and Minutes Bullet is Deflected					
		By 1, 5, 7, and 11 o'Clock Winds		By 2, 4, 8 and 10 o'Clock Winds		By 3 and 9 o'Clock Winds	
		Inches	Min.	Inches	Min.	Inches	Min.
50 Yards	5	.22	.45	.38	.77	.45	.9
1 Minute = ½ Inch	10	.45	.90	.78	1.57	.90	1.8
	15	.67	1.35	1.19	2.38	1.35	2.7
	20	.90	1.80	1.57	3.15	1.80	3.6
100 Yards	5	.90	.90	1.57	1.57	1.80	1.8
1 Minute = 1 inch	10	1.80	1.80	3.15	3.15	3.60	3.6
	15	2.70	2.70	4.82	4.82	5.40	5.4
	20	3.60	3.60	6.30	6.30	7.20	7.2
200 Yards	5	3.60	1.80	6.30	3.15	7.20	3.6
1 Minute = 2 Inches	10	7.20	3.60	12.60	6.30	14.40	7.2
	15	10.80	5.40	18.90	9.45	21.60	10.8
	20	14.40	7.20	25.20	12.60	28.80	14.4

Table is approximately correct for .22 L. R. High-Speed Cartridges also.

Some types of bullets are affected more by wind than others. The better the bullet retains its velocity over long ranges, the less it is affected by the wind. Long, heavy, sharp-pointed bullets with superior sectional densities are affected less than short, light, round-nosed, flat-nosed, or hollow-point bullets with low sectional densities. This is why the hunter should use slightly heavier and pointed bullets under strong wind conditions, provided the heavier bullet has as long range as needed. Boat-tail bullets also buck the wind better than others.

A formula for wind compensation which gives the minutes of angle (MOA) required to compensate for wind blowing at 90° to the bullet's path is given below.

$$\frac{\text{Range in Hundreds of Yds} \times \text{Wind Velocity in mph}}{\text{A Set Constant For Each Cartridge Load}} = \text{Minutes of Angle}$$

For example, if the shooter is using a .30/06 M-2 cartridge, the set constant is 10. If the range is 200 yards, and the wind velocity is 10 mph from the left, the correction needed is:

$$\frac{2 \times 10}{10} = \text{2 minutes of angle into the wind, or 4″ at the 200 yards}$$

Shooting at Angles Uphill or Down

When a target is at a considerable range above or below the level of the shooter, the tendency is to shoot high, or overshoot, because the bullet drop is over the horizontal range and not over the greater distance of the slant range, so the total pull of gravity is not able to deflect the bullet downward as much.

If, in shooting uphill, the gun is at an angle of 10° above the line of sight, this places the sights right on the target. On the other hand, if the gun angle is at 10° + 30° (the angle uphill), the result is the trajectory of the bullet passing over and beyond the target. The same thing would happen if shooting at a 30° angle downhill as well. This means the hunter must hold low. The table shows the relationship between the "slant range" (or actual distance over which the bullet passes) the "horizontal range" (which governs the bullet's drop).

Relationship Between Estimated Slant Range and Horizontal Range

Angle of Slope (Up or Down)	Divide Estimate Range by
0°	1.0
5°	1.0
10°	1.02
15°	1.04
20°	1.06
25°	1.10
30°	1.15
40°	1.31
45°	1.41

Another way of calculating the same thing is with the following formula:

$$\text{Horizontal Range} = \text{Estimated Slant Range} \times \text{Cosine of Angle Elevation}$$

Let us see how this works with the table above and with the formula. Suppose one's angle of elevation = 30° uphill, and the estimate slant range = 350 yards. By the table above:

$$\text{Horizontal Range} = \frac{350 = 305 \text{ yards}}{1.15}$$

By the formula above:

$$\text{Horizontal Range} = 350 \times \text{Cosine } 30° = 350 \times .87 = 305 \text{ yards.}$$

Range Estimation

Several ways of learning to estimate ranges will be discussed here.

1. Memorize distances so you can compare distances while hunting.
2. Estimate range with your scope reticle.
3. Use a range-finding scope.

The best way to learn to estimate ranges is by memorizing distances with which you can compare ranges while hunting. Then practice your range estimation. Everyone knows, for example, that a football field is 100 yards long. Go look at it; see how long 100 yards is when you are looking over the flat ground. Then try to visualize 100 yards over flat ground, over a valley or draw, or canyon, and through bushes. Go to different spots and estimate ranges. If you are not sure of the distance, pace it off. (But first measure your stride to learn how to pace off approximately 3' per stride.)

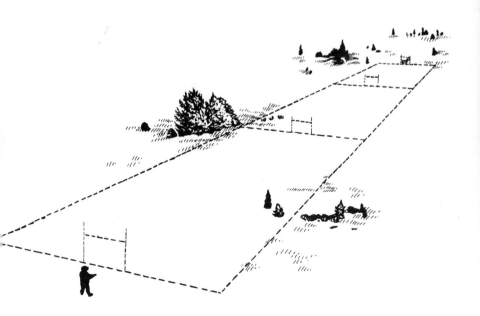

By remembering the length of a football field or other convenient distance, a hunter can visualize it in multiples to estimate the range of a game animal.

After you are good at estimating 100-yard ranges, try estimating distances of 200, 300, and 400 yards, if you are likely to be shooting this far. By remembering the length of a football field and being able to judge 100 yards accurately, you can then begin to estimate multiples of 100 yards.

The only way to become expert at range estimation is to practice. Take walks and estimate ranges between widely separated telephone poles. Estimate distances to trees, to houses, to bushes, to other people. Then check your estimates by pacing off the distance, and you'll soon discover you are an expert.

The second way to estimate ranges is by using your scope reticule. But to do this you have to know how many minutes or fractions of minutes of angle your reticule covers. For example, if you have a scope with a 4-minute dot reticule, you know this will cover 4″ of target at 100 yards, 8″ at 200 yards, or 16″ at 300 yards. If an adult buck deer measures about 18″ from withers (points between shoulders) to his brisket (belly line), and your dot covers this entire vertical area, you know your buck is slightly over 300 yards away. If your dot covers about half the distance, your buck is a little over 200 yards away.

The same principle applies if you have a post reticule. An excellent post reticule subtends (covers) about 4 to 6 minutes of angle (4″ to 6″ at 100 yards). By knowing the size of your animal, and the post, you can quickly determine the range of an animal. While usually slimmer than a post reticule, crosshairs can also be used. An excellent crosshair for a 2½X hunting scope is about 2 minutes, or subtends 2″ at 100 yards. So if you are gopher shooting (total measurement standing full length is about 8″), and the horizontal crosshair subtends his entire body, you know the range is about 8″ ÷ 2″/100 yards = 400 yards. Furthermore, suppose you know your bullet will drop 8″ at that distance. Hold a crosshair's width over the middle of the body of the gopher, and you should hit dead center. Thus, the reticule can be used not only to determine range but also to determine how far to hold over the target when necessary.

You should know the measurements of various animals. The table shows some common animals' measurements.

The third way of estimating range is by using a range-finding scope. As discussed in the previous section on reticules, some reticules are designed as range-finder reticules. The simplest is No. 14, shown in the figure on types of reticules. If the two horizontal crosshairs are subtended at a 6-minute angle, they will cover 6″ at 100 yards, or 18″ at 300 yards.

Measurements of Common Animals

Animal	Where Measured	Distance
Elk	Shoulder to brisket	24″
Deer	Shoulder to brisket	18″
Bear	Shoulder to brisket	18″
Sheep	Shoulder to brisket	22″
Antelope	Shoulder to brisket	14″
Mountain Lion	Shoulder to brisket	12″
Coyote	Shoulder to brisket	9″
Chuck	Standing full length	18″
Gopher	Standing full length	8″

If they cover only half the 18″ body of a deer from shoulders to belly, you know the range is 150 yards.

Reticule No. 8, the Redfield Accu-Range, was also discussed in the previous section. On this type, the horizontal wires are adjusted until they subtend the deer's body, and then the range is read directly. But it is important to note that a correct range reading is obtained on this reticule only if the animal's body is 18″ and the two horizontal crosshairs are correctly adjusted to fit the body 18″ apart. If a small animal is the target, such as a coyote (measuring 9″), the correct range is only half of the scale reading. The table shows how to calculate the correct yardage using the Redfield Accu-Range when the animal's measurement is less or more than 18″.

Of course, these rapid-fire calculations are virtually impossible under actual hunting conditions. Therefore, this type of reticule does not seem as wise a choice for hunting as some others that can also be used in range estimation.

Calculating Yardage with Redfield Accu-Range

Animal Measurement	Yardage
6″	⅓ of scale reading
9″	½ of scale reading
12″	⅔ of scale reading
15″	82% of scale reading
18″	direct scale reading
21″	scale reading plus 17%
24″	scale reading plus ⅓
27″	scale reading plus ½
30″	scale reading plus ⅔
36″	twice scale reading

The Realist Autorange (No. 11 in the figure on reticules) was also discussed in the section on reticules. Since this involves an automatic adjustment for range when the horizontal crosshairs are adjusted to subtend the animal, it is fast and accurate.

Shot Placement Areas for Big Game

No hunter likes to cripple game, which may run off to die. But some hunters are careless about their aim or lack sufficient understanding to shoot in a vital area. For this reason, some knowledge of where to aim to assure a quick kill is essential.

Where is the best spot to aim on a deer? The best place of all is the lung area back of the shoulder. The reasons are several:

1. This is the largest, most vital area to aim at. The chances of getting an accurate hit are far greater than if the hunter aims at a vital but small target, such as the brain, spinal column, or jugular vein. It is too easy to miss a brain or spinal shot, and to only wound the animal. Then you have to track the wounded beast for miles.

2. A clean hit with an adequate bullet, one that has sufficient weight and expanding qualities, usually means a one-shot kill. Death may not be instantaneous, but it is very fast. The bullet tears up the lungs, causing terrific bleeding and shock to the whole system, and it usually ruptures the heart or stops it.

3. Strangely, a lung shot is better than a heart shot. The heart is small and low. If your bullet goes very low, you will miss the animal or only break a foreleg. Also, a large deer can be shot in the heart and still run several hundred yards before falling dead, making the hunter think he has missed it and leave a dead animal in the woods.

4. A lung shot ordinarily does not destroy much edible meat. A spine shot destroys a lot of deer chops; a shoulder shot splinters bone into some fine roasts.

There are several spots a hunter must avoid hitting if at all possible. (1) A leg (not a shoulder), low on the leg. The animal can have a leg blown off or a broken leg and suffer terribly, but escape. (2) A paunch or gut shot. The deer may have his intestines and stomach literally blown out and still keep going. If the hunter does find him, the meat is often badly tainted. (3) A ham shot, primarily because it destroys a lot of edible meat. If the shot misses the hip or leg bone, it will never stop the animal. If it hits the hip, he will go down only wounded, and have to be dispatched quickly, but a lot of meat will still be destroyed. If the shots hit

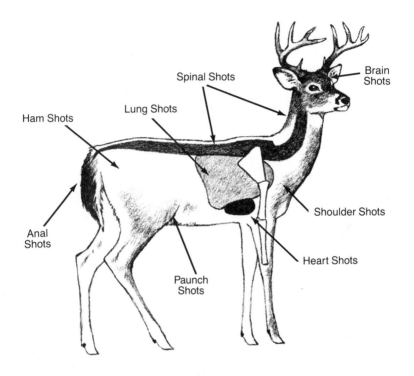

Placement of shots on a big-game animal.

the lower leg, the animal will usually go down, then get up and keep traveling.

The basic principles just outlined apply to many other animals as well: antelope, mountain sheep and goats, elk, caribou, and moose. The best shot placement for these animals is the lung area. Try to avoid hitting the shoulder of an elk, caribou, or moose, particularly with the type of rapid expansion bullets usually selected for this game. These are tough animals with large bones. The shoulder bone may turn the fast-expanding bullets designed for thin-skinned game such as deer. So, shoot behind the shoulder not right into it.

The game that must be shot into the shoulder to be stopped are dangerous bears: grizzlies, polar bears, and Alaskan brown bears. The first task of the hunter, in this instance, is to stop the animal, and by holding to break one or both shoulders. True, this only wounds the animal unless the bullet also enters the lungs or heart, but the bear is stopped and can be readily dispatched with quick finishing shots. On angling shots, the hunter can hold to break the near shoulder and have the bullet penetrate the chest cavity to go through the heart-lungs area or also break the opposite shoulder. Of course, high-velocity, heavy, tough, deep-penetrating bullets must be used for this type of hunting.

How to Lead a Moving Target

There are basically two methods of hitting a moving target. One is with the fast swing; the other is with the sustained lead. In the *fast swing,* the hunter aims exactly as does the shotgunner on waterfowl: he starts the swing behind the animal, swings in the direction the animal is moving, but at a somewhat faster rate than the animal is traveling, pulls ahead of the animal and, as he keeps his rifle moving, squeezes off the shot. The secret of this method is to follow through in the direction the animal is moving, keeping the rifle moving as the rifle barrel gets ahead of the animal and the shot is squeezed off. If the shooter stops or slows his swing to check his sight picture, he will shoot behind a fast-running animal.

In the fast swing, the rifle is aimed behind the animal, swung rapidly past, and fired when the lead looks right.

The second method is the *sustained lead.* In using this technique, the hunter must decide how much to lead the target, place his sight the correct distance in front of the game, and then keep swinging his rifle at the same speed and in the same direction the animal is moving, so as to sustain the correct lead. The shot is fired without stopping the swing.

FIRE

In the sustained lead, the sight is placed the correct distance in front of the animal, the lead is held for a few yards, and the trigger squeezed without stopping the swing.

The question often asked is: How much do you lead a running animal? Of course, this depends on the range, the bullet's velocity, how fast the animal is running and at what angle, and the reaction time of the hunter between the time he decides to shoot and the time he actually pulls the trigger. The fast swing or sustained lead will ordinarily take care of the problem of the angle the deer is running, and of the hunter's reaction time, because the rifle continues to swing along the path of the animal while the hunter decides to shoot and actually pulls the trigger. The variables remaining are the bullet's velocity (which determines how long it takes the bullet to travel from muzzle to target), the range, and the speed of the animal. The time (in seconds) it takes for the bullet to reach the target is:

$$\frac{\text{Time}}{\text{(in seconds)}} = \frac{\text{Distance to Target (in feet)}}{\text{Average Bullet Velocity (in feet per second)}}$$

Of course, the bullet gradually slows down after firing, so its velocity can be approximately calculated as an average of muzzle velocity and velocity at the time it hits the target. Let's see how this works. Suppose the hunter is using a .30/06 with a 150-grain bullet, muzzle velocity of 2,970 fps, and velocity at 200 yards of 2,400 fps, on a deer crossing at 30 mph at 200 yards away. How long will it take for the bullet to reach the target?

The first task is to calculate the average velocity of the bullet.

$$\text{Average Velocity} = \frac{2{,}970 \text{ fps} + 2{,}400 \text{ fps}}{2} = \frac{5370}{2} = 2{,}685 \text{ fps}$$

$$\text{Time} = \frac{\text{Distance (in feet)}}{\text{Average Velocity (in fps)}} = \frac{200 \text{ yds} \times 3'/\text{yds.}}{2{,}685 \text{ fps}}$$

$$\text{Time} = \frac{600'}{2{,}685 \text{ fps}} = .22 \text{ sec.}$$

Once you know how long it will take the bullet to get to the target, it is easy to calculate the lead distance required according to the speed of the game.

$$\text{Lead Distance (in feet)} = \frac{\text{Time} \times \text{Speed of Deer} \times 5{,}280'/\text{mile}}{3{,}600 \text{ sec./hr.}}$$

In the case sighted above, the answer is as follows:

$$\text{Lead Distance (feet)} = \frac{.22 \text{ sec.} \times 30 \text{ mph} \times 5{,}280'/\text{mile}}{3600 \text{ sec./hour}}$$

$$\text{Lead Distance} = \frac{.22 \times 30 \times 5{,}280'}{3{,}600} = 9.68'$$

A deer about 5' long should be led about two body lengths ahead of the desired aiming point. Of course, these solutions assume the deer is running at a 90° angle across at about 30 mph.

Handloading Rifle Cartridges

Case Sorting and Inspection

Before starting to load, all cartridge cases should be sorted and inspected. Separate the cases into groups according to caliber, make, and type. It is helpful if those purchased together have been kept separated by lots, so you know that those of the same brand name and date of purchase, and those which have been reloaded a particular number of times, are loaded together. Check all cases for splits, cracks, or other signs of excessive fatigue. Discard those not in good condition. Those cases that have been lengthened after numerous firings and reloadings need trimming at the mouth. Also, new or once-fired cases have sharp edges inside the case mouth. These edges are trimmed by a process known as *chamfering*. Hold the case in one hand while you lightly turn a reamer in the case mouth with the other hand. Be certain not to remove much material or a sharp knife edge will be cut on the edge of the case.

Selecting the Components

Reloading handbooks have charts that recommend the right components for your cartridge. Make certain you select the proper bullet diameter and primer size for your cartridge case. Bullet weight should be selected according to recommendations and the type of shooting you are doing. Generally speaking, long-range shooting requires lighter bullets than short-range shooting. Pointed bullets do not lose velocity as fast as rounded or flat bullets. Hunting in brush and woods requires heavy, round-nosed bullets to minimize brush deflection. Large animals obviously require heavier bullet weights than small animals. Some bullets expand rapidly, others not at all, so jacket, design, and bullet material are important. For full information, see the discussion of "Bullets" in a previous section.

Powder type and amount must also be selected. If you are uncertain, use a starting load recommended for the caliber and bullet you have selected. Do not make the mistake of overloading the cartridge, or even of loading to the maximum if you are unfamiliar with the process or result.

Steps in Handloading a Rifle Cartridge

There are six mechanical operations involved in reloading a cartridge.

1. *Full-length resizing.* This involves reducing the stretched outside diameter of the case, including the neck, shoulder, and body.

2. *Decapping.* Removing the fired primer.

3. *Inside neck expanding.* Enlarging the diameter of the neck to receive and hold the bullet firmly.

4. *Priming.* Inserting a new primer.

5. *Charging powder.* Weighing the powder and pouring it into the case.

6. *Bullet seating.* Putting the bullet firmly into the case.

Usually, these six mechanical operations are performed in four basic steps. In actual practice, though, operations 1 and 2 (full-length resizing and decapping) are both accomplished in step 1. Inside neck expanding and priming (operations 3 and 4) are both accomplished in step 2.

PART TWO

Shotguns and Shotshells

Types of Shotguns

There are six basic types: *single-shot break action; side-by-side double barrel; over-and-under double barrel; bolt-action repeater; pump-action repeater,* and *autoloader.* The single shot is light, inexpensive, and safe for the beginner, and comes in either hammer or hammerless design, with most having automatic extractors. Double barrels, either side-by-side or over-and-under, have the advantage of two different chokes. Triggers are double, single selective, or single non selective. The barrel you shoot first may be selected with the double trigger, or the single-selective trigger. The over-under design has less recoil than the side-by-side double, plus the advantage of a narrower sighting plane. The pump action is light, but fast, and somewhat chepaer than the autoloaders. It may come with interchangeable barrels or with variable-choke devices. The autoloader has the distinct advantage of faster firing and one more shot than the double. It is expensive, heavy to handle, and dangerous if not handled with caution.

U.S. Shotguns: Autoloading

Model	Gauge	Action	Barrel & Choke	Weight	Features
Browning Auto-5 Light 12 or 20	12,20	Recoil operated	26"–20 g–Skt., C,IC,M–12 g–Skt. 28"–12 g–Skt., M,F 30"–12 g–F	12 g–7¼ lbs 20 g–6⅜ lbs	Double extractors, extra bbls., from Japan by Browning
Browning Auto-5 Magnum 12 or 20	12,20 for 2¾" or 3"	Recoil operated	28"–12,20 g–M,F 30"–12 g–F 32"–12 g–F 26"–20 g–F,M,IC	12 g–8¾ lbs 20 g–7½ lbs	With vent. rib, recoil pad
Browning Auto-5 Light Skeet	12,20	Recoil operated	26",28"–12,20 g–Skt.	12 g–6⅜ lbs 20 g–7½ lbs	With vent. rib
Browning Auto-5 Light 12,20, or 12 Buck Special	12,20 Mag. 12,20	Recoil operated	24"–12,20, Mag. 12–choked for slugs	12 g–7 lbs 20 g–6 lbs 2 oz Mag. 12–8¼ lbs	Gold bead front sight on ramp, rear sight adj., with carrying sling

U. S. Shotguns: Autoloading (*cont.*)

Model	Gauge	Action	Barrel & Choke	Weight	Features
Browning B-80 Auto	12,20 for 2¾" or 3"		22"–Slug 26"–IC,C,Skt., F,M 28"–F,M 30"–F 32"–F	About 6½ lbs	Vent. rib, cross-bolt safety, interchangeable bbls., from Belgium by Browning
Ithaca Model 51A Automatic	12,20	Gas operated	30"–F 28"–F,M 26"–IC, Skt.	About 7½ lbs	Raybar front sight, safety reversible for left-hand shooter
Ithaca 51A Magnum	12,20 for 3"				Same as std. models
Ithaca 51A Supreme Skeet	12,20		26"–Skt.		Same as Model 51 Skt. with fancy walnut stock
Ithaca 51A Deerslayer	12,20	Gas operated	24"–special bore	12 g–7½ lbs 20 g–7¼ lbs	Raybar front, open rear, adj. sight, grooved for scope
Ithaca Mag-10 Gas Operated Shotgun	10, 3½"	"Counter-coil" gas system	26",28",32" – F,M	11¼ lbs	Vent. rib, crossbolt safety, comes in Std., Deluxe, Supreme, Presentation models
Ithaca Mag-10 Deerslayer	10, 3½"		22"		Similar to Std. Mag-10 except has rifle sights, comes in Std., Deluxe, Supreme grades

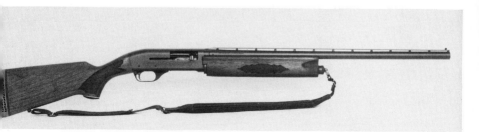

Ithaca Model 51A Automatic

U. S. Shotguns: Autoloading (*cont.*)

Model	Gauge	Action	Barrel & Choke	Weight	Features
Ljutic Bi-Matic Auto Shotgun	12, 2¾"	Left- or right-hand ejection	26" to 32" –choked to customer specs	About 10 lbs	Two-shot, pull or release trig., custom-made
Mossberg 5500 Auto Shotgun	12, 2¾" or 3"		18½"–C 24"–Slugster 26"–IC 28"–M 30"–F (2¾" or 3")	7½ lbs	Bead front sight, safety on top, interchangeable bbls. or choke tubes
Remington 1100 Auto	12	Gas operated	26"–IC 28"–M,F 30"–12 g–F	12 g–7½ lbs	Interchangeable bbls., crossbolt safety, left or right hand
Remington 1100 Magnum	12,20		30"–12 g–M,F 28"–20 g–M,F	7¾ lbs	With or without vent. rib, right or left hand
Remington 1100 "Special Field"	12,20		21"–IC,M,F	12 g–7¼ lbs 20 g–6½ lbs	Like Std. model, vent. rib only
Remington 1100 Small Gauge	28, 2¾" .410, 2½" or 3"		25"–F,M,IC		Same as 1100
Remington 1100 Lt.-20	12,20, also in Lt.–20 Mag. or Lt.–20 Deer Gun		28"–12,20 g–F,M 26"–12,20 g–IC 20"–Lt.-20 Deer Gun 23"–Lt.-20 Mag.– M,IC	6½ lbs	Same as 1100 but with weight-saving features
Remington 1100 TA Trap	12		30"–M,Trap,F	8¼ lbs	With or without Monte Carlo stock, right or left hand, also comes in tournament grade, Model 1100D is Tournament Auto
Remington 1100F Premier Auto					Like 1100D except select wood, better engraving, with or without gold inlay
Remington 1100SA Skeet	12, 20, 28, .410		26"–Skt. 25"–28,.410 g–Sk.	7½ lbs	12 g in right or left hand, 20 g available in Lt. Skt., also available in Tournament Skt., ivory bead front and metal bead middle sights

U. S. Shotguns: Autoloading (*cont.*)

Model	Gauge	Action	Barrel & Choke	Weight	Features
Remington 1100 Deer Gun	12		22"–IC	7¼ lbs	Rifle sights, right or left hand
Smith and Wesson 1000 Auto	12, 2¾" or 3"	Gas operated	26"–Skt., IC 28"–M,F Also with choke tubes 22"–C 30"–M,F with 3" chamber	7½ lbs	22" bbl. has rifle sights, all have interchangeable crossbolt safety
Smith and Wesson 1000 20 Gauge and 20 Magnum	20, 20 Mag.	Self-cleaning gas system	26"–IC, Skt. 28"–M,F Or Multi-Choke system with IC,M,F tubes		Four interchangeable bbls., 3" has M,F choke
Smith & Wesson 1000 Trap Shotgun	12		30"–Multi-Choke bbl. with F,M,IM tubes		Monte Carlo stock, white middle bead, Bradley front, tuned trig.
Smith and Wesson 1000 Waterfowler Auto	12, 3"		30"–F		Metal and stock have dull finish to reduce glare
Smith and Wesson 1000S Super Skeet Shotgun			25"–Skt. choke with compensator	8¼ lbs	Double sighting beads, front is fluorescent red
Weatherby Eighty-Two Auto	12, 2¾" or 3"	Gas operated	26"–M,IC,Skt. 28"–F,M 30"–F,Full Trap, Full 3" Mag. Or Multi-Choke interchange-able tubes	7½ lbs	Crossbolt safety, gold-plated trig., Field, Skt., or Trap grade, from Japan by Weatherby
Winchester 1500 XTR Auto Shotgun	12,20, 2¾"	Gas operated	28"–F,M,IC choke tubes	7–7¼ lbs	Metal bead front, crossbolt safety, with or without choke tubes, also comes in deer slug bbl.
Winchester Ranger Auto Shotgun	12,20, 2¾"		28" vent. or plain–IC,M,F	7–7¼ lbs	Metal bead front, crossbolt safety, plain bbl. or vent.

U.S. Shotguns: Pump Action

Model	Gauge	Action	Barrel & Choke	Weight	Features
Browning BPS Pump Shotgun	12	Bottom ejection	26",28",30" ,32" –IC,M,F. Also choke tubes	28"–7 lbs 12 oz	Bottom feeding action, top safety, comes in Hunting, Trap, Buck Special models, from Japan by Browning
Ithaca 37 Featherlight	12,20	Bottom ejection	26",28",30" –12 g–F,M,IC 26",28"–20 g– F,M,IC	12 g–6½ lbs 20 g–5¾ lbs	Raybar front sight, crossbolt safety, std. or vent, also 2500 and Presentation series
Ithaca 37 Ultralight	12,20		26"–12 g– F,M,IC 25"–20 g– F,M,IC 20"–20 g– Ultra- Deerslayer	5 lbs	Gold-plated trig.
Ithaca 37 English Ultralight	12,20				Same as Std. 37 except vent. bbl. and straight stock
Ithaca 37 Magnum	12,20 Mag.		30"–F 28"–M 26"–IC	7¼ lbs	Similar to Std. 37 except 3" shells
Ithaca 37 Supreme	12,20		Like Std. 37 but also available in Supreme model with Skt. or Trap		Same as Std. 37 except hand checkered
Ithaca 37 Field Grade	12,20, 2¾" only				Raybar front sight, similar to Std. 37
Ithaca 37 Deerslayer	12,20		20", 26" –designed for rifle slugs		Sporting rear sight, Raybar front sight, or grooved for scope, also comes in Super Deluxe model
Ithaca 37 DeLuxe Featherlight	12,20			12 g–6¾ lbs	Checkered stock, beavertail forend, vent. rib, recoil pad, otherwise same as Std. 37
Marlin 120 Magnum Pump Gun	12	Side ejecting	20"–Slug 26"–IC 28"–M 30"–F–vent, rib 38"–F–plain	8 lbs	Interchangeable bbls., crossbolt safety

U. S. Shotguns: Pump Action (*cont.*)

Model	Gauge	Action	Barrel & Choke	Weight	Features
Marlin Glenfield 778 Pump Gun	12, 2¾" or 3"		20" –Slug/sights 26"–IC 28"–M 30"–F 38"–F	7¾ lbs	Interchangeable bbls., plain or rib
Mossberg 500 AGVD, CGVD	12,20,3"	Takedown, side ejecting	28"–ACCU-CHOKE tubes for IC,M,F	6¾ lbs	Top tang safety, interchangeable bbls., also in youth model (20 g, 13" butt, 25" bbl.–M)
Mossberg 500 Medallion	12,20		28"–F,M,IC choke tubes, vent.		Same as Std. 500 except game bird medallions
Mossberg 500 AHT/AHTD	12		30"–F, or tubes 28"–ACCU-CHOKE tubes for M,IC,F		Same as Std. 500
Mossberg 500 ASG Slugster	12,20		18½"–12 g 24"–12,20 g For slugs		Ramp front sight, open adj. folding-leaf rear
Mossberg 500 EGV	.410		26"–F, 2½",3"	6 lbs	Similar to Std. 500
Remington 870 Wingmaster Pump Gun	12,20	Takedown	26"–IC 28"–M,F 30"–12 g–F 23"–IC,M	12 g–7 lbs 20 g–6½ lbs	Crossbolt safety, plain or vent. bbl., lightweight, 23" model has vent. rib only
Remington 870 Magnum	12,20,3"		30"–12 g–M,C 28"–20 g–M,F	12 g–8 lbs 20 g–7½ lbs	Same as Std. 870 except 3" chamber, also comes in 870DU Commemorative in 3" Mag. with 32" bbl. (F) with engraving
Remington 870 F Premier					Same as Std. 870 except better walnut, engraving, with or without gold inlay
Remington 870 Small Gauges	28,.410,20 Mag.		25"–F,M,IC	Ltwght. Mag. 20–5¾ lbs	Ltwght. Mag. 20 with plain or vent. rib bbl.
Remington 870 Brushmaster Deluxe	12,20		20"–IC. Carbine version for slugs	6½ lbs.	Adj. rear, ramp front sights

U. S. Shotguns: Pump Action (*cont.*)

Model	Gauge	Action	Barrel & Choke	Weight	Features
Remington 870D Tournament	12,20				Same as Std. 870 except better walnut hand checkering, engraved receiver, stock dimensions to order
Remington 870 20 Gauge Lightweight	20		26"–IC 28"–F,M 30"–F	6 lbs	Same as Std. 870 except ltwght., plain or vent rib
Remington 870 TA Trap	12		30"–M,F	8 lbs	Vent. rib bbl., ivory front and white metal middle beads, with or without Monte Carlo stock
Smith & Wesson 3000 Pump	12,20, 3"		22"–C 26"–IC 28"–M 30"–F Also multi-Choke system	7½ lbs	Crossbolt safety right or left hand, slug bbl. has rifle sights
Smith & Wesson 3000 Watefowler Pump	12,30, 3"		30"–F		Similar to Std. 3000 except dull finish to reduce glare
Stevens 67 Pump Shotgun	12,20, 2¾" or 3" .410, 2½" or 3"		26"–.410 g– F 28"–M,F 30"–12 g–F Also interchangeable choke tubes 21"–Slug	7 lbs	Metal bead front, top tang safety, with or without vent. rib, slug model has rifle sights
Weatherby Ninety-Two Pump	12, 3"	Short stroke	26"–M,IC,Skt. 28"–F,M 30"–F,FT (3" Mag.–F) Also interchangeable choke tubes	7½ lbs	Comes in Field, Skt., Trap grades, interchangeable bbls. or Multi-Choke models

Stevens Model 67 Pump Shotgun

U. S. Shotguns: Pump Action (*cont.*)

Model	Gauge	Action	Barrel & Choke	Weight	Features
Winchester Ranger Pump Gun	12,20,3"		28"–F,M,IC or tubes 30"–F,M,IC or tubes	7–7¼ lbs	Metal bead front, crossbolt safety, plain or vent. rib bbl.
Wincester Ranger Youth Pump gun	20, 3"		22"–F,M,IC tubes or fixed M choke	6½ lbs	
Winchester Pump Gun Combination	12, 3"		Comes with two inter-changeable bbls.: 24⅛"–C deer bbl. with rifle sights 28"–F,M,IC choke tubes		Similar to Std. Ranger
Wincester 1300 XTR Pump Gun	12,20, 3"		28"–F,M,IC tubes Also comes with deer slug bbl.	7¼ lbs	Metal bead front, crossbolt safety, with or without vent. rib bbl.
Wincester 1300 XTR Deer Gun	12		24⅛"–C	6½ lbs	Rifle-type sights
Winchester 1300 XTR Waterfowl Pump Gun	12		30"–with choke tubes		Like 1300 XTR with vent. rib bbl.

U.S. Shotguns: Over-Under

Model	Gauge	Action	Barrel & Choke	Weight	Features
Browning Citori Over-Under Shotgun	12,20,28, .410		26",28"–all gauges–M-F, IC-M 30"–12 g–M-F,F-F Also with choke tubes	.410–26"–6 lbs 8 oz 12 g–30"– 7 lbs 13 oz	Medium raised beads, bbl. selector integral with safety, from Japan by Browning, comes in different grades

U. S. Shotguns: Over-Under (*cont.*)

Model	Gauge	Action	Barrel & Choke	Weight	Features
Browning Citori Over-Under Trap	12		32″ –F-F,IM-F,M-F 34″–in combo.–F, IM,M		Monte Carlo, conventional target rib and high post target rib, comes in different grades
Browning Citori Over-Under Skeet	12,20,28, .410		26″–S-S 28″–S-S		Similar to Std., comes in different grades
Browning Citori Over-Under Sporter	12,20,28, .410		26″–M-F,IC-M		Similar to Std. except straight grip stock
Browning Superlight Citori Over-Under	12,20,28, 3″		26″–12,20 g–3″–IC-M 28″–12,20 g–M-F	12 g–26″– 6 lbs 9 oz 20 g–26″– 5 lbs 12 oz	Different grades
Browning Citori Sideplate 20 Gauge	20		26″–IC-M, M-F		
Browning Superposed Super-Light Presentation Series	12,20,2¾″		26½″ –M-F,IC-M	6⅜ lbs	Four grades
Browning Presentation Superposed Magnum 12	12, 3″		30″–F-F,F-M	8 lbs	
Browning Presentation Superposed Lightning Skeet	12,20,28, .410			6½–7¾ lbs	Special Skt. stock
Browning Presentation Superposed Lightning Trap 12	12		30″ –F-F,F-IM,F-M		Same as Superposed Lightning
Browning Limited Edition Waterfowl Superposed	12		28″–M-F		Same specs as Superposed Lightning, limited edition of 500 guns, gold inscription, lined black-walnut case

U. S. Shotguns: Over-Under (*cont.*)

Model	Gauge	Action	Barrel & Choke	Weight	Features
Ljutic Bigun Over-Under Shotgun	12		28″ to 24″ to specs	To customer specs	Custom, with or without screw-in chokes
Remington 3200 Competition Trap	12		30″–F-F,F-M 32″–F-IM 28″–IM,M (Pigeon)	8¼ lbs–30″	With or without Monte Carlo stock
Remington 3200 Combination Skeet			26″,28″– S-S	7¾ lbs–26″	
Ruger "Red Label" Over-Under Shotgun	12,3″ 20,3″ or 2¾″		26″–12,20g– S-S,IC-M,F-M 28″–20 g–S-S,IC-M, F-M	7 lbs–26″	Auto. safety
Weatherby Orion Over-Under Shotgun	12,3″ 2¾″ on 20 g trap		30″–12 g–F-M 28″–12 g–F-M, M-IC,S-S 28″,26″–20 g–F-M, M-IC,S-S	12g, 26″–7 lbs 8 oz	Selective auto. ejectors, single selective trig., from Japan by Weatherby
Weatherby Athena Over-Under Shotgun	12,20, 3″, 2¾″ on trap		28″– F-M,M-IC,S-S	12 g–7⅜ lbs 20 g–6⅞ lbs	Mechanically operated trig., top tang safety, Field, Skt., or Trap models
Winchester 101 Winchoke Over-Under Gun	12,20, 3″	Top lever, break open	27″–inter-changeable choke tubes	12 g–7 lbs others 6½ lbs	Single selective trig., auto. ejectors, from Japan by Winchester

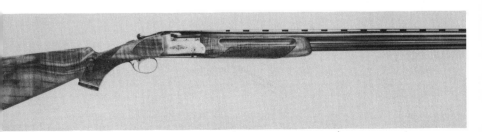

Weatherby Orion O/U Shotgun

U. S. Shotguns: Over-Under (*cont.*)

Model	Gauge	Action	Barrel & Choke	Weight	Features
Winchester 101 Diamond Grade Target Guns	12,20,28, .410–Skt. 12–Trap		Variety of bbl. lengths, available with Winchoke system		Straight or Monte Carlo stocks, similar to 101 Winchoke except for trap and skt. competition
Winchester 101 Waterfowl Winchoke	12, 3"		32"–M,IM,F, Extra-F tubes		From Japan by Winchester
Winchester 501 Grand European Over-Under	12–Trap 12,20–Skt. With 2¾" chambers		27"–S-S 30"–IM-F 32"–IM-F	7½ lbs–Skt. 8½ lbs–Trap	Slide-button selector safety, selective auto. ejectors, trap gun has regular or Monte Carlo stock
Winchester 101 Pigeon Grade	12,28– Ltwght. 12,20– Ltwght.– Winchoke 12,20– Fthwght. All with 3" chambers		28"–12,28 g–Ltwght.–M-F, M-IC, 27"–12,20 g–Ltwght.– Winchoke–6 choke tubes for 12 g, 4 for 20 g 25½"–12,20 g–Fthwght. –IC-M		Vent. rib bbl., middle bead, from Japan by Winchester

U.S. Shotguns: Side-by-Side

Model	Gauge	Action	Barrel & Choke	Weight	Features
Browning B-SS	12,20, 2¾"	Break open	26"–12,20 g– M-F,IC-M 28"–12 g–M-F 30"–12 g–F-F, M-F	12 g–30"– 7½ lbs 20 g–26"– 6¾ lbs	Auto. safety and ejectors, single selective trig., from Japan by Browning, two grades
Browning B-SS Sporter	12,20				Similar to Std. B-SS except straight grip stock
Savage Fox B-SE Double	12,2¾" 16,2¾" 20,2¾" and 3" .410,2½" and 3"	Hammer-less, takedown	26"–12,20 g–IC-M 26"–.410-F-F 26"–12 g–M-F	12 g–7 lbs 16 g–6¾ lbs 20 g–6½ lbs .410–6¼ lbs	Nonselective trig., auto. safety and ejectors

U. S. Shotguns: Side-by-Side (*cont.*)

Model	Gauge	Action	Barrel & Choke	Weight	Features
Savage-Stevens 311 Double	12,20, .410, 3" 16, 2¾"	Top lever	26"–12,16,20 g– IC-M 26"–.410–F-F 28"–12 g–M-F 30"–12 g–M-F	7 to 8 lbs– 30"	Double trig., auto. top tang safety
Winchester 23 Pigeon Grade Double	12,20,3"		26"–IC-M 28"–M-F	12 g–7 lbs 20 g–6½ lbs	Mechanical trig., vent. rib, selective ejectors, from Japan by Winchester
Winchester 23 Pigeon Grade Winchoke	12,20		25½"–inter- changeable Winchoke tubes		Same as 23 Pigeon Grade
Winchester 23 XTR Lightweight	12,20		25½"– IC-M		English style, straight stock, engraved scenes
Winchester 23 Heavy Duck	12,20,3"		30"–F-EF		Same as Std. 23

Browning B-SS Double-Barreled Shotgun

U.S. Shotguns: Bolt Action

Model	Gauge	Action	Barrel & Choke	Weight	Features
Marlin 55 Goose Gun Bolt gun	12, 2¾" or 3"	Bolt	36"–F	8 lbs	Thumb safety, 2-shot clip, tapped for receiver sights, brass bead front sight, U rear sight
Marlin Supergoose 10 M5510	12, 3½" or 2⅞"	Bolt	34"–F	10½ lbs	Thumb safety, 2-shot clip
Mossberg 183K Bolt Action	.410, 3"	Top loading, 3-shot	25" –C-Lect-Choke	5¾ lbs	Monte Carlo comb, gold bead front sight
Mossberg 395K Bolt Action	12, 3" 20, 3"	Bolt, 3-shot	26"–12 g– C-Lect- Choke 38"–12 g–F 28"–20 g– C-Lect- Choke	7½ lbs	Monte Carlo comb, top safety, grooved rear sight

Mossberg 595K Bolt-Action Shotgun

U.S. Shotguns: Single Shot

Model	Gauge	Action	Barrel & Choke	Weight	Features
Remington 870 Competition Trap	12,20	Pump	30"–F		Vent. rib bbl.
Harrington & Richardson 099 Deluxe	12,20, .410, 3" 16,2¾"		28"–12 g–F,M 28"–16 g–M 26"–20 g–F,M 25"–.410–F	About 5½ lbs	Bead front
Harrington & Richardson 088	Most popular gauge and choke combinations		Most popular bbl. and choke combinations incl. 30", 32", 36"–12 g–F		Junior model also available
Harrington & Richardson 162	12,20	Push-button action release	24"–cyl. bored	5½ lbs	Adj. folding leaf rear sight, blade front, crossbolt safety
Harrington & Richardson 490 and 490 Greenwing	20,.410		26"–20 g–M 26"–.410–F	5 lbs	Stock proportioned for the smaller shooter, Greenwing is fancier, designed for steel-shot use
Harrington & Richardson 176 Magnum	10, 3½"		36"–F 32"–F		
Harrington & Richardson 176 10 Slug Gun	10 g slugs, 3½"		28"–C	9¼ lbs	Ramp front sight, adj. folding leaf rear
Ithaca SE Single Barrel Trap Gun	12	Top lever, break open	32",34"–Trap		Monte Carlo comb, engraving and gold inlay
Ljutic Mono Gun Single Barrel	12	Push-button opener	34"–choked to specs 32"–choked to specs	9 lbs	Custom-made, also available with choke tubes
Ljutic Dyna Trap II Shotgun			33"–Trap		Monte Carlo or straight stock, similar to Mono Gun
Ljutic Recoilless Space Gun Shotgun	12, 2¾"		30"–F	8½ lbs	Choice of front sight or vent. rib, choice of pull or release button trig., anti-recoil

U. S. Shotguns: Single Shot (*cont.*)

Model	Gauge	Action	Barrel & Choke	Weight	Features
Savage-Stevens 94 Single Barrel Gun	12,20, .410,3" 16, 2¾"	Top lever, break open	28"–12,16, 20 g–F 30"–12 g–F 32"–12 g–F 36"–12 g–F 26"–.410–F	6 lbs	Hammer, auto. ejector
Stevens M94-Y Youth's Gun	20, .410		26"–20 g–M 26"–.410 g–F	5½ lbs	Short stock for youth
"Snake Charmer" Shotgun	.410,3"		18½"–C	3½ lbs	Molded plastic stock, from H. Koon, Inc.
Stevens 9478 Single Barrel	10,12,20, .410	Bottom opening action lever	26"–F,M 28"–F 30"–F 32"–F 36"–F	6¼ lbs– 9½ lbs 10 g	Manually cocked hammer, auto. ejector, youth model available in 20 g or .410 (26" bbl.), weighs 5½ lbs

Imported Shotguns: Pump Action

Model	Gauge	Action	Barrel & Choke	Weight	Features
Kassnar-Squires Bingham Model 30 D Shotgun	12, 2¾"		20"–IC,Slug 24"–Slug 26"–IC 28"–M 30"–F	7 lbs	Slug or Field model, slug guns have ramp front, open rear sights, from Philippines

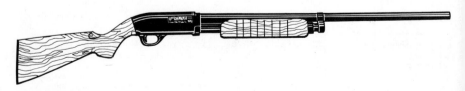

Kawaguchiya M-250 Auto Shotgun

Imported Shotguns: Autoloading

Model	Gauge	Action	Barrel & Choke	Weight	Features
Benelli Autoloading Shotgun	12		26"–Skt.,IC,M 28"–F,IM,M	6¾ lbs	Interchangeable bbls., crossbolt safety, comes in std. or engraved models, also in slug model or SL201 (20 g)
Beretta A-302 Auto Shotgun	12,20	Gas operated	22"–12 g–Slug 26"–12,20 g– IC,Skt. 28"–12 g–M,F, Multi-choke 28"–20 g–M,F	20 g–6½ lbs	Push-button safety, Multi-Choke models come with four choke tubes, 12 g trap comes with Monte Carlo stock
Franchi 48/A1 Auto Shotgun	12,20, 2¾" or 3" Mag.	Recoil operated	24"–IC,C 26"–IC,M 28"–Skt.,M,F 30",32"–F	12 g–6¼ lbs 20 g–5 lbs 2 oz	Std. or engraved model (Hunter model)
Franchi Slug Gun	12,20 g		22"–C		Adj. rifle sights, Std. or Hunter grades
Kawaguchiya K.F.C. M-250 Auto Shotgun	12 g, 2¾"	Gas operated	24½"–IC,M,F, interchange-able choke tubes 26"–IC 28"–M 30"–full or std. chokes	7 lbs 6 oz	Crossbolt safety, Std. or Deluxe grades
Tradewinds H-170 Auto Shotgun	12, 2¾"	Recoil operated	26",28"–M 28"–F	7 lbs	From Italy

Kassnar-Squires Bingham Model 30D Shotgun

Imported Shotguns: Over-Under

Model	Gauge	Action	Barrel & Choke	Weight	Features
Astra 750 Over-Under Shotgun	12, 2¾″		28″-M-F,S-S 30″-Trap-M-F	6½ lbs	Single selective trig., selective auto. ejectors
Astra 650 Over-Under Shotgun					Same as Model 750 except double trig.
Armsport Model 2500 Over-Under	12,20		26″-IC-M 28″-M-F	8 lbs	Single selective trig., auto. ejectors
Beretta 680 Over-Under	12, 2¾″		29½″- Trap-IM-F,IM 28″-S-S	8 lbs	Luminous front sight and center bead, trap Monte Carlo stock, Skt., Trap or Field models, also single-barrel Trap, 32″ or 34″
Beretta SO-3 Over-Under Shotgun	12, 2¾″	Back-action sidelock	26″,27″,28″,30″ -chokes to specs		Comes in three grades
Beretta SO-4 Traget Shotgun	12		28″-S-S 30″- Trap-IM-F, M-F	7 lbs 10 oz 7 lbs 12 oz	Inlaid in gold
Caprinus Sweden Over-Under Shotgun	12, 2¾″	Gas pressure auto. ejectors	28″,30″- interchange-able choke tubes for C,S, IC,M,IM,F	6.8 lbs	Single selective trig., double safety, Skt., Trap, or Game models, from Sweden
Clayco 6 Over-Under Shotgun	12, 2¾″		26″-IC-M 28″-M-F	7 lbs 15 oz	Single trig., auto. safety, from China
ERA "The Full Limit" Over-Under Shotgun	12,20, 2¾″		28″-M-F	7¾ lbs	Auto. safety, extractors, double trig., from Brazil
Franchi Diamond Grade Over-Under	12, 2¾″		28″-M-F	6 lbs 13 oz	Top tang safety, auto. ejectors, single selective trig., from Italy
Franchi Falconet Super	12		27″-IC-M 28″-M-F		Similar to Diamond grade except ltwght. alloy receiver, single selective mech. trig.
Franchi Alcione Super Deluxe					Similar to Falconet Super except hand engraved, gold-plated trig., elephant ivory bead front

Imported Shotguns: Over-Under (*cont.*)

Model	Gauge	Action	Barrel & Choke	Weight	Features
Francisco Sarriugarte 101E Over-Under	12		26"–IC-M 28"–M-F	7 lbs	Single trig., bead front, auto. ejectors, from Spain, also with selective trig.
Franciso Sarriugarte 200 Trap	12		30"–F-F	8 lbs	Monte Carlo stock, similar to 101E
Francisco Sarriugarte 400 Trap, 501E Special		Sidelock	To order		Custom-made, four grades
Heym 55/77 Over-Under Shotgun	12,16,20, 2¾" or 3"	Boxlock or full sidelock	28"–F-M. Other lengths, chokes to specs. Also O/U rifle bbls., or rifle-shotgun bbls.	6¾–7½ lbs	Double crossbolt, interchangeable bbls., optional single selective trig., from West Germany
K.F.C. "FG" Over-Under Shotgun	12, 2¾"		26",28"–IC-IM	6.8 lbs	Sterling silver front bead, single selective trig., selective auto. ejectors, nonaut. safety, from Japan
K.F.C. OT-Skeet Shotgun	12, 2¾"		26", 28"–S-S	7½ lbs	Skt. version of FG model
K.F.C. OT-Trap-EI Shotgun	12		30"–IM-F	7.9 lbs	Trap version of FG, white and middle front beads
K.F.C. OT-Trap-E2 Shotgun	12				Same as E-1 model except has engraving, deluxe Walnut stock
Kassnar/ Fias SK-1 Over-Under Shotgun	12,20, 3"	Top lever break open	26"–IC-M 28"–M-F 30"–M-F 32"–F-F	6–6½ lbs	Double trig., nonauto. extractors, SK-3 has single selective trig., SK-4D has deluxed receiver engraving
Lanber 844 Over-Under Shotgun	12, 2¾" or 3"		28"–IC-IM 30"–M-F	7 lbs	Single selective or nonselective trig., double trig. on Mag. models, with or without ejectors, from Spain
Lanber 2004 Over-Under	12		Interchangeable choke tubes		Trap, Skt., Field, and Pigeon models

Imported Shotguns: Over-Under *(cont.)*

Model	Gauge	Action	Barrel & Choke	Weight	Features
Marocchi America Target Shotgun	12,20, 2¾″		26″ to 29″–Skt. 27″ to 32″–Trap 32″–Trap mono. 30″–O/U with extra 32″ single	7¼–8 lbs	Special stock dimensions and finish, from Italy
Marocchi Contrast Target Shotgun	12,20, 2¾″		26″ to 29″–Skt. 27″ to 32″–Trap	7¼–8 lbs	Std. or engraved
Marocchi SM23 SXS Shotgun					Similar to Contrast except totally custom-made
Rottweil Olympia '72 Skeet Shotgun	12	Boxlock	27″–Skt.	7¼ lbs	Metal bead front, selective single trig., trap model has 30″ bbl. (IM,F)
Rottweil AAT Trap Gun	12		32″–IM-F 32″–extra single lower bbl. 34″–extra single lower bbl.	8 lbs	Monte Carlo stock, special trig. groups available
Rottweil 72 American Skeet	12		26¾″–S-S	7½ lbs	Plastic front sight in metal sleeve, center bead, interchangeable trig. groups, from West Germany
Rottweil American Trap Combo	12	Boxlock	32″–IM-F 34″–single(F)	8½ lbs	Monte Carlo stock, plastic front sight in metal sleeve, center bead
Rottweil Field Supreme Over-Under Shotgun	12	Boxlock	28″–M-F,IC-M	7¼ lbs	Metal bead front
Secolo Model 250 Over-Under Shotgun	12		28″–M-F	7 lbs	Single or double trig., ejectors optional, from Spain

Imported Shotguns: Over-Under (*cont.*)

Model	Gauge	Action	Barrel & Choke	Weight	Features
Secolo 550 Trap Over-Under	12		30″,32″–five interchange-able choke tubes		Monte Carlo stock, also with mono-trap upper or under bbl. and skt. models
Valmet 412K Over-Under	12,20, 2¾″ or 3″		26″–IC-M 28″–M-F 30″–M-F	7½ lbs	Interchangeable bbls. to double rifle model, combo gun, bbl. selector, auto. top tang safety, double trig. optional, with extractors or ejectors
Valmet 412KE Target Series	12, 2¾″ or 3″ 20, 3″		30″– F-T,I-T,S-S	7⅝ lbs–T 7½ lbs–S	Nonauto. safety, from Finland
A Zoli Delfino S.P. Over-Under	12,20, 3″		28″–M-F	5½ lbs	Auto. sliding safety double trig., ejectors
Zoli Silver Snipe Over-Under Shotgun	12,20, 3″	Purdey-type double boxlock, crossbolt	26″–IC-M 28″–M-F 30″–12 g–M-F	6½ lbs	Auto. safety except trap and skt., single trig., from Italy
Zoli Golden Snipe Over-Under Shotgun			26″–S-S 30″–Trap–F-F		Same as Silver Snipe except selective auto. ejectors

Imported Shotguns: Side-by-Side

Model	Gauge	Action	Barrel & Choke	Weight	Features
Armera "Winner" Double	12,20		Length and choke to specs		Auto. ejectors, all options available, from Spain
Armsport Western Double Barrel	12, 3″		20″	6½ lbs	Metal front bead, exposed hammers

Imported Shotguns: Side-by-Side (*cont.*)

Model	Gauge	Action	Barrel & Choke	Weight	Features
Armsport Goosegun Side-by-Side	10, 3½"		32"–F-F	11 lbs	Double trig.
Aya 117 Double Barrel	12, 2¾" 20, 3"		26"–IC-M 28"–M-F		Single selective trig., auto. ejectors, cocking indicators, from Spain
Aya No. 2 Side-by-Side	12,16,20, 28,.410	Sidelock	26",27",28"– choked to specs	5 lbs 15 oz–7½ lbs	Auto. ejectors, double trig. std., single trig. optional
Aya No. 1 Side-by-Side			Barrel lengths and chokes to specs		Similar to No. 2
Aya 56 Side-by-Side	12,16,20				Similar to No. 1
Aya 4 Deluxe Side-by-Side	12,16,20, 28,.410	Boxlock	26",27",28"– IC-M,M-F	5 lbs 2 oz–6½ lbs	Auto. ejectors, double trig. single trig. available
Aya XXV BL, SL Double	12,16,20	Boxlock– BL Sidelock– SL	25"–chokes to specs	5 lbs 15 oz–7 lbs 8 oz	Auto. ejectors, double trig., from Spain
Bernardelli XXVSL Double	12	Sidelock	25"–choice of chokes	6½ lbs	Manual or auto. safety, selective auto. ejectors, from Italy
Beretta M-424 Side-by-Side	12, 2¾" 20, 3"	Boxlock	26"–IC-M 28"–M-F	20 g–6 lbs 14 oz	Double trig., auto. safety
Baretta M-426 Side-by-Side					Same as M-424 except action body is engraved, single selective trig., selective auto. ejectors
Industrias Danok "Red Prince" Double	12		28"–M-F	7 lbs	Auto. ejectors, double trig., from Spain
Erbi 76 Double	12,16,20, 28		26" (28 g) 28"–M-F	7 lbs	Medium bead front, double trig., with extractors or auto. ejectors, also Model 80 has sidelock action
Ferlib F VII Double Shotgun	12,20,28, .410	Boxlock	25" to 28"	5½ lbs	Double trig. std., single trig. optional, from Italy

Imported Shotguns: Side-by-Side (*cont.*)

Model	Gauge	Action	Barrel & Choke	Weight	Features
F.I.E. "The Brute" Double Barrel	12,16,20, 2¾" .410, 3"	Boxlock	18"–C 28"–M-F	5 lbs 2 oz	Smallest. lightest double bbl. available, Riot and Brute models have 18" bbl.
Gib 10 Gauge Magnum	10,3½"	Boxlock	32"–F	10 lbs	Double trig., front and center metal bead sights, from Spain
Garbi 51 Side-by-Side	12,16,20, 2¾"	Boxlock	28"–M-F	5½–6½ lbs	Double trig, extractors, from Spain
Garbi 60 Side-by-Side	12,16,20	Sidelock	26",28",30"– choked to specs	5½–6½ lbs	Double trig., extractors
Garbi 62			Choked M-F		Similar to Model 60, jointed trig., extractors
Garbi 71 Double	12,16,20	Sidelock	26",28"– choked to specs	20 g–5 lbs 15 oz	Auto. ejectors, double trig. std., five other models
Garbi 103A, B Side-by-Side			Nickel-chrome steel bbls.–103B		Similar to 71 except engraving, better quality, from Spain
Garbi 101 Side-by-Side	Like 71 plus available in pigeon or waterfowl gun				Churchill or vent. top rib
Garbi 200 Side-by-Side			Nickel-chrome steel bbls.		Like 71 except engraving
Garbi Special Side-by-Side					Like 71 except best quality wood and metal work, with or without gold inlay
Garbi 102 Shotgun	12,16,20	Sidelock ejector	25"–30"–12 g 25"–28"–16, 20 g Chokes to specs	20 g–5 lbs 15 oz to 6 lbs 4 oz	Double trig., nonselective single trig. available, many options available
Garbi 110 Double	12,20,28		Bbl. length and chokes to specs		Stock dimensions to specs, two grades
IGA Side-by-Side Shotgun	12,20,28, 2¾" .410, 3"		26"–.410– F-F 26"–IC-M 28"–M-F	6¾–7 lbs	Auto. safety, extractors, double trig., from Brazil

Imported Shotguns: Side-by-Side (*cont.*)

Model	Gauge	Action	Barrel & Choke	Weight	Features
Miguel Larranaga "The Traditional" Double	12,20		28"–M-F	6½ lbs	Medium bead front, exposed hammers, from Spain
Mercury Magnum Double Barrel Shotgun	10, 3½" 12,20,3"		28"–12,20 g–F-M 32"–10 g–F-F	12 g–7½ lbs 20 g–6½ lbs 10 g–10⅛ lbs	Double trig., auto. safety, extractors, from Spain
Parquemy 48E Double	12,20,28, 2¾" .410, 3"	Model 45E– boxlock	28"–M-F	5½–7 lbs	Medium bead front, auto. ejectors, double trig., from Spain, .410 has extractors
Piotti King No. 1 Side-by-Side	12,16,20, 28,.410	Sidelock	25"–30"–12 g 25"–28" –12,16,20,.410 g Chokes to specs	6½–8 lbs	Stock custom, auto. ejectors, double or single trig. (nonselective), from Italy
Piotti Monte Carlo Side-by-Side					Like No.1 except not as fine, no gold
Piotte Lunik Side-by-side		Sidelock			Like No. 1 except better over-all quality
Piotti King EELL Side-by-Side					Similar to No. 1 except highest quality wood and metal, engraving, gold inlays
Piotti Pluma Side-by-Side	12,16,20, 28,.410	Boxlock	25"–30"–12 g 25"–28"– 16,20,28,.410; chokes to spec.	5½–6¼ lbs	Stock dimensions to specs, double trig. std., single, nonselective trig. optional
Rossi "Squire" Double Barrel	20,.410, 3"		26"–20 g–IC-M 28"–20 g–M-F 26"–.410–F-F	7½ lbs	Double trig.,
Rossi Overland Double Barrel	12,20, .410, 3" chambers	Sidelock	20"–12 g–IC-M 20"–20 g–M-F 28"–12 g–M-F 26"–.410–F-F	6½–7 lbs	External hammers

Imported Shotguns: Side-by-Side (*cont.*)

Model	Gauge	Action	Barrel & Choke	Weight	Features
J.J. Sarasqueta 119E Double	12		28″–M-F,IC-M	7 lbs	Medium bead front, auto. ejectors, double trig., also available custom
W&C Scott Chatsworth Grande Luxe Deluxe	12,16,20, 28	Boxlock	25″,26″,27″ ,28″,30″–IC-M or to order	6½ lbs	Stock std. or to specs, from England
W&C Scott Bowood Deluxe Game Gun					Similar to Grande Luxe except less ornate
W&C Scott Kinmount Game Gun					Similar to Bowood Deluxe except less ornate
Toledo Armas "Valezquex" Double	12		Length and choke to specs	To specs	Auto. ejectors, all options available, from Spain
Urbiola 160E Double	12,20		28″–12 g–M-F 26″–20 g-IC-F	7 lbs	Medium bead front, auto. ejectors, double trigs., from Spain
Ventura 66/66 XXV-SL Doubles	12,28, 2¾″ 20, 3″	Sidelock	25″,27½″ 30″–12 g–std. chokes available	12 g–6½ lbs 28 g–5¾ lbs	Single selective or double trig., auto. ejectors, can be made to specs, from Spain
Ventura 53/53XXV-BL Doubles	12,28, 2¾″ 20, 3″		25″,27″ 30″–12 g	12g–6½ lbs 28g–5¼ lbs	Single selective or double trig., auto. ejectors, from Spain
Ventura 51 Double	12, 2¾″ 20, 3″		27½″ 30″–12 g Chokes according to preference	6–6½ lbs	Single selective trig., auto. ejectors

Imported Shotguns: Single Shot

Model	Gauge	Action	Barrel & Choke	Weight	Features
Beretta 680 Mono Single Barrel	12	Boxlock	32″,34″–F	8 lbs	Auto. ejector, manual safety, from Italy
FIE "S.O.B." Single Barrel	12,20, 2¾″ .410, 3″	Button break on trig. guard	18½″–12, 20 g–C 28″–F 26″–.410–F	6½ lbs	Metal bead front, exposed hammer, auto. ejector, from Brazil
FIE "C.B.C" Single Barrel Shotgun	12,16,20, 2¾″ .410, 3″	Button break on trig. guard	28″–12,20, .410–F	6½ lbs	Metal bead front, exposed hammer, auto. ejector
Galef Companion Single Barrel Shotgun	12,20, .410, 3″ 16,28, 2¾″	Folding boxlock	28″–16,20, 28 g 30″–12 g 26″–.410 All full choke	12 g–5½ lbs .410–4½ lbs	Nonauto. safety, folds, from Italy

Shotgun Stock and Fit

Stock Measurements
Five measurements are important in determining whether or not a shotgun stock fits. These are:
  1. Length of pull.
  2. Drop at comb.
  3. Drop at heel.
  4. Pitch.
  5. Cast-off (or "on" for a left-handed shooter). These measurements are shown in the three drawings on this and the next page.

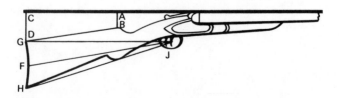

Measurements of shotgun stock.

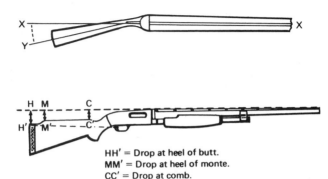

HH' = Drop at heel of butt.
MM' = Drop at heel of monte.
CC' = Drop at comb.

Measurements of Monte Carlo stock

F-J is length of pull. On a shotgun with two triggers, this measurement is taken from the front trigger as shown. *A-B* is drop at comb; *C-D* is drop at heel. When you see a shotgun with measurements of 14″ × 1½″ × 2½″, you know the 14″ is length of pull, the 1½″ is drop at comb, the 2½″ is drop at heel. The difference between *X* and *Y* is cast-off. Pitch is simply the angle at which the butt is cut. It is measured at the muzzle by determining the distance vertically from the muzzle of a shotgun to a line drawn at right angles to the butt and tangent to the standing breech. One way to do this is to stand the shotgun with its butt on the floor and the action touching a wall. The measurement from the muzzle to the wall is the pitch.

Length of Pull

Length of pull is the measurement from the trigger to the middle of the buttplate; *F-J* on the diagram. If this measurement is too long, the shooter will catch the heel of the stock on his clothes under his armpit as he tries to raise the shotgun to his shoulder. Or, once at his shoulder, the gun will feel uncomfortable as he strains to reach the trigger. If pull length is too short, the recoil will drive the shooter's thumb into his nose each time the gun is fired. The proper length of pull is one that allows the shooter to mount the gun to his shoulder easily, clearing his clothes and keeping his thumb a safe distance from his nose. This usually requires a gap of at least ¾″ between thumb and nose. Recoil drives the gun back about half an inch, so a ¾ " gap prevents the nose blow.

Factory guns for field use and skeet shooting have a length of pull of about 14", which is average for a man 5'8" to 5'10" tall. A taller man usually needs a pull of from 14¼ " to 14½ ". A woman or boy from about 5' to 5'6" needs a pull length of about 13½ ". Many youth shotguns have pull lengths of 12½ ". Shotguns used for trap shooting have longer lengths of pull, because the shooter mounts his gun before he calls for his target. Lengths of 14½ " to 14⅜ " are most common.

Drop at Comb

The drop at comb is the distance from the top of the comb to the line of sight. (See *A-B* on the diagram illustrating stock measurements.) Comb drop is one of the most important measurements, since the cheek rests on the comb so the eye can be aligned along the barrel. If the comb is too high, the eye is too high, and the shooter sees too much barrel and raises the gun muzzle in compensation. As a consequence, he shoots high. If the comb is too low, the eye is too low, so the shooter will try to lower the muzzle to see along the line of sight. As a result, he shoots too low. Improper comb height prevents the gunner from developing speed in his shooting, since he must try constantly to adjust his sighting plane. The right amount of drop will enable the shooter to press his cheek hard against the comb and to look directly down the shotgun rib or barrel. Unless he gets his eye in the proper sight plane, his shooting will be off.

The typical standard comb has a drop of 1½ inches. A few have less or more than this: 1¼ ", 1⅜ ", or 1⅝ ". Some youth models have a drop of 2¼ ". Generally, shotguns for trap shooting have a higher comb than shotguns for field or skeet shooting, since the trap shooter's targets are rising sharply and he needs a built-in lead so he can shoot *at* a bird going straightaway and still hit it. If the comb is low, the trap shooter must raise his barrel over the target and blot it out in order to hit it. This aiming procedure is not easy and is not conducive to accurate shooting. Therefore, comb drop for trap guns usually varies from 1¼ " to 1½ ", with 1⅜ " very common. Many trap guns utilize a Monte Carlo bomb, since the cheek piece is high and is carried all the way back in a straight line, dropping down to the heel only several inches short of the butt itself.

Drop at Heel

The drop at heel is the distance between the line of sight and the heel of the stock. (See *C-D* on diagram illustrating stock measurements.) The typical factory-made stock has a drop at heel of 2½". Fat, round-shouldered, bull-neck shooters may need an even greater drop than this, as might beginning shooters, primarily because they have trouble getting their cheek down on the stock. Guns with excessive drop at heel are hard to mount and shoot, however, and recoil is felt more when using them than when using a straighter stock, since the crooked comb rises with the recoil and cracks the shooter on the cheek. For these reasons, some experts like stocks that are almost straight, with very little drop at heel or with heel drop not much greater than comb drop. Trap guns often have quite a straight stock, with drop at heel ranging from 1½" to 1⅞". Trap shooters like these because the straight stock lessens recoil and aids in fast pointing. In fact, with the level Monte Carlo comb, it does not matter where the shooter positions his cheek; the elevation of the barrel will be the same. With a stock sloping sharply downward, the farther back the shooter places his cheek, the lower it will be, necessitating his lowering the elevation of the muzzle to see over it. The point is, it is hard to mount the gun with the cheek at the same position each time, so unless the cheekpiece is fairly level, the variation in cheek positions results in variations in muzzle elevation while sighting, causing inaccurate shooting. Therefore, one should shoot the gun with the straightest stock one can easily mount to one's shoulder.

Pitch

Pitch is the angle at which the buttplate is set on, and it is measured from the muzzle. This angle is important, because it determines whether or not the butt of the shotgun fits firmly against the shoulder. If there is too little downward pitch (too short a stock at the heel), the butt has a tendency to slip down, throwing the gun muzzle up so the shot goes high. If there is too much downward pitch (too long a stock at the heel and too short at the toe), the butt slips up on the shoulder, throwing the gun muzzle downward so the shot goes low.

The only way to determine whether or not your gun has the proper pitch is to throw the gun to your shoulder as in normal shooting. If the pitch is right, the butt will stick evenly and firmly under your armpit. If the butt slips up or down, and you are sure both the pull and the drop are right, you can alter the angle of the buttplate or recoil pad by removing it and taking off or adding to some of the heel or toe, depending on the change of angle needed. A proper correction should allow the whole butt to rest firmly against the shoulder. After the correction, the buttplate or recoil pad is replaced. (See a later section of this book on altering a stock to fit.)

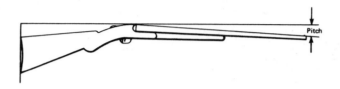

How pitch of shotgun stock is measured.

Cast-Off

Cast-off is the diversion of the stock to one side, so when the butt is placed against the shoulder your aiming eye will look down a line drawn up the center of the barrel or rib. (See the drawing of cast-off under the section on stock measurements.) The degree of cast-off is the length of the horizontal distance from your eye to the center line of the barrel. Cast-off is intended to compensate for the lateral distance between the eye and cheekbone, much as drop at comb does for the vertical distance. Most guns come with a slight cast-off, approximately ¼″, with the toe cast off more than the heel to allow the stock face to follow the structure of the shooter's cheek. British-made shotguns are more commonly made with cast-off than are United States-made guns.

The Shotgun Grip

Shotgun grips may be classified in four basic types:
1. Straight or English grip.
2. Full pistol grip.
3. Half pistol grip.
4. Monte Carlo grip.

Most American-made shotguns have a full pistol grip. Since automatics and pump shotguns became so popular, and single triggers on double and over-under guns became common, the pistol grip has become almost universal in the United States. Such grips allow the shooter to maintain a firm hold on the stock, giving maximum control over the gun while the wrist and hand are at a natural, comfortable angle. The so-called "half pistol grip" is a compromise between a straight grip and a full pistol grip.

SHOTGUN GRIPS

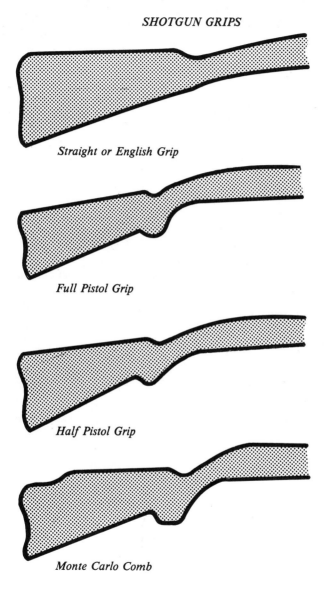

Straight or English Grip

Full Pistol Grip

Half Pistol Grip

Monte Carlo Comb

It can be obtained by special order, or comes as standard equipment on some models of Browning shotguns. On this type of grip, the stock does not curve as rapidly downward back of the trigger guard as it does on the full pistol grip.

The straight or "English" grip was developed in the days of the breech-loading double shotgun, to permit the movement of the hand front and back on the stock to shift from one trigger to the other. This type of grip is still manufactured on British and other European shotguns and on a few specially made American guns. Some shooters feel the lines of such guns are sleeker and more graceful in appearance than are those with full pistol grips, but they have never become very popular in the United States. The straight grip tends to cramp the wrist and give the shooter less control over his gun. Also, there is an occasional tendency for the gun to shoot high.

Stocks with pistol grips and high combs and cheekpieces, such as those with Monte Carlo stocks, reflect a German, Austrian, and Czech influence. They often have a lot of drop at heel, but far back on the stock, and are often relief engraved with animals, birds, oak leaves, or other designs on the stock and breech. A high cheekpiece is really not necessary on a hunting gun, but those with high, level cheekpieces are favorites of trap shooters. However, the trap shooter does not have to carry his gun through the brush all day. If he did, he would probably agree with the hunter, that a lighter, shorter stock is more practical. Monte Carlo stocks look bulky and unwieldy. Whatever advantages they may have for the trap shooter, they are not very graceful looking guns.

Barrel, Gauge, Choke, and Pattern

Gauge and Bore Diameter
At the present time, United States shotshells are manufactured in six gauges: 10, 12, 16, 20, 28, and .410. Originally, gauge (except for the .410) was determined by the number of lead balls of a particular bore diameter it took to weigh a pound. Thus, it took ten 10-gauge, or twelve 12-gauge, round lead balls to weigh a pound. Today, however, twelve round balls would not weigh a pound. The reason is that the balls have to be made smaller than the bore diameter to get through the choke. Therefore, gauge is now a designation of a particular bore diameter. Actually, the .410 was never a gauge; it was always a caliber indicating bore diameter.

Barrel Length
There is really no need to buy a shotgun with a barrel length over 28″, except perhaps for trap shooting, for which a 30″ barrel gives a longer sighting plane. In fact, for upland game shooting, a barrel length

SHOTGUN BORES

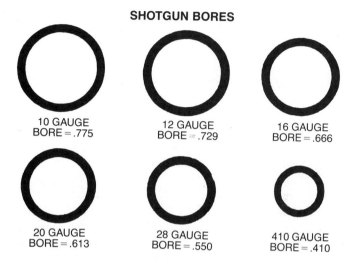

10 GAUGE
BORE = .775

12 GAUGE
BORE = .729

16 GAUGE
BORE = .666

20 GAUGE
BORE = .613

28 GAUGE
BORE = .550

410 GAUGE
BORE = .410

of 24″ to 26″ is best since it gives a light, fast gun that is easy to swing on target and not tiring to carry. The waterfowl gun, even for pass shooting, need not be over 28″, even though 30″ is more commonly used. For an all-around gun for upland game, waterfowl, and deer slugs, the preferred length is 26″.

Why, then, are there so many hunters who think a long barrel is needed in order to have a hard-hitting, long range shotgun? The reason is that old ideas die hard, and hunters hesitate to change opinions that have been handed down from generation to generation. When slow-burning black powder was used to propel shot charges, a gun did need a long barrel to give time for the shot to gain velocity before leaving the barrel. But with modern, smokeless, fast-burning powder, the extra barrel length is no longer necessary. Maximum velocity is reached in 24″ to 26″ of barrel. If the barrel is much longer, the friction of the shot passing through the inside of the barrel will actually decrease velocity. Therefore, shot velocity should not be a consideration in selecting barrel length except to suggest that maximum velocity does not demand a barrel longer than 26″. Even a barrel as short as 22″ does not signifi-cantly reduce shot velocity. For example, if a hunter has a 22″ barrel and shoots at a crossing bird flying at a speed of 6 mph at a distance of 20 yards, he would have to increase his lead by only 5″ over the man using a 30" barrel. Remember, this is while using a shotgun with only a 22" barrel. Therefore, a difference in barrel length of 5" (25" versus 30") makes no significant difference in shot velocity, but it may make considerable difference in ease of handling the gun. A double or over-under 12 gauge barrel weighs about 1½ ounces per inch, so the difference in weight between a 26" and 32" barrel is 9 ounces, enough to make quite a difference when hanging on the end of a shotgun. Put a half-pound weight on the end of your shotgun barrel sometime and see how much difference it makes in your ability to swing, aim, and shoot fast. Use a barrel of fairly reasonable length, therefore: 26" is best all-around, 24" is better for upland game, 28" is alright for waterfowl if you insist on one this long, and 28" or 30" is standard if for trap shooters.

Common Chokes and Pattern Percentage

Choke is the constriction on the end of the barrel, which keeps the shot from scattering so as to assure a fairly tight pattern of shot at medium to far ranges. Full choke gives the maximum constriction and the tightest pattern, so is most useful at long ranges. Open cylinder means no constriction of the barrel and thus allows a wide separation of shot. There is also a reverse cylinder where the end of the barrel is of greater diameter than the bore, allowing for maximum spread of shot.

The most common chokes are listed in the table. Pattern percentage is the percent of the total shot found within a 30" circle at 40 yards.

The table actually gives approximate pattern percentages. Since there is no standardization that requires the manufacturer to design his chokes to conform to these figures, there may be considerable variations in guns that supposedly have the same choke. One gun marked "full" may provide the same pattern as another gun marked "modified." Furthermore, the same gun may perform somewhat differently with different

Common Chokes and Pattern Percentages

Choke	Pattern Percentage
Full	70–80 percent
Improved Modified (¾ choke)	65–70 percent
Modified (½ choke)	55–65 percent
Quarter choke (¼ choke)	50–55 percent
Improved cylinder	45–50 percent
Skeet No. 2	50–60 percent
Skeet No. 1 (Cylinder)	35–40 percent

shotshells and size of shot. Therefore, the only practical way to ascertain the degree of choke of a particular gun is to pattern it. (See the directions in a succeeding section.)

Size of Shotgun Patterns
The shooter needs to be aware of the size of patterns at various ranges with different degrees of choke. The table gives the average spread of shot charges at various ranges. There is some difference in the patterns made by shells from different manufacturers, so the figures are only approximate.

Spread of Shot Charges (in inches) at Various Ranges with Different Degrees of Choke

| Degree of Choke | Range In Yards | | | | | | | | |
	10	15	20	25	30	35	40	45	50
Cylinder	19	26	32	38	44	51	57		
Improved Cylinder	15	20	26	32	38	44	51		
Half Choke (modified)	12	16	20	26	32	38	46	54	66
Full Choke	9	12	16	21	26	32	40	48	60

The upland game hunter who shoots quail, grouse, or woodcock in the brush at close ranges, usually at ranges under 20 yards, needs a barrel with a very open choke: cylinder or improved cylinder. One local woodcock hunter uses a reverse choke gun, hitting his birds as soon as he flushes them. He seldom misses, primarily because he throws an ideal pattern for close ranges. A duck hunter shooting at ranges from 40 to 50 yards, however, needs a modified or full choke to throw a dense enough pattern.

For most shooting, the hunter should confine his shots to ranges where at least 50 percent of his shot is in a 30″ circle. This means maximum ranges of about 38 yards for improved cylinder, 52 yards for modified choke, and 60 yards for full choke.

Patterning the Shotgun
How do you go about patterning your shotgun? The easiest way is to get a roll of wrapping paper 48″ wide and cut it into 4″ squares. Tack the squares to a wooden frame or to a piece of hardboard as you need them. In addition, in order to have a point of aim, paint a black bullseye in the exact center. A bullseye about 1′ in diameter is about right. Set the target

up securely, measure off exactly 40 yards away, and fire a test shot. Before doing anything else, be sure your point of aim has been in the center, as indicated by the location of most of the shot. If for any reason you have shot high, low, or to one side, correct this on the next shot by adjusting your point of aim. When your shot is well centered on the paper, shoot five times, using a separate sheet of paper for each. Since pattern is determined by counting the percentage of shot in a 30″ circle at 40 yards, inscribe a 30″ circle enclosing the most holes on each of the five targets. Then count the holes within each circle, and compare each total on a percentage basis with the total number of shot in a charge. To determine the total shot in a charge, open a shell and count the pellets, but be certain to do this with the make shell and size shot you are using in the patterning, for shot loads vary slightly from one manufacturer to another. Finally, to determine the choke of your gun, see the table in the previous section on common chokes and pattern percentage.

Since much shooting is done at ranges less than 40 yards, it is also helpful to know how your gun performs at 10-, 20-, and 30-yard ranges also. Mark off these distances and fire at your paper targets to ascertain the pattern. You may be surprised at how tight the pattern of your gun is and decide to use barrels with more open choke.

Choke Constriction

Choke is the difference between bore diameter and muzzle diameter measured in thousandths of an inch. The measurement is also designated in points. For example, a difference between bore diameter and muzzle diameter of .040″ is a choke of 40 points. In the old days, a full choke, 12-gauge barrel was one with a choke of 40 points. Three-fourths choke (improved modified) for this barrel was 30 points; ½ choke (modified) was 20 points; ¼ choke (strong improved cylinder) was 10 points. Today, however, there is a tendency for manufacturers to vary the size of the bore of a particular gauge gun. The 12-gauge gun is supposed to have a bore of .729″, yet some run as small as .722 and others as large as .747. Manufacturers tend to "overbore" their barrels rather than underbore. Because of this, the same choke device on different size barrels will result in different amounts of constriction and variations in patterns.

There are various systems of choke construction. These may be listed and described as follows.

1. The taper choke, also called the American choke. This type utilizes a gradual decreasing diameter of the bore as one gets closer to the muzzle. Actually the taper is not cut in a straight line, but with a slightly curved radius.

2. The standard choke, also called an English choke. It utilizes a taper plus a parallel portion, or "lede," at the end of the barrel.

3. The swaged choke is made by tapering both the outside and inside of the muzzle. It is used on inexpensive guns and is made by driving the muzzle into a die, rather than inserting a reamer inside the barrel.

4. The recess or jug choke is not a factory made choke, but is usually made by hand by cutting a recess in the inside of the end of the barrel with a rod and emery cloth. It can be made to give patterns up to 60 percent.

5. The bell or reverse choke is made by boring out the inside of the end of the muzzle so this section is wider than the bore.

TYPES OF CHOKE CONSTRICTION

Simplified diagram of the standard or English choke which has a parallel portion at muzzle.

PARALLEL OR LEDE | CONE | BORE

Cone choke, sometimes known as the American or taper choke.

Swaged choke is made by merely tapering the muzzle itself.

Recess or jug choke is usually made by hand with a rod and emery cloth.

Bell or reverse choke for extra-wide patterns.

Variable or Interchangeable Choke Devices
Choke devices can be divided into five basic types.
1. The plain collet.
2. The collet with muzzle brake.
3. The automatic choke.
4. The plain screw-on tube.
5. The tube with ventilated cage.

The *plain collet* is a variable choke device, which gives different degrees of constriction with the same adjustable tube by simply turning a knurled sleeve. Turn the sleeve clockwise (looking at the end of the muzzle) and the fingers of the tube are squeezed together to decrease the diameter and increase the degree of choke. Turning the sleeve counterclockwise opens the tube and decreases the amount of choke. This type of choke device can be adjusted by hand and is the easiest of all types to adjust. The setting may include reverse choke, which is more open than true cylinder and is used with rifled slugs, or at the other extreme it may include a full, full choke, giving tighter patterns than just full choke. Any choke device that is screwed too tight will start to give an uneven pattern, however, so the shooter needs to learn, by patterning, the maximum choke he can obtain with his device. Also, he should pattern at each setting to determine the optimum settings for various types of shooting. He may find, for example, that a modified (½) setting will give him a full choke pattern and that a tighter adjustment is not necessary. The only way to really find out is to pattern the gun with the device attached.

Sometimes, the variable device is put on carelessly. If it is not properly aligned, the device may throw the shot to one side or low. Or if it is not properly attached, the device itself may fly off when the gun is fired.

There are several fine adjustable choke devices on the market. One of the most well-known and easily adjusted is the Poly Choke, which it comes in either a standard or a ventilated model. The barrel is sent to the company, cut off to the proper length, and the Poly Choke installed. The writer has used a Poly Choke for years and finds it gives marvelous versatility to his old 12-gauge automatic. The gun can now be used on the smallest birds, the largest geese, or even with slugs for deer. Variable chokes are also offered by Lyman, Herter's (which sells the Vari-Choke), Emsco, and other manufacturers. Some gun manufacturers, such as Hi-Standard, Mossberg, Smith and Wesson, and Western, offer variable choke devices on some models of their guns as optional equipment.

The *collet with muzzle brake* is like the plain collet except that venting slots or holes have been added to let gas escape to reduce shotgun recoil.

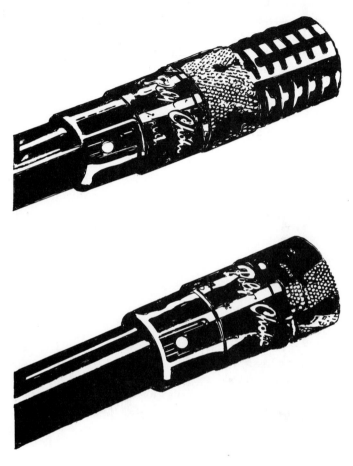

Two types of polychoke: with ventilated rib (top) and standard.

The Poly Choke and Lyman and Herter's variable chokes can be obtained with or without recoil reducers.

The *automatic choke* is a variable choke device whose setting changes automatically each time the gun is fired. The first manufactured was one called the jarvis Flex Choke. It changed in three shots from open or modified to full. However, it was heavy, expensive, and complicated, so was never widely accepted. After that the Adjustomatic (Hartford Gun Choke Company) and Poly-Matic (Poly Choke Company) were introduced, but they never really became popular and were discontinued.

The *plain screw-on tube or the tube with ventilated cage* are the last two types of choke devices. These are interchangeable choke tubes, which are screwed into the end of a muzzle attachment to give various degrees of choke. The plain tube has no vents to reduce recoil; the tube with ventilated cage does. These are quite popular and widely used. The Cutts Compensator is one of the best known. Manufactured by Lyman, it is available with either a steel or aluminum body. The full, modified, and spreader chokes are available in 12, 16, 20, 28, and .410 gauges. The adjustable tube is available in 12, 16, 20, and 28 gauges. The 755 tube (improved cylinder) and long-range tubes No. 2 and No. 3 are available in 12 gauge only. Note that the choke tubes of this compensator fit on any expansion chamber which, in turn, gives recoil reduction by venting excess expanding gases. The expansion chamber is attached to an adapter fitted to the barrel.

Shotshells, Loads, and Shot

Shell Designation
Every shell is labeled according to gauge, drams of powder, ounces of shot, and shot size. A shell labeled No. 12, 3¾—1¼—6 is 12 gauge, has 3¾ drams of powder and 1¼ ounces of shot of No. 6 size. In addition shells are given designations like brush loads, scatter loads, field loads, express loads, magnum loads, buckshot loads, or rifled slug loads. Also, each manufacturer uses its own nomenclature on the different types of shotshells. Remington has its "Shur Shot Field Loads," its "Express Long Range Loads," or its "Power-Pakt Express Magnum Buckshot Loads." Winchester-Western refers to its "Super-X Mark 5 Game Loads," its "Super-X Mark 5 with Lubaloy (Copperized Shot)," or its "Super-X Rifled Slug Loads (not Mark 5)." Peters sells its "Plastic Target Loads—Power Piston Wad," "Victor Shotgun Loads—Power Piston Wad," or "High-Velocity Extra Long Range Shotgun Shells—Power Piston Wad." Is it any wonder that the various designations get confusing?

The nomenclature is not as difficult as it sounds, however. All manufacturers offer one or more, or all, of the following types of loads.

Magnum loads. These can be of two types: 2¾" magnums, which are used in shotguns with standard-size chambers, or 3" magnums (3½" for 10 gauge), which require especially long chambers to accommodate

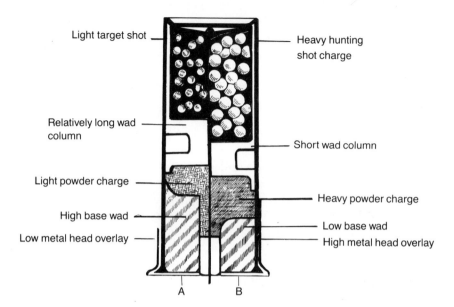

Light target shot

Heavy hunting shot charge

Relatively long wad column

Short wad column

Light powder charge

Heavy powder charge

High base wad

Low base wad

Low metal head overlay

High metal head overlay

A   B

The components of two types of shotshells are shown in this composite drawing. Section A shows a typical high-base/low-brass shell with light shot and powder charge; section B shows a typical low-base/high-brass shell for heavy game loads.

them. In most cases, the shorter magnum shells can also be used in guns with the longer magnum chambers.

Long-range loads. So-called express, hi-power, or high-base shells. These are the most commonly used shells for all-around hunting, lacking the maximum power of the magnums but also having less recoil. They have adequate range, sufficient shot charge, and enough killing power for all but the largest birds at longest ranges.

Field loads. These are the lowest power used in ordinary hunting. They are sometimes designated low-base shells because of the shorter brass base at the foot of the shell. They are used for short-range, small game and bird hunting situations. They are more than adequate for quail, woodcock, squirrels, and other small game.

Scatter loads. Also called brush loads, these are low-base shells especially designed to scatter small shot over a wide pattern for close-range upland bird shooting.

Target, skeet, and trap loads. The name implies, they are especially designed to meet official requirements for trap and skeet shooting or to meet the needs of the home target shooter.

Buckshot loads. These are manufactured in regular 2¾ " shells, or in 3″ magnums. Their uniqueness is in the fact that they are loaded with buckshot, obtainable in sizes 00, 0, 1, 3, or 4.

Rifled slug loads. This is a single projectile in each shell, used primarily in close range deer hunting.

Shotshell Loads

The following table lists the various shotshells manufactured in the United States today. Manufacturers may differ slightly in the shot sizes offered, but in general all makes offer equivalent loads.

The table shows the comparative size of different shot and the average number of pellets per load. The actual number of pellets will differ slightly from one manufacturer to another.

Shotshell Loads:
Winchester-Western, Remington-Peters, Federal

In certain loadings one manufacturer may offer fewer or more shot sizes than another, but in general all makers offer equivalent loadings. Sources are indicated by letters, thus: W-W (a); R-P (b); Fed. (c).

Gauge	Length Shell (Inches)	Powder Equiv. Drams	Shot (Ozs.)	Shot Size
Magnum Loads				
10 (a)	3½	4½	2¼	BB, 2, 4
10 (a¹, b)	3½	Max	2	BB, 2, 4
12 (a, b, c)	3	Max	1⅞	BB, 2, 4
12 (a¹, b)	3	4	1⅝	2, 4, 6
12 (a¹, b)	2¾	Max	1½	2, 4, 5, 6
16 (a, b, c)	2¾	Max	1¼	2, 4, 6
20 (a, b, c)	3	Max	1¼	2, 4, 6, 7½
20 (a¹)	3	Max	1³⁄₁₆	4
20 (a¹, b, c)	2¾	2¾	1⅛	4, 6, 7½
Long-Range Loads				
10 (a, b)	2⅞	4¾	1⅝	4
12 (a¹, b, c)	2¾	3¾	1¼	BB, 2, 4, 5, 6, 7½, 8, 9
16 (a, b, c)	2¾	3¼	1⅛	4, 5, 6, 7½, 9
20 (a¹, b, c)	2¾	2¾	1	4, 5, 6, 7½, 9
28 (a, b)	2¾	2¼	¾	6, 7½, 9
40 (b)	2½	Max	½	6, 7½
410 (b)	3	Max	11⁄16	4, 6, 7½, 8
Field Loads				
12 (a, b, c)	2¾	3¼	1¼	7½, 8, 9
12 (a, b, c)	2¾	3¼	1⅛	4, 5, 6, 7½, 8, 9
16 (a, b, c)	2¾	2¾	1⅛	4, 5, 6, 7½, 8
20 (a, b, c)	2¾	2½	1	4, 5, 6, 7½, 8, 9

Gauge	Length Shell (Inches)	Powder Equiv. Drams	Shot (Ozs.)	Shot Size
Skeet and Trap				
12 (a, b, c)	2¾	3	1⅛	7½, 8
12 (a, b, c)	2¾	2¾	1⅛	7½, 8, 9
20 (a, b, c)	2¾	2½	⅞	9
28 (a, c)	2¾	2	¾	9
.410 (a, b, c)	2½	Max	½	9
Buckshot				
10 (c)	3½ Sup. Mag.		—	4 Buck—54 pellets
12 (a, b, c)	3 Mag.	4½	—	00 Buck—12 pellets
12 (a, b, c)	3 Mag.	4½	—	4 Buck—41 pellets
12 (b)	2¾ Mag.	4	—	1 Buck—20 pellets
12 (a, b, c)	2¾ Mag.	4	—	00 Buck—12 pellets
12 (a, b, c)	2¾	Max	—	00 Buck—9 pellets
12 (a, b, c)	2¾	3¾	—	0 Buck—12 pellets
12 (a, b, c)	2¾	Max	—	1 Buck—16 pellets
12 (a, b, c)	2¾	Max	—	4 Buck—27 pellets
12 (a)	2¾ Mag.		—	000 Buck—8 pellets
12 (a)	3 Mag.		—	000 Buck—10 pellets
16 (a, b, c)	2¾	3	—	1 Buck—12 pellets
20 (a, b, c)	2¾	Max	—	3 Buck—20 pellets
Rifled Slugs				
10	3½	Max	1¾	Slug 5-pack
12 (a, b, c)	2¾	Max	1	Slug 5-pack
12 (c)	2¾	Max	1¼	Slug 5-pack
16 (a, b, c)	2¾	Max	⅘	Slug
20 (b)	2¾	Max	⅝	Slug
20 (a, b)	2¾	Max	¾	Slug
.410 (a, b, c)	2½	Max	⅓	Slug
Steel Shot Loads				
10 (c)	3½	Max	1⅝	BB, 2
12 (c)	2¾	3¾	1⅛	1, 2, 4
12 (a, c)	2¾	Max	1¼	BB, 1, 2, 4
12 (b)	3	Max	1¼	1, 2, 4
12 (b)	2¾	Max	1⅛	1, 2, 4
20 (c)	3	3¼	1	4

1—These loads available from W-W with Lubaloy shot at higher price.

Shot Size Considerations

Shot size is important in hunting, for the larger the shot, the farther its effective killing range. Killing power depends not only on shot size, however, but on the number of pellets that hit the game and on velocity and penetration. In fact, shocking power increases in direct ratio to the square of the number of pellets that hit, regardless of size. Thus, four pellets striking home have sixteen times the shocking power of one. From this point of view, there is an advantage of using small shot at close ranges, so the pattern is denser and the number of pellets striking the target is at a maximum. If No. 2 shot is used as a basis for comparison,

There are 50 percent more No. 4s, than 2s in an ounce.
There are 89 percent more No. 5s than 2s in an ounce.
There are 150 percent more No. 6s than 2s in an ounce.
There are 289 percent more No. 7½s than 2s in an ounce.

If No. 4 shot is used as a basis for comparison,
There are 26 percent more No. 5s than 4s in an ounce.
There are 67 percent more No. 6s than 4s in an ounce.

Since it is generally agreed that it takes four or five pellets to kill a large duck or pheasant, the hunter needs to use small enough shot at close

Recommended Shot Sizes and Ranges for Different Game

Bird	Average Weight	Average Max. Range	Average Shot Size
Woodcock	4 to 7 oz.	Under 35 yds.	9 to 7½
Jacksnipe	4 to 7 oz.	Under 35 yds.	9 to 7½
Bobwhite Quail	4 to 6 oz.	Under 35 yds.	9 to 7½
Valley or Calif. Quail	4 to 7 oz.	Up to 35 yds.	8 to 7½
Gambel's Quail	4 to 7 oz.	Up to 35 yds.	8 to 7½
Mearn's Quail	4 to 7 oz.	Up to 35 yds.	8 to 7½
Scaled Quail	7½ oz.	Under 40 yds.	8 to 7½
Mountain Quail	9 to 16 oz.	Under 40 yds.	8 to 7½
Hungarian Partridge	12 to 13 oz.	Under 40 yds.	8 to 7½
Doves	3 to 4 oz.	Under 40 yds.	8 to 6
Ptarmigan	12 to 20 oz.	Under 40 yds.	7½ to 6
Franklin's and Spruce Grouse	12 to 24 oz.	Under 40 yds.	7½ to 6
Chukar Partridge	18 to 20 oz.	Under 40 yds.	7½ to 6
Small Ducks	12 to 21 oz.	Up to 40 yds.	7½ to 6
Squirrels	1 lb.	Up to 40 yds.	7½ to 6
Ruffed Grouse	1 to 1¾ lbs.	Up to 45 yds.	7½ to 6
Cottontail Rabbit	2 lbs.	Up to 45 yds.	7½ to 6
Pinnated Grouse	1½ to 2 lbs.	Under 50 yds.	6 to 5
Sharp-tailed Grouse	2 lbs.	Under 50 yds.	6 to 5
Large Ducks	2 lbs. and over	Up to 50 yds.	6 to 4
Pheasants	2½ to 3 lbs.	Up to 50 yds.	6 to 4
Snowshoe Rabbit	2½ to 3½ lbs.	Up to 50 yds.	6 to 4
Blue Grouse	Up to 4 lbs.	Under 55 yds.	5 to 4
Small Geese	5 lbs. 5 oz.	Up to 55 yds.	4 to 2
Sage Grouse	5 to 8 lbs.	Under 60 yds.	4 to 2
Large Canada Geese	8 lbs. 4 oz.	Up to 60 yds.	2 to BB
Wild Turkey	12 to 15 lbs.	Up to 60 yds.	4 to BB
Deer		Up to 60 yds.	1, 3, 4 Buck 0 to 000 BB Buckshot
Deer		Up to 100 yds.	Rifled Slug

ranges so that the pattern will be dense enough to assure that enough pellets penetrate the bird at these ranges. Obviously, the larger the bird, the larger the shot can be and still get the required minimum of four to five pellets into the body.

At longer ranges, however, small shot begins to scatter, and those remaining in the pattern lose their velocity quickly. Therefore, as ranges increase, the hunter needs to use larger and larger shot. At far ranges, only the larger shot maintains enough striking power to kill the game. Deciding what size shot to use, therefore, is a fairly complicated process. The table gives recommended shot sizes for different game. Select the smaller sizes for the closest ranges and the larger sizes for the longest, within the range of shot size suggested for each type of game.

Shotshell Ballistics

The table summarizes the muzzle velocities of four of the most popular shot sizes in each of four gauges. This data relates to the most powerful high-velocity shells made by Winchester-Western, Remington-Peters, and Federal. The table also summarizes the ballistic behavior of BB, No. 2, 4, and 6 size shot at 40 yards when fired at each of the five muzzle velocities mentioned. The larger the pellets, the more they retain their velocity and energy at 40 yards range. Also, the larger the gauge, the greater the velocity at which the pellets are delivered. And since the larger gauges throw larger shot charges, the energy they deliver is correspondingly greater.

To find the foot-pounds of energy delivered by a particular shot charge at 40 yards, multiply the number of pellets in the shotshell by the foot-pounds of energy per pellet (from the previous table). For example, assume you are shooting a 12-gauge gun whose 2¾" magnum shell is loaded with 1½ ounces of No. 6 shot. How much energy is delivered at 40 yards? From the table in a previous section entitled "Shot Size and Number of Pellets per Load," you find that the total number of pellets in this shell is 337. Thus, the energy = 337 pellets × 2.47 foot-pounds per pellet = 832 foot-pounds. If No. 2 shot is used in this load, the number of pellets is 135. The energy delivered = 135 × 7.86 = 1,061 foot-pounds. If No. 4 shot is used, the number of pellets is 203. The energy delivered = 203 × 4.71 = 956.13 foot-pounds.

All this energy could not be transmitted to the target unless every pellet hit home. The actual energy delivered is found by multiplying the number of pellets striking the target times the foot-pounds of energy per pellet. Thus, if four No. 6 pellets of this charge hit a bird, the actual energy delivered is 2.47 × 4 = 9.88 foot-pounds. If only one No. 2 pellet hits a bird, the actual energy delivered is 7.86. Whether or not one or more pellets hit vital spots is also important in determining whether the bird is downed or not.

Thus, as mentioned in a previous section, the decision regarding what shot size to use is hard, because it depends upon how many pellets will hit vital spots of the game at a particular range and with how much foot-pounds of energy. It is obvious from the calculations at 40 yards that each No. 2 shot delivers considerably more foot-pounds of energy at that range than does either No. 4 or No. 6 shot, so only if there are significantly more pellets of smaller size hitting the target will the smaller shot be a better choice. Also, whether more pellets will actually hit depends not only on the range and shot charge, but on the choke and pattern of the particular gun. It is helpful, therefore, for the shooter to know: (1) how his gun patterns at different ranges (a 50 percent pattern at any range is considered minimum for effective killing power), (2) the loads and ballistics of the shotshells he uses, and (3) the estimated ranges at which he proposes to shoot. Knowing these things, he has a fairly good idea about the shot sizes to use on different game at various ranges. If in doubt, he should make life size silhouettes of his game, shoot at them at various ranges and with different shot charges, count the pellets hitting the game, and figure out which charges seem to be best for different ranges. He should keep in mind that for large birds like ducks, more and larger pellets are needed to penetrate for effective killing power.

Muzzle Velocities and Ballistic Behavior at 40 Yards of Four Sizes of Shot

Gauge	Shell Length	Drams Powder	Ounces Shot	Shot Size	Muzzle Vel. (FPS)
10	2⅞	4¾	1⅝	BB, 2, 4	1,330
12	2¾	3¾	1¼	2, 4, 6	1,330
12	2¾ Mag	4	1½	2, 4, 6	1,315
12	3 Mag	4	1⅜	2, 4, 6	1,315
12	3 Mag	4¼	1⅝	2, 4, 6	1,315
16	2⁹⁄₁₆	3	1⅛	2, 4, 6	1,240
16	2¾	3¼	1⅛	2, 4, 6	1,295
16	2¾ Mag	3½	1¼	2, 4, 6	1,295
20	2¾	2¾	1	2, 4, 6	1,220
20	2¾ Mag	3	1⅛	2, 4, 6	1,220

At each of these five velocities, here is how each of the four shot sizes will perform in flight:

Shot Size	Muzzle Velocity	Velocity (FPS) 40 yds.	Pellet Energy 40 yds. in Ft.-lbs. (Each pellet)	Drop In Inches 40 yds.
BB	1,330	915	16.27	2.4
2	1,330	860	7.98	2.6
4	1,330	815	4.77	2.7
2	1,315	855	7.86	2.6
4	1,315	810	4.71	2.8
6	1,315	760	2.47	3
2	1,295	845	7.71	2.6
4	1,295	800	4.62	2.8
6	1,295	750	2.43	3.1
2	1,240	820	7.28	2.8
4	1,240	780	4.38	3
6	1,240	730	2.30	3.3
2	1,220	815	7.13	2.9
4	1,220	775	4.29	3.1
6	1,220	725	2.26	3.6

Ballistic and Trajectory Data: Rifled Slugs

Gauge	Shell Length	Slug Wt. Oz.	Velocity in fps at Muzzle	25 Yds.	50 Yds.	75 Yds.	100 Yds.
12	2¾	1	1,600	1,365	1,175	1,040	950
16	2¾	⅞	1,600	1,365	1,175	1,040	950
20	2¾	⅝	1,600	1,365	1,175	1,040	950
28	2¾	½	1,600	1,365	1,175	1,040	950
.410	2½	⅕	1,830	1,560	1,335	1,150	1,025

Gauge	Shell Length	Wt. Oz.	Drop in inches at 25 Yds.	50 Yds.	75 Yds.	100 Yds.
12	2¾	1	.5	2.1	5.3	10.4
16	2¾	⅞	.5	2.1	5.3	10.4
20	2¾	⅝	.5	2.1	5.3	10.4
28	2¾	½	.5	2.1	5.3	10.4
.410	2½	⅕	.4	1.6	4.1	8.2

Ballistic and Trajectory Data: Buckshot

Gauge	Shell Length	Size	No. of Pellets	Velocity in fps at Muzzle	10 Yds.	20 Yds.	30 Yds.
12	2¾	00	9	1,325	1,220	1,135	1,070
12	2¾	00	12	1,325	1,220	1,135	1,070
12	3	00	15	1,250	1,160	1,085	1,030
12	2¾	0	12	1,300	1,200	1,120	1,055
12	2¾	1	16	1,250	1,135	1,050	990
12	2¾	4	27	1,325	1,195	1,095	1,020
16	2 9/16	1	12	1,225	1,115	1,040	975
or	2¾						
20	2½	3	20	1,200	1,100	1,025	970
or	2¾						

	Energy in ft.-lbs. at			
Muzzle	25 Yds.	50 Yds.	75 Yds.	100 Yds.
2,485	1,810	1,350	1,040	875
2,175	1,585	1,175	920	765
1,555	1,130	840	655	550
1,245	905	670	525	440
650	475	345	255	205

Midrange Trajectory in In. for a Range of				
25 Yds.	50 Yds.	75 Yds.	100 Yds.	Barrel Length In.
.1	.6	1.5	3.1	30
.1	.6	1.5	3.1	28
.1	.6	1.5	3.1	26
.1	.6	1.5	3.1	26
.1	.4	1.2	2.5	26

			Energy in ft.-lbs. per pellet at					
40 Yds.	50 Yds.	60 Yds.	Muzzle	10 Yds.	20 Yds.	30 Yds.	40 Yds.	50 Yds.	60 Yds.
1,015	970	930	210	180	155	135	125	110	105
1,015	970	930	210	180	155	135	125	110	105
985	940	900	185	160	140	125	115	105	95
1,005	960	915	185	160	135	120	110	100	90
935	885	835	140	115	100	90	80	70	65
960	905	860	80	65	55	50	45	40	35
925	875	830	135	110	95	85	75	70	60
915	870	825	75	65	55	50	45	40	35

Ballistics and Trajectory Data: Buckshot (*cont.*)

Gauge	Shell Length	Size	No. of Pellets	Drop In Inches at		
				10 Yds.	20 Yds.	30 Yds.
12	2¾	00	9	.1	.4	1.0
12	2¾	00	12	.1	.4	1.0
12	3	00	15	.1	.5	1.2
12	2¾	0	12	.1	.5	1.1
12	2¾	1	16	.2	.7	1.7
12	2¾	4	27	.1	.5	1.1
16 or	2⁹⁄₁₆ 2¾	1	12	.2	.7	1.8
20 or	2½ 2¾	3	20	.1	.5	1.3

Range and Aiming

Estimating Game Range

For all hunters, learning to estimate ranges is an important prerequisite for successful shooting. Any person can shoot at game, flying or running, at all ranges, but to shoot at ranges beyond established maximums is useless, wasteful, and cripples much game. But even if he knows established maximums, he needs to be able to judge when that maximum is reached, so that he will not fire his gun at game beyond that range.

As indicated in the table, "Recommended Shot Sizes and Ranges for Different Game," the average maximum killing ranges for upland game and waterfowl are 35 to 60 yards. Actually, since not many gunners can hit flying birds consistently at ranges much beyond 45 to 50 yards, up to 50 yards is considered the usual maximum range, provided the choke is sufficiently tight. Of course, a lot of game is killed much closer—20 to 25 yards—so for most situations the hunter should learn to judge distances from about 20 to 50 yards. He should seldom shoot closer than 20 yards, even with open cylinder chokes, since the pattern is so dense and small that the game may either be missed or blown up. With modified and full choke guns, the hunter should wait until his game is at least 25 yards away before firing.

How do you learn to estimate 20-to-50-yard distances? There are three separate problems here: making estimates on land, water, and in the air. Of the three, estimating on land is the easiest. The best way to make estimates of distances on land is to measure off different distances at 10-yard intervals, from 20 to 50 yards over open ground, through thick grass, and in the woods, and to try to memorize how far these distances

Drop in Inches at				
40 Yds.	50 Yds.	60 Yds.	Barrel Length In.	Choke
2.0	3.2	4.8	30	Full
2.0	3.2	4.8	30	Full
2.2	3.5	5.2	30	Full
2.0	3.3	4.9	30	Full
3.2	5.2	7.8	30	Full
2.1	3.4	5.1	30	Full
3.3	5.4	8.0	28	Full
2.4	3.9	5.9	26	Full

are. Look at trees, another hunter, bushes, fence posts, telephone poles, to see how they look at 20, 30, 40, and 50 yards. Practice until you can estimate accurately with a minimum of error. By learning to estimate distances on land, the hunter will be able to tell when a rabbit, pheasant, or other game is within acceptable range for the gun he is using.

Making estimates over water is a different proposition. It is harder, because there are fewer landmarks to help in judging distance. However, there are several things that help. If you are going to be shooting over decoys, place the decoys within acceptable range and vow not to shoot beyond that range. If you have a lone decoy at a maximum range of 45 yards and the other decoys scattered within that radius, it is easy not to shoot beyond the 45 yards, simply by not shooting at birds outside the radius. If you're hunting a stream or river, know the width of the body of water and estimate killing ranges by making comparisons. Or you can measure ahead of time the distance to a weed bed, stump, rock, the opposite bank of a stream, or other objects above the water. The important point is that a little planning ahead of time will enable you to judge shooting ranges much more accurately.

Estimating distances in the air is the hardest of all. I have seen hunters fire at geese that were at least 200 yards high, and wonder why they didn't bring them down! Judging distances in the air is easier if there are objects around with which to make comparisons. For example, a 100-foot high tree enables one to visualize just how high 100 feet is. Then observe a duck flying at 100 feet, tree-top level, and learn how it looks. Or look at the heights of various buildings in town, estimating stories at about nine to twelve feet high each. How high is the five-story building? How large do pigeons look sitting or flying around the roof? By repeatedly trying to estimate heights and ranges of different objects, one can begin to become quite expert.

Of course, most shots in the air are not taken right overhead, but at an angle up and across. The hunter is really shooting a certain distance across and another distance up in the air. In the drawing, this slant range is represented as the hypotenuse of a triangle, labeled *A—C*. The horizontal range is *A—B*. The vertical height is *B—C*. The angle between the slant range and horizontal range is angle *CAB*.

One simple way of figuring the vertical height of an object, such as a tree or building, is to position yourself at *A* so that angle *CAB* is 45°. This will occur when the horizontal distance, *A—B,* is equal to the vertical

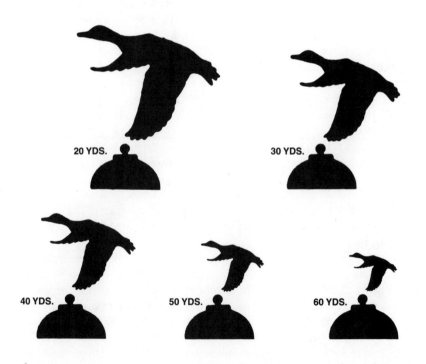

These drawings show the relative sizes ducks would appear over the barrel of a shotgun at various distances.

height, *B—C.* Thus, to find the vertical height all you have to do is measure the horizontal distance, *A—B,* and the vertical distance, *B—C,* will be equal to it. (Note: This is true only in the instance given where you have an equilateral triangle with both legs the same distance and with the angle *CAB* 45°.)

Slant range, *A—C,* can be found as the square root of the sum of the squares of the legs of the triangle.

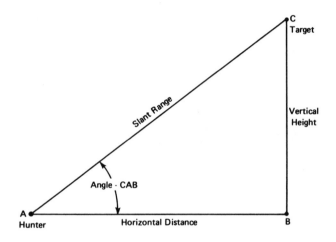

Estimating slant range in the field.

Thus, slant range $= \sqrt{(A\text{-}B)^2 + (B\text{-}C)^2} = A\text{-}C$

If *A-B* $= 40$ yards and *B-C* $= 30$ yards,

$A\text{-}C = \sqrt{(40)^2 + (30)^2} = \sqrt{1600 + 900} = \sqrt{2500} = 50$ yards

Of course, no hunter is going to calculate square roots while the ducks are flying, but it is helpful to be able to estimate ahead of time slant ranges by knowing horizontal and vertical distances. The table shows slant ranges in yards with various combinations of vertical and horizontal ranges.

Slant Ranges (in yards)* with Various Vertical and Horizontal Ranges

Horizontal Range (in yards)

	5	10	15	20	25	30	35	40	45	50
5	7	11	16	21	26	30	35	40	45	50
10	11	14	18	22	27	32	36	41	46	51
15	16	18	22	25	29	34	39	43	47	52
20	21	22	25	28	32	36	40	45	49	54
25	26	27	29	32	35	39	43	47	52	56
30	30	32	34	36	39	42	46	50	54	58
35	35	36	39	40	43	46	50	53	57	61
40	40	41	43	45	47	50	53	57	60	64
45	45	46	47	49	52	54	57	60	67	67
50	50	51	52	54	56	58	61	64	67	71

*Total yards have been rounded off to nearest whole number.

Vertical Range (in yards)

Styles of Shooting

There are basically three styles of shooting when firing at birds on the wing: (1) the *fast swing,* (2) the *sustained lead,* and (3) *snap shooting.* In the *fast swing,* the shooter starts his gun muzzle behind the target, moves the muzzle rapidly along the line of flight of the target, past it and in front, firing when experience tells him he is out in front enough. The important thing is to follow through, to keep the gun moving as it passes the target and is fired. If the shooter stops the muzzle, the time he takes to stop and pull the trigger, and the time the shot takes to travel the distance to the target, will allow the target to move beyond the point where the shooter is aiming. Thus the target will be missed.

It does not matter how fast a bird is going with this method. The faster the bird, the faster the shooter must swing the gun as he pulls ahead and squeezes the trigger. If a bird is crossing slowly, an easy swing will be sufficient to pass it and only a short lead will result by the time he pulls the trigger. If the bird is moving rapidly across, the gun must be whipped past, resulting in a longer lead when the trigger is pulled. This system works regardless of range, as long as the range is reasonable, since moving the muzzle ahead of a bird a few inches will result in many feet of lead at 40 yards but only a foot or so at very close ranges. Thus, the lead is automatically adjusted.

In the *sustained lead,* the gunner starts his swing ahead of the bird, estimates the lead needed, and maintains his lead as he keeps the muzzle moving ahead of the bird along the angle of flight. To be successful with that method, the shooter must be able to estimate the proper lead needed

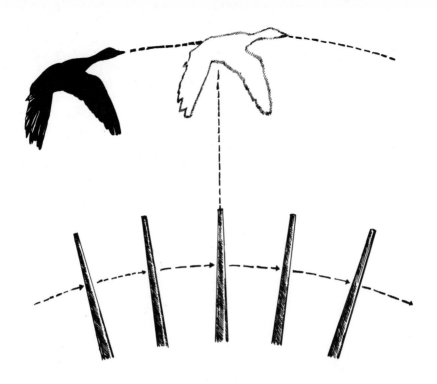

THE FAST SWING

THE SUSTAINED LEAD

at various ranges and speeds, and to continue to move the gun muzzle ahead of the bird at the necessary distance. This method is most useful with slow, deliberate, pass shooting, whereas the fast swing is more appropriate for upland game hunting where the action must be fast.

The third style of shooting is known as *snap shooting.* This style is only useful on nearly stationary targets. With this method, the shooter raises his gun to his shoulder, points it at the bird (which does not appear to be moving), and gets off a quick shot.

When a bird flushes this way, hunter must lead above the target.

Necessary Leads for Various Game Birds

In order to show the necessary leads for various game birds, Captain Charles Askins compiled a list of the speed of these birds with the theoretical and practical leads at 40 yards. The theoretical lead is how far the gun should be pointed in front of the bird so the shot charge can intercept the target. The practical lead will vary, depending upon the angle of flight, the reaction time of the shooter, and the speed of his swing, but in general it is the distance the gunner thinks he is ahead of the bird when the gun goes off.

A low-flying overhead bird might seem like a dead-on hold. Actually, the hunter must shoot slightly under.

When a bird flushes in front of the hunter and flies straightaway, no lead is required. This is a true dead-on hold.

Leads Necessary for Various Game Birds

Bird	Speed in Feet Per Second	Average	Theoretical Lead at 40 Yds.	Practical Lead
Quail	60 to 80	70	8.7 ft.	4 or 5 ft.
Ruffed Grouse	65 to 80	72.5	9	5
Dove	70 to 90	80	9.8	5
Mallard	50 to 90	70	8.7	4 or 5
Canvasback	90 to 100	95	11.66	6 or 7
Canada goose	80 to 90	85	10.4	5 to 6

Skeet and Trap Shooting

Skeet Shooting

The layout for skeet shooting has two trap houses: the high house, located behind station one, and the low house, located behind station seven. The targets from these houses always follow the same path. Those from the high house emerge at a height of 10′; those from the low house emerge at a height of 3½′. The shooter gets different angles by moving around a semicircle that starts at the high house (station 1), and shooting at seven stations, ending at the low house (station 7). He also shoots at a forward station (8), which is midway between the two trap houses. In skeet shooting, the shooter must fire a single shot at a target from each

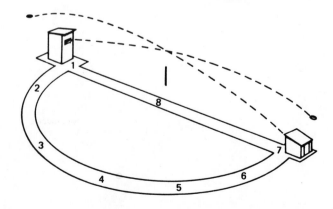

Layout of a skeet field.

house from a position in each of eight stations, with a target from the high house always shot first. Then, after firing the singles, he fires doubles from stations 1, 2, 6, and 7 with the two targets thrown simultaneously. The going away target is shot first and the incoming target second. This makes a total of 24 shots. A twenty-fifth shot is taken immediately following the first target missed, with the shot coming from the same station and house as the one missed. If no misses occur, the shot may be taken from any station, but shooters usually prefer the easy shot from station 7 at the high house target. No. 9 shot is the size preferred by most shooters.

Shooting is conducted with groups of five or fewer persons. Groups are known as squads. Each shooter takes his turn on each station in the order in which he is signed up. Each person in the squad fires a round of 25 shots in the manner already described. Each time a target needed, the shooter calls "pull" and the target is thrown. The shooter can have the gun mounted before a bird is called for, but it is better practice to bring the gun to the shoulder after calling for the target and at the time you are moving the gun after the target. The gun should be moved with the target and past it until the correct lead is reached and the shot fired. The shooter should always continue swinging the gun as the shot is fired; otherwise the shot will go behind the target. The table gives suggested leads at each station for the target from each house.

Suggested Leads in Skeet Shooting

Station	High House	Low House
1	Under 6″	1′
2	1′	1½′
3	1½′	3′
4	2½′	2½′
5	3½′	1½′
6	1½′	1′
7	1′	0′
8	Blot out target with muzzle	Blot out target with muzzle

Trap Shooting

In trap shooting, the gunner fires from five different positions spaced 3 yards apart with each position exactly 16 yards from the trap house.

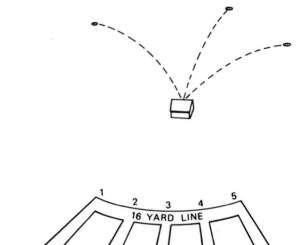

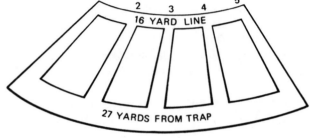

Layout of a trap field.

After each string of five shots, the shooter moves to another station until he has fired from all five positions, thus completing a round.

In ordinary singles shooting, the targets come out of the trap 16 yards from the gun and must go a minimum of 48 yards and not over 52 yards. The targets must be thrown 8' to 12' high, but at an angle and position unknown to the shooter, since each trap moves automatically to the next position. The trap has to be adjusted to throw a normal distribution of angles so that the right angle is not less than straightaway from position one. Ordinarily, the fast shooter will break his birds as close as 30 yards, the slow shooter at 35. Birds allowed to go 40 yards or more are frequently missed.

There are three different events in trap shooting. In *16-yard singles,* shooters are arranged by classes according to their ability. The mechanics of shooting are simple: The shooter takes his place at the station and mounts and aims his gun. At his command of "pull," the bird is electrically tripped. Its flight may vary from straightaway to fairly sharp left and right obliques. Since the shooter never knows at what angle the bird will be thrown, he has to track its path with his gun muzzle, swinging along and beyond the flight path before pressing the trigger. The varying angles provide excellent practice for the upland game hunter.

The second event in trap shooting is *handicap shooting.* Each shooter is given a certain distance from the trap, depending on his ability and his handicap. The distances vary from 18 to 27 yards. There are no classes in this event. All shooters compete against one another.

The third event is *doubles.* This is quite difficult, since two targets are thrown simultaneously along predetermined, fixed flight paths, with the left and right targets following the path of the extreme left and right 16-yard targets. The shooter knows ahead of time where the first target will be, so he aims at that before calling "pull." After firing at the first target, he must quickly swing to the second target and break it before it hits the ground. This requires fast shooting.

The most usual gun for trap shooting is the 12 gauge. The shells may be loaded with no more than 1⅛ ounces of shot and 3 drams of powder, with shot no longer than 7½s. The maximum gauge is 12 gauge.

Shotgun Care

Cleaning Equipment

The following equipment is suggested in cleaning shotguns.

1. Jointed wooden cleaning rod.

2. Brass, copper, or bronze brushes of proper size to use with gauge being cleaned.

3. Felt balls.

4. Jap of proper gauge with serrated tip to screw on the end of the cleaning rod.

5. Cut flannel patches of proper size.

6. Powder solvent such as Hoppe's No. 9.

7. A grease solvent such as cleaning fluid or gasoline.

8. A high-quality gun oil, preferably a good synthetic lubricant such as WD-40, which remains fluid at extremes of cold and hot temperatures. Powdered graphite is also helpful.

9. Small, stiff brushes such as tooth brushes, paint brushes, or electric shaver brushes for cleaning dirt and debris out of action recesses.

10. Soft, clean wiping cloths, plus a silicone-treated cloth.

11. Paste wax or linseed oil for protecting the stock.

12. Assorted screwdrivers and/or pin punches as required for disassembling gun.

Barrel Cleaning

1. Always remove the barrel from the gun before cleaning, so that it can be cleaned from the breech end.

2. Put a clean patch over the felt ball, saturate it with powder solvent, and gently push it through the barrel.

3. Holding the end of the barrel up to the light, rotate the barrel slowly to inspect all the insides of the barrel.

4. If the barrel shows any leading, squirt some solvent into it, attach the wire brush to the cleaning rod, and brush back and forth to loosen the lead. The sections nearest the breech and muzzle are more likely to show lead deposits than is the center.

5. Saturate another patch with solvent and push through the barrel once more. Inspect the barrel as before to make certain it is clean.

6. After the barrel is free of lead, push a clean patch through it to remove all solvent.

7. Complete the barrel cleaning by pushing an oil-soaked patch through, followed by additional dry patches until the patches come through clean.

8. Wipe the outside of the barrel clean with the silicone-treated cloth. The silicone will leave a protective film to prevent rust.

Cleaning the Shotgun Action

The worst thing the gunner can do is squirt oil into every hole and crevice in his gun. Some oils will congeal or collect dirt, causing parts to malfunction. Oil also rots the stock. It is better, therefore, to use oil sparingly, after all parts are free of dirt.

The first step is to remove all dirt. Use the small brushes to brush out every available part of the action. Use a cleaning or gasoline solvent if there is some grease or dirt that is hard to remove. If there are inside parts such as those associated with the trigger mechanism that the shooter cannot and should not reach, the gun should be taken to a gunsmith at the end of each hunting season, as needed, for a thorough take-down and cleaning of the inside mechanism. A gas-operated automatic should have the gas port and gas cylinder cleared of carbon. Doubles with hand detachable locks should have the locks removed once a year for a thorough cleaning.

After all dirt is removed, all movable parts should be very lightly oiled (a drop or two is sufficient) and the excess wiped off. If the gunner uses a synthetic oil such as the WD-40 suggested in the list of cleaning equipment, it will not congeal in cold weather as will standard light oils.

Moving parts can also be lubricated with powdered graphite, but all excess should be wiped off, leaving only the slightest trace to provide lubrication. The metal surfaces that cover the mechanisms should be wiped clean with the silicone-treated cloth.

Care of the Stock

The stocks of most factory guns are finished with varnish, lacquer, or synthetics, all of which have a tendency to break and chip. If the stock is badly in need of complete refinishing, see the section on "Refinishing the Stock" in Part IV. If the stock needs only to be protected, first wipe it clean to remove dirt, dust, and fingerprints. Then apply a small amount of linseed oil, rubbing it into the stock with the fingers and palm of the hand. Then rub hard with a clean, dry cloth. Or a small amount of paste wax can be used for basic protection of the finish.

If the stock is oil finished, wipe off dirt and rub in a few drops of linseed oil. Wipe off excess oil and polish the stock with a cloth. Scratches can be removed by rubbing oil into them. Be certain all excess oil is wiped off each time and a tough, dry hard oil finish left on the stock. Also, keep oil out of the checkering, or it will become gummy and dirty looking.

General Care and Storing

Most important, clean the gun each time it is used. It is especially important to wipe it dry to prevent rust and corrosion. Make certain both gun and gun case are dry before putting the gun away in the case. If the gun is to be stored for a long period of time, it should be lightly coated with rust-preventing oil. The best storage is in an upright position in a regular gun cabinet and behind closed doors, but the cabinet should allow free circulation of air at all times. The gun should not be permanently stored in a moisture-collecting sheepskin case, or on a wall gun rack that cradles the gun in a horizontal position. Such a position may warp the stock over a period of time.

Handloading Shotshells

Steps and Stations in Handloading

There are essentially 8 steps in handloading shotshells. As shown in the figure below, these steps are:

1. *Decapping*—pushing out the old primer.

2. *Priming*—replacing the old primer with a new one.

3. *Charging powder*—putting the required amount of powder into the old shell case.

4. *Seating wads*—inserting wads over powder before shot is put in. Wads are used to hold and seal the powder, cushion the shot, and (with the newer types of wads) to enclose the shot column as it passes out the gun barrel so the shot is not deformed by rubbing the sides of the barrel.

5. *Charging shot*—putting the required amount and size of shot into the case.

6. *Crimp starting*—since modern plastic cases do not bend into crimp form easily, the crimping is done in two stages. The crimp is started when fold creases are pressed in the top of the case.

7. *Crimping*—closing the top of the case with a good firm crimp.

8. *Resizing*—resizing the case to its original dimensions.

In order to accomplish these eight steps, the shot-shell is moved through five different stations on the handloader, as shown in the drawings.

Station 1—Step 1—Decapping

Station 2—Steps 2, 3—Priming, Charging Powder

Station 3—Steps 4, 5—Seating Wads, Charging Shot

Station 4—Step 6—Crimp Starting

Station 5—Steps 7, 8—Crimping and Sizing

Some inexpensive loaders provide only one station, and all the operations are performed with the shotshell at that one station. This procedure is more time consuming, however, since the eight steps must be accomplished with a large number of changes and adjustments in the reloader as one moves from one step to the other. The most expensive loaders move the shotshell automatically from one station to the other with a minimum of effort on the part of the operator.

Tips on Shotshell Loading

Cases. Plastic cases are far superior to paper for handloading. Plastic will not absorb moisture or dry out; it is far stronger and more resistant to abrasion, and is dimensionally more stable. The head usually remains firmly attached to the case body. Plastic cases have a much longer reloading life and provide smoother, more trouble-free gun functioning than do paper cases. They have one disadvantage: they become brittle at Arctic temperatures, so paper cases are still preferred in Arctic areas.

Before starting to load, carefully inspect and sort out your cases.

Separate them by length, since 3″ magnums require a separate operation. Also sort by make and type and by height of base wad. Highbase (wad, not metal) cases are used for light target loads; low-base (wads) for heavy field loads. High-base wads take light powder loads; low-base wads take more powder and shot.

Cases should be inspected for condition. Look for bent metal heads (to be rejuvenated later, if possible), loose heads (throw the case away), split, torn, and crushed bodies. Inspect the inside to see if the base wad is present (they are occasionally blown out in firing). If the mouth is torn or cracked, it will not hold a good crimp and must be discarded or shortened. (Lyman makes a shotshell trimmer.) Soft, paper mouths can be rewaxed. Mushy, plastic mouths can be reformed under heat. Wipe all cases to be used free of water and dirt.

Primers. If the reloader does not have a decapping rod over which the old primer is placed for decapping, so that correct alignment is assured, make sure the decapping pin enters the center of the cup. If it does not, the primer pocket may be enlarged or the base wad torn. Similarly, in inserting a new primer, be certain the priming rod enters without snagging the case mouth and that enough pressure is exerted to seat the primer firmly without bulging the case head inward. If the primer goes in too easily, the pocket is oversized and ought to be discarded.

Charging. Check loading data tables carefully, selecting loads and other components you will need. Remember large bores and light loads need fast powders; small bores and heavy loads need slow powders. Use a powder that is right for your shell. Recheck powder and shot charge bushings to be certain of their measures.

Wads. One decision the shooter will have to make is the type of wad he is going to use. Basically, he can use separate over-powder (O-P) wads, along with filler wads and plastic shot shields to provide a shooting column around the shot so that it does not rub the inner sides of the gun barrel, or he can use the newer plastic single-unit wad columns, which fit over the powder, providing a cushion and filler between the powder and shot and a shot cup as well. Separate O-P wads have evolved from cardboard to plastic cups. Some shooters still use card wads, and even cut their own. These card wads are perfectly suitable for close-range hunting or fun shooting over a hand trap, but plastic cup wads give superior performance because of better fit. This means a better gas seal, so plastic wads ought to be selected for the best shooting.

As for separate filler wads, they have been made from paper pulp, hair felt, cord, and pressed composition materials of various kinds. Usually, felt and cork give the best results. When using this separate filler wad you can still use a shot-protector shield. Alcon makes a polyethylene shot-strip which is inserted over the filler wad before the shot is poured.

The single-unit plastic wads are now provided in all but the cheapest factory loads. The base forms a cup-type over-powder wad, the middle provides the necessary cushion, and the top a shot-protecting cup. It must be emphasized that these single-unit wads are more expensive than old-style cut wads, and also the reloader must stock several lengths or heights to accommodate different shells and loads. But the single-unit wads are much more convenient to load, and they do provide superior performance.

Crimping. With some older reloaders, you will have to turn the shell case so a crimp fold falls under the index mark facing you. Newer tools provide a self-indexing start die, which automatically rotates to accommodate the location of the crimp folds. Fired paper cases and new plastic ones always require a separate crimp-starting operation to reestablish the fold locations before the final crimping is done. Fired plastic cases do not always require a crimp-start die, but its use insures better crimping. Paper cases use 6-fold crimps; plastic uses 6- or 8-point crimps. Paper cases that had rolled crimps may be folded crimps if the case is in good condition. The final crimping requires considerable pressure, which could budge the case walls, and that is one reason resizing is accomplished at the same time as the final crimping. A proper crimp is one where the crimp folds meet precisely in the center without a hole or bulge. Some reloaders put a drop or two of melted wax over the crimp center to waterproof the shell. Others stick circular patches over the completed crimp, color-coding the load enclosed.

PART THREE

*Handguns
and Ammunition*

U.S. Handguns

Types of Handguns and Their Actions
There are three major types of handguns: (1) *single-shot pistols,* (2) *revolvers,* and (3) *semi-automatic pistols.* The *single-shot pistol* is generally used only for plinking and target shooting. It comes in a variety of shapes, sizes, and designs. The most common type has a hinged frame and standing breech. In this type, the barrel is hinged to a forward exterior of the receiver. When the latch is released, the muzzle of the barrel is tipped down to expose the cartridge chamber and to operate the extractor. Single-shot pistols are not often used today.

The *revolver* may be subdivided into two types: the *single-action* and the *double-action revolver.* The *single-action revolver* requires the hammer to be cocked manually for each shot. When the hammer is pulled back, a pawl connected to the foot of the hammer rotates the cylinder so the next loaded cartridge is in position ready to be fired. Generally, this revolver is of solid-frame construction with a fixed cylinder. Fired cases are extracted individually by a rod.

The *double-action revolver* only requires the trigger to be pulled to fire it. Pulling the trigger raises the hammer, rotates the cylinder, and releases the hammer to fire the cartridge. The hammer may be cocked manually (in which case the revolver is being used like a single-action gun), but the double action is the cocking and dropping of the hammer in the one act of pulling the trigger.

Revolvers differ also in the way they are designed for loading or for extracting empty cartridges. The so-called *break frame, break-open, top-breaking, hinged-frame, hinged action,* or *tip-up top* is an older design in which the barrel is swung downward to open the revolver. Empty cartridges are pushed out by a star-shaped extractor mounted on a central stem in the cylinder. This type of revolver is used for light sporting purposes but not for target shooting.

The *solid-frame revolver with a swing-out cylinder* is the most common type for both target and hunting use. In this type, the frame is not hinged or jointed, but the cylinder swings out to the side so that empty cartridges can be pushed out by the extractor.

One obsolete type of revolver has a *solid frame with removable cylinder.* In this type, the cylinder is taken out of the frame during unloading or loading. Another obsolete type of revolver has a *solid frame with nonremovable cylinder.* In this type, the cartridges are put into the cylinder one at a time through a loading gate, and the empty cartridges

A break-frame revolver opens this way; the cartridges are pushed out by an extractor mounted on the cylinder.

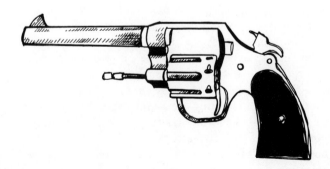

Solid-frame revolver's cylinder swings out to the side so extractor can push out empty cartridges.

are pushed out one at a time by a ramrod attached to the lower side of the barrel.

Semiautomatic pistols may be divided into two types according to the way the automatic action works: (1) those with *blowback* or *recoil action* and (2) those with *breechblock* or *gas-operated action.* In the *blowback* or *recoil action,* the breech-block is held against the case by a spring. When the pistol is fired, the breechblock is blown to the rear against the spring tension and ejects the empty case. The spring then moves the breechblock forward, cocking the pistol and picking up a fresh cartridge for the chamber. This type of action is most frequently found in .22 caliber pistols. In the *breech-block* or *gas-operated action,* part of the gas from the exploding shell is channeled off to provide power to work the action. The gas drives a piston that unlocks the breechbolt and pushes it to the rear to eject the case. At this point a compressed recoil spring drives the breechbolt back forward, picking up a new cartridge and chambering it for the next shot. This type of action is most frequently found in semiautomatic pistols of the larger calibers.

Barrels

Barrels of handguns must be designed long enough to deliver maximum velocities, to minimize muzzle blast and noise for the shooter, and to provide a long-enough sight radius for good accuracy. They must also be heavy enough to provide a steady hold for target shooting.

First, maximum velocity requires a long enough barrel. For example, a .41 Magnum cartridge develops a muzzle velocity of 1,500 fps with an 8⅜" barrel but only 1,250 fps with a 4" barrel. Extra velocity is needed for big-game hunting or for fairly long ranges.

Second, if the barrel is too short, excessive muzzle blast and noise may cause the shooter to flinch, thus destroying accuracy.

Third, the longer the distance between the front and rear sights, the greater the accuracy in aiming. A long barrel in a handgun allows the maximum sight radius.

Fourth, the barrel must be heavy enough to provide a steady hold for target shooting. Target shooters do not have to carry their guns far, so weight is no handicap. In fact, a heavier gun will hold steadier, so some target guns come equipped with extra-heavy barrels, or with adjustable weights that can be added or taken out to provide the desired balance.

The handgun used for hunting or target shooting should have a barrel length of not less than 6". In hunting models, 6" to 8" is most common; in target handguns, 6" to 9" is usual unless one uses one of the highly specialized competition pistols, such as the .45 caliber Colt Gold Cup National Match Pistol, which has a 5″ barrel. The tables of handguns on the following pages list only those guns that can be obtained with barrels of adequate length for hunting plus the specialized handguns used in competition.

Sights

For hunting and/or target shooting, handguns should also be equipped with sights that can be adjusted for both windage and elevation. Most commonly, the front sight is fixed and the rear sight adjustable, although the occasional gun, such as the H&R Sportsman Model 999 revolver, has the front sight adjustable for elevation and the rear for windage. Front sights are usually of blade type, with or without a ramp mount. Some target handguns have removable, interchangeable blade-front sights. Blades may vary in design, but a square type, Patridge front, ⅛″ is common. Rear sights may be notch adjusted or micrometer click adjustable. For additional information on sights, see the section on "Iron Sights" in Part I. The handguns described in the tables that follow include only those with adjustable sights. All guns that have both the front and rear sights fixed have been omitted from the list.

Handguns may also be mounted with scopes for hunting. Such scopes have a long eye relief, generally 6″ to 17″, allowing the shooter to hold the gun well away from his face. Magnification is low, usually 1.3X or 2.5X, which allows a broad field of view. The big advantage of a scope is that it allows the shooter to bring both sights and target into sharp focus, something that becomes more difficult to do with iron sights, particularly as the hunter advances in years.

U.S. Handguns: Single-Action Revolvers, .22 Caliber

Model	Caliber	Capacity	Barrel	Length Overall
Colt New Frontier .22	.22LR	6-shot	4¾″, 6″, 7½″	9⅝″
Ruger New Model Super Single-Six Convertible Revolver	.22S, .22L, .22LR, .22 Mag.	6-shot	4⅝″, 5½″, 6½″, 9½″	11¹³⁄₁₆″

Ruger New Model Super Single-Six Convertible Revolver

Weight	Sights	Features
29½ oz	Ramp-style front, adj. rear	Crossbolt safety
34½ oz	Patridge front on ramp, adj. rear	Transfer bar ignition, wide trig., music wire springs

U.S. Handguns: Single Action Revolvers, Larger Caliber

Model	Caliber	Capacity	Barrel	Length Overall
Abilene Single-Action Revolver	.357 Mag., .44 Mag., .45 Colt	6-shot	4⅝", 6", 7½", 10" (.44 Mag. only)	
Colt Single-Action Army–New Frontier	.44 Spec., .45 Colt	6-shot	.44 Spec.–5½", 7½" .45 Colt–4¾", 7½"	
Ruger New Model Blackhawk Revolver	.357 or .41 Mag.	6-shot	4⅝" or 6½"	12½"
Ruger New Model 357/9mm Blackhawk				
Ruger New Model 30 Carbine Blackhawk	.30		7½"	13⅛"
Ruger New Model Super Blackhawk Stainless	.44 Mag. Also fires .44 Spec.	6-shot	7½", 10½"	13⅜"
Ruger New Model Super Blackhawk RMR	.44 Mag.		10½"	
Ruger New Model Blackhawk 357 Maximum	.357 Mag.		7½", 10½"	13⅜"
Seville Single-Action Revolver	.357 Mag., 9mm Win. Mag., .41 Mag., .44 Mag., .45 ACP, .45 Colt, .45 Win. Mag.	6-shot	4⅝", 5½", 6½", 7½"	
Seville Stainless Super Magnum	.357 Mag., .454 Mag.		7½" or 10½"	
The Virginian Dragoon Revolver	.357 Mag., .41 Mag., .44 Mag., .45 Colt		.44 Mag.–6", 7½", 8⅜" .357 Mag., .45 Colt–5", 6", 7½"	10"
Virginian Dragoon Engraved Models	.44 Mag., .45 Colt		6", 7½"	

Weight	Sights	Features
48 oz	Serrated ramp front, adj. rear	Wide hammer spur, from Mossberg
	Ramp front and target rear, adj.	Flat-top frame, high-polish finish
42 oz	⅛″ ramp front, micro-click rear adj. for W & E	Interlocked mechanism, independent firing pin, music wire springs
		Same as .357 Mag. except interchangeable cylinders for 9mm Para. and .357 Mag.
44 oz		Like .44 Blackhawk except fluted cylinder, round-back trig. guard
48 oz	⅛″ ramp front, micro-click adj. rear	Nonfluted cylinder, sq.-back trig. guard, wide trig. and wide spur hammer
54 oz	Target-type front and rear	Similar to Std. New Model
53 oz		Similar to Std. New Model
52 oz	Ramp front with red insert, adj. rear	Blue or stainless steel
		Similar to Std. Seville except cal., available in stainless steel only
50 oz	Ramp-type Patridge front blade, micro adj. target rear	Spring-loaded firing pin, coil main spring
		Same as Std. Dragoon, fluted or unfluted cylinder, stainless or blued

Colt Single-Action Army Revolver

U.S. Handguns: Double-Action Revolvers, .22 Caliber

Model	Caliber	Capacity	Barrel	Length Overall
Charter Arms Pathfinder	.22LR, .22M	6-shot	2″, 3″, 6″	
Colt Trooper MK III Revolver	.22LR, .22WMR	6-shot	4″, 6″, 8″	9½″
Colt Lawman/Trooper Mark V Revolvers	.22LR, .22WMR	6-shot	Trooper–4″, 6″, 8″ Lawman–2″, 4″	
Colt Diamondback Revolver	.22LR		4″, 6″	9″–4″ bbl.
Harrington & Richardson M686 Revolver	.22LR, .22WMRF	6-shot	4½″, 5½″, 7½″, 10″, 12″	
Harrington & Richardson 649 Revolver	.22LR, .22WMRF	6-shot	5½″, 7½″	
Harrington & Richardson M929	.22S, .22L, .22LR	9-shot	2½″, 4″, 6″	
Harrington & Richardson 999 Revolver	.22S, .22L, .22LR	9-shot	4″, 6″	10½″
Harrington & Richardson 604, 904, 905	.22LR–M904, 905 .22WMR–M604	.22LR–9 shot .22WMR–6 shot	4″, 6″	

Harrington & Richardson Model 686 Revolver

Weight	Sights	Features
18½ oz	Ramp front, adj. rear	Wide trig. and hammer spur
39 oz–4" 42 oz–6"	Ramp front with ⅛" blade, adj. notch rear	Blued or nickel
	Trooper has red insert front sight, adj. rear, Lawman has fixed sights	Like MK III except reduced trig. pull, faster lock time
28½ oz–4"	Ramp front, adj. notch rear	Crisp trig., swing-out cylinder
41 oz–12"	Blade front, adj. rear	Comes with extra cylinder
32 oz	Blade front, adj. rear	Like 686, loads and ejects from side
26 oz–4"	Blade front, adj. rear on 4", 6" models	Swing-out cylinder with auto. extractor, grooved trig.
34 oz–6"	Front adj. for elevation, rear for windage	Auto. ejection, trig. guard extension
32 oz	Blade front, adj. rear	Swing-out cylinder, single-stroke ejection

U. S. Handguns: Double-Action Revolvers, .22 Caliber (*cont.*)

Model	Caliber	Capacity	Barrel	Length Overall
Harrington & Richardson 603, 903				
High Standard Camp Gun	.22LR, .22 Mag.	9-shot	6"	11⅛"
Smith & Wesson 17 K-22 Masterpiece	.22LR	6-shot	6", 8⅜"	11⅛"
Dan Wesson 22 Revolver	.22LR, .22 Mag.	6-shot	2½", 4", 6", 8", 10"	9¼"–4" bbl.

U.S. Handguns: Double-Action Revolvers, Larger Caliber

Model	Caliber	Capacity	Barrel	Length Overall
Colt Python Revolver	.357 Mag. Also fires .38 Spec.	6-shot	2½", 4", 6", 8"	9¼"–4" bbl.
Colt Trooper MK III Revolver	.38 Spec., .357 Mag.	6-shot	4", 6", 8"	9½"–4" bbl.
Colt Trooper Mark V Revolver				
Colt Diamondback Revolver	.38 Spec.	6-shot	4" or 6"	9"–4" bbl.
High Standard Crusader Commemorative Revolver	.44 Mag., .45 Long Colt		6½", 8⅜"	
Ruger Security-Six 117	.357 Mag.	6-shot	2¾", 4", 6", or 4" heavy bbl.	9¼"–4" bbl.
Ruger Stainless Security-Six 717	.357 Mag. Also fires .38 Spec.	6-shot	2¾", 4", 6"	9¼"–4" bbl.
Ruger Redhawk	.44 Rem. Mag.	6-shot	7½"	13"
Smith & Wesson 357 Combat Magnum 19	.357 Mag., .38 Spec.	6-shot	2½", 4", 6"	9½"–4" bbl.
Smith & Wesson 24 44 Special	.44 Spec.	6-shot	4", 6½"	9½"–4" bbl.

Weight	Sights	Features
		Similar to 604, 904 except has flat-sided bbl.
28 oz	⅛″ ramp front, adj. rear	Comes with two cylinders
38½ oz–6″	Patridge front, microclick rear, adj.	Grooved tang and trig.
44 oz–6″	⅛″ serrated, interchangeable front, white outline rear	Smooth, wide trig., wide spur hammer, blue or stainless steel

Weight	Sights	Features
38 oz–4″	⅛″ ramp front, adj. notch rear	Swing-out cylinder
39 oz–4″	Ramp front with ⅛″ blade, adj. notch rear	Target hammer and stocks
		Modified MK III with reduced trig. pull and faster lock time
28½ oz–4″	Ramp front, adj. notch rear	Swing-out cylinder
48 oz–6½″	Blade front on ramp, adj. rear	Smooth, light double-action trig.
33½ oz–4″	Front on ramp, white outline adj. rear	Music wire coil springs
33 oz–4″	Patridge-type front, adj. rear	Similar to regular Security-Six
3¼ lbs	Patridge-type front, adj. rear	Stainless steel
35 oz	⅛″ front on 2½″, 4″ bbl., Patridge on 6″ bbl., click rear	Blue or nickel
41½ oz–4″	Ramp front on 4″, Patridge on 6½″ bbl., adj. rear	Limited production to 7,500 pieces

U. S. Handguns: Double-Action Revolvers, Larger Caliber (*cont.*)

Model	Caliber	Capacity	Barrel	Length Overall
Smith & Wesson 25 Revolver	.45 Colt	6-shot	4", 6", 8"	11⅞"–6" bbl.
Smith & Wesson Highway Patrolman 28	.357 Mag., .38 Spec.	6-shot	4", 6"	11¼"–6" bbl.
Smith & Wesson .44 Magnum 29 Revolver	.44 Mag., .44 Spec., .44 Russian	6-shot	4", 6", 8⅜", 10⅝"	11⅞"–6½" bbl.
Smith & Wesson 41 Magnum Model 57 Revolver	.41 Mag.	6-shot	4", 6", 8⅜"	11⅜"–6" bbl.
Smith & Wesson 66 Stainless Combat Magnum	.357 Mag., .38 Spec.	6-shot	2½", 4", 6"	9½"
Smith & Wesson 586 Distinguished Combat Magnum	.357 Mag.	6-shot	4", 6"	
Dan Wesson 9–2 and 15–2 Revolvers	.38 Spec. or .357 Mag.	6-shot	2½", 4", 6", 8"	9¼"
Dan Wesson 41V and 44V	.41 Mag. or .44 Mag.	6-shot	4", 6", 8", 10"	12"–6" bbl.

Smith & Wesson Model 25 Revolver

Weight	Sights	Features
45 oz	⅛" red ramp front, white outline click rear	Blue or nickel, target trig. and hammer
44 oz.–6"	⅛" on ramp front, micro-click rear, adj.	Blue
47 oz	⅛" ramp front, click rear	Blue or nickel
48 oz–6"	⅛" ramp front, click rear	Blue or nickel
35 oz	⅛" ramp front, click rear	Satin, stainless-steel finish
46 oz–6"	Red ramp front, click rear	Ejector rod, combat-type trig., semitarget-type hammer, also stainless (Model 686)
30 oz–2½"	⅛" front, adj. rear	Interchangeable bbls., grips, wide trig. and hammer, blue or stainless
48 oz–4"	⅛" front, white outline rear, adj.	Blue or stainless

U.S. Handguns: Autoloaders, .22 Caliber

Model	Caliber	Capacity	Barrel	Length Overall
Browning Challenger III Sporter	.22LR	10-shot	6¾"	10⅞"
Bushmaster Auto Pistol	.223	30-shot	11½"	20½"
Charter Explorer II and SII Pistol	.22LR	8-shot	8"	15½"
Ruger Mark II Standard Auto Pistol	.22LR	10-shot	4¾" or 6"	8¾"

Charter Arms Explorer II .22 LR Pistol

U.S. Handguns: Autoloaders, Larger Caliber

Model	Caliber	Capacity	Barrel	Length Overall
AMT 45 ACP Hardballer Long Slide	.45 ACP		7"	10½"
Iver Johnson PP30 "Super Enforcer" Pistol	.30 U.S. Carbine	15- or 30-shot	9"	17"
L.A.R. Grizzly Winchester Magnum Pistol	.45 Win. Mag.	7-shot	5⁷⁄₁₆"	8⅞"

Weight	Sights	Features
29 oz	⅛" blade front, rear screw, adj.	Blue, steel
5¼ lbs	Post front, open "y" rear, adj.	AK-47 gas system
28 oz	Blade front, open rear, adj.	Semiauto.
36 oz	Wide blade front, sq.-notch rear, adj.	Bolt hold-open device, mag. catch, safety trig.

L.A.R. Grizzly Winchester Magnum Pistol

Weight	Sights	Features
	Micro rear, adj.	Combat safety, adj. trig.
4 lbs	Blade front, click adj. peer rear	Shortened version of M1 Carbine
51 oz	Ramped blade front, adj. rear	Interchangeable cal., conversion units available

U. S. Handguns: Autoloaders, Larger Caliber (*cont.*)

Model	Caliber	Capacity	Barrel	Length Overall
Universal Enforcer 3000 Auto	.30M1 Carbine	5-, 15-, or 30-shot	10¼"	17¾"
Wildey Auto Pistol	.45 Win. Mag.	8-shot	5", 6", 7", 8", 10"	
Wilkinson "Linda" Pistol	9mm Para.	31-shot	8⅝"	12¼"

U.S. Handguns: Competition Handguns, Larger Caliber

Model	Caliber	Capacity	Barrel	Length Overall
Colt Gold Cup National Match MK IV Series 70	.45 ACP	7-shot	5"	8⅜"
Detonics Scoremaster Target Pistol	.45 ACP, .451 Detonics Mag.	7-shot	5"	8¾"
M-S Safari Arms Matchmaster Pistol	.45 ACP	7-shot	5"	8.7"
M-S Safari Arms 81NM Pistol				8.2"
M-S Safari Arms 81 Pistol	.45 or .38 Spec.			
M-S Safari Arms 81BP		Magazine chute		
M-S Safari Arms Enforcer Pistol			3.8"	7.7"
M-S Safari Arms Unlimited Silhouette Pistol	Any cal. with .308 head size or smaller		14¹⁵⁄₁₆" tapered	21½"
Navy Grand Prix Silhouette Pistol	.44 Mag., .30/30, 7mm Spec., .45/70	Single shot	13¾"	
Remington XP-100 Silhouette Pistol	7mm BR Rem.	Single shot	14¾"	21¼"

Weight	Sights	Features
4½ lbs	Gold bead ramp front, peer rear	Various finishes available
51 oz	Blade front, rear adj.	Interchangeable bbls., single or auto., double-action trig.
4 lbs 13 oz	Blade front, adj. rear	Semiauto., crossbolt safety, blow-back action

Weight	Sights	Features
38½ oz	Ramp-style front, Colt-Elliason rear, adj.	Arched or flat housing; wide, grooved trig. with adj. stop, top slide
41 oz	Blade front, low-base Bomar rear	Stainless steel, Detonics recoil, grip safety, mag. release
45 oz	Combat adj.	Beavertail grip safety, slide release, combat hammer, various finishes
28 oz	Ron Power match sights	Similar to Matchmaster
	Extended front sight optional	Similar to Matchmaster
	Combat adj.	Similar to Matchmaster
40 oz		Shortened version of the Matchmaster
72 oz	Open iron	Electronic trig., bolt-action single shot
4 lbs	Adj. target type	Rolling block action, adj. aluminum barrel rib
4⅛ lbs	Tapped for scope	Right or left hand, match-type grooved trig., thumb safety

U. S. Handguns: Competition Handguns, Larger Caliber (*cont.*)

Model	Caliber	Capacity	Barrel	Length Overall
Seville "Silhouette" Single Action	.357, .41, .44, .45 Win. Mag.	6-shot	10½"	
Smith & Wesson 1955 Model 25, 45 Target	.45ACP, .45AR	6-shot	6"	11⅞"
Smith & Wesson K-38 S.A. M-14	.38 Spec.	6-shot	6"	11⅛"
Smith & Wesson 29 Silhouette	.44 Mag.	6-shot	10⅝"	16⅛"
Smith & Wesson 38 Master 52 Auto	.38 Spec.	5-shot	5"	8⅝"
Thompson-Center Super 14 Contender	6.5 TCU, 7mm TCU, .30 Herrett, .357 Herrett, .30/30 Win., .35 Rem., .41 and .44 Mag., .45 Win. Mag.	Single shot	14"	17½"
Virginian Dragoon Stainless Silhouette	.357 Mag., .41 Mag., .44 Mag.		7½", 8⅜", 10½"	11½"–7½" bbl.
Wichita MK-40 Silhouette Pistol	7mm IHMSA, .308 Win., others on special order	Single shot	13"	19⅜"
Wichita Silhouette Pistol	7mm IHMSA, .308, 7mm × .308, others on special order	Single shot	10¾" or 14¹⁵⁄₁₆"	21⅜"
Wichita Classic Pistol	Any up to and incl. .308		11¼"	

U.S. Handguns: Competition Handguns, .22 Caliber

Model	Caliber	Capacity	Barrel	Length Overall
High Standard X Series Custom 10-X	.22LR	10-shot	5½" bull	9¾"
High Standard Supermatic Citation Military	.22LR	10-shot	5½", 7¼" fluted	9¾"–5½" bbl.

Weight	Sights	Features
55 oz	Undercut Patridge-style front, adj. rear	Steel or blue
45 oz	⅛" Patridge front, micro-click rear, adj.	Target trig., swing-out cylinder
38½ oz	⅛" Patridge front, micro-click rear, adj.	Same as M-14 except single action
58 oz	Four-position front, micro-click rear, adj.	For silhouette shooting
41 oz	⅛" Patridge front, micro-click rear, adj.	Moving bbl.
45 oz	Adj. target type	Break-open action with auto. safety, interchangeable bbls. for centerfire or rimfire
51 oz–7½"	Blade front, adj. square notch rear	Stainless steel
4½ lbs	Wichita Multi-Range sighting system	Aluminum receiver, adj. trig.
4½ lbs	Wichita Multi-Range sighting system	Right or left hand, tapped for scope, adj. trig.
5 lbs	Micro open, also tapped for scope	Adj. trig.

Weight	Sights	Features
44½ oz	Ramp front, adj. rear	Custom, adj. trig., slide lock
46 oz	Ramp front, click adj. rear	Adj. trig., double-acting safety, rebounding firing pin

U. S. Handguns: Competition Handguns, .22 Caliber (*cont.*)

Model	Caliber	Capacity	Barrel	Length Overall
High Standard Victor	.22LR	10-shot	5½"	9⅝"
High Standard Supermatic Trophy Military	.22LR	10-shot	5½", 7¼" fluted	9¾"–5½" bbl.
Ruger Mark II Target Auto Pistol	.22LR	10-shot	6⅞", 5½" bull	10⅞"–6⅞" bbl.
Smith & Wesson 22 Match Heavy Barrel M-41	.22LR	10-shot	5½"	9"
Smith & Wesson 22 Auto Pistol Model 41	.22LR	10-shot	7⅜"	12"
Thompson-Center Super 14 Contender	.22LR, .222 Rem., .223 Rem.	Single	14"	17¼"

Cartridges and Caliber

Caliber and Groove Diameter
The following table shows the basic groove diameter of different pistol calibers.

Basic Groove Diameter for Pistols

Caliber	Groove Dia.	Caliber	Groove Dia.
.22 Jet	.222	.38/40	.400
.30 Mauser	.309	.41 Colt	.406
.30 Luger	.310	.41 S&W Mag.	.410
.32 Auto	.311	.44/40 (revolver)	.425
.32/20	.312	.44 S&W Spec. and 44 Russian	.429
.32 S&W and .32 Colt NP	.314	.44 Mag. (S&W and Ruger)	.430
9mm Luger	.354	.45 ACP.	.450
.38 Spec. and .357 Mag. (Colt)		.45 Auto Rim	.451
.38 ACP. and .380 Auto	.355	.45 Colt (postwar)	.451
.38 Spec. and .357 Mag. (S&W)	.357	.45 Colt (prewar)	.454
.38 S&W	.360	.455 Webley	.457

Weight	Sights	Features
47 oz	Ramp front, click adj. rear	Interchangeable bbl., 2–2¼ lb trig. pull
44½ oz		Adj. trig.
42 oz	⅛" blade front, micro-click rear, adj.	Blued
44½ oz	⅛" front on ramp base, micro-click rear, adj.	⅜" wide grooved trig., adj. trig. stop
43½ oz	⅛" Patridge front, micro-click rear, adj.	⅜" wide trig. with adj. stop
45 oz	Adj. target type	Break-open action with auto. safety, interchangeable bbls. for both centerfire and rimfire

Centerfire Handgun Cartridges

.22 Remington Jet. This cartridge was designed in 1961 for the S&W Magnum M53 revolver which handles not only the .22 Jet but also .22 shorts, longs, and long rifles when inserts are used. This cartridge delivers a muzzle velocity of 1,870 fps with a 6" barrel and 2,100 fps and 390 foot-pounds of energy with a 8⅜" barrel, so is a respectable varmint cartridge.

.221 Remington Fireball. This cartridge has the distinction of being the first to be chambered in an American commercial bolt-action pistol in 1963. The 50-grain soft-point bullet fired in a 10½" barrel develops 2,650 fps muzzle velocity with 780 foot-pounds of energy: far greater than any commercially made .38 or .45 caliber cartridge. It is the most powerful .22 caliber available.

.256 Winchester Magnum. The 60-grain bullet with an 8½" barrel develops almost as much velocity and muzzle energy as the .221 Remington Fireball. It is used both as a handgun and as a rifle cartridge, and is the most powerful .25 caliber on the market.

.25 (6.35mm) Auto. This is a weak cartridge for use in tiny automatics.

The 50-grain bullet develops only 810 fps velocity and 73 foot-pounds of energy, so is the least powerful of all pistol cartridges larger than the standard .22s.

.25 ACP. The 45-grain bullet has an expanding point which makes it more destructive than the .25 Auto with its metal case. Ballistics of the two cartridges are similar.

.30 Carbine. Used in both rifles and handguns, this cartridge is a high-speed (1,400 to 1,530 fps with a 7½ " barrel), flat-shooting load without the heavy recoil of the .40 calibers. It should never be used as a deer cartridge, but is adequate for varmints.

.30 Luger. The large 93-grain bullet with full metal case lacks necessary expansion qualities to stop large varmints, but it is fairly flat shooting and powerful with a muzzle velocity of 1,220 fps and muzzle energy of 307 foot-pounds.

.32 (7.65mm) Auto (ACP). This caliber is available in a 60-grain semi-jacket hollow-point bullet, or in 71- or 77-grain metal case bullets, which have poor expansion qualities. Muzzle velocity (900, 905, or 970 fps) and energy (125, 129, or 162 foot-pounds) are fair. Actually, since the energy delivered is about the same as the Hi-Velocity .22, the load is not suitable for hunting. It is most used by foreign police who label it the 7.65mm.

.32 Colt New Police. In 98- or 100-grain lead bullets this is a weak, slow-moving cartridge, delivering only 100 foot-pounds of muzzle energy: not as much as the .22LR.

.32 S&W Short, and .32 S&W Long. The Short has an 88-grain lead bullet and delivers only 90 foot-pounds of muzzle energy (less than the .22 Long), so ranks second to the .25 Auto as the weakest cartridge made above .22 caliber. The .32 S&W Long with the 98-grain bullet is more powerful, delivering 115 foot-pounds of energy, about equivalent to the regular .22 LR. This cartridge has been used extensively in the past for short-barrel, bureau-drawer guns, but is not really powerful enough for police work, and is not useful in hunting except for very small game at short ranges.

.32 Colt Short and Long. Available in 80- or 82-grain lead bullets, they are less accurate and powerful than the .32 S&W Long. They are obsolete since they will not chamber in modern .32 caliber revolvers.

.32/20 Winchester. This caliber is available in both pistol and rifle loads, but the "Hi-Speed" cartridge should be used only in rifles. The 100-grain bullet is available in lead or soft point, and delivers 271 foot-pounds of muzzle energy at 1,030 fps: about minimum for serious police work. It is useful in hunting only for varmints and small game, but is the best choice of all the .32 calibers.

9mm Luger. A versatile cartridge, internationally used for police work, available in 95-grain jacketed soft point, in 115-grain full metal case, semijacketed hollow point, and jacketed hollow point, or 125 grain with full metal case or jacketed soft point. Muzzle velocities range from 1,100 to 1,355 fps (with a 4″ barrel). The foot-pounds of muzzle energy range from 335 to 387, depending on the load. Makes a fairly powerful varmint load at close ranges.

.357 Magnum. Ties with the .45 Winchester Magnum as the third most powerful and long-range handgun cartridge (the .44 Remington Magnum is first; the .41 Remington Magnum is second). Available in 110-grain jacketed hollow point, or semijacketed hollow point, in 125-grain jacketed soft point, or jacketed hollow point, in 140-grain jacketed hollow point, 150-grain full metal jacket, and in 158-grain lead, jacketed soft point, jacketed hollow point, metal point, or semi–wad cutter bullets. Muzzle energies depend upon the load and barrel lengths, and range from 410 foot-pounds for the 110-grain bullet (in a 4″ barrel) to a high of 1,001 foot-pounds of energy in the 125-grain jacketed soft point. This cartridge is adequate for deer, and for coyotes, bobcats, and other large varmints if the shooter restricts the range. One advantage of this caliber is that the gun will also accept the .38 Special, a popular target load. (The .38 Special can be fired in the .357 Magnum, but the .357 Magnum cannot be shot in the .38 Special.) A fine choice for all-around use.

.38 Auto and .38 Super Auto. The .38 Auto is designed for use in the original Colt .38 Automatic pistols of 1900 and 1902. The .38 Super Auto was used in the Colt Super .38 of 1925. However, both cartridges will work in the .38 Super, but the .38 Super Auto cartridge cannot be used in the regular .38 Auto. Both of these are powerful cartridges. The .38 Super Auto is more powerful than both the .30 Luger Auto (7.65mm) and the 9mm Luger Auto. The .38 Auto is not as powerful as the 9mm Luger. If the metal case or full metal case bullets are used, the expansion qualities of the bullets are limited, so the cartridges have limited usefulness for hunting purposes. However, if the jacketed hollow-point Super Auto bullets are selected, it makes a good varmint load.

.380 Auto. The commercially loaded 95-grain bullet with full metal case and low power has limited usefulness for hunting, but the 88- and 90-grain jacketed hollow-point bullets delivering 191 and 200 foot-pounds of energy, and the 85-grain semijacketed hollow-point bullet with 189 foot-pounds of energy make this a respectable cartridge for small varmint hunting and a minimum load for defensive purposes.

.38 S&W. The 146-grain lead bullet delivers a maximum of 172 foot-pounds of muzzle energy in a 4″ barrel, so this is a fairly low-power weapon. It was used by the British military during World War II and is often used in pocket revolvers.

.38 Colt Short and Long. The Short is available in 125- or 130-grain lead bullets and delivers only a fraction greater muzzle energy than the Hi-Velocity .22LR. The Long comes in a 150-grain lead bullet and delivers 175 foot-pounds of muzzle energy with a 6″ barrel. Both may be used in a .38 Special revolver, but are far outclassed by those cartridges for all purposes.

.38 Special. One of the most versatile cartridges because of the wide selection of loadings. It is now available in 95-, 110-, 125-, 140-, 148-, 150-, and 158-grain bullets with a wide variety of bullet styles. It continues to be one of the most accurate and widely used target cartridges for handguns. Muzzle energies range from 166 foot-pounds for one of the target loads to a maximum of 580 foot-pounds for the special Norma. A fine all-around cartridge.

.38/40 Winchester. This cartridge is used both in rifles and handguns. Its large 180-grain soft-point bullet punches a big hole, but it develops less than half the power of the .357 Magnum and about ⅓ that of the .44 Remington Magnum. So in spite of the fact that it has shot a lot of deer at close ranges, it is really not recommended as a deer load. It makes a fine defensive weapon or a large varmint gun at close ranges.

.41 Remington Magnum. The second most powerful handgun cartridge on the market. (The .44 Magnum is the most powerful.) The 210-grain bullet packs a huge wallop. The cartridge is available with the lower-powered load with a lead bullet, developing 515 foot-pounds of muzzle energy at 1,050 fps, or in the higher-powered load with a soft-point bullet, developing 1,050 foot-pounds of muzzle energy at 1,500 fps. It is now widely used as a potent weapon for police, although weight and recoil are heavy. It is useful on deer and large varmints at close ranges in the faster load. Recoil is about ¾ that of the .44 Magnum.

.44/40. This cartridge is used both in rifles and handguns. It shoots a heavy (200 grain), slow-moving (975 fps) soft-point bullet which develops only fair muzzle energy (420 foot-pounds in a 7½″ barrel). It is not recommended as a deer load, but may be used on large varmints or as a defensive weapon at close ranges.

.44 S&W Special. The large caliber cartridges (200 and 246 grain) are lightly loaded for target use, the 246-grain lead bullet moving at only 755 fps as it leaves the muzzle. This is satisfactory on the range, but only with hand loads is the power of this cartridge great enough to make it very useful for other purposes.

.44 Remington Magnum. This is the most powerful handgun cartridge made. Regular loads with 240-grain jacketed soft-point bullets develop a muzzle energy of 1,406 foot-pounds at 1,625 fps. The cartridge also comes in 180- and 200-grain bullets. Recoil and gun weight are very heavy, so this is recommended only for experienced handgunners. However, where maximum power and range are needed, this is the weapon for deer and large varmints. Target shooters use the .44 S&W Special rather than this load.

.45 Colt. The large 225-, 250-, or 255-grain revolver bullets punch a big hole at close ranges, which is why it "won the West" and swung from many a hip for a number of years. Muzzle energy is about equivalent to the .38 Special Hi-Speed. When loaded with semi–wad cutter hollow-point bullets, stopper power is further increased.

.45 Auto. With the 230-grain metal case bullet, this has been the official U.S. Army sidearm since 1911. It is not quite as powerful as the .45 Colt, but has proven to be an effective defensive weapon as well as an accurate target gun. Target loads include a 185-grain wad-cutter bullet and a 185-grain match bullet. The lightly loaded target cartridge produces slower velocities, but is more pleasant to use than heavier loads, and often supplant the .38 Special in the centerfire matches. The most powerful cartridge is the 200-grain jacketed hollow-point bullet moving at 1,020 fps and developing 466 foot-pounds of muzzle energy. This load is preferred for hunting purposes.

.44 Auto Magnum. This is a powerful cartridge with a large 240-grain jacketed power-cavity bullet delivering 976 foot-pounds of muzzle energy at 1,350 fps in a 6½" barrel. It is not as powerful as the .44 Remington Magnum, but packs considerably more punch than the .44 S&W Special, the .45 Colt, or the .45 Auto.

.45 ACP. With its 230-grain bullet, this cartridge is identical to the 230-grain .45 Auto in ballistics, but comes loaded with a jacketed hollow-point bullet which gives better stopping power than the metal case bullets of the .45 Auto.

.45 Auto Rim. This thick-rimmed cartridge was developed for use in revolvers chambered for the .45 Auto. The 230-grain lead bullet develops 335 foot-pounds of muzzle energy, slightly less than the .45 Auto.

.45 Winchester Magnum. This ties with the .357 Magnum as the third most powerful and long-range handgun cartridge. It comes only in a 230-grain full metal case bullet which is designed to penetrate without expansion, thus wounding but without leaving a large hole.

Interchangeability Chart for Pistol and Revolver Cartridges

Caliber	Rimfire	Remarks
.22LR	5.6mm LFB	.22 BB and CB Cap, .22 Short, .22 Long may be fired in .22LR chamber
.22 Magnum Rimfire	.22 Winchester Magnum Rimfire	.22 WRF may be fired in .22 MF chamber

Caliber	Centerfire Pistol and Revolver	Remarks
.22 Rem. Jet	.22 Centerfire Magnum; .22 Jet	
.221 Remington	.221 Fireball; .221 Rem. Fireball	
.256 Win. Magnum	.256 Magnum; .256 Win.	
.25 ACP	6.35mm Browning; DWM 508A; 25 ASP, .25 Auto Pistol; .25 Colt Auto; 6.35mm Auto; 6.35mm ACP; 6.35mm Fur Selbstlader Pistole	
.30 Luger	7.65mm Luger; 7.65mm Parabellum; 7.65mm Borchardt-Luger; 7.65mm Luger, Swiss, M1900	
.30 Mauser	7.63mm Mauser, DWM 403; .30 Auto, Mauser, and Borchardt; 7.63mm Mauser, M1896; .30/7.63 Mauser	7.62mm Tokarev may be used
.32 ACP	DWM 479A; GR 619; .30 Browning; .32 Browning; 7.65mm Browning; .32 ASP; .32 Colt Auto; .32 Auto; .32 Auto Colt; .32/7.65 Auto; 7.65mm Auto; 7mm-65 Pour Pistolet Automatique; 7.65mm ACP; 7.65mm Browning M1897; 7.65mm Browning M1900; 7.65mm Browning, Mauser, Beretta; 7.65mm Pist. Patronen No. 19; 7.65mm Pist. Patronen 260 (h); 7.65mm for Browning Pistole	
7.65 Long Auto Pistol (French)	7.65mm French Long; 7.65mm L Pistolet-Mitrailleur Mod. 1938	
.32 Colt NP	.32 Colt New Police, .32 Police; .32 Colt Police Positive	Interchangeable with .32 S&W Long; .32 Long and Short Colt may be fired but cases will bulge; .32 S&W may be used
.32 Short Colt	.32 Short CF	
.32 Long Colt	.32 Colt; .32 Long Colt, outside lube	.32 Short Colt may be used
.32 S&W Long	.32 Long S&W; .32 S&W Long Revolver	Interchangeable with .32 Colt NP; .32 S&W may be used; also .32 Short and Long Colt, but cases will bulge

Interchangeability Chart for Pistol and Revolver Cartridges (*cont.*)

Caliber	Rimfire	Remarks
32 S&W	.32 Smith & Wesson; DWM 202; 8.15 × 15.80 Smith & Wesson cal. .32 Revolver	.32 Short Colt may be used, but case will bulge
32/20 Win.	.32/20 WCF; .32 Winchester; 8.33mm (cal. .32) Winchester; 8.0 × 33.0 Winchester .32	
.62mm Russian Nagant	7.62mm Rev. Patr. 2602 (r); 7.5mm Russian Nagant; 7.62mm Nagant; 8mm Russian Nagant; 8 × 38 GR 684	
.62mm Tokarev	7.62mm Russian Tokarev Auto Pistol; 7.62mm Pist. Patr. 2601 (r); 7.62mm Tokarev M30	7.63mm Mauser may be used
mm Nambu	8mm Nambu Auto Pistol 8mm Japanese Nambu	
mm Lebel Revolver	GR 662; 7.7mm Clair Auto Pistol; 8mm Reglementaire M1892; 8mm Revolver M1892; 8.3 × 27.5 Lebel Revolver; 8mm French Ord. Rev. M1892	
mm Browning Long	9mm Army Browning; 9mm Auto Pistol; 9mm Long; 9mm Long Browning; 9mm Swedish M1907	
mm Bergman-Bayard	9mm Largo; DWM 456,456B; 9mm Bayard; 9mm Bayard Armee Pistol; 9mm Bergmann Mars #6; 9mm Mars; 9mm Star Auto Pistol	9mm Steyr may be used; .38 ACP and .38 Super will *usually* work
mm Japanese Revolver Pattern 6 (M1893)	9mm Nambu	
mm Mauser	DWM 487; 9mm Mauser, Export Model; 9mm Mauser Selbstlader Pistole; 9.08 × 25.0 Kal. 9mm Mauser	
mm Luger	9mm Parabellum; DWM 480C and D, 487C; 9mm Beretta M1915; 9mm Glisenti; 9mm Pistolen Patrone 400(b); 9mm Pist. Patr. 08; 9mm Pist. Patr. M1941; 9mm Pour Mi 34 et GP; 9mm Suomi; 9mm Swedish M39; 9mm 40M Parabellum	
mm Steyr	DWM 577; GR 892; 9mm Mannlicher; 9mm M12	9mm Bergman Bayard may be used; .38 ACP and .38 Super may *sometimes* be used.

Interchangeability Chart for Pistol and Revolver Cartridges (*cont.*)

Caliber	Rimfire	Remarks
.357 Magnum .380 ACP	.357 S&W Magnum DWM 540; .38 Colt Auto Hammerless; .380 Auto Hammerless Pistol; .380 Auto Webley; .380 CAPH; .380(9mm) Auto; 9mm Auto Pistol (.380); 9mm Beretta M1934; 9mm Browning Short; 9mm Corto; 9mm Kurz; 9mm Pist. Patr. 400(h); 9mm Pist. Patr. No. 21; 9mm Short; 9mm Short Browning	.38 Special may be used
.38 ACP	.38 Automatic Pistol; .38 Automatic Colt; .38 Colt Automatic; .38 CAP; .38 Super	
.38 Colt NP	.38 Colt New Police; .38 Colt Police Positive Revolver; .380 Revolver	Interchange with .38 S&W
.38 Special	.38 Colt Special; .38 S&W Special; .38/44; .38/44 Special	
.38 S&W	.38 Smith & Wesson; DWM 261; .38 S&W Revolver; .38 S&W Short; .38 Super Police; 9.2 × 19.8 Smith & Wesson Kal. .38 Revolver; .380 Revolver	Interchange with .38 Colt NP
.38/40 Win.	.38/40 WCF; .38 WCF; .38 Win. M73	
.41 Long Colt	.41 L.DA; .41 Long Colt Double Action; .410 Extra Long Colt	.41 Short Colt may be used
.41 Short Colt	.41 S.D.A.; .41 Short CF; .41 Short Colt Double Action	
.41 Magnum	.41 Remington; .41 Remington Magnum; .41 S&W Magnum	
.44 Special	.44 S&W Special; .44 Smith & Wesson Special	.44 Russian may be used
.44 Magnum	.44 S&W Magnum; .44 Remington Magnum	.44 Russian and .44 Spcl. may be used
.44/40 .45 ACP	.44 WCF; .44/40 Win.; .45 Colt Auto; .45 Automatic Colt; .45 Automatic Colt, Govt. Model; 11.25mm Auto Pistol	
.45 Auto-Rim	.45 AR	.45 ACP may be used
.45 Colt	.45 Colt U.S.A.; .45 Colt Army and Double Action; .45 Colt DA; .45 Colt M1909	
.455 Webley	.455 Enfield; .455 Enfield MKI, MKII; .455 Govt. Pattern 1881; DWM 228; .455 Eley; .455 Colt; 11.7 × 22.0 RN .455	

Win.-Western, Rem.-Peters, Norma, PMC, and Federal

Most loads are available from W-W and R-P. All available Norma loads are listed. Federal cartridges are marked with an asterisk. Other loads supplied by only one source are indicated by a letter, thus: Norma (a); R-P (b); W-W (c); PMC (d); CCI (e). Prices are approximate.

Cartridge	Bullet Gr.	Bullet Style	Muzzle Velocity	Muzzle Energy	Barrel Inches	Price Per Box
22 Jet (b)	40	SP	2100	390	8⅜	$ NA
221 Fireball (b)	50	SP	2650	780	10½	NA
25 (6.35mm) Auto*	50	MC	810	73	2	15.85
25 ACP (c)	45	Exp. Pt.	835	70	2	16.95
256 Winchester Magnum (c)	60	HP	2350	735	8½	31.20
30 (7.65mm) Luger Auto	93	MC	1220	307	4½	25.95
32 S&W Blank (b, c)		No bullet	—	—	—	15.10
32 S&W Blank, BP (c)		No bullet	—	—	—	15.10
32 Short Colt	80	Lead	745	100	4	15.20
32 Long Colt IL (c)	82	Lub.	755	104	4	15.85
32 Auto (c)	60	STHP	970	125	4	19.60
32 (7.65mm) Auto*	71	MC	905	129	4	18.15
32 (7.65mm) Auto Pistol (a)	77	MC	900	162	4	18.15
32 S&W	88	Lead	680	90	3	15.30
32 S&W Long	98	Lead	705	115	4	16.15
32-20 Winchester	100	Lead	1030	271	6	19.75
32-20 Winchester	100	SP	1030	271	6	24.45
357 Magnum	110	JHP	1295	410	4	23.80
357 Magnum	110	SJHP	1295	410	4	23.80
357 Magnum	125	JHP	1450	583	4	23.80
357 Magnum (d)	125	JHC	1450	583	4	23.80
357 Magnum (e)	125	JSP	1900	1001	—	23.80
357 Magnum (e)	140	JHP	1775	979	—	23.80
357 Magnum (e)	150	FMJ	1600	852	—	23.80
357 Magnum*	158	SWC	1235	535	4	20.15
357 Magnum (b) (e)	158	JSP	1550	845	8⅜	23.80
357 Magnum	158	MP	1410	695	8⅜	23.80
357 Magnum	158	Lead	1410	696	8⅜	20.15
357 Magnum	158	JHP	1450	735	8⅜	23.80
9mm Luger (c)	115	FMC	1155	341	4	22.50
9mm Luger (c)	115	STHP	1255	383	4	23.65
9mm Luger*	115	JHP	1165	349	4	22.50
9mm Luger*	125	MC	1120	345	4	22.50
9mm Luger (e)	125	JSP	1100	335	—	22.50
38 S&W Blank		No bullet	—	—	—	18.30
38 Smith & Wesson	145	Lead	685	150	4	17.05
38 Special Blank		No bullet	—	—	—	18.40
38 Special (e)	110	JHP	1200	351	—	NA
38 Special	158	Lead	855	256	6	17.10
38 Special	158	MP	855	256	6	21.70
38 Special (b)	125	SJHP		Not available		NA
38 Special Match, IL	148	Lead	770	195	6	17.85
38 Special Match, IL (b)	158	Lead	855	256	6	NA
38 Special*	158	LRN	755	200	4	17.10

Cartridge	Bullet Gr.	Bullet Style	Muzzle Velocity	Muzzle Energy	Barrel Inches
38 Special	158	SWC	755	200	4
38 Special Match*	148	WC	710	166	4
38 Special +P (c)	95	STHP	1100	255	4
38 Special +P (b)	110	SJHP	1020	254	4
38 Special +P	125	JSP	945	248	4
38 Special +P*	158	SWCHP	915	294	4
38 Special +P*	158	LSWC	915	294	4
38 Special +P (e)	140	JHP	1275	504	—
38 Special +P*	110	JHP	1020	254	4
38 Special +P*	125	JHP	945	248	4
38 Special Norma +P (a)	110	JHP	1542	580	6
38 Short Colt	125	Lead	730	150	6
38 Long Colt	150	Lead	730	175	6
38 Super Auto +P (b)	130	MC	1280	475	5
38 Super Auto +P (b)	115	JHP	1300	431	5
38 Auto	130	MC	1040	312	4½
380 Auto (c)	85	STHP	1000	189	3¾
380 Auto*	95	MC	955	190	3¾
380 Auto (g)	88	JHP	990	191	4
380 Auto*	90	JHP	1000	200	3¾
38-40 Winchester	180	SP	975	380	5
41 Remington Magnum	210	Lead	1050	515	8¾
41 Remington Magnum	210	SP	1500	1050	8¾
44 S&W Spec.*	200	LSW	960	410	7½
44 S&W Special	246	Lead	755	311	6½
44 Remington Magnum*	180	JHP	1610	1045	4
44 Remington Magnum (e)	200	JHP	1650	1208	—
44 Remington Magnum (e)	240	JSP	1625	1406	—
44 Remington Magnum (b)	240	SP	1470	1150	6½
44 Remington Magnum	240	Lead	1470	1150	6½
44 Remington Magnum (g)	240	SJHP	1180	741	4
44 Remington Magnum (a)	240	JPC	1533	1253	8½
44-40 Winchester	200	SP	975	420	7½
45 Colt*	225	SWCHP	900	405	5½
45 Colt	250	Lead	860	410	5½
45 Colt, IL (c)	255	Lub., L	860	410	5½
45 Auto (c)[1]	185	STHP	1000	411	5
45 Auto (e)	200	JHP	1025	466	—
45 Auto	230	MC	850	369	5
45 Auto WC*	185	MC	775	245	5
45 Auto*	185	JHP	950	370	5
45 Winchester Magnum (c)	230	FMC	1400	1001	5
45 Auto Rim (b)	230	Lead	810	335	5½

[1]20 rounds per box. IL—Inside Lub. JSP—Jacketed Soft Point WC—Wad Cutter RN—Round Nose HP—Hollow Point Lub—Lubricated MC—Metal Case SP—Soft Point MP—Metal Point LGC—Lead, Gas Check JHP—Jacketed Hollow Point SWC—Semi Wad Cutter SJHP—Semi Jacketed Hollow Point PC—Power Cavity

Courtesy Shooter's Bible

WINCHESTER-WESTERN CENTERFIRE PISTOL & REVOLVER BALLISTICS

	BULLET	
CALIBER	WT. GRS.	TYPE
25 Automatic (6.35mm)	50	FMC
256 Winchester Magnum Super-X	60	OPE(HP)
30 Luger (7.65mm)	93	FMC
32 Automatic	71	FMC
32 Automatic	60	STHP
32 Smith & Wesson (inside lubricated)	85	Lead
32 Smith & Wesson Long (inside lubricated)	98	Lead
32 Short Colt (greased)	80	Lead
32 Long Colt (inside lubricated)	82	Lead
357 Magnum Jacketed Hollow Point Super-X	110	JHP
357 Magnum Jacketed Hollow Point Super-X	125	JHP
357 Magnum Super-X (inside lubricated)	158	Lead
357 Magnum Jacketed Hollow Point Super-X	158	JHP
357 Magnum Jacketed Soft Point Super-X	158	JSP
357 Magnum Metal Piercing Super-X (inside lubricated, lead bearing)	158	Met. Pierc.
9 mm Luger (Parabellum)	95	JSP
9 mm Luger (Parabellum)	100	JHP
9 mm Luger (Parabellum)	115	FMC
9 mm Luger (Parabellum)	115	STHP
9 mm Winchester Magnum Super-X	115	FMC
38 Smith & Wesson (inside lubricated)	145	Lead
38 Special (inside lubricated)	158	Lead
38 Special Metal Point (inside lubricated, lead bearing)	158	Met. Pt.
38 Special Super Police (inside lubricated)	200	Lead
38 Special Super-X Jacketed Hollow Point+P	110	JHP
38 Special Super-X Jacketed Hollow Point+P	125	JHP
38 Special Super-X+P	95	STHP
38 Special Super-X (inside lubricated)+P	150	Lead
38 Special Metal Piercing Super-X (inside lubricated, lead bearing) +P	150	Met. Pierc.
38 Special Super-X (inside lubricated) +P	158	Lead-HP
38 Special Super-X Semi-Wad Cutter (inside lubricated) +P	158	Lead-SWC
38 Special Super-Match and Match Mid-Range Clean Cutting (inside lubricated)	148	Lead-WC
38 Special Super Match (inside lubricated)	158	Lead
38 Short Colt (greased)	130	Lead
38 Long Colt (inside lubricated)	150	Lead
38 Automatic Super-X (For use only in 38 Colt Super and Colt Commander Automatic Pistols)	125	JHP
38 Automatic Super-X +P (For use only in 38 Colt Super and Colt Commander Automatic Pistols)	130	FMC
38 Automatic (For all 38 Colt Automatic Pistols)	130	FMC
380 Automatic	95	FMC
380 Automatic	85	STHP
41 Remington Magnum Super-X (inside lubricated)	210	Lead
41 Remington Magnum Super-X Jacketed Soft Point	210	JSP
44 Smith & Wesson Special (inside lubricated)	246	Lead
44 Remington Magnum Super-X (Gas Check) (inside lubricated)	240	Lead
45 Colt (inside lubricated)	255	Lead
45 Automatic	185	STHP
45 Automatic	230	FMC
45 Automatic Super-Match Clean Cutting	185	FMC-WC
45 Winchester Magnum Super-X	230	FMC

Met. Pierc.-Metal Piercing   FMC-Full Metal Case   SP-Soft Point   JHP-Jacketed Hollow Point
JSP-Jacketed Soft Point   Met. Pt.-Metal Point   OPE-Open Point Expanding   HP-Hollow Point
PP-Power Point   WC-Wad Cutter   SWC-Semi Wad Cutter   STHP-Silvertip Hollow Point
Specifications are nominal. Test barrels are used to determine ballistics figures. Individual firearms
may differ from these test barrel statistics.

VELOCITY-FPS			ENERGY FT-LBS.			MID-RANGE TRAJECTORY INCHES		BARREL LENGTH INCHES
MUZZLE	50 YDS.	100 YDS.	MUZZLE	50 YDS.	100 YDS.	50 YDS.	100 YDS.	
810	755	700	73	63	54	1.8	7.7	2
2350	2030	1760	735	550	415	0.3	1.1	8½
1220	1110	1040	305	255	225	0.9	3.5	4½
905	855	810	129	115	97	1.4	5.8	4
970	895	835	125	107	93	1.3	5.4	4
680	645	610	90	81	73	2.5	10.5	3
705	670	635	115	98	88	2.3	10.5	4
745	665	590	100	79	62	2.2	9.9	4
755	715	675	100	93	83	2.0	8.7	4
1295	1094	975	410	292	232	0.8	3.5	4 V
1450	1240	1090	583	427	330	0.6	2.8	4 V
1235	1104	1015	535	428	361	0.8	3.5	4 V
1235	1104	1015	535	428	361	0.8	3.5	4 V
1235	1104	1015	535	428	361	0.8	3.5	4 V
1235	1104	1015	535	428	361	0.8	3.5	4 V
1355	1140	1008	387	274	214	0.7	3.3	4
1320	1114	991	387	275	218	0.7	3.4	4
1155	1047	971	341	280	241	0.9	3.9	4
1225	1095	1007	383	306	259	0.8	3.6	4
1475	1264	1109	556	408	314	0.6	2.7	5
685	650	620	150	135	125	2.4	10.0	4
755	723	693	200	183	168	2.0	8.3	4 V
755	723	693	200	183	168	2.0	8.3	4 V
635	614	594	179	168	157	2.8	11.5	4 V
1020	945	887	254	218	192	1.1	4.8	4 V
945	898	858	248	224	204	1.3	5.4	4 V
1100	1002	932	255	212	183	1.0	4.3	4 V
910	870	835	276	252	232	1.4	5.7	4 V
910	870	835	276	252	232	1.4	5.7	4 V
915	878	844	294	270	250	1.4	5.6	4 V
915	878	844	294	270	250	1.4	5.6	4 V
710	634	566	166	132	105	2.4	10.8	4 V
755	723	693	200	183	168	2.0	8.3	4 V
730	685	645	150	130	115	2.2	9.4	6
730	700	670	175	165	150	2.1	8.8	6
1245	1105	1010	430	340	285	0.8	3.6	5
1280	1140	1050	475	375	320	0.8	3.4	5
1040	980	925	310	275	245	1.0	4.7	4½
955	865	785	190	160	130	1.4	5.9	3¾
1000	921	860	189	160	140	1.2	5.1	3¾
965	898	842	434	376	331	1.3	5.4	4 V
1300	1162	1062	788	630	526	0.7	3.2	4 V
755	725	695	310	285	265	2.0	8.3	6½
1350	1186	1069	971	749	608	0.7	3.1	4 V
860	820	780	420	380	345	1.5	6.1	5½
1000	938	888	411	362	324	1.2	4.9	5
810	776	745	335	308	284	1.7	7.2	5
770	707	650	244	205	174	2.0	8.7	5
1400	1232	1107	1001	775	636	0.6	2.8	5

+P with (+P) on the case head stamp is loaded to higher pressure. Use only in firearms designated for this cartridge and so recommended by the gun manufacturer. V-Data is based on velocity obtained from 4" vented barrels for revolver cartridges (38 Special, 357 Magnum, 41 Rem. Mag. and 44 Rem. Mag.) and unvented (solid) test barrels of the length specified for 9mm and 45 auto pistols.

Courtesy Shooter's Bible

REMINGTON BALLISTICS

Remington Ballistics

CALIBER	REMINGTON Order No.	Primer No.	Wt. Grs.	BULLET Style	VELOCITY (fps) Muzzle	50 Yds.	100 Yds.	ENERGY (FT LB) Muzzle	50 Yds.	100 Yds.	TRAJECTORY 50 Yds.	100 Yds.	BARREL LENGTH
(1) 22 REM. "JET" MAG.	R22JET	6½	40*	Soft Point	2100	1790	1510	390	285	200	0.3"	1.4"	8⅜"
(2) 221 REM. "FIRE BALL"	R221F	7½	50*	Pointed Soft Point	2650	2380	2130	780	630	505	0.2"	0.8"	10½"
(3) 25 (6.35mm) AUTO. PISTOL	R25AP	1½	50*	Metal Case	810	755	700	73	63	54	1.8"	7.7"	2"
(4) 32 S. & W.	R32SW	5½	88*	Lead	680	645	610	90	81	73	2.5"	10.5"	3"
(5) 32 S. & W. LONG	R32SWL	1½	98*	Lead	705	670	635	115	98	88	2.3"	10.5"	4"
(6) 32 SHORT COLT	R32SC	1½	80*	Lead	745	665	590	100	79	62	2.2"	9.9"	4"
(7) 32 LONG COLT	R32LC	1½	82*	Lead	755	715	675	100	93	83	2.0"	8.7"	4"
(8) 32 (7.65mm) AUTO. PISTOL	R32AP	1½	71*	Metal Case	905	855	810	129	115	97	1.4"	5.8"	4"
(9) 357 MAG. Vented Barrel	R357M7	5½	110	Semi-Jacketed H.P.	1295	1094	975	410	292	232	0.8"	3.5"	4"
	R357M1	5½	125	Semi-Jacketed H.P.	1450	1240	1090	583	427	330	0.6"	2.8"	4"
	R357M2	5½	158*	Semi-Jacketed H.P.	1235	1104	1015	535	428	361	0.8"	3.5"	4"
	R357M3	5½	158	Soft Point	1235	1104	1015	535	428	361	0.8"	3.5"	4"
	R357M4	5½	158	Metal Point	1235	1104	1015	535	428	361	0.8"	3.5"	4"
	R357M5	5½	158	Lead	1235	1104	1015	535	428	361	0.8"	3.5"	4"
	R357M6	5½	158	Lead (Brass Case)	1235	1104	1015	535	428	361	0.8"	3.5"	4"
(10) 9mm LUGER AUTO. PISTOL	R9MM1	1½	115*	Jacketed H.P.	1110	1030	971	339	292	259	1.0"	4.1"	4"
	R9MM2	1½	124	Metal Case	1115	1047	971	341	302	241	0.9"	3.9"	4"
(11) 380 AUTO. PISTOL	R380AP	1½	95	Metal Case	955	865	785	190	160	130	1.4"	5.9"	4"
	R380A1	1½	88*	Jacketed H.P.	990	920	868	191	165	146	1.2"	5.1"	4"
(12) 38 AUTO. COLT PISTOL	R38ACP	1½	130*	Metal Case	1040	980	925	310	275	245	1.0"	4.7"	4½"
(13) 38 SUPER AUTO. COLT PISTOL	R38SU1	1½	115*	Jacketed H.P. (+P)†	1300	1147	1041	431	336	277	0.7"	3.3"	5"
	R38SU2	1½	130	Metal Case (+P)†	1280	1140	1050	475	375	320	0.8"	3.4"	5"
(14) 38 S. & W.	R38SW	1½	146*	Lead	685	650	620	150	135	125	2.4"	10.0"	4"
(15) 38 SPECIAL Vented Barrel	R38S1	1½	95	Semi-Jacketed H.P. (+P)†	1175	1044	959	291	230	194	0.9"	3.9"	4"
	R38S10	1½	110	Semi-Jacketed H.P. (+P)†	1020	945	887	254	218	192	1.1"	4.9"	4"
	R38S2	1½	125	Semi-Jacketed H.P. (+P)†	945	898	858	248	224	204	1.3"	5.4"	4"
	R38S3	1½	148	"Targetmaster" Lead W.C.	710	634	566	166	132	105	2.4"	10.8"	4"
	R38S4	1½	158	"Targetmaster" Lead	755	723	692	200	183	168	2.0"	8.3"	4"

Order No.		Wt. Grs.	Bullet Style	Velocity (ft/sec) Muzzle	50 yds	100 yds	Energy (ft-lbs) Muzzle	50 yds	100 yds	Mid-Range Traj. 50 yds	100 yds	Barrel Length
R38S5	1½	158*	Lead (Round Nose)	755	723	692	200	183	168	2.0"	8.3"	4"
R38S6	1½	158	Semi-Wadcutter	755	723	692	200	183	168	2.0"	8.3"	4"
R38S7	1½	158	Metal Point	755	723	692	200	183	168	2.0"	8.3"	4"
R38S8	1½	158	Lead (+P)†	915	878	844	294	270	250	1.4"	5.6"	4"
R38S12	1½	158	Lead H.P. (+P)†	915	878	844	294	270	250	1.4"	5.6"	4"
R38S9	1½	200	Lead	635	614	594	179	168	157	2.8"	11.5"	6"
(16) 38 SHORT COLT												
R38SC	1½	125*	Lead	730	685	645	150	130	115	2.2"	9.4"	6"
(17) 41 REM. MAG. Vented Barrel												
R41MG1	2½	210*	Soft Point	1300	1162	1062	788	630	526	0.7"	3.2"	4"
R41MG2	2½	210	Lead	965	898	842	434	376	331	1.3"	5.4"	4"
(18) 44 REM. MAG. Vented Barrel												
R44MG5	2½	180*	Semi-Jacketed H.P.	1610	1365	1175	1036	745	551	0.5"	2.3"	6"
R44MG1	2½	240	Lead Gas Check	1350	1186	1069	971	749	608	0.7"	3.1"	4½"
R44MG2	2½	240	Soft Point	1180	1081	1010	741	623	543	0.9"	3.7"	4½"
R44MG3	2½	240	Semi-Jacketed H.P.	1180	1081	1010	741	623	543	0.9"	3.7"	4½"
R44MG4	2½	240	Lead (Med. Vel.)	1000	947	902	533	477	433	1.1"	4.8"	4½"
(19) 44 S. & W. SPECIAL												
R44SW	2½	246*	Lead	755	725	695	310	285	265	2.0"	8.3"	6½"
(20) 45 COLT												
R45C	2½	250*	Lead	860	820	780	410	375	340	1.6"	6.6"	5½"
(21) 45 AUTO.												
R45AP1	2½	185	Metal Case Wadcutter	770	707	650	244	205	174	2.0"	8.7"	5"
R45AP2	2½	185*	Jacketed H.P.	940	890	846	363	325	294	1.3"	5.5"	5"
R45AP4	2½	230	Metal Case	810	776	745	335	308	284	1.7"	7.2"	5"
(22) 45 AUTO. RIM												
R45AR	2½	230*	Lead	810	770	730	335	305	270	1.8"	7.4"	5½"
38 S. & W. R38SWBL	1½	-*	Blank	-	-	-	-	-	-	-	-	-
32 S. & W. R32BLNK	5½	-	Blank	-	-	-	-	-	-	-	-	-
38 SPECIAL R38BLNK	1½	-	Blank	-	-	-	-	-	-	-	-	-

†Ammunition with (+P) on the case headstamp is loaded to higher pressure. Use only in firearms designated for this cartridge and so recommended by the gun manufacturer.

*Illustrated (not shown in actual size).

FEDERAL BALLISTICS

Automatic Pistol Ballistics (Approximate)

Federal Load No.	Caliber	Bullet Style	Bullet Weight in Grains	Velocity in Feet Per Second		Energy in Foot/Lbs.		Mid-range Trajectory 50 yds.	Test Barrel Length
				Muzzle	50 yds.	Muzzle	50 yds.		
25AP	25 Auto Pistol (6.35mm)	Metal Case	50	810	775	73	63	1.8"	2"
32AP	32 Auto Pistol (7.65mm)	Metal Case	71	905	855	129	115	1.4"	4"
380AP	380 Auto Pistol	Metal Case	95	955	865	190	160	1.4"	3¾"
380BP	380 Auto Pistol	Jacketed Hollow Point	90	1000	890	200	160	1.4"	3¾"
9AP	9mm Luger Auto Pistol	Metal Case	123	1120	1030	345	290	1.0"	4"
9BP	9mm Luger Auto Pistol	Jacketed Hollow Point	115	1160	1060	345	285	0.9"	4"
45A	45 Automatic (Match)	Metal Case	230	850	810	370	335	1.6"	5"
45B	45 Automatic (Match)	Metal Case, S.W.C.	185	775	695	247	200	2.0"	5"
45C	45 Automatic	Jacketed Hollow Point	185	950	900	370	335	1.3"	5"

Revolver Ballistics—Vented Barrel* (Approximate)

Federal Load No.	Caliber	Bullet Style	Bullet Weight in Grains	Velocity in Feet Per Second		Energy in ft./lbs.		Mid-range Trajectory 50 yds.	Test Barrel Length
				Muzzle	50 yds.	Muzzle	50 yds.		
38A	38 Special (Match)	Lead Wadcutter	148	710	634	166	132	2.4"	4"
38B	38 Special	Lead Round Nose	158	755	723	200	183	2.0"	4"
38C	38 Special	Lead Semi-Wadcutter	158	755	723	200	183	2.0"	4"
▲ 38D	38 Special (High Velocity + P)	Lead Round Nose	158	915	878	294	270	1.4"	4"
▲ 38E	38 Special (High Velocity + P)	Jacketed Hollow Point	125	945	898	248	224	1.3"	4"
▲ 38F	38 Special (High Velocity + P)	Jacketed Hollow Point	110	1020	945	254	218	1.1"	4"
▲ 38G	38 Special (High Velocity + P)	Lead, Semi-Wadcutter Hollow Point	158	915	878	294	270	1.4"	4"
▲ 38H	38 Special (High Velocity + P)	Lead Semi-Wadcutter	158	915	878	294	270	1.4"	4"
▲ 38J	38 Special (High Velocity + P)	Jacketed Soft Point	125	945	898	248	224	1.3"	4"
357A	357 Magnum	Jacketed Soft Point	158	1235	1104	535	428	0.8"	4"
357B	357 Magnum	Jacketed Hollow Point	125	1450	1240	583	427	0.6"	4"
357C	357 Magnum	Lead Semi-Wadcutter	158	1235	1104	535	428	0.8"	4"
357D	357 Magnum	Jacketed Hollow Point	110	1295	1094	410	292	0.8"	4"
357E	357 Magnum	Jacketed Hollow Point	158	1235	1104	535	428	0.8"	4"
NEW 44SA	44 S&W Special	Semi-Wadcutter Hollow Point	200	900	830	360	305	1.4"	6½"
oo 44A	44 Rem. Magnum	Jacketed Hollow Point	240	1180	1081	741	623	0.9"	4"
oo 44B	44 Rem. Magnum	Jacketed Hollow Point	180	1610	1365	1045	750	0.5"	4"
45LCA	45 Colt	Semi-Wadcutter Hollow Point	225	900	860	405	369	1.6"	5½"

*To simulate service conditions, these figures were obtained from a 4" length vented test barrel with a .008" cylinder gap and with the powder positioned horizontally inside the cartridge case. 445A and 45LCA data from revolvers of indicated barrel length.

**Both 44A and 44B can be used in either pistols or rifles of this caliber. However, the 44B is accurate only in pistols.

▲This ammunition is loaded to a higher pressure, as indicated by the "+P" marking on the case headstamp, to achieve higher velocity. Use only in firearms especially designed for this cartridge and so recommended by the manufacturer

Gunnery Shooter's Bible

22 RIMFIRE CARTRIDGES

Cartridge Type	Bullet Wt. Grs.	Type	Velocity (fps) 22½" Barrel			Energy (ft. lbs.) 22½" Barrel			Velocity (fps) 6" Barrel		Energy (ft. lbs.) 6" Barrel	
			Muzzle	50 Yds.	100 Yds.	Muzzle	50 Yds.	100 Yds.	Muzzle	50 Yds.	Muzzle	50 Yds.
22 CB Short (CCI & Win. only)	29	Solid	727	667	610	34	29	24	706	—	32	—
22 CB Long (CCI only)	29	Solid	727	667	610	34	29	24	706	—	32	—
22 Short Standard Velocity	29	Solid	1045	—	810	70	—	42	865	—	48	—
22 Short High Velocity (Fed., Rem., Win.)	29	Solid	1095	—	903	77	—	53	—	—	—	—
22 Short High Velocity (CCI only)	29	Solid	1132	1004	920	83	65	55	1065	925	73	—
22 Short High Velocity HP (Fed., Rem., Win.)	27	Hollow Point	1120	1013	904	75	62	49	—	—	—	—
22 Short High Vel. HP (CCI only)	27	Hollow Point	1164	—	920	81	—	51	1077	—	69	—
22 Long Standard Vel. (CCI only)	29	Solid	1180	1038	946	90	69	58	1031	—	68	—
22 Long High Velocity (Fed., Rem.)	29	Solid	1240	—	962	99	—	60	—	—	—	—
22 Long Rifle Stand. Velocity (CCI only)	40	Solid	1138	1046	975	115	97	84	1027	925	93	76
22 Long Rifle Stand. Velocity & Sil. (Fed., Rem., Win.)	40	Solid	1150	—	976	117	—	85	—	—	—	—
22 Long Rifle High Vel. (CCI only)	40	Solid	1341	1150	1045	160	117	97	1150	1010	117	90
22 Long Rifle High Velocity (Fed., Rem., Win.)	40	Solid	1255	—	1017	140	—	92	—	—	—	—
22 Long Rifle High Velocity HP (CCI only)	37	Hollow Point	1370	1165	1040	154	111	89	1190	1040	116	88
22 Long Rifle High Velocity HP (Fed., Rem., Win.)	36-38	Hollow Point	1280	1105	1010	131	100	82	—	—	—	—
22 Long Rifle Hyper Velocity (Fed., Rem., Win.(4))	33-34	Hollow Point	1500	1240	1075	165	110	85	—	—	—	—
22 Long Rifle Viper (Rem. only)	36	Solid	1410	1187	1056	159	113	89	—	—	—	—
22 Stinger (CCI only)	32	Hollow Point	1687	1300	1158	202	120	95	1430	1100	145	86
22 Winchester Magnum Rimfire (Win., Fed.)	40	FMC or HP	1910	—	1326	324	—	156	1339	1110	159	109
22 Winchester Magnum Rimfire (CCI only)	40	FMC or HP	2025	1688	1407	364	253	176	—	—	—	—
22 Long Rifle Pistol Match (Win., Fed.)	40	Solid	—	—	—	—	—	—	1060	950	100	80
22 Long Rifle Match (Rifle) (CCI only)	40	Solid	1138	1047	975	116	97	84	1027	925	93	76
22 Long Rifle Shot (CCI, Fed., Win.)	—	#11 or #12 shot	1047	—	—	—	—	—	950	—	—	—
22 Winchester Magnum Rimfire Shot (CCI only)	—	#11 shot	1126	—	—	—	—	—	—	—	—	—
22 Short Match (CCI only)	29	Solid	830	752	695	44	36	31	786	—	39	—
22 Long Rifle Super Silhouette (Win. only)	42	Solid	1220	—	1003	139	—	85	1000	—	93	—

Please note that the actual ballistics obtained in your gun can vary considerably from the advertised ballistics. Also, ballistics can vary from lot to lot, even within the same brand. All prices were correct at the time this table was prepared. All prices are subject to change without notice.
(1) 20 to a box. (2) per 250 rounds. (3) Also packaged 200 rounds per box. (4) Also packaged 250 rounds per box.

Courtesy Shooter's Bible

WINCHESTER-WESTERN
RIMFIRE PISTOL AND REVOLVER CARTRIDGES

FMC—Full Metal Case

*—Wax Coated

L—Lubaloy

JHP—Jacketed Hollow Point

Cartridge	Bullet		Barrel Length	Muzzle Velocity (ft/s)	Muzzle Energy (ft. lbs.)
	Wt. Grs.	Type			
22 Short Blank	—	—	—	—	—
22 Short Super-X	29	L*	6"	1010	66
22 Short T22	29	Lead*	6"	865	48
22 Long Super-X	29	L*	6"	1095	77
22 Long Rifle Super-X	40	L*	6"	1060	100
22 Long Rifle T22	40	Lead*	6"	950	80
22 Long Rifle Super-Match Mark IV	40	Lead*	6¾"	1060	100
22 Winchester MAGNUM Rimfire Super-X	40	JHP	6½"	1480	195
22 Winchester MAGNUM Rimfire Super-X	40	FMC	6½"	1480	195

Specifications are nominal. Test barrels are used to determine ballistics figures. Individual firearms may differ from these test barrel statistics.

PART FOUR

Miscellaneous

Safety Rules

Rifle and Shotgun Handling

1. *Treat each gun as if it were loaded.* Always examine a rifle when you pick it up to be certain if it is empty, but even if you are sure it is, treat it as if it were loaded.

2. *Always keep the muzzle of the gun pointed in a safe direction.* This means in a direction where no person, object, or animal can be accidentally hit.

3. *Always keep the safety on until ready to shoot.* This means release the safety only when pointing at the target or animal and just before firing.

4. *Unload guns when they are not in use.* This means to be certain that all cartridges are out of both chambers and magazine. Never leave a loaded gun in a tent or house or carry one in a car. It is against the law even to have cartridges in the magazine when your gun is in the car. When not in use, take down, or leave actions open. Guns should be carried to shooting areas in cases.

5. *Always open the action of a gun and point the muzzle in a safe direction when passing it to another person or when receiving it from another person.* Do not receive a gun from another person unless the action is open and the muzzle is pointed in a safe direction.

6. *Never point a gun at anyone or anything you do not wish to shoot.* Avoid all horseplay in gun handling.

7. *When loading a gun, keep the muzzle pointing in a safe direction.* This is really an extension of rule 2, but it is to emphasize the importance of keeping the muzzle pointed safely even while only loading the gun.

8. *Never climb a tree, fence, or wall or jump a ditch with a loaded gun.* Put the gun down and go over or through the obstace, then let your partner hand you the gun, or reach for it yourself, making certain never to pull the gun toward you by the muzzle. If you have to climb something with your gun, unload it first, then climb.

9. *Be sure of your target before you pull the trigger.* You must positively identify all game before firing and be certain that what you are shooting at is legal and desirable game. The wanton destruction of birds or animals, whether legal game or not, is unsportsmanlike and unforgivable. It is also foolish to shoot at signboards, telephone wire insulators, or other property that deserves to be respected.

10. *Be sure of your backstop.* On the range, a proper backstop will stop the bullet behind the target. In the field, watch for natural objects behind

your game that will prevent the bullet from traveling farther than necessary. Never shoot in directions or at objects that are likely to cause the bullet to ricochet dangerously, such as a flat, hard surface or water.

11. *Know your gun and ammunition.* Keep your rifle in clean, operating condition. Be certain you only use ammunition appropriate for your gun, and that you know its range and power. Keep the barrel of your gun free of all obstructions.

12. *Store guns and ammunition in a safe, dry, cool place.* Preferably, keep all guns and their ammunition under lock and key when not in use.

13. *Avoid alcoholic beverages and drugs before or during shooting.*

Handling Pistols or Revolvers

The following rules are a paraphrase of those used by the armed services in instructing personnel in the safe use of revolvers and pistols. These rules apply to all persons using handguns.

1. *Unload the weapon every time it is picked up for any purpose.* Never trust your memory. Consider every gun as loaded until you have proved otherwise. This first safety rule is the cardinal rule upon which all other safety rules are based. Having made certain that a gun is empty, do not hesitate to look again. Continue to assume that it is loaded even if you, yourself, have unloaded it. If you do this, you will never have an accident and you will automatically obey all other safety rules.

2. *Always unload the gun if it is to be left where someone else may handle it.* This is especially important if there is any possibility that it might be picked up by children or by adults who are not trained to handle firearms properly.

3. *Always point the gun up when snapping it after examination. Keep the hammer fully down when the gun is not loaded.* If the gun is pointed up and a shot is accidentally fired, there is less probability of hurting anyone. It is practically impossible to discharge most firearms when the hammer is fully down, even if they are loaded. In addition, keeping the hammer down relieves the spring from tension and prolongs the life of that part.

4. *Never place the finger within the trigger guard until you intend to fire or to snap for practice.* This reduces the possibility of an accidental discharge.

5. *Never point the gun at anyone you do not intend to shoot, or in a direction where an accidental discharge may do harm.* On the range, do not snap for practice while standing back of the firing line. You may know that your weapon is unloaded, but bystanders do not.

6. (a) *Before loading a revolver, open the cylinder and look through the bore to see that it is free from obstruction.*

(b) *Before loading a semiautomatic pistol, draw back the slide and look through the bore to see that it is free from obstruction.*

7. (a) *On the range do not load the revolver until the time for firing.*

(b) *On the range do not insert a loaded magazine in a semiautomatic pistol until the time for firing.*

8. *Never turn around at the firing point while you hold a loaded pistol or revolver in your hand, because by so doing you may point it at the man firing alongside of you.*

9. (a) *On the range do not cock the revolver until immediate use is anticipated. If there is any delay, lower the hammer and recock it only when ready to fire.*

(b) *On the range do not load the semiautomatic pistol with a cartridge in the chamber until immediate use is anticipated. If there is any delay, lock the pistol and only unlock it while extending the arm to fire. Do not lower the hammer on a loaded cartridge; the pistol is much safer cocked and locked.*

10. (a) *If the revolver fails to fire, open the cylinder and unload if the hammer is down. If the hammer is cocked or partly cocked, a break has occurred. In this case, hold the revolver at the position of raise pistol and announce the fact to the person in charge of the firing line.*

(b) *If a semiautomatic pistol is jammed, first remove the magazine.* Further instruction on this difficulty is given in the rule below.

11. (a) *To remove a cartridge not fired from a revolver, open the cylinder and eject the cartridge, first lowering the hammer if it is cocked.*

(b) *To remove the cartridge not fired from a semi-automatic pistol, first remove the magazine and then extract the cartridge from the chamber by a drawing back the slide.*

12. (a) *While hunting, or in a military campaign, the revolver is carried in the holster fully loaded with the hammer down. The cocked revolver should never be put in the holster whether or not it is loaded.*

(b) *While hunting, or in a military campaign, when the early use of the semiautomatic pistol is not foreseen, it should be carried with a fully loaded magazine in the socket, chamber empty, hammer down. When early use of the pistol is probable, it should be carried loaded and locked in the holster or hand. In a military campaign, extra magazines should be carried fully loaded.*

(c) *When the semiautomatic pistol is carried in the holster loaded, cocked, and locked, the butt should be rotated away from the body when drawing the pistol in order to avoid displacing the safety lock.*

13. *Safety devices on both revolvers and semiautomatic pistols should be tested frequently.* A safety device is a dangerous device if it does not work properly.

In addition to the foregoing rules, Chapel* lists four additional common sense precautions that should be observed in using handguns.

1. *Know the range and penetrating power of the cartridge you are using and shoot only where the bullet will not hit anything except the target.* For example, the bullet from a .22 Long Rifle cartridge can go through two ordinary doors or the side of an ordinary frame house and still have enough velocity to kill a man. For this reason, it is wrong to hang a target on a door or the side of a house where people whom you cannot see might be hurt or even killed.

2. *Be sure you have a proper target and backstop.* Do not shoot at rocks, bottles, chunks of ice, or other hard-surfaced objects, because the bullets will ricochet (glance off) and may injure or even kill someone you cannot see.

3. *In case of a misfire, which occurs when a cartridge does not fire after being struck by the firing pin, leave the gun closed and keep it pointed down the range toward the target for at least 30 seconds.* It may be a case of a *hang-fire,* which occurs when a cartridge does not fire at the instant of being struck by the firing pin, but fires later; hence extreme care is necessary.

4. *At a shooting match always carry a revolver with the cylinder swung out and carry a semiautomatic pistol with the slide locked back.*

Binoculars, Field Glasses, and Spotting Scopes

Binocular and Field Glass Construction
In its simplest form a field glass is a small, double telescope with a separate viewing tube and set of lenses for each eye. Thus, it is really two telescopes mounted side by side. The focus can be adjusted by means of a knob, which moves the lenses in each tube closer together or farther apart.

But a field glass is not a binocular according to modern terminology unless it is made with prisms. In binoculars, two prisms reflect the light in each tube before it reaches the eye. The light enters the binocular through the front magnifying lens, strikes one prism, is reflected forward and strikes another prism, and from there is reflected to the lens or lenses in the eyepiece of the binocular, where the viewer sees it.

The prisms do three things. They turn the reversed image that the magnifying lens brings in right side up. They help make the binoculars

*Charles E. Chapel, *The Art of Shooting.* New York: A. S. Barnes and Co., 1960.

smaller than field glasses of the same power, because the light is reflected from one prism to another, not in a straight line. And they allow the magnifying lenses to be set farther apart than the eyepieces to make for better stereoscopic vision at distances. Stereoscopic vision is depth perception, which is achieved because the two eyes see slightly different views owing to the difference in angle at which they look. The farther apart are the objective lenses, the greater the angle of view and the better the depth perception.

The best glasses have *achromatic lenses,* which compensate for the bending of the different light rays. The best also have specially coated lenses to reduce glare and to cut down reflection. There are two different types of focusing arrangements used. Some have a single central adjustment, so that both lenses adjust with one knob. Others have oculars that adjust individually; these are more suited for persons whose eyes do not test the same. For shooters who wear glasses, special flat eye caps are available. The regular eye caps are unscrewed from the eyepiece and replaced with flat eye caps, allowing the eyeglass wearer to see a full field of view. Or expensive binoculars can be obtained, which have an individual's prescription for corrective lenses included.

. In general, it is best to get binoculars of fine quality. Cheap ones have lenses of defective quality, which can cause eyestrain and headaches, particularly if anything is wrong with the alignment of the lenses and prisms.

Binocular Numbers, Relative Brightness

Manufacturers make binoculars in different magnifying powers and with lenses of different diameters. The magnifying power and lens diameter are usually given together, such as 6X, 30; 7X, 35; 7X, 50; or 9X, 35. The magnifying power is given first, so that in a 6X binocular, the object is six times larger than when seen with the naked eye. Also, the object appears at ⅙ the distance. Thus, the first figure always means power or magnification.

It is possible to check the magnification of your binoculars. Suppose you have bought a pair of glasses that are supposedly 7X. If you want to be certain of their power, set up an object (a 7' length of lumber will do) 100' away. Rest your glasses on something firm, and focus them on the object. Then look at the object, with one eye exposed and the other looking through the tube of the binoculars. The result will be two images side by side. Move the binoculars until the two images overlap. If the smaller object is ⅐ the size of the larger, you have seven-power magnification.

The second number refers to the diameter of the front, or object lens, in millimeters. The larger the diameter of the objective lens, the greater the light-gathering power of the binocular. Under some circumstances, such as poor light conditions, the brightness of the image is more important than magnification. Therefore, there is some advantage to having a large enough objective lens.

However, as discussed in the sections on "Telescopic Sights" in Part I, there is no point in having an objective lens that is too large, because the eye cannot absorb more than a certain maximum amount of light. (See the previous section under "Telescopic Sights" on "Objective Lens Diameter, Exit Pupil Diameter, and Brightness.") The maximum amount of light the eye can absorb is obtained with a binocular having a relative brightness of 25. Brightness is calculated by dividing the objective lens diameter, in millimeters, by the magnification, and squaring the result. Thus, if a binocular is 7X, 35, the relative brightness is:

$$\text{Relative brightness} = \frac{35}{7} = (5)^2 = 25$$

If a binocular is 7X, 50 the relative brightness is:

$$\text{Relative brightness} = \frac{50}{7} = (7.1)^2 = 50.4$$

Actually, the relative brightness of the 7X, 50 binocular is greater than the eye can handle, so the buyer is spending more money than necessary on an objective lens that is too large. However, the relative brightness of a 9X, 35 binocular is as follows.

$$\text{Relative brightness} = \frac{35}{9} = (3.88)^2 = 15.1$$

Such a binocular is fine under excellent light conditions but inadequate when available light is poor.

Field of View
Another important consideration is selecting a binocular that has a wide enough field of view. It is important to have as wide a field of view as possible, but other things being equal, the greater the magnification, the smaller the field of view. As magnification increases, it becomes harder and harder to locate your game in the more limited field of view. Binocu-

lars of very high power appear extremely unsteady when you are trying to locate an object through them. For target work, spotting scopes are preferred, since the power has to be quite high to locate bullet holes.

Of course, the manufacturer may change internal design and dimensions to increase the magnification and still keep an adequate field of view. Bausch and Lomb have accomplished this on their 9X binocular, which has the same field of view as does their 7X binocular. The table shows the specifications of their 7X, 35; 9X, 35; and 7X, 50 binoculars.

Bausch and Lomb Binocular Specifications

	7X, 35	9X, 35	7X, 50
Magnification	7X	9X	7X
Catalog number center focus	61-2010	61-2030	61-2020
Objective diameter	35mm	35mm	50mm
Angular field	7° 17′	7° 17′	7° 16′
Linear field (1,000 yards)	382′	382′	381′
Exit pupil diameter	5mm	3.8mm	7.1mm
Relative brightness	25	14.4	50.4
Height	5⅜″	5⅜″	7⅛″

The relative brightness of the 9X, 35 binocular is considerably less than of the 7X, 35, even though the field of view of the two glasses is the same.

If you want to calculate the linear field of view, in feet, of a particular binocular at various distances from the viewer, the following formula can be used.

$$\text{Linear field of view (in feet)} =$$

$$\text{Tangent of } \left(\frac{\text{Angular field of view}}{2} \right) \times \text{Distance (Feet)} \times 2$$

Thus, if a binocular has an angular field of view of 7°17′, the linear field of view at 1,000 yards (3,000′) is as follows:

$$\text{Linear field of view} =$$

$$\text{Tangent of } \left(\frac{7°17′}{2} \right) \times 3,000′ \times 2 = \text{Tangent of } (3°38½′) \times 6,000$$

(From mathematical tables, the tangent of the angle 3°38½′ = .06365.)

$$\text{Linear field of view} = .06365 \times 6,000 = 382′$$

Using the same formula, the linear field of view can be calculated at other distances. Several of the results for the same binocular with an angular field of view of 7°17′ are shown in the table.

Linear Field of View at Different Distances of a Binocular with an Angular Field of View of 7°17′

	Distances from Viewer (in feet)										
	3,000	2,700	2,400	2,100	1,800	1,500	1,200	900	600	300	150
Linear field of view	382	344	306	267	229	191	153	115	76	38	19

Selecting a Binocular

Which binocular should the hunter buy? For all-around hunting use, the most popular is the 7X, 35. This provides as much relative brightness as the eye can handle, a seven-power magnification, which is usually adequate for all but the longest-distance big-game hunting, and a large-enough field of view to insure easy location of the object. The table gives Bausch and Lomb's recommendations for binoculars for different purposes.

Binocular Applications

Use	7X, 35	9X, 35	7X, 50
Spectator sports			
Baseball	A	B	C
Football	A	B	C
Horse racing	A	B	C
Auto racing	A	B	C
Track and field	A	B	C
All-purpose viewing	A	B	C
Long-distance viewing	B	A	C
Poor-light viewing	B	C	A
Astronomy	B	C	A
Surveillance	C	B	A
Hunting			
Woods and heavy brush	A	C	B
Open country	B	A	C
Mountains	B	A	C
Varminting	B	A	C
Big game	A	B	C
Mountain goats	B	A	C
Flying	A	B	C
Boating	B	C	A
Travel	A	B	C
Hiking	A	B	C
Theater	A	B	C
Bird watching	A	B	C
Advanced nature study	B	A	C

A—First Choice. B—Second Choice. C—Third Choice.

Spotting Scopes

Spotting scopes are usually much more high power than binoculars, varying in magnification from 9X up to 60X. Some are variable power, allowing the magnification to be adjusted over broad ranges, such as 9X–30X, 15X–30X, 15X–60X, 20X–45X, 20X–60X, 25X–50X, and other combinations. Other scopes are fixed power. Still others have interchangeable eyepieces to give different magnification. Very high power scopes are usually used for spotting shots in target shooting. Some even have right-angle or 45°-angle eyepieces, which allow the target shooter to see his shot simply by turning his head and without any shift in body position. Scopes may also be obtained that are less than 1′ in length, with medium or better magnification. These scopes are extremely useful in long-range hunting, such as for sheep, goats, or antelope. Such scopes may be tucked in a knapsack and carried about easily. By glassing from ridges, canyons, basins, or other uneven terrain, the hunter can locate game at far ranges before it has been alerted to his presence. This allows the hunter to stalk game he might otherwise miss.

In contrast to the small spotting scopes, the largest ones may have objective apertures of 100mm and be mounted on heavy tripods. Such large scopes are used primarily for long-range, big-bore matches. Sunshades, dust covers, carrying cases, and other extras can be purchased as optional equipment by the serious target shooter.

Carriers, Storage, and Cabinets

Gun Cases

One of the secrets of keeping your gun looking new is having a proper gun case. The most usual cases are long leather, leatherette, canvas, or plastic cases lined with sheepskin, flannel, or artificial fleece. These are adequate to protect your gun from scratches but will not protect it from hard knocks as will a trunk-type case. Always put your gun in some type of case before you transport it anywhere by auto, truck, boat, plane, and so on. If you are carrying your gun yourself, a fleece-lined case is adequate as long as you are careful not to bang it around, put heavy objects on it, or otherwise abuse it. If you are shipping your gun or checking it on a plane, however, a trunk-type tote case is necessary.

Be certain your gun is dry when you put it in a fleece-lined case and make certain that a case that has been exposed to rain, spray, or other moisture is thoroughly dried after each outing. One disadvantage of such a case is that the fleece retains moisture, and any gun put away damp, or in a damp case, will rust very quickly.

I like the fleece-lined cases of the proper size for the gun, particularly if made of a fairly heavy leatherette or real leather on the outside, with a convenient carrying handle and a zipper that works. Guns with scopes should have cases broad enough to fit right over the scope.

Never store your gun in a fleece-lined case for very long, especially in humid weather. Your gun is better off out in the air, especially if it is in its own rack or in a well-ventilated gun cabinet.

Ammunition Storage

All ammunition is subject to deterioration over a long period of time, particularly if it is not properly stored. Also, some ammunition deteriorates faster than others. During the 1920s, millions of pounds of powder and ammunition left over from World War I had to be destroyed because it deteriorated in storage magazines. During the years following World War II, ordnance inspectors tested samples of stored military ammunition regularly, and when deterioration was discovered the ammunition was condemned and was often dumped into the sea.

The reason for this deterioration was acid, not from outside sources but from within the powder itself. Acid is vital to powder manufacture, yet if all traces are not removed in the final stages of manufacture, powder deteriorates rapidly with age. Therefore, whether or not your ammunition will deteriorate over the years will depend somewhat on its manufacture. The older it is, the more likely it will deteriorate because of residual acid in the powder itself. Therefore, if you have some old World War I surplus ammunition, or some old shells of Grandpa's passed down from World War I days, better think twice before taking them along on that once-a-year deer hunt. They might not have any more power than your son's BB gun.

Generally speaking, most of the powder manufactured since World War II has been produced by new methods that have eliminated some of the process of deterioration to which older powder was subject. Therefore, this powder does not deteriorate rapidly with age, unless it is subject to adverse environmental conditions.

Two environmental conditions are harmful to all rifle and pistol ammunition and shotshells: (1) excessive heat and (2) moisture. Excessive heat dries out the moisture in the powder itself and changes its characteristics. The wax of paper-case shotshells stored at the critical temperature of above 135° will start to melt and run into the powder, causing a great loss of power. Or the shell may only go "poof" when someone fires it. Alternating heat and cold dries and loosens seals in many types of cartridges, reducing pressures, velocities, and power. Of course, heat can become so excessive that powder and primers will explode, so don't put your box of shells on the top of the wood stove when you come in tired from hunting!

To avoid heat, store ammunition near the floor in rooms, never in attics or near ceilings, or over stoves, radiators, or other sources of excessive heat. Similarly, shells left in closed automobiles or auto trunks, or out in the hot sun, may be subject to far too much heat.

Shells should be kept away from high humidity and excessive moisture. Damp basements will eventually destroy the power of ammunition, especially of shells with inadequate moisture-proof seals. Paper-case shotshells are especially subject to deterioration. If the wax is rubbed off of spots on the cases, moisture will be absorbed into the case itself and work its way into the wadding and powder. Not only is power reduced, but the case swells and may not even work in your gun. Plastic shells are much more waterproof, but even they will not keep out moisture indefinitely. I have seen duck hunters leave a box of shells out in the rain and never dry them before storing them in an air-tight container. Such carelessness is asking for trouble. Moisture also has a corrosive effect on metal cartridge cases, so these too should be stored away from dampness.

The rule is: Store your ammunition in a cool, dry place.

The National Association for Fire Prevention recommends that ammunition and/or powder be stored in a wood chest or cabinet, constructed of lumber not less than 1″ thick and fitted with a tight lid or door. Wood is preferred over metal since wood prevents heat from being transferred through to the powder in the early stages of fire. If the wood burns and the ammunition ignites, the wood gives way more easily, eliminating the dangerous fragments of shrapnel a metal container would produce.

What about carrying ammunition in your car or boat? Some shooters have specially made wooden ammunition boxes, which serve admirably. I generally use the metal ammunition boxes that can be obtained from war surplus stores. But I keep the ammunition within these metal boxes in their own cardboard containers until ready to use. The metal boxes are especially waterproof for use in boats, have convenient carrying handles, and are inexpensive. But do not leave them in the hot sun or in a hot, closed-up automobile where temperatures become excessive. If you hunt in hot climates, wooden ammunition boxes make better carriers, primarily because they do not heat up as fast as metal boxes.

I do not like to have loose ammunition rattling around in any kind of carrier. If you do not have the original cardboard carton for your cartridges, drill holes in a block of wood to put rifle or pistol shells in it. Ammunition belts or vests will hold a lot of cartridges or shotshells, and are fine means for transporting your ammunition. After shooting, however, put unused shells away in their storage boxes, and these in drawers or cabinets. Never let shells of any kind lie around loose where children can find them. I once saw a five-year-old boy sitting on the front steps of his house hitting one of his father's shotshells with a hammer! Fortunately, the shell did not explode. Persons have been injured, also, by shells carelessly thrown into trash and burned. Therefore, put your ammunition away, and preferably keep it and your guns under lock and key at all times when not in use.

Gun Stock Alterations

Adding Checkering

Checkering is a series of parallel V grooves cut to a depth of about $\frac{1}{16}''$ into a stock and crossed at a sharp angle (usually 30° to 45°) by another series of parallel grooves at the same depth. The spaces between these two series of grooves are formed into diamond-like pointed pyramids. Checkering is described by the number of grooves per inch. For example, "20-line checkering" indicates 20 grooves per inch. Generally, if the grooves are spaced closer than 22 to 24 lines per inch, the diamonds are too small to provide a rough gripping surface. If the grooves are fewer than 16 to 18 per inch, however, the checkering is usually too rough for comfortable gun handling. Woods that are too soft or porous cannot take lines closer than 16 to 20 per inch.

The best checkering is done by hand. (The total process will be described in this section.) However, less-expensive commercially made guns frequently have checkering that is pressed into the wood under high heat and pressure. Impressed checkering is generally of the *negative type;* that is, instead of the diamond-shaped pyramids rising above the wood, they are pressed into the wood. However, a new *positive type* of checkering is now being impressed commercially, which more closely approximates the hand-cut checkering found on the finest guns. If done properly, checkering not only enhances the beauty of the stock, but provides a better gripping surface on the forend and pistol grip.

Checkering is a job that requires much time, patience, careful work, and skill, so if you're the type that can't stand tedious work, better let someone else do your checkering for you. However, if you like tedious, fussy tasks, and have the temperament to work slowly and patiently, you might try checkering for yourself. The following outline gives the basic steps in the process.

Holding the Stock: The Checkering Cradle. The first step in checkering your stock is to provide a way to hold the stock so that you can work on it. By far the best way is to use a checkering cradle. These may be purchased from gun supply houses.

Necessary Tools. Only a few basic tools are needed: a metal scribe, a border tool, a spacing tool, a V-tool or single cutter, a V-chisel, a flexible ruler, grease pencil, toothbrush, paper for border pattern, and linseed oil or stock oil to darken the checkering to match the rest of the stock.

The Pattern. The first task is to select or design a pattern. Where will the checkering be placed: forend, pistol grip, other parts of the stock? Many patterns, such as those found on the pistol grip of a stock, consist of two sections—one on each side of the grip. These are mirror images of each other. Others, such as those on the forend, consist of one design on the underneath side. There are wide variations in patterns, so you will have to decide on the pattern you want. Patterns can be purchased from gun supply houses but must frequently be modified to fit the individual gun. One way to decide on a pattern is to look at the checkering on a number of guns. If you find a pattern you like, tape a piece of typewriter paper over it and rub the side of a soft pencil against the paper. This will transfer the basic pattern onto the paper, which in turn can be transferred to the wood of your gun.

After you have a pattern, tape a paper cut out of it to the proper position on your stock. Draw around the outside edges with the grease pencil to form the border lines of the pattern on your stock.

The Border. Trace over the border of the pattern lightly with a sharp metal scribe, making certain you follow the grease pencil line exactly. Then use the V-tool or single cutter to cut a groove at the border where the checkering lines will end, but do not cut this groove too deep. Later, if you decide on a deep, permanent border line, you can trace over the border with the special border tool, but do this after the checkering is complete.

Master Lines. After the border is cut, the next important step is to draw and cut the master lines for the diagonal checkering. These are two basic lines running diagonally across the pattern, intersecting at an angle so the diamonds are about 3½ times longer than they are wide. The

Two rifles and a shotgun, all custom-stocked, display fine checkering on their grips and forends. The rifle and shotgun at left and center have classic border checkering; the rifle at right has borderless checkering.

Winchester Model 70 XTR Featherweight features scrolled banners interrupting the checkering—an intricate and difficult pattern to cut.

This Browning A-Bolt High Grade is checkered with a fancy skip-line pattern and a sculptured border.

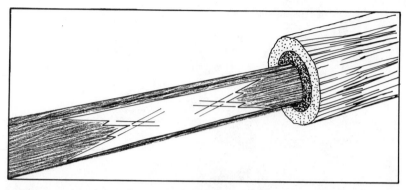

1. After securing the stock in a vise or cradle, attach a paper pattern to the area —in this case the forend—which you intend to checker. Here the pattern is held by cellophane tape.

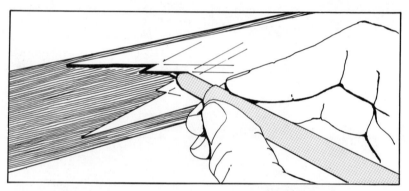

2. Use a wax china marking pencil to trace the outline of the pattern onto the wood. The wax marks are easily wiped off when you've finished checkering.

flexible plastic ruler can be held against the stock while the lines are drawn, then scribed, and then cut with the V-tool (single cutter).

Spacing Lines. The parallel spacing lines are cut one by one, with each previous line acting as a guide for the succeeding line. Begin by running the spacing tool along each master line. Note that one blade of the spacing tool traces along the master line while the other blade cuts the next groove parallel to the master line. After each line is cut, run the spacing tool blade along that so the other blade can cut the line next to it. Continue this until all the lines are in along both diagonals. At this stage, the lines are not cut to their full depth, nor are all the diamond

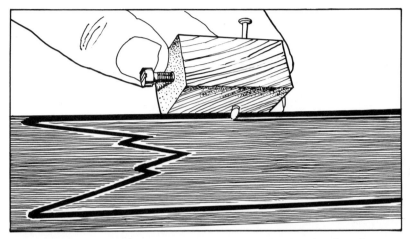

3. This simple tool is made from a block of wood, a sharpened nail, and a screw. Use it to cut the top edge of the checkering border. Since it rides along the top of the stock, the line will be straight and even.

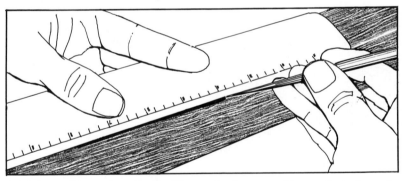

4. With a scribing tool, and a flexible metal ruler as a guide, cut the bottom edge of the panel.

pyramids fully formed. The important thing is to cut to about ½ or ⅔ depth, forming perfectly spaced parallel lines so the pattern is even and the lines do not cross the border lines or nick the outside of the border lines. Use the V-chisel as needed to get into the corners or other hard-to-reach places.

Deepen the Lines to Form Diamond Pyramids. Use the single cutter or V-tool to deepen the lines until the diamonds are no longer flat topped. Deepen first along one set of diagonals, then along the diagonals running across. Usually about two cuts are needed before the lines are cut to their full depth.

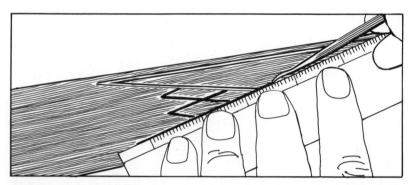

5. *Again using the flexible ruler, which follows the contour of the stock, cut the master-lines for the checkered, diamond-shaped panels. The lines should intersect at an angle so the diamonds are about 3 to 3½ times as long as they are wide.*

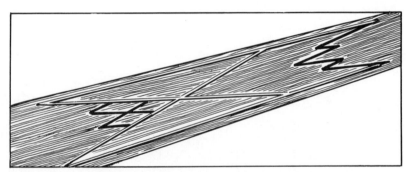

6. *This is how the panel should look after the master cuts have been made.*

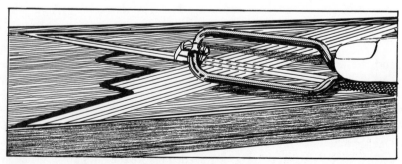

7. *With a spacing tool, cut the lines one by one, using the previous line as a guide.*

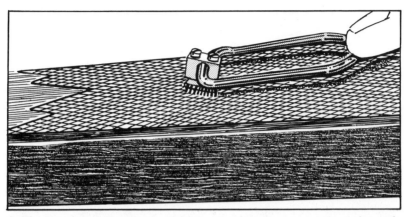

8. *The V-tool is used to deepen the lines. It takes about two passes to bring the diamonds to full depth.*

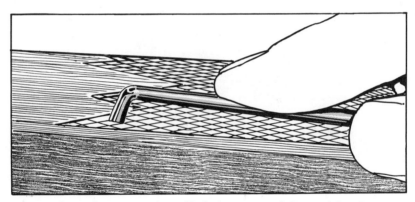

9. *To work in tight areas, use a small, close-quarter tool. Be careful in the corners to avoid overruns.*

Forming the Border. If the border lines are nicked or crossed at all, use the border tool to deepen and widen the border lines until they are cut neatly and deep enough for all nicks to be eliminated. If the initial border lines have not been marked at all, it may not be necessary to use the border tool. Some of the finest checkering has no border lines, but this skill is very difficult for the beginner to achieve. Usually using the border tool gives the job a finished look.

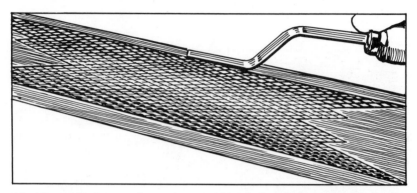

10. A Brownell edging tool is used to cut a straight line along the edge of a border, which deepens the border and adds a finished look to the pattern.

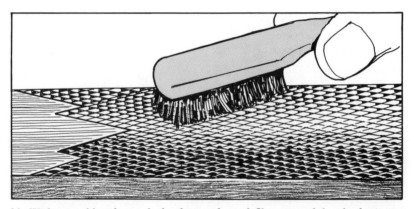

11. With a toothbrush, scrub the dust and wood fibers out of the checkering.

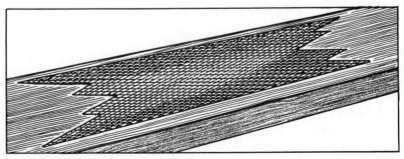

12. The finished checkering.

Brush Out All Dust and Wood Fibers. Use the toothbrush to thoroughly clean out all lines.

Finish. Apply linseed oil, TruOil, or some other stock oil so the cuttings are colored the same tone as the rest of the stock. Apply sparingly, being careful not to fill up the cuts with gummy oil.

Shortening or Lengthening Pull, Adding a Recoil Pad

Installing a recoil pad is warranted if one or more of the following conditions exist:

1. The length of pull of the stock is too long and needs to be shortened. It is sometimes easier to cut the stock down and install a recoil pad than to reinstall the original buttplate after the stock is cut off.

2. The length of pull is too short and must be lengthened.

3. The recoil of the gun disturbs the shooter and a pad will help minimize the problem.

The first consideration in installing the recoil pad is to determine at what point and at what angle (pitch) the stock is to be cut off. Therefore, two questions must be answered: (1) What total length of pull does the shooter require, and (2) Is the present pitch of the gun (particularly of a shotgun) satisfactory? Length of pull is discussed in sections of Parts I and II; see those sections for measuring and determining length of pull. After this is done, the thickness of the recoil pad must be taken into consideration. The place at which the stock is to be cut off should be the distance of the length of pull minus the center thickness of the recoil pad.

If the present pitch of your gun is satisfactory, the stock butt should be cut off exactly at the original angle. Ordinarily, a rifle has no pitch, so the stock is cut at a 90° angle to the line of the barrel. If either the heel or toe is slightly long on a shotgun, the pitch and angle of the butt must be correspondingly altered. (See the sections on Shotgun Stock and Fit in Part II.) Note that if there is a tendency for the butt to slip down so that you are overshooting, the heel is too short and the stock must be cut off more at the toe (to increase the pitch). If the butt is slipping up so that you are undershooting, the toe is too short and the stock must be cut off more at the heel (to decrease the pitch).

If you are not sure of the angle, cut off the butt at the same angle, but ¼" long. Attach the pad temporarily according to the instructions that follow. Then take your gun to a trap range or field and fire it with the pad as is. If you are undershooting or overshooting because the stock tends to slip up or down, try putting a wooden wedge between pad and stock at either the heel or toe as needed. (A wedge about 2½" long, 1¼" wide, and tapered from 0" to ⅛" thick is about right.) Shoot with the wedge in place at either the heel or toe to determine the correction needed. Back in your workshop, draw lines to show which way the angle is to be corrected and to be sure the butt is cut off the right length.

Once the proper stock length and angle are determined, extreme care must be taken to avoid splintering the far sides of the stock with the saw. There are several ways of minimizing this. One, is to cut the stock ¹⁄₁₆" long and then use sandpaper, or a sharp cabinet scraper and files, to reduce to the length wanted and to cut away the splintered edges. Another way to minimize splintering is to use saw blades with only the finest, sharpest teeth. I can do the best job using very fine teeth on a crosscut blade of a table saw. I saw straighter and neater with such a saw also. I cut the stock ¹⁄₁₆" long and then sand with a belt sander. If you prefer, you can use a new, sharp, hacksaw blade to cut ¹⁄₁₆" long and go on from there. I have far more trouble cutting straight with a hacksaw than with other types of saws. Whatever you do, do not use standard wood saws with coarse teeth; you will splinter your stock edges.

After sawing the stock, locate the pad on the butt, mark, drill, and tap the pad holes in the butt, and attach the pad with screws. If your gun is a take-down type, it is better to remove the barrel and so on before starting to attach the recoil pad. If your gun has a solid frame-type arm, held to the butt by a screw from the back end, you will have to remove the stock, fit the pad, then take off the pad, rescrew the stock to the gun, then reinstall the pad.

After the pad is screwed to the stock, the excess parts of the pad that stick out from the flat sides of the stock must be removed. A belt or disc sander is usually best for this job, since the hard portions of the pad are difficult to cut. But before sanding the pad, wind two layers of masking tape around the bottom portions of the stock to protect the stock finish from the sander. The final sanding must be done carefully, with the masking tape removed from the stock. If you have marred the stock finish with the sander, refinish or repolish the spots. Minor markings can often be polished out. If the stock is finished with varnish, lacquer, or plastic, touch up the surface finish with one of these. Stock oil or linseed oil can be used to restore the gloss to oil finishes, or even to slightly darken light spots on a stained stock. (If the stock has to be completely refinished, see a subsequent section.)

Cutting Down Comb Height
Sometimes a shooter discovers that a gun does not fit because of the height of the comb. (For a complete discussion of comb height see the sections on "Rifle Stock and Fit" in Part I and on "Shotgun Stock and

Fit" in Part II.) A comb of proper height, whether on a rifle or shotgun, should allow the shooter to rest his cheek comfortably on the comb so that his eye is aligned along the proper sighting plane.

The easiest situation to remedy is one in which the comb is too high. The problem is solved by cutting off the top of the comb to the proper height, and reshaping and refinishing the stock. There are three useful tools for cutting down the comb. The first is a plane. Get a so-called smooth plane or bench plane, about 8″ or 9″ long. The second needed tool is a wood rasp. Get a four-in-hand or shoe rasp. This rasp is really four in one; one side is flat and the other side is partially rounded. Each side has a rough cut at one end and a smooth cut at the other, so there are four different cuts from which to choose. The third tool is sandpaper of different grits: sizes 120, 220, 280, 320, and 400 will do nicely. (The larger the number, the finer the grit.) A belt sander (which goes straight back and forth, not orbiting) will speed your work along in the early stages, but is not necessary. In using the sander, hold it in a clamp and hold the stock by hand up to it. Never use a disc sander, as any movement across the grain will make noticeable scratches in the wood.

Use the wood rasp to start the cutting, beginning with the flat, roughest end of the rasp first if much is to be taken off. From time to time, hold the stock up to your eye and sight along the top plane to see if any portions are cut more than others. If there are ridges or valleys, use the plane to smooth out the surface before continuing the cutting with your wood rasp, using the flat, smooth surface of the rasp to do the finer finish work and then the plane to smooth that out.

After your comb is cut to a proper height and shape, use varying grades of sandpaper to do the finish work, ending up with the extra fine grit, #320 or #400. Be certain to sand only with the grain of the stock, not against the grain.

One final step is needed before refinishing the stock: your stock must be "dewhiskered." Whiskers in a stock are really ends of wood fibers that break loose from the body of the wood when it is cut down. These loose fiber ends will stick up when the finish is applied, so that the entire stock surface feels like a day's growth of beard. Obviously, the whiskers must be removed. The best way to do this is to dampen the cut portions of the stock by wiping with a wrung-out but slightly damp sponge. After dampening, hold the stock over the burner of your stove, close enough to evaporate the moisture but without scorching the wood. Move the sanded portion back and forth over the burner until dry. As the water evaporates, the steam raises the splintered fiber ends until they protrude enough to be removed.

The best way to remove the whiskers is with #320 or #400 sandpaper or with fine steel wool. Always move against (but not across) the grain of the wood to cut off the whiskers. If you move with the grain, you will only press the whiskers back down into the wood and have to start the whole process over again.

After removing the whiskers, wet the stock again and repeat the procedure until no whiskers remain. The stock must be sanded completely before any finish is applied. (For directions in applying the finish, see a subsequent section.)

Adding to Comb Height

If the comb of a gun is too low and the shooter does not want to buy a whole new stock, there are two principal methods by which the comb may be built up. The simplest method is to install a laced sleeve. Such a sleeve is best made of leather and padded on top under the leather to provide a comfortable cheek rest for the shooter. Such a sleeve is quite practical for the shooter with a "glass jaw" who objects to the recoil of a high, hard, wooden comb, but it does detract from the beauty of the gun.

For a shooter who objects to the sleeve, a comb may be built up by gluing another piece of wood to the top and shaping and finishing it to match the rest of the comb as closely as possible. There are a number of steps to this process, and they are outlined here.

1. Select a piece of a kind of wood whose grain matches that of the existing stock as closely as possible. Stocks are most commonly made of walnut or maple.

2. Cut off the top, rounded portion of the comb of your stock so that the surface is flat and broad enough to provide a proper base for the piece you plan to glue on. The broader the base needed, the more you will have to cut down the existing comb. If much is to be cut off, it can be marked, sawed with a table saw that has a blade with very fine teeth, and finished off with a plane. Or all the cutting can be done with the bench plane, removing a little wood at a time and continuing until the surface of the cut is smooth and level. Any dips or waves in the wood can be detected by laying a flat-edge ruler or piece of metal on the planed surface and holding it at eye level against a strong light.

3. After the stock is prepared, plane the gluing surface of the new comb piece until it is also flat and smooth and will fit tightly against the top

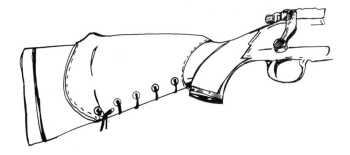

One way to build up the comb on a stock is to install a laced sleeve.

of the stock. Be certain the new piece is slightly larger than needed to give plenty of wood to work with in shaping the new comb.

4. Glue the new piece to the old stock with epoxy glue. Epoxy comes in two tubes, one with resin and the other with hardener. When the two are properly mixed and applied the result is a bond stronger than the wood around it. Mix the resin and hardener according to directions, stirring until they turn a cream color. Apply the glue to both the pre-pared surfaces of the stock and to the new comb piece using a small piece of clean wood for an applicator. Press the two glued surfaces together, sliding firmly back and forth to spread the glue evenly, ending with the new piece correctly aligned. Clamps or large rubber bands may be used to hold the two pieces firmly together. In addition, tape can be wrapped around the two sections until the glue is dry.

5. After drying, usually overnight, remove the bands, clamp, and tape, and check to be certain the new piece is in correct position.

6. Shape the new piece with a wood rasp, plane, and sandpaper as described in the previous section on cutting down comb height.

7. Refinish the stock according to the directions in a following section of this chapter.

Refinishing the Stock

Removing Dents

Before the dents can be removed, the finish over them must be removed. Use a high-quality paint and varnish remover, scrape off the finish, wipe, and sandpaper. Sanding down past the dents will require the removal of too much wood, so the dents must be raised until level with the surrounding surface of the stock.

To raise the dents, two pieces of equipment are needed: (1) a piece of metal that can be heated and placed over the dents to warm them and (2) an ink blotter or a soft piece of flannel cloth. The warming metal can be an electric soldering iron, or you can make a suitable substitute. One way is to put a handle on a 12″ piece of ½″ copper tubing. Drive the tubing up into a common file handle, bend it slightly, and hammer the exposed end until flat.

In removing the dent, heat the electric soldering iron, or if one is not available, heat the homemade warmer metal over the kitchen stove until only slightly hot. The metal should be about as hot as a clothes iron: hot enough to iron clothes, but not so hot it will scorch them. The amount you warm the metal is extremely important, because you will scorch the wood of your stock if you get it too hot.

Next, wet the blotter or cotton flannel and lay it directly over the dent. Then touch the heated metal to the blotter or cloth at the point where the wood is dented. The water will be turned to steam, which will penetrate the bent fibers of wood and will cause them to swell up. As they swell, they will return to their original shape, and the dent will be gone.

If one application of moisture and heat is not sufficient, repeat the process two or more times until the bent wood fibers are level with the rest of the wood.

Sometimes the wood fibers are broken. In this case, they will not return to their original position, or if they do, they will look and feel rough because an evident abrasion remains. In this case, there are two possibilities. The dent area can be sanded out if it is small and shallow, or the hole can be filled or patched.

If the hole is to be filled, first clean out the gouge, removing all dirt and loose fibers. Next, collect a spoonful of sawdust from the stock you are working on and mix with epoxy glue until the mixture takes on the appearance of putty. Press the filler into the hole to overflowing. Be certain the mixture is pressed firmly to expel any air trapped in the dent, and add a little extra to allow for shrinkage. Allow to dry, then sand the mound down even with the surface of the stock. The stock is now ready to refinish.

If the dent is large and deep, the hole will have to be patched. A popular patch is a precut diamond patch of wood or plastic, which can be purchased from gunsmith supply houses. It does not matter if the patch is not the same color as the wood of the stock. Contrasting colors add decoration to the stock.

To insert the patch, lay it over the dent, mark the patch outline, and cut out the gouge to the shape of the diamond about ⅛ " deep. Glue in the diamond-shaped patch with epoxy glue. After drying, sand the patch until it is even with the surface of the stock.

Refinishing with Varnish

Most American-made factory-produced guns have stocks finished with varnish, lacquer, or one of the newer polyurethane plastic finishes. Only the finer commercially produced European stocks are oil finished, but many American gun enthusiasts refinish their stocks with an oil finish, since this finish is considered the most handsome. There are advantages and disadvantages to each type of finish. The custom stockmaker who uses several coats of marine-type spar varnish, carefully sanding between coats, produces a handsome product. Spar varnish is one of the old favorite sealers and is still a good choice if it is thinned with turpentine and brushed thoroughly into the wood. If such a stock becomes scratched, it can be retouched with varnish, provided all old wax, dirt, or grease has been thoroughly removed with a solvent. After cleaning the surface, apply several thin coats (thinned with turpentine), one at a time, sanding bad spots in between coats and making certain each coat is thoroughly dry before sanding. Finish off with a final light rubdown with #400 grit paper.

When applied in the preceding manner, a varnished finish is tough, and not easily scratched or chipped. It will dent, scratch, or chip with rough handling, however, and should never be exposed to rain, snow, or excessive moisture for long periods of time. If you hunt in the rain, be certain the gun is wiped dry before putting it away. If moisture soaks into the wood through cracks, at ends, or in the spaces between wood and metal, the finish may crack and the stock may warp. It is best, therefore, to protect a varnished finish with rubbed coats of good-quality, hard paste wax.

If the stock is to be refinished completely, first remove the old varnish with varnish remover, scraping off the softened finish with a knife and wiping with a rough cloth. Wash thoroughly with alcohol. When completely dry, sand thoroughly, ending with #320 or #400 fine grit sandpaper. Remove the "whiskers" by the method discussed in the section on "Cutting Down Comb Height." Then apply several coats of varnish, lightly sanding between coats as described.

The secret of a good varnish finish is to apply thin coats, sanding in between. Thick coats, carelessly brushed on, will be lacking in good appearance and are more likely to chip easily. Varnish may also be applied from a spray gun, which produces fine results if thinly and evenly applied.

Refinishing with Lacquer

Refinishing with lacquer is usually more difficult than varnish refinishing. Many inexpensive gun stocks are finished with sprayed-on lacquer, which does not penetrate the wood and which chips and flakes off in large chunks, leaving bare wood underneath. Therefore, unless the lacquer needs only a little retouching, the total finish must be removed before the new one is applied. The steps in lacquer refinishing are as follows.

1. Remove old finish with lacquer remover. Brush on, let soak, scrape off with a knife, wipe dry.

2. Sand entire wood surface, ending with #320 or #400 grit paper. Remove "whiskers" as outlined in the section on "Cutting Down Comb Height."

3. If the wood has an open grain, apply a wood filler especially made for stocks and to go under lacquer. It is important that the correct type of filler be used. One made for varnish will be dissolved by lacquer. After filler is applied, repolish stock with a very fine grit sandpaper. In applying filler, rub it in both with and across the grain. Let it dry partially and continue rubbing until it takes on a light sheen. Apply more filler if necessary, to be certain all wood pores and cracks are filled. Wipe off excess only across the grain. If you wipe with the grain, you will remove the filler. Let dry thoroughly.

4. Apply a thin coating of lacquer especially made for gun stocks. A spray can or a paint brush may be used. After drying, polish with #400 fine grit paper. Apply another coat of lacquer. Some workers prefer three or more coats, sanding in between. Use your own judgment about the number of coats. Too many or too thick applications are likely to crack and peel, so be certain the coats are thin and well polished in between.

Sealing, Filling, Refinishing with Polyurethane Plastic
Polyurethane is the toughest of all finishes. It is practically impervious to water and will stand a lot of use, and even abuse, without cracking or peeling. It comes in either a high gloss or a soft or satin finish. It may be used just as a wood sealer, and/or as a filler, or for the final finish as well. No wood filler is required, since it is its own filler if several coats are applied, with excess rubbed and polished off between coats.

In using polyurethane as a wood sealer, thin it with naphtha and brush into the wood. Wait 15 minutes, and with a rag damp with naphtha rub off the surface coat cross-grain, leaving the wood pores filled. If other types of wood fillers or finishes are to be used over the polyurethane sealer, let it dry 24 hours before other fillers and finishes are applied.

If the polyurethane is to be used as a wood filler as well as a sealer, apply a thick coat of it over the thin sealer coat, about four hours after the sealer has been applied. If you allow the polyurethane sealer to dry, it is so hard that subsequent coats will not stick to it. If you are using a final finish of something other than polyurethane, allow the filler coat to dry a full 24 hours before polishing it back down to the base wood with steel wool. This should leave every wood pore filled completely so that the regular, final finish can be applied.

If you are using the polyurethane for the final finish, it may be applied from a spray can or with a soft, camel hair brush. It brushes on better if thinned fifty-fifty. When used as a final finish, wait no more than 12 hours between coats, so that subsequent coats will stick to those already applied. This means the final coat must be applied over the filler coat, before the latter has a chance to dry completely hard. If a satin or soft finish is desired, it is best to use this type of polyurethane. If the glossy type is used, it can be rubbed down to produce a soft, velvety look, but it requires a lot of rubbing.

Applying an Oil Finish to the Stock
An oil finish is considered by many gun owners to be the most handsome of all, especially if the wood of the stock is especially fine. The reason an oil finish is not usually applied by commercial gun makers is that it is a time-consuming process. However, the individual gun owner can get

a lot of pleasure out of refinishing his stock, and have a beautiful product as a result. While time-consuming, the process is quite simple. The following suggestions should prove helpful.

Use a regular gun-stock oil rather than boiled linseed oil. LinSpeed Oil, TrueOil, and Genuine Oil are three of the better-known brands. They are much easier and faster to use than linseed oil, and leave a handsome finish.

After the old finish is removed, the stock is thoroughly sanded and the whiskers sanded off (see the section on "Cutting Down Comb Height"). Apply a first heavy coat of oil cross-grain, with the grain, or against the grain—any way at all. This initial coat is used as a sealer and filler. When the stock has been filled with oil, hang it outdoors in the sun and wind to dry completely.

Repeat, putting on a second and third heavy coat of oil, drying completely outdoors between coats. Allow the third coat to dry for a full twelve hours at least.

Polish the stock with steel wool, rubbing until all the oil is removed and you are down to the bare wood again. The pores of the wood, however, remain completely filled, with the surface smooth. If there are dimples in the skin, repeat one or two more sloppy coats and cut the finish back to the wood again. Never start the final finish until all the pores are filled.

Apply the first final coat very lightly, with the fingertips, rubbing in and smoothing as you go along. The secret of a fine finish is to smooth out each drop of oil over as broad a surface as possible. Rub each drop in completely until it starts to "pull" as you rub your finger over it. Cover each section in turn, going on to the next without going back over a section already done. Make certain all spots are covered completely.

Allow this coat to dry in the sun and wind. Apply a thin second coat as you did the first, and hang the stock up to dry once more. Repeat this process until the stock takes on a sheen. Usually about five coats are required to obtain a good finish. Some wood requires more coats than others.

If you prefer a high gloss, wipe the stock clean with a special stock rubbing compound, and apply one final coat of stock oil. If you prefer a rubbed finish, rub the entire stock very lightly with the special stock-rubbing compound, rubbing just enough to remove some of the gloss but leaving a satin-glow look to the finish.

Whether you prefer the high-gloss or rubbed look, the final step is to wax the stock completely with good-quality paste wax, rubbing until hard. Finish off by wiping with a soft flannel cloth.

Blueing the Gun

Methods

There are essentially three methods for blueing a gun: (1) the accelerated process, (2) the fast, one-shot "hot blue" process, and (3) the traditional, slow-blue, slow-rust method, which requires repeated applications. In addition, "tough-up blueing" has been developed for refinishing small spots where the regular blueing has been scratched or worn off. Touch-up blueing is usually an accelerated process also, but it will be discussed separately because it may utilize either hot or cold methods.

The Accelerated Process

The accelerated process is based upon the principle that metal oxidizes more rapidly when it is warm. After cleaning and polishing, the gun metal is heated before the blueing solution is applied. As the solution dries, the metal oxidizes, leaving a heavy coating of rust. When the rust is removed, the metal is left a bluish tint. Repeated applications give the desired shade. Finally, a finishing oil is applied to stop all rusting action and to dry the surface. After this oil is removed, regular gun oil is applied, and the metal is polished to bring out the shiny blue luster of the coating.

There are several blueing products made to use in the accelerated process. Herter's Belgium Blue, Stoeger's Yankee Bluer, and Brownell's Dicropan IM are three of the most common. In addition to blueing solutions, a number of items of equipment are needed.

1. *A heating tank.* This should be about 6″ wide, 6″ deep, and 36″ long to handle the longest barrel. A long metal flower or window box is a good choice, or a tank especially made for the purpose may be purchased. Galvanized tanks should not be used since the blueing chemicals react with them and cause problems.

2. *Electric hotplate for heating the tank of water.*

3. *Electric grinder* with wire brush, hard rubber wheel, buffing pad attachments, and buffing compounds.

4. *Fine steel wool.*

5. *Large tongs or forceps* for handling cotton balls.

6. *Absorbent cotton, Q-tips, and soft wiping cloths.*

7. *Finishing oil* especially made for gun blueing.

8. *Regular gun oil.*

9. *Rubber gloves* to protect your hands, since blueing solution should never be allowed on your hands.

10. *Washing soda or a regular gun cleaner* such as Blu-Blak Cleaner or Brownell's Picro-Clean No. 909.

11. *Wooden dowel* small enough in diameter and long enough to go through the gun barrel and stick out both ends.

12. *Heavy string, picture wire, or coat hanger wire* to use in lowering barrel and other metal parts into the tank.

13. *Quart glass jar* to hold blueing solution. *Picture wire* to wrap around the neck of the jar to lower it into the tank.

14. *Mineral spirits* for cleaning finishing oil off the metal parts.

The following steps are used in the accelerated process of blueing.

1. Disassemble the gun. If only the barrel is to be blued, only this must be removed, but if the receiver and smaller parts are to be blued, the stock must be taken off and various small parts removed from the receiver. All aluminum and pot metal must be removed, because blueing salts will eat them up. Receivers made of cast powdered iron will not take blueing. Also, case-hardened receivers such as those found on some double-barrel shotguns will not blue by regular methods. They can be blued, but it requires special knowledge.

2. Polish the barrel and other parts to be blued. Use the electric grinder with the wire brush and the hard rubber wheel to remove rusted or pitted spots. Polish with buffing compounds and pad until metal is bright.

3. Place the dowel through the barrel and attach suspension wires or string to each end of the dowel. Tie strings or wires to every other metal part to be cleaned also. These strings or wires are used to hang the metal parts in the hot tank.

4. Heat a tankful of water, to which the proper amount of cleaning substance has been added. Boil the metal parts in this cleaning solution for five minutes. Remove metal parts and rinse in plain water. Be careful not to touch any metal with your fingers, as it leaves prints that prevent proper blueing. It is best to suspend all parts in the air with the strings or wires, so the parts do not touch any surface.

5. After you are certain all metal is thoroughly cleaned, dump out the cleaning water, rinse and clean the tank thoroughly, and partially fill it with plain, clean water. Place the quart jar containing the blueing solution in the tank so that the top of the jar sticks out several inches from the top of the water, making certain the water does not get into the jar. Turn on the heat, and bring the water to a hard boil.

6. When the water is boiling hard, lower the barrel and other gun parts into the tank, boiling them until you are sure they have reached the maximum temperature (usually about 5–10 minutes).

7. Meanwhile roll several pieces of cotton into round swabs the size

of golf balls to use in applying the blueing solution. Put on your rubber gloves, pick up a cotton swab with the tongs, and soak it in the blueing solution. Remove the barrel and, with even strokes the full length of the barrel, apply the solution to the barrel, doing this rapidly to take advantage of the metal's high temperature. The solution dries almost as soon as it is applied, but keep applying it as long as the hot metal will dry it. Do the same for all smaller metal parts. Use Q-tips dipped in the blueing for difficult-to-reach cracks and corners.

8. After about five minutes, or after the solution is thoroughly dry, you will notice a heavy coat of rust on the metal. This rust must be completely removed. The easiest way is to rub the metal surfaces hard with a handful of steel wool. Each time a ball of steel wool becomes clogged with rust, discard it and use a new piece. After cleaning away the rust, the metal should evidence a light bluish tint, but the color will deepen with each application.

9. Repeat heating, blueing, and polishing until the metal has reached the desired shade of blue-black. Be certain the metal is thoroughly reheated each time before another coating of blueing is applied. Rub the final application hard with the steel wool to remove every bit of rust, but do not return the metal to the boiling water.

10. To be certain all the solution and rust is removed, apply a thick coating of finishing oil to all blued parts, allowing the oil to remain on the parts (suspended in the air) overnight.

11. Wash the metal parts in mineral spirits the next day, and apply a coat of regular gun oil as you reassemble the gun. Leave the gun out of the case for a few days, recoat once or twice with gun oil until the oil is absorbed into the metal surface, then wipe clean with a soft cloth.

Some gunsmiths advocate pouring oil into the barrel and sealing up the ends of the barrel with proper-size wooden plugs before immersing it into the hot water. The only problem is that the heat often causes the plugs to blow out, allowing the oil to flow out into the tank. Therefore, the suggestions given here do not require you to seal off the barrel during water immersion. But this does mean you will have to dry and oil the inside of the barrel thoroughly as part of the total process. Any rust spots inside the barrel can usually be removed by ordinary cleaning methods.

The Hot-Blue Process

The blueing process just described is called the accelerated process. But there is still a faster method, known as the "hot-blue" process. It is a one-shot procedure. For this method, a minimum of two tanks is required: one for use for the cleaning solution and later the neutralizing solution, and one to hold the blueing solution. A third tank is helpful so that the cleaning solution, blueing solution, and neutralizing solution can each be put in its own tank at the same time. Professionals even use a fourth tank for soluble oil, but this is not necessary since the oil can be put on by hand. A number of different blueing solutions are used. Lynx-Line Blu-Blak and Brownell's Oxynate-7 are commonly used in professional shops. Stoeger's Lightning Bluer has also been used widely for many years. The following steps are used in the "hot-blue" method.

1. Disassemble the gun, sorting out the parts to be blued (see step 1 under the accelerated process).

2. Remove all old blueing and rust, and polish all parts to be blued (see step 2 under the accelerated process). The process of removing old blueing, rust, and so on may be further speeded up by dunking all parts in a stripping bath consisting of a 10 percent solution of nitric acid or a 10 to 20 percent solution of muriatic acid. Start with the 10 percent solution, running a test strip of blued metal through it, and increasing the percentage if the solution is not strong enough. However, be certain the metal is not immersed too long, for a deep etching will require too much polishing. After the old blueing is removed, rinse thoroughly with clear water and polish the metal bright on the polishing wheel. Be certain not to touch the metal with your bare hands.

3. Heat the tank of blueing solution to 285°. Also, heat the tank of cleaning solution to a good rolling boil. Washing soda, Blu-Blak Cleaner, or Brownell's Picro-Clean No. 909 may be used as cleaning solutions. If you are using a separate third tank, heat the neutralizing solution in it until it comes to a boil.

4. Lower the metal into the boiling cleaning solution and allow to remain for the period stipulated for the particular cleaner. Remove metal and rinse in clear water to wash off cleaning solution. If you do not have a third tank, empty the cleaning solution at this time, clean the tank, fill with the neutralizing solution, and heat this to a boil.

5. Place the metal in the tank of hot blueing solution, suspending the parts carefully so as not to touch the sides or bottom of the tank. The metal should start to blue in about five minutes, but a good color is usually reached in about 15 minutes. If a part is not taking the blueing well, remove it, wipe it with a pad of surgical gauze, and place it back in the blueing tank. After the parts are blued, rinse them in clear water.

6. Place all blued, rinsed parts in the neutralizer tank and boil for 30 minutes to neutralize the remaining blueing solution.

7. Finally, immerse the parts in a tank of soluble finishing oil for about 10 minutes, or if no separate oil tank is provided, coat the parts thoroughly with the oil, rubbing it on with large cotton swabs. Hang up the parts to drip oil and dry until the following day.

8. Rinse all parts in mineral spirits, recoating with regular gun oil as the gun is reassembled. Reoil the gun thoroughly, allowing the oil to stand for several days until absorbed into the pores of the metal. Wipe clean with a polishing cloth.

The Slow-Blue Process

The third process of gun blueing, the traditional slow-blue, slow-rust method will not be described here, since it is very time consuming. It is slow because the blueing is put on cold, and each time the blueing compound is applied, several days must elapse to give the metal a chance to oxidize before the following step is employed. However, the process produces a beautiful finish with a minimum of equipment. Stoeger's Gunsmith Bluer is a good example of a solution to use in this process. Directions for use come with the bottle.

Touch-up Blueing

Touch-up blue is designed for touching up a scratched place on the surface of your gun. Two brands, Minute Man and Numrich's 44–40, use an accelerated process, especially if the metal is slightly heated. The metal is first polished and cleaned, then heated slightly. The touch-up is applied with a Q-tip in long, even strokes. It is allowed to work for a few minutes, then wiped clean. If the color is not deep enough, another coat is applied after the metal is reheated. After the desired color is achieved, the area is rubbed thoroughly with gun oil.

Oxpho-Blue and Stoeger's Instant Blue are touch-up solutions that may be used cold. The metal surface is first polished. Oxpho-Blue is applied with a Q-tip and rubbed hard with steel wool. Then a second coat is put on with long, even strokes to complete the finish. Stoeger's Instant

Blue is applied, wiped off when milky, and followed by an acid solution, which produces the blue color. The process is repeated for a deeper color. Finally, gun oil is rubbed on to halt the oxidizing process. The surfaces are then polished lightly with very fine steel wool. For best results, carefully follow the instructions for each brand.

Directory of Manufacturers and Suppliers

Action Arms. Ltd. (UZI)
P.O. Box 9573
Philadelphia, Pennsylvania 19124
(215) 744-0100

AKM
(see Gun South Inc.)

Anschutz
(rifles and airguns available through Precision Sports)

Armsport, Inc. *(rifles, shotguns, black powder)*
3590 NW 49th Street
Miami, Florida 33142
(305) 635-7850

Astra
(handguns available through Interarms; shotguns available through L. Joseph Rahn, Inc.)

AUG
(available through interarms)

Auto-Ordnance Corporation *(rifles)*
Box 588
West Hurley, New York 12491

BSA Guns Ltd.
Armoury Road
Birmingham
B11 2PX England

Baikal International Trading Corp.
(shotguns)
12 Farview Terrace
Paramus, New Jersey 07652
(201) 845-8710

Bauer Firearms Corporation *(handguns, rifles)*
34750 Klein Avenue
Fraser, Michigan 48026
(313) 294-9130

Beeman's Precision Air Guns, Inc.
(also Anschutz, Feinwerkbau, Webley, Weihrauch, Wischo air guns)
47 Paul Drive
San Rafael, California 94903
(415) 472-7121

Benjamin Air Rifle Company
3205 Sheridan Road
Racine, Wisconsin 53403
(414) 633-5424

Beretta U.S.A. Corp. *(handguns, shotguns)*
17601 Indianhead Highway
Acco Keck, Maryland 20607
(301) 283-2191

Bernardelli *(handguns)*
(available through Interarms)

Bersa *(handguns)*
(available through Interarms)

Birchwood Casey *(gun care products)*
7900 Fuller Road
Eden Prairie, Minnesota 55344
(612) 937-7931

Bonanza Sports Manufacturing Co.
(reloading tools)
412 Western Avenue
Faribault, Minnesota 55021
(507) 332-7153

Maynard P. Buehler, Inc. *(mounts, screws)*
17 Orinda Highway
Orinda, California 94563
(415) 254-3201

Burris Company, Inc. *(scopes, mounts)*
331 East Eighth Street
Greeley, Colorado 80632
(303) 356-1670

Bushnell Optical Company *(scopes)*
(Div. of Bausch & Lomb)
2828 East Foothill Boulevard
Pasadena, California 91107
(213) 577-1500

CCI *(ammunition, primers)*
(see Omark Industries, Inc.)

CVA *(black powder guns)*
Connecticut Valley Arms, Inc.
5988 Peachtree Corners East
Norcross, Georgia 30092
(404) 449-4687

C-H Tool & Die Corporation *(reloading)*
P.O. Box L
Owen, Wisconsin 54460
(715) 229-2146

Charter Arms Corporation *(handguns, rifles)*
430 Sniffens Lane
Stratford, Connecticut 06497
(203) 377-8080

Churchill *(shotguns)*
(available through Kassnar)

Colt Industries, Firearms Division *(handguns, rifles, black powder guns)*
150 Huyshope Avenue
Hartford, Connecticut 06102
(203) 236-6311

Crosman Air Guns
980 Turk Hill Road
Fairport, New York 14450
(716) 223-6000

Daisy *(airguns)*
P.O. Box 220
Rogers, Arkansas 72756
(501) 636-1200

Dakota *(handguns)*
(see E.M.F. Company, Inc.)

Detonics Manufacturing Corporation *(handguns)*
2500 Seattle Tower
Seattle, Washington 98101
(206) 747-2100

Dixie Gun Works, Inc. *(black powder guns)*
Gunpowder Lane
Union City, Tennessee 38261
(901) 885-0561

E.I. Du Pont de Nemours & Co., Inc. *(gunpowder)*
Explosives Department
1007 Market Street
Wilmington, Delaware 19898
(302) 774-1000

Dynamit Nobel of America, Inc. *(Rottweil shotguns)*
105 Stonehurst Court
Northvale, New Jersey 07647
(201) 767-1660

E.M.F. Company, Inc. *(Dakota handguns, black powder)*
1900 East Warner Avenue, One D
Santa Ana, California 92705
(714) 966-0202

Erma *(rifles)*
(available through Beeman Precision Arms)

Euroarms of America *(black powder guns)*
1501 Lenoir Drive
Winchester, Virginia 22601
(703) 662-1863

Exel Arms of America, Inc. *(shotguns)*
14 Main Street
Gardner, Massachusetts 01440
(617) 632-5008

Fabrique Nationale Sports *(rifles)*
(available through Gun South, Inc.)

FAS *(pistols)*
(available through Beeman Precision Arms)

Federal Cartridge Corporation *(ammunition, primers, cases)*
2700 Foshay Tower
Minneapolis, Minnesota 55402
(612) 333-8255

Feinwerkbau *(air guns)*
(available through Beeman Precision Arms)

FIAS *(shotguns)*
(available through Kassnar Imports)

FIE *(shotguns, black powder guns, Franchi)*
P.O. Box 4866 Hialeah Lakes
Hialeah, Florida 33014
(305) 685-5966

Fox *(rifles, shotguns)*
(see Savage Arms)

Franchi *(shotguns)*
(available through FIE)

Freedom Arms *(handguns)*
One Freedom Lane
Freedom, Wyoming 83120
(307) 883-2468

Galil *(paramilitary, rifles)*
(available through Magnum Research Inc.)

Garbi *(shotguns)*
(available through L. Joseph Rahn, Inc.)

Griffin & Howe, Inc. *(sights, mounts)*
589 Broadway
New York, New York 10012
(212) 966-5323

Gun South Inc. *(Steyr-Mannlicher, Fabrique Nationale, AKM)*
P.O. Box 6607
7605 Eastwood Mall
Birmingham, Alabama 35210
1-800-821-3021

Harrington & Richardson, Inc. *(handguns, rifles, shotguns)*
Industrial Rowe
Gardner, Massachusetts 01440
(617) 632-9600

Heckler & Koch *(handguns, rifles, shotguns)*
14601 Lee Rd.
Chantilly, Virginia 22021
(703) 631-2800

Hege-Siber *(black powder)*
(available through Beeman Precision Arms)

Hercules, Inc. *(gunpowder)*
910 Market Street
Wilmington, Delaware 19899
(302) 575-5000

Heym *(rifles, shotguns)*
(see Paul Jaeger, Inc.)

High Standard, Inc. *(handguns)*
31 Prestige Park Circle
East Hartford, Connecticut 06108
(203) 289-9531

Hodgdon Powder Co., Inc.
7710 West 63rd Street
Shawnee Mission, Kansas 66202
(913) 362-5410

Hopkins & Allen Arms *(black powder guns)*
3 Ethel Avenue
Hawthorne, New Jersey 07507
(201) 427-1165

Hoppe's Gun Care Products
Penguin Industries, Inc.
Coatesville, Pennsylvania 19320
(215) 384-6000

Hornady Manufacturing Company *(reloading, ammunition)*
P.O. Box 1848
Grand Island, Nebraska 68801
(308) 382-1390

IGA
(available through Stoeger Industries)

Interarms *(handguns, also Astra and Virginian handguns, Bernardelli, Bersa, Rossi Star, Walther)*
10 Prince Street
Alexandria, Virginia 22313
(703) 548-1400

Ithaca Gun Company, Inc. *(shotguns)*
123 Lake Street
Ithaca, New York 14850
(607) 273-0200

Paul Jaeger, Inc. *(mounts, Heym, Schmidt & Bender)*
211 Leedom Street
Jenkintown, Pennsylvania 19046
(215) 884-6920

Iver Johnson's Arms, Inc. *(handguns, rifles)*
Wilton Avenue off South Avenue
Middlesex, New Jersey 08846
(201) 752-4994

Judd and Associates
P.O. Box 919
Madison, Connecticut 06443
(203) 245-7373

Kahles of America *(scopes)*
Main Street

Margaretsville, New York 12455
(914) 586-4103

Kassnar Imports *(rifles, black powder guns; FIAS shotguns)*
P.O. Box 6097
Harrisburg, Pennsylvania 17112
(717) 652-6101

Kimber *(rifles)*
9039 S.E. Jannsen Road
Clackamas, Oregon 97015
(503) 656-1704

Kleinguenther's Inc. *(rifles)*
P.O. Box 1261
Seguin, Texas 78155
(512) 379-8141

Krico *(rifles)*
(see Beeman Precision Arms)

Krieghoff Gun Company *(shotguns)*
(available through Shotguns of Ulm)

Leupold & Stevens, Inc. *(scopes, mounts; Nosler bullets)*
P.O. Box 688
Beaverton, Oregon 97075
(503) 646-9171

Llama *(handguns)*
(available through Stoeger Industries)

London Guns *(sights, mounts)*
1528 20th Street
Santa Monica, California 90404
(213) 828-8486

Luger *(handguns)*
(see Stoeger Industries)

Lyman Products Corporation *(black powder guns, sights, scopes, reloading tools)*
Route 147
Middlefield, Connecticut 06455
(203) 349-3421

Magnum Research Inc. *(Galil)*
2825 Anthony Lane South
Minneapolis, Minnesota 55418

MEC, Inc. *(reloading tools)*
Mayville Engineering Company, Inc.

P.O. Box 267
Mayville, Wisconsin 53050
(414) 387-4500

MTM Molded Products Company *(reloading tools)*
5680 Webster Street
Dayton, Ohio 45414
(513) 890-7461

Mandall Shooting Supplies, Inc. *(Sig-Hammerli air guns)*
7150 East Fourth Street
Scottsdale, Arizona 85252
(602) 945-2553

Mannlicher *(rifles)*
(see Gun South, Inc.)

Marksman Products, Inc. *(air guns)*
2133 Dominguez Street
Torrance, California 90509
(213) 775-8847

Marlin Firearms Company *(rifles shotguns)*
100 Kenna Drive
North Haven, Connecticut 06473
(203) 239-5621

Merit Gunsight Company *(optical aids)*
P.O. Box 995
Sequim, Washington 98382
(206) 683-6127

Millett Sights
16131 Gothard St.
Huntington Beach, California 92647
(714) 847-5245

O.F. Mossberg & Sons, Inc. *(rifles, shotguns)*
7 Grasso Avenue
North Haven, Connecticut 06473
(203) 288-6491

Navy Arms Company *(handguns, black powder guns, replicas)*
689 Bergen Boulevard
Ridgefield, New Jersey 07657
(201) 945-2500

Norma Precision *(ammunition, gun-*

powder, reloading cases)
(see Outdoor Sports Headquarters, Inc.)

Nosler Bullets, Inc.
(available through Leupold & Stevens, Inc.)

ODI
(see Omega Defensive Industries)

Olin Industries, Inc. *(Winchester ammunition, primers, cases, imported shotguns)*
East Alton, Illinois 62024
(618) 258-2000

Omark Industries, Inc. *(CCI, RCBS, Speer)*
Box 856
Lewiston, Idaho 83501
(208) 746-2351

Omega Defensive Industries *(handguns)*
124A Greenwood Avenue
Midland Park, NJ 07432

Outdoor Sports Headquarters, Inc. *(Norma)*
P.O. Box 1327
Dayton, Ohio 45401
(513) 294-2811

Pachmayr Gun Works, Inc. *(scope mounts)*
1220 South Grand Avenue
Los Angeles, California 90015
(213) 748-7271

Pacific Tool Company *(reloading tools)*
(Div. of Hornady Manufacturing Company)

Ponsness-Warren, Inc. *(reloading tools)*
P.O. Box 8
Rathdrum, Idaho 83858
(208) 687-1331

Precise International *(air guns)*
3 Chestnut Street
Suffern, New York 10901
(914) 357-6200

Precision Sports *(Norma)*
(Div. of General Sporting Goods Corporation)
798 Cascadilla Street
Ithaca, New York 14850
(607) 273-2993

RCBS, Inc. *(reloading tools)*
(see Omark Industries, Inc.)

L. Joseph Rahn, Inc. *(Astra, Garbi, Secolo shotguns)*
P.O. Box 94
104 E. Main St.
Manchester, Michigan 48158
(313) 428-9290

Redding-Hunter, Inc. *(reloading tools)*
114 Starr Road
Cortland, New York 13045
(607) 753-3331

Redfield *(sights, scopes)*
5800 East Jewell Avenue
Denver, Colorado 80224
(303) 757-6411

Remington Arms Company, Inc. *(rifles, shotguns, ammunition, primers)*
939 Barnum Avenue
Bridgeport, Connecticut 06602
(203) 333-1112

Rossi *(handguns, rifles, shotguns)*
(available through Interarms)

Rottweil *(shotguns)*
(available through Dynamit Nobel of America, Inc.)

Ruger *(handguns, rifles, shotguns, black powder guns)*
(see Sturm, Ruger & Company, Inc.)

Sako *(rifles, scope mounts)*
(available through Stoeger Industries)

Saver *(rifles, shotguns)*
(available through Judd and Assoc.)

Savage Arms *(shotguns, rifles; also Fox, Stevens)*
Springdale Road
Westfield, Massachusetts 01085
(413) 562-2361

Schmidt and Bender *(scopes)*
(available through Paul Jaeger, Inc.)

W & C Scott *(shotguns)*
(available through L.J. Rahn)

Secolo *(shotguns)*
(available through L. Joseph Rahn, Inc.)

Sheridan Products, Inc. *(air guns)*
3205 Sheridan Road
Racine, Wisconsin 53403
(414) 633-5424

Shiloh Products Co., Inc. *(black powder guns)*
100 Centennial Drive
P.O. Box 885
Big Timber, Montana 59011
(406) 932-4454

Shotguns of Ulm *(also Krieghoff)*
P.O. Box L
Ringoes, New Jersey 08850
(609) 466-9452

Sierra Bullets
10532 South Painter Avenue
Santa Fe Springs, California 90670
(213) 941-0251

Sig-Hammerli *(air guns)*
(available through Mandall Shooting Supplies, Inc.)

Sig-Saver *(handguns)*
(available through Interarms)

Smith & Wesson *(handguns, shotguns)*
2100 Roosevelt Avenue
Springfield, Massachusetts 01101
(413) 781-8300

Speer *(bullets)*
(see Omark Industries, Inc.)

Springfield Armory *(rifles)*
420 West Main Street
Geneseo, Illinois 61254
(309) 944-5138

Star *(handguns)*
(available through Interarms)

Sterling *(air guns)*
(available through Benjamin Air Rifle Co.)

Stevens *(rifles, shotguns)*
(see Savage Arms)

Steyr *(handguns)*
(See Gun South, Inc.)

Steyr Mannlicher *(rifles)*
(See Gun South, Inc.)

Stoeger Industries *(IGA, Llama, Luger, Sako, gun care products)*
55 Ruta Court
South Hackensack, New Jersey 07606
(201) 440-2700

Sturm, Ruger & Company, Inc. *(Ruger firearms)*
Lacey Place
Southport, Connecticut 06490
(203) 259-7843

Tasco *(scopes)*
7600 N.W. 26th Street
Miami, Florida 33122
(305) 591-3670

Taurus International, Inc. *(Taurus handguns)*
4563 Southwest 71st Avenue
Miami, Florida 33155
(305) 662-2529

Texan Reloaders, Inc. *(reloading tools)*
P.O. Box 74
Watseka, Illinois 60970
(815) 432-5065

Tecni-Mec *(shotguns)*
(available through L.J. Rahn)

Thompson/Center Arms *(black powder guns, handguns)*
Farrington Road
Rochester, New Hampshire 03867
(603) 332-2333

Tikka (see Armsport, Inc.) *(rifles, shotguns)*
SF-41160
Tikkakoshi, Finland

U.S. Repeating Arms Co. *(Winchester rifles, shotguns)*
275 Winchester Avenue
New Haven, Connecticut 06504
(203) 789-5000

UZI *(paramilitary)*
(see Action Arms Ltd.)

Valmet, Inc. *(rifles, shotguns)*
7 Westchester Plaza
Elmsford, New York 10523
(914) 347-4440

Ventura Imports *(shotguns)*
P.O. Box 2782
Seal Beach, California 90740
(213) 596-5372

Walther *(air guns, handguns)*
(available through Interarms)

Weatherby, Inc. *(rifles, shotguns, scopes, ammunition)*
2781 Firestone Boulevard
South Gate, California 90280
(213) 569-7186

Weaver Arms *(rifles)*
115 North Market Place
Escondido, California 92025
1-800-227-4896

Weihrauch *(air guns)*
(available through Beeman Precision Arms)

Dan Wesson Arms, Inc. *(handguns)*
293 Main Street
Monson, Massachusetts 01057
(413) 267-4081

Whitworth *(rifles)*
(available through Interarms)

Wichita Arms *(rifles, shotguns)*
444 Ellis Avenue
P.O. Box 11371
Wichita, Kansas 67211
(316) 265-0661

Williams Gun Sight Company *(sights, scopes, mounts)*
7389 Lapeer Road
Davison, Michigan 48423
(313) 653-2131

Winchester *(domestic rifles, shotguns)*
(see U.S. Repeating Arms Co.)

Winchester *(rifles, imported shotguns, ammunition, primers, cases)*
(see Olin Industries)

Winslow Arms Company *(rifles)*
P.O. Box 783
Camden, South Carolina 29020
(803) 432-2938

American and Foreign Associations of Interest to the Hunter and Shooter

UNITED STATES

ALABAMA
Alabama Gun Collectors Assn.
Dick Boyd, Secy., P.O. Box 5548, Tuscaloosa,
AL 35405

ARIZONA
Arizona Arms Assn.
Clay Fobes, Secy., P. O. Box 17061,
Tucson,
AZ 85731

CALIFORNIA

Calif. Hunters & Gun Owners Assoc.
V.H. Wacker, 2309 Cipriani Blvd.,
Belmont,
CA 94002

Greater Calif. Arms & Collectors Assn.
Donald L. Bullock, 8291 Carburton
St., Long
Beach, CA 90808

Los Angeles Gun & Ctg. Collectors Assn.
F.H. Ruffra, 20810 Amie Ave., Apt.
#9,
Torrance, CA 90503

COLORADO

Pikes Peak Gun Collectors Guild
Charles Cell, 406 E. Uintah St.,
Colorado
Springs, CO 80903

CONNECTICUT

Ye Conn. Gun Guild, Inc.
Robert L. Harris, P.O. Box 8, Cornwall Bridge,
CT 06754

FLORIDA

Florida Gun Collectors Assn., Inc.
John D. Hammer, 5700 Mariner Dr.,
304-W.
Tampa, FL 33609

Tampa Bay Arms Collectors' Assn.
John Tuvell, 24611—67th Ave. S.,
St. Petersburg, FL 33712

Unified Sportsmen of Florida
P.O. Box 6565, Tallahassee, FL 32314

GEORGIA

Georgia Arms Collectors
Cecil W. Anderson, P.O. Box 218,
Conley, GA
30027

HAWAII

Hawaii Historic Arms Assn.

John A. Bell, P.O. Box 1733,
Honolulu, HI
96806

IDAHO

Idaho State Rifle and Pistol Assn.
Tom Price, 3631 Pineridge Dr., Coeur
d'Alene,
ID 83814

ILLINOIS

Fox Valley Arms Fellowship, Inc.
P. O. Box 301, Palatine, IL 60067

Illinois State Rifle Assn.
224 S. Michigan Ave., Room 200, Chicago, IL
60604

Illinois Gun Collectors Assn.
P.O. Box 1694, Kankakee, IL 60901

Little Fort Gun Collectors Assn.
Ernie Robinson, P.O. Box 194, Gurnee, IL
60031

Mississippi Valley Gun & Cartridge Coll. Assn.
Lawrence Maynard, R.R. 2, Aledo, IL
61231

NIPDEA
c/o Phil Stanger, 1029 Castlewood
Lane,
Deerfield, IL 60015

Sauk Trail Gun Collectors
Gordell M. Matson, 3817–22 Ave.,
Moline, IL
61265

Wabash Valley Gun Collectors Assn., Inc.
Eberhard R. Gerbsch, 416 South St.,
Danville,
IL 61832

INDIANA

Indiana Sportsmen's Council-Legislative
Maurice Latimer, P.O. Box 93,
Bloomington,
IN 47402

Indiana State Rifle & Pistol Assn.
Thos. Glancy, P.O. Box 552, Chesterton, IN
46304

Southern Indiana Gun Collectors Assn., Inc.
Harold M. McClary, 509 N. 3rd St., Boonville,
IN 47601

IOWA
Central States Gun Collectors Assn.
Avery Giles, 1104 S. 1st Ave., Marshtown, IA
50158

KANSAS
Four State Collectors Assn.
M.G. Wilkinson, 915 E. 10th, Pittsburg, KS
66762

Kansas Cartridge Coll. Assn.
Bob Linder, Box 84, Plainville, KS
67663

Missouri Valley Arms Collectors Assn.
Chas. F. Samuel, Jr., Box 8204, Shawnee
Mission, KS 66208

KENTUCKY
Kentuckiana Arms Coll. Assn.
Tony Wilson, Pres., Box 1776, Louisville, KY
40201

Kentucky Gun Collectors Assn., Inc.
Ruth Johnson, Box 64, Owensboro, KY 42302

Kentucky Rifle Assn.
Ronald Gabel, 158 W. Unionville, RD 1,
Schnecksville, PA 18078

LOUISIANA
Washitaw River Renegades
Sandra Rushing, P.O. Box 256, Main St.,

Grayson, LA 71435

MARYLAND
Baltimore Antique Arms Assn.
Stanley I. Kellert, E-30, 2600 Insulator Dr.,
Baltimore, MD 21230

MASSACHUSETTS
Bay Colony Weapons Collectors, Inc.
Ronald B. Santurjian, 47 Homer Rd., Belmont,
MA 02178

Massachusetts Arms Collectors
John J. Callan, Jr., P.O. Box 1001, Worcester, MA 01613

MICHIGAN
Royal Oak Historical Arms Collectors, Inc.
Nancy Stein, 25487 Hereford, Huntingdon
Woods, MI 48070

MINNESOTA
Minnesota Weapons Coll. Assn., Inc.
Box 662, Hopkins, MN 55343

MISSISSIPPI
Mississippi Gun Collectors Assn.
Mrs. Jack E. Swinney, P.O. Box 1332, Hattiesburg, MS 39401

MISSOURI
Mineral Belt Gun Coll. Assn.
D.F. Saunders, 1110 Cleveland Ave., Monett,
MO 65708

MONTANA
Montana Arms Collectors Assn.
Lewis E. Yearout, 308 Riverview Dr. East,
Great Falls, MT 59404

The Winchester Arms Coll. Assn.
Lewis E. Yearout, 308 Riverview Dr. East,
Great Falls, MT 59404

NEW HAMPSHIRE
New Hampshire Arms Collectors, Inc.
Frank H. Galeucia, Rte. 28, Box 44,
  Windham,
NH 03087

NEW JERSEY
Englishtown   Benchrest   Shooters
  Assn.
Tony Hidalgo, 6 Capp St., Carteret,
NJ 07008

Experimental Ballistics Associates
Ed Yard, 110 Kensington, Trenton,
NJ 08618

Jersey Shore Antique Arms Collectors
Joe Sisia, P.O. Box 100, Bayville, NJ
08721

New Jersey Arms Collectors Club,
  Inc.
Angus Laidlaw, 230 Valley Rd.,
  Montclair, NJ
07042

NEW YORK
Empire State Arms Coll. Assn.
P.O. Box 2328, Rochester, NY 14623

Hudson-Mohawk   Arms   Collectors
  Assn., Inc.
Bennie S. Pisarz, 6 Lamberson St.,
  Dolgeville,
NY 13329

Iroquois Arms Collectors Assn.
Dennis Freeman, 12144 McNeeley
  Rd., Akron,
NY 14001

Mid-State Arms Coll. & Shooters
  Club
Jack Ackerman, 24 S. Mountain Terr.,
Binghamton, NY 13903

NORTH CAROLINA
North Carolina Gun Collectors Assn.
Jerry Ledford, Rt. 10, Box 144, Hick-
  ory, NC
28601

OHIO
Central Ohio Gun and Indian Relic
  Coll. Assn.
Coyt Stookey, 134 E. Ohio Ave.,
  Washington
C.H., OH 43160

Ohio Gun Collectors, Assn., Inc.
Drawer 24F, Cincinnati, OH 45224

The Stark Gun Collectors, Inc.
William I. Gann, 5666 Waynesburg
  Dr.,
Waynesburg, OH 44688

OKLAHOMA
Indian Territory Gun Collectors Assn.
P.O. Box 4491, Tulsa, OK 74104

OREGON
Oregon Cartridge Coll. Assn.
Richard D. King, 3228 N.W. 60th,
  Corvallis,
OR 97330

Oregon Arms Coll. Assn., Inc.
Ted Dowd, P. O. Box 25103, Portland,
  OR
97225

PENNSYLVANIA
Presque Isle Gun Coll. Assn.
James Welch, 156 E. 37 St., Erie, PA
16504

SOUTH CAROLINA
Balton Gun Club, Inc.
J.K. Phillips, Route 1, Belton, SC
29627

South Carolina Arms Coll. Assn.
P.O. Box 115, Irmo, SC 29063

SOUTH DAKOTA
Dakota Territory Gun Coll. Assn.,
  Inc.
Curt Carter, Castlewood, SD 57223

TENNESSEE
Memphis Antique Weapons Assn.

Jan Clement, 1886 Lyndale #1, Memphis TN 38107

Smoky Mountain Gun Coll. Assn., Inc.
Hugh W. Yarbro, P.O. Box 286, Knoxville, TN 37901

Tennessee Gun Collectors Assn., Inc.
M.H. Parks, 3556 Pleasant Valley Rd., Nashville, TN 37204

TEXAS
Houston Gun Collectors Assn., Inc.
P.O. Box 37369, Houston, TX 77237

Texas State Rifle Assn.
P.O. Drawer 340809, Dallas, TX 75234

UTAH
Utah Gun Collectors Assn.
Nick Davis, 5676 So. Meadow Lane #4, Ogden, UT 84403

VIRGINIA
Virginia Arms Collectors & Assn.
Clinton E. Jones, P.O. Box 333, Mechanicsville, VA 23111

WASHINGTON
Washington Arms Collectors, Inc.
J. Dennis Cook, P.O. Box 7335, Tacoma, WA 98407

WISCONSIN
Great Lakes Arms Coll. Assn., Inc.
E. Warnke, 1811 N. 73rd St. Wauwatosa, WI 53213

Wisconsin Gun Collectors Assn., Inc.
Rob. Zellmer, P.O. Box 181, Sussex, WI 53089

WYOMING
Wyoming Gun Collectors
Bob Funk, Box 1805, Riverton, WY 82501

NATIONAL ORGANIZATIONS
Amateur Trap Shooting Assn.
P.O. Box 458, Vandalia, OH 45377

American Association of Shotgunning
P.O. Box 3351, Reno, NV 89505

American Committee for International Conservation
c/o Natural Resources Defense Council, Inc.
917 15th Street, NW
Washington, DC 20005
Thomas B. Stoel, Secretary-Treasurer

American Coon Hunters Assn.
Ingraham, IL 62434
Floyd E. Butler, Secretary

American Defense Preparedness Assn.
Rosslyn Center, Suite 900, 1700 N. Moore St.,
Arlington, VA 22209

American Institute of Biological Sciences
1401 Wilson Boulevard
Arlington, VA 22209
Arthur Gentile, Ph.D., Executive Director

American Pheasant and Waterfowl Society
Route 1
Granton, WI 54436
Lloyd Ure, Secretary-Treasurer

American Police Pistol & Rifle Assn.
1100 N.E. 125th St., No. Miami, FL 33161

American Single Shot Rifle Assn.
L.B. Thompson, 987 Jefferson Ave., Salem, OH 44460

American Society of Arms Collectors, Inc.
Robt. F. Rubendunst, 6550 Baywood Lane,
Cincinnati, OH 45224

Armor & Arms Club
J.K. Watson, Jr., c/o Lord, Day & Lord, 25
Broadway, New York, NY 10004

Association for Conservation Information
c/o Arch Andrews
Colorado Division of Wildlife
6060 Broadway
Denver, CO 82016
Arch Andrews, President

Association of American Rod and Gun Clubs, Europe
First Perscom APO MSD
New York, NY 09081
Lee E. Miethke, Executive Officer

Association of Firearm and Toolmark Examiners
Eugenia A. Bell, Secy., 7857 Esterel Dr.,
LaJolla, CA 92037

Association of Midwest Fish and Game Commissioners
Forestry, Fish and Game Commission
Box 1028
Pratt, KS 67124
Fred Warders, Treasurer

Big Thicket Assn.
Box 198
Saratoga, TX 77585
Gene Feigelson, President

Boone & Crockett Club
205 South Patrick, Alexandria, VA 22314

Bounty Information Service
c/o Stephens College Post Office
Columbia, MO 65201
H. Charles Laun, Director

Brigade of the American Revolution
The New Windsor Cantonment

P.O. Box 207
Vails Gate, NY 12584
George Woodbridge, Commander

Cast Bullet Assn., Inc.
Ralland J. Fortier, 14193 Van Doren Rd.,
Manassas, VA 22111

Citizens Committee for the Right to Keep and Bear Arms
Natl. Hq.: 12500 N.E. Tenth Pl.,
Bellevue, WA
98005

Committee for Handgun Control
109 N. Dearborn, 13th Fl.
Chicago, IL 60602
Katherine Zartman, President

Committee for the Study of Handgun Misuse
109 N. Dearborn St., 13th Fl.
Chicago, IL 60602
Margaret Douaire, President

Company of Military Historians
North Main Street
Westbrook, CT 06498
Major William R. Reid, Administrator

Conservation Education Assn.
c/o Robert A. Darula
School University Programs
University of Wisconsin, Green Bay
Green Bay, WI 54302
Robert A. Darula, Secretary-Treasurer

Conservation Foundation
1717 Massachusetts Avenue, NW
Washington, DC 20036
William K. Reilly, President

Conservation and Research Foundation
Box 1445
Connecticut College
New London, CT 06320
Richard H. Goodwin, President

Conservation Services
Massachusetts Audubon Society

South Great Road
Lincoln, MA 01773
Wayne Hanley, Editor

Deer Unlimited of America, Inc.
P.O. Box 509, Clemson, SC 29631

Defenders of Wildlife
1244 19th Street, NW
Washington, DC 20036
John W. Grandy, IV, Executive Vice-
President

Ducks Unlimited, Inc.
One Waterfowl Way, Long Grove, IL
60047

Experimental Ballistics Associates
Ed Yard, 110 Kensington, Trenton,
NJ 08618

Federation of Western Outdoor Clubs
208 Willard North
San Francisco, CA 94118
Winchell T. Hayward, President

Firearms Research and Identification Assn.
18638 Alderbury Dr.
Rowland Heights, CA 91748
John Armand Caudron, President

Game Conservation International
900 NE Loop, 410, Suite D-211
San Antonio, TX 78209
Bob Holleron, Executive Director

Handgun Control
810 18th St., NW, Suite 607
Washington, DC 20006
Nelson T. Shields, Chairman

Handgun Hunters International
J. D. Jones, Dir., P. O. Box 357 MAG,
Bloomingdale, OH 43910

International Association of Wildlife Agencies
1412 16th Street, NW
Washington, DC 20036
Jack H. Berryman, Executive Vice
President

International Benchrest Shooters
Evelyn Richards, 411 N. Wilbur Ave.
Sayre, PA
18840

International Cartridge Coll. Assn., Inc.
Victor v. B. Engel, 1211 Walnut St.,
Williamsport, PA 17701

International Handgun Metallic Silhouette Assn.
Box 1609, Idaho Falls, ID 83401

International Wild Waterfowl Assn.
Box 1075
Jamestown, ND 58401
Carl E. Strutz, Secretary

Izaak Walton League of America
1800 North Kent Street, Suite 806
Arlington, VA 22209
Jack Lorenz, Executive Director

J.N. "Ding" Darling Foundation
209 South Village Drive
West Des Moines, IA 50265
Mr. Sherry R. Fisher, Chairman

Marlin Firearms Coll. Assn., Ltd.
Dick Paterson, Secy., 407 Lincoln
Bldg., 44
Main St., Champaign, IL 61820

Miniature Arms Collectors/Makers Society Ltd.
Joseph J. Macewicz, 104 White Sand
Lane,
Racine, WI 53402

National Assn. of Federally Licd. Firearms Dealers
Andrew Molchan, 2801 E. Oakland
Park Blvd.,
Ft. Lauderdale, FL 33306

National Association to Keep and Bear Arms
P.O. Box 78336
Seattle, WA 98178
Gerry Unger, President

National Audubon Society
950 Third Avenue
New York, NY 10022
Russell W. Peterson, President

National Automatic Pistol Collectors Assn.
Tom Knox, P.O. Box 15738, Tower Grove
Station, St. Louis, MO 63163

National Bench Rest Shooters Assn., Inc.
Stella Buchtel, 5735 Sherwood Forest Dr.,
Akron, OH 44319

National Board for the Promotion of Rifle Practice
Room 1205
Pulaski Building
20 Massachusetts Avenue, NW
Washington, DC 20314
Col. Jack R. Rollinger, Executive Officer

National Coalition to Ban Handguns
100 Maryland Ave., NW
Washington, DC 20002
Michael K. Beard, Executive Director

National Deer Hunter Assn.
1415 Fifth St. So., Hopkins, MN 55343

National Muzzle Loading Rifle Assn.
Box 67, Friendship, IN 47021

National Police Officers Assn. of America
Frank J. Schira, Ex. Dir., 609 West Main St.,
Louisville, KY 40202

National Reloading Mfrs. Assn., Inc.
4905 S.W. Griffith Dr., Suite 101, Beaverton,
OR 97005

National Rifle Assn.
1600 Rhode Island Ave., N.W., Washington,
DC 20036

National Shooting Sports Fdtn., Inc.
Arnold H. Rohlfing, Exec. Director,
1075 Post
Rd., Riverside, Ct 06878

National Skeet Shooting Assn.
Ann Myers, Exec. Director, P.O. Box 28188,
San Antonio, TX 78228

National Sporting Goods Assn.
717 North Michigan Avenue
Chicago, IL 60611
James L. Faltinek, Executive Director

National Trappers Assn.
15412 Tau Road
Marshall, MI 49068
Don Hoyt Sr., President

National Waterfowl Council
c/o Arkansas Game and Fish Commission
Game and Fish Building
Little Rock, AR 72201
Steve Wilson, Chairman

National Wildlife Federation
1412 16th Street, NW
Washington, DC 20036
Thomas L. Kimball, Executive Vice President

National Wild Turkey Federation, Inc.
P.O. Box 530, Edgefield, SC 29824

Natural Resources Council of America
Box 220
Tracys Landing, MD 20869
Michael Rawson, Executive Secretary

New England Advisory Board for Fish and Game Problems
115 Summit Avenue
West Warwick, RI 02839
Theodore Boyer, Secretary

North American Wildlife Foundation
1000 Vermont Avenue, NW
Washington, DC 20005
L.R. Jahn, Secretary

North-South Skirmish Assn., Inc.
T.E. Johnson, Jr., 9700 Royerton Dr.,
Richmond, VA 23228

Outdoor Writers Association of America
4141 West Bradley Road
Milwaukee, WI 53209
Edwin W. Hanson, Executive Director
Founded 1927

Pacific International Trapshooting Assn.
4408 Fourth Street, NW
Puyallup, WA 98371
Richard T. Stoner, Secretary-Manager

Pheasant Trust
Great Witchingham
Norwich, Norfolk, England
Philip Wayre, Honorary Director

Prairie Chicken Foundation
4122 Mineral Point Road
Madison, WI 53705
Paul J. Olson, President

Remington Society of America
Fritz Baehr, 3125 Fremont Ave.,
Boulder, CO
80302

Ruffed Grouse Society
994 Broadhead Road, Suite 304
Corapolis, PA 15108
Samuel R. Pursglove Jr., Executive
Director

Ruger Collector's Assn., Inc.
Nancy J. Padua, P.O. Box 211, Trumbull, CT
06611

SAAMI, Sporting Arms and Ammunition Manufacturers' Institute, Inc.
P.O. Box 218, Wallingford, CT 06492

Safari Club International
Holt Bodinson, 5151 E. Broadway,
Suite 1680,
Tucson, AZ 85711

Second Amendment Foundation
James Madison Building, 12500 N.E.

10th Pl.,
Bellevue, WA 98005

Sierra Club
530 Bush Street
San Francisco, CA 94108
Michael McCloskey, Executive Director

Society of Tympanuchus Cupido Pinnatus
433 East Michigan Street
Milwaukee, WI 53202
Robert T. Foote, President

Southeastern Association of Fish and Wildlife Agencies
P.O. Box 40747
Nashville, TN 37204
Gary T. Myers, Secretary-Treasurer

Southern California Schuetzen Society
Thomas Trevor, 13621 Sherman Way,
Van
Nuys, CA 91405

U.S. Revolver Assn.
Stanley A. Sprague, 59 Alvin St.,
Springfield,
MA 01104

Western Association of Fish and Wildlife Agencies
P.O. Box 25
Boise, ID 83707
Robert L. Salter, Secretary-Treasurer

Wilderness Society
1901 Pennsylvania Avenue, NW
Washington, DC 20006
William A. Turnage, Executive Dir.

Wildlife Management Institute
709 Wire Building
Washington, DC 20005
Daniel A. Poole, President

Wildlife Society
7101 Wisconsin Avenue, NW, Suite 611
Washington, DC 20014
Richard N. Denney, Executive Dir.

Winchester Arms Collectors Assn.
Lewis E. Yearout, 308 Riverview Dr., E., Great
Falls, MT 59404

World Fast Draw Assn.
Gene Cozzitorto, 1026 Llagas Rd., Morgan
Hill, CA 95037

World Wildlife Fund
1601 Connecticut Avenue, NW
Washington, DC 20009
Russell E. Train, President

AUSTRALIA
Sporting Shooters' Assn. of Australia Inc.
Mr. K. MacLaine, P.O. Box 210, Belgrave, Vict. 3160, Australia

CANADA

ALBERTA
Canadian Historical Arms Society
P.O. Box 901, Edmonton, Alb., Canada T5J 2L8

BRITISH COLUMBIA
B.C. Historical Arms Collectors
Ron Tyson, Box 80583, Burnaby, B.C. Canada V5H 3X9

NEW BRUNSWICK
Canadian Black Powder Federation
Mrs. Janet McConnell, P.O. Box 2876, Postal Sta. "A", Moncton, N.B. E1C 8T8, Can.

ONTARIO
Ajax Antique Arms Assn.
Monica A. Wright, P.O. Box 145, Millgrove, Ont., LOR 1VO, Canada

The Anglers and Hunters of Ontario
P.O. Box 15141, Peterborough, Ont., K9J 7H7, Canada

Glengarry Antique Arms
P.O. Box 122, R.R. #1, North Lancaster,
Ont., Canada

National Firearms Assn.
P.O. Box 4610 Sta. F, Ottawa, Ont., K1S 5H8
Canada

The Ontario Handgun Assn.
135 Centre St. East, Richmond Hill, Ont.,
L4C 1A5, Canada

Oshawa Antique Gun Coll. Inc.
Monica A. Wright, P.O. Box 145, Millgrove,
Ont., LOR 1VO, Canada

ENGLAND
Arms and Armour Society of London
A.R.E. North, Dept. of Metalwork, Victoria & Albert Museum, South Kensington, London SW7 2RL

British Cartridge Collectors Club
Peter F. McGowan, 15 Fuller St., Ruddington,
Nottingham

Historical Breechloading Smallarms Assn.
D.J. Penn, M.A., Imperial War Museum,
Lambeth Rd., London SE1 6HZ,
England Journal and newsletter are $8 a yr.
seamail; surcharge for airmail

National Rifle Assn. (British)
Bisley Camp, Brookwood, Woking, Surrey,
GU24 OPB, England

FRANCE
Syndicat National de l'Arquebuserie du Commerce de l'Arma Historique
B.P. No 3, 78110 Le Vesient, France

GERMANY (WEST)
Deutscher Schützenbund
Lahnstrasse, 6200 Wiesbaden-Klaren-
thal, West Germany

NEW ZEALAND
New Zealand Deerstalkers Assn.
Mr. Shelby Grant, P.O. Box 6514,
Wellington, New Zealand

SOUTH AFRICA
Historical Firearms Soc. of South
Africa
P.O. Box 145, 7725 Newlands, Repub-
lic of South Africa

South African Reloaders Assn.
Box 27128, Sunnyside, Pretoria 0132,
South
Africa

Fish and/or Game Departments

FEDERAL GOVERNMENT
Bureau of Sport Fisheries and Wildlife
Fish and Wildlife Service
Department of the Interior
18th and C Streets, N.W.
Washington, DC 20240

Environmental Protection Agency
401 M Street, S.W.
Washington, DC 20460

Forest Service
Department of Agriculture Building E
Rosslyn Plaza
Rosslyn, VA 22209

**Migratory Bird Conservation Com-
mission**
Department of the Interior Building
Washington, DC 20240

National Zoological Park
Smithsonian Institution
Adams Mill Rd.
Washington, DC 20009

STATE GOVERNMENTS

ALABAMA
Game and Fish Division
Department of Conservation and Nat-
ural Resources
64 North Union Street
Montgomery, AL 36104

ALASKA
Department of Fish and Game
Subport Building
Juneau, AK 99801

ARIZONA
Game and Fish Department
2222 West Greenway Road
Phoenix, AZ 85023

ARKANSAS
Game and Fish Commission
Game and Fish Commission Building
Little Rock, AR 72201

CALIFORNIA
Department of Fish and Game
Resources Agency
1416 Ninth Street
Sacramento, CA 95814

Wildlife Conservation Board
Resources Agency
1416 Ninth Street
Sacramento, CA 95814

COLORADO
Division of Wildlife
Department of Natural Resources
6060 Broadway
Denver, CO 80216

CONNECTICUT
Fish and Wildlife Unit
Department of Environmental Protection
State Office Building
165 Capitol Avenue
Hartford, CT 06115

DELAWARE
Division of Fish and Wildlife
Department of Natural Resources and
  Environmental Control
Tatnall Building
Legislative Avenue and D Street
Dover, DE 19901

DISTRICT OF COLUMBIA
Department of Environmental Services
1875 Connecticut Avenue, N.W.
Washington, DC 20009

FLORIDA
Game and Fresh Water Fish Commission
Farris Bryant Building
620 South Meridian Street
Tallahassee, FL 32304

GEORGIA
Game and Fish Division
Department of Natural Resources
270 Washington Street, S.W.
Atlanta, GA 30334

HAWAII
Fish and Game Division
Department of Land and Natural Resources
1179 Punchbowl Street
Honolulu, HI 96813

IDAHO
Fish and Game Department
600 South Walnut
P.O. Box 25
Boise, ID 83707

ILLINOIS
Wildlife Resources Division
Department of Conservation
605 State Office Building
400 South Spring Street
Springfield, IL 62706

INDIANA
Fish and Wildlife Division
Department of Natural Resources
State Office Building
Indianapolis, IN 46204

Land, Forests, and Wildlife
Resources Advisory Council
Department of Natural Resources
State Office Building
Indianapolis, IN 46204

IOWA
Fish and Wildlife Division
Conservation Commission
300 Fourth Street
Des Moines, IA 50319

KANSAS
Forestry, Fish and Game Commission
P.O. Box 1028
Pratt, KS 67124

KENTUCKY
Department of Fish and Wildlife Resources
State Office Building Annex
Frankfort, KY 40601

LOUISIANA
Game Division
Wildlife and Fisheries Commission
Box 44095
Capitol Station
Baton Rouge, LA 70804

MAINE
Department of Inland Fisheries and Game
284 State Street
Augusta, ME 04330

MARYLAND
Wildlife Administration
Department of Natural Resources
Tawes State Office Building
580 Taylor Avenue
Annapolis, MD 21401

MASSACHUSETTS
Department of Natural Resources
Leverett Saltonstall Building
100 Cambridge Street
Boston, MA 02202

MICHIGAN
Wildlife Division
Department of Natural Resources
Mason Building
Lansing, MI 48926

MINNESOTA
Game and Fish Division
Department of Natural Resources
Centennial Office Building
St. Paul, MN 55155

MISSISSIPPI
Game and Fish Commission
Game and Fish Building
402 High Street
P.O. Box 451
Jackson, MS 39205

MISSOURI
Game Division
Department of Conservation
2901 North Ten Mile Drive
P.O. Box 180
Jefferson City, MO 65101

MONTANA
Game Management Division
Department of Fish and Game
Helena, MT 59601

NEBRASKA
Game and Parks Commission
2200 North 33rd Street
P.O. Box 30370
Lincoln, NE 68503

NEVADA
Department of Fish and Game
P.O. Box 10678
Reno, NE 89510

NEW HAMPSHIRE
Game Management and Research Division
Department of Fish and Game
34 Bridge Street
Concord, NH 03301

NEW JERSEY
Wildlife Management Bureau
Fish, Game and Shellfisheries Division
Department of Environmental Protection
Labor and Industry Building
P.O. Box 1809
Trenton, NJ 08625

NEW MEXICO
Game Management Division
Department of Game and Fish
State Capitol
Sante Fe, NM 87503

NEW YORK
Division of Fish and Wildlife
Department of Environmental Conservation
50 Wolf Road
Albany, NY 12233

NORTH CAROLINA
Wildlife Resources Commission
Albermarle Building
325 North Salisbury Street
P.O. Box 27687
Raleigh, NC 27611

NORTH DAKOTA
Department of Game and Fish
2121 Lovett Avenue
Bismarck, ND 58505

OHIO
Wildlife Division
Department of Natural Resources
1500 Dublin Road
Columbus, OH 43224

OKLAHOMA
Department of Wildlife Conservation
1801 North Lincoln Boulevard
P.O. Box 53465
Oklahoma City, OK 73105

OREGON
Wildlife Commission
1634 Southwest Alder Street
P.O. Box 3503
Portland, OR 97208

PENNSYLVANIA
Game Commission
P.O. Box 1567
Harrisburg, PA 17120

RHODE ISLAND
Division of Fish and Wildlife
Department of Natural Resources
83 Park Street
Providence, RI 02903

SOUTH CAROLINA
Department of Wildlife Resources
1015 Main Street
P.O. Box 167
Columbia, SC 29202

SOUTH DAKOTA
Department of Game, Fish and Parks
State Office Building No. 1
Pierre, SD 57501

TENNESSEE
Game and Fish Commission
Ellington Agricultural Center
P.O. Box 40747
Nashville, TN 37220

TEXAS
Fish and Wildlife Division
Parks and Wildlife Department

John H. Reagan State Office Building
Austin, TX 78701

UTAH
Division of Wildlife Resources
Department of Natural Resources
1596 West North Temple
Salt Lake City, UT 84116

VERMONT
Department of Fish and Game
Agency of Environmental Conservation
Montpelier, VT 05602

VIRGINIA
Commission of Game and Inland Fisheries
4010 West Broad Street
P.O. Box 11104
Richmond, VA 23230

WASHINGTON
Department of Game
600 North Capitol Way
Olympia, WA 98501

WEST VIRGINIA
Division of Wildlife Resources
Department of Natural Resources
1800 Washington Street, East
Charleston, WV 25305

WISCONSIN
Game Management Bureau
Forestry, Wildlife and Recreation Division
Department of Natural Resources
P.O. Box 450
Madison, WI 53701

WYOMING
Game and Fish Division
P.O. Box 1589
Cheyenne, WY 82001

CANADA

ALBERTA
Alberta Fish and Wildlife Division
Natural Resources Building
9833—109th Street
Edmonton, Alberta T5K 2E1

BRITISH COLUMBIA
Environment and Land Use Commission
Parliament Building
Victoria, British Columbia V8V 1X4

BRITISH COLUMBIA
Department of Land, Forest and Water Resources
Parliament Building
Victoria, British Columbia V8V 1X4

MANITOBA
Department of Lands, Forests and Wildlife Resources
9—989 Century Street
Winnipeg, Manitoba R3H 0W4

NEWFOUNDLAND
Canadian Wildlife Service
Sir Humphrey Gilbert Building
Duckworth St.
St. John's, Newfoundland A1C 1G4

Department of Tourism
Wildlife Division
Confederation Building, 5th Floor
St. John's, Newfoundland

NORTHWEST TERRITORIES
Game Management Branch
Government of the Northwest Territories
Yellowknife, Northwest Territories

NOVA SCOTIA
Department of Environment
Box 2107
Halifax, Nova Scotia

Department of Land and Forests
Dennis Building
Granville Street
Halifax, Nova Scotia

ONTARIO
Wildlife Branch
Ministry of Natural Resources
Whitney Block
Toronto, Ontario M7A 1W3

PRINCE EDWARD ISLAND
Department of Fish and Wildlife
Environmental Control Commission
Box 2000
Charlottetown, Prince Edward Island C1A 7N8

QUEBEC
Department of Environment and Tourism
Box 2000
Charlottetown, Prince Edward Island C1A 7N8

QUEBEC
Department of Tourism, Fish and Game
150 St. Cyrille East—15th Floor
Quebec, Quebec G1R 4Y3

SASKATCHEWAN
Department of Natural Resources
Fisheries and Wildlife Branch
Administrative Building
Regina, Saskatchewan S4S 0B1

YUKON TERRITORY
Game Branch
Government of the Yukon Territory
Whitehorse, Yukon Territory

Measures of Weight

Avoirdupois or Commercial Weight
1 gross or long ton equals 2240 pounds.
1 net or short ton equals 2000 pounds.
1 pound equals 16 ounces equals 7000 grains.
1 ounce equals 16 drachms equals 437.5 grains.

The following measures for weight are now seldom used in the United States:
1 hundredweight equals 4 quarters equals 112 pounds (1 gross or long ton equals 20 hundredweights); 1 quarter equals 28 pounds; 1 stone equals 14 pounds; 1 quintal equals 100 pounds.

Troy Weight, Used for Weighing Gold and Silver
1 pound equals 12 ounces equals 5760 grains.
1 ounce equals 20 pennyweights equals 480 grains.
1 pennyweight equals 24 grains.
1 carat (used in weighing diamonds) equals 3.168 grains.
1 grain Troy equals 1 grain aviordupois equals 1 grain apothecaries' weight.

Apothecaries' Weight
1 pound equals 12 ounces equals 5760 grains.
1 ounce equals 8 drachms equals 480 grains.
1 drachm equals 3 scriples equals 60 grains.
1 scruple equals 20 grains.

NATIONAL RIFLE ASSOCIATION
Official Rules for
Highpower Rifle Matches

These Rules establish uniform standards for NRA sanctioned Highpower rifle competition. Where alternatives are shown, the least restrictive conditions apply unless the tournament program sets forth limitations. The Rules do not apply to Silhouette or International Shooting Union type competition. They supersede the January 1, 1982 and all earlier editions and remain in effect until specifically superseded.

Tournament sponsors may not alter these Rules. If sponsors require additional rules for special conditions, the additions must be fully set forth in the program for the competition concerned.

The arrangement and Rule numbering systems are such that corresponding Rules for other types of NRA competition are correspondingly located and numbered in the Rule Books for those competitions. Gaps in the sequence of Rule numbers result from there being a Rule in one or more of the other Rule Books which does not apply in this book.

Anyone wishing to submit recommendations for Rules changes may forward those recommendations to the Highpower Rifle Rules Committee in care of the National Rifle Association.

NOTE: *Rules in which major changes have been made since publication of the previous Rule Book are marked thus:* (• 1.1). All the revised wording is underlined.

1. NRA COMPETITION

1.0 NRA Competition—Competition which is authorized in advance of firing by the National Rifle Association. The program, range facilities and officials must comply with standards established by the NRA.

1.1 Sanctioned Tournament—A series of matches covered by an Official Program. Such matches may be all individual matches, all team matches, or a combination of both, which must be conducted by an NRA Affiliated Club or organization. They may be all fired matches or a combination of fired and aggregate matches. A tournament may be conducted on one day, or successive days, or may provide for intervening days between portions of the tournament, such as tournaments programmed to be conducted over more than one weekend.

1.2 Authorization—Before being publicized in programs or otherwise, the sponsoring organization of each type of competition mentioned in Rule 1.6 shall have agreed to comply with the current regulations for such competition and shall have received notice from the NRA that the competition applied for has been authorized.

1.3 Rules—The local sponsor of each type of competition must agree to conduct the authorized competition according to NRA Rules, except as these Rules have been modified by the NRA in the General Regulations for that type of competition.

1.4 General Regulations—The local sponsor of each type of competition must agree to comply with the General Regulations published by the NRA for the competition concerned.

1.5 Refusal or Withdrawal of NRA Authorization—The NRA may refuse to authorize or may withdraw its authorization for any competition which cannot, or does not, comply with the requirements for that competition.

1.6 Types of Tournaments—The types of tournaments listed below are those which are Sanctioned by NRA in its Competitive shooting program.

(a) *International Matches*—Arranged by the NRA with the recognized national shooting organization(s) of the countries concerned. The officials thereof are appointed by the NRA.

(b) *International Team Tryouts*—Are U.S. tournaments conducted under UIT or NRA International Rules organized or authorized by the NRA as Preliminary or Final Tryouts for the selection of International Team members. The officials thereof are appointed or approved by the NRA.

(c) *National Championships*—Organized by the NRA, and in some cases in conjunction with the National Board for the Promotion of Rifle Practice, Department of the Army, to form the National Matches. The officials thereof are appointed by the NRA, in some circumstances in cooperation with the NBPRP. These tournaments will be registered.

(d) *Regional and Sectional Championships*—Arranged between the NRA and a local sponsoring organization. These tournaments will be registered.

(e) *State Championships*—Annual tournaments conducted by State Rifle and/or Pistol Associations, affiliated with the NRA. Such State Associations may if desired, authorized local organizations to sponsor and conduct State Championships. In states where there is no NRA affiliated State Association the NRA may authorize a local organization to sponsor and conduct the State Championship. State Championships will be Registered Tournaments.

(f) *Registered Tournaments*—May be authorized by the NRA after application has been filed by the local NRA affiliated member organization which will act as the sponsor. Application forms are available from NRA on request. National Records may only be established in Registered Tournaments (Rule 17.1). All competitors in Registered Tournaments must be individual members of NRA, except for Junior (Rules 2.3, 2.3.1, and 2.3.2), who may be either members of NRA Affiliated Junior Clubs or individual members of NRA; except in the outdoor National Championships, where all competitors, junior or adult, must be individual members of NRA.

(g) *Approved Tournaments*—May be authorized by the NRA after application has been filed by the local NRA affiliated member organization which will act as the sponsor. Application forms are available from NRA on request.

(h) *Sanctioned Leagues*—(shoulder-to-shoulder or postal) May be authorized by the NRA after application has been filed by a local group or organization. Application forms are available from NRA on request. Sanctioned League and Sanctioned Postal League scores are used for classification.

(i) *Postal Matches*—Organized by the NRA and publicized to groups concerned through the AMERICAN RIFLEMAN and THE AMERICAN MARKSMAN announcements and special mailings.

1.7 Types of matches—

(a) *Match*—A complete event as indicated in the program for the awarding of certain specific prizes. A match may consist of one or of several stages. It may, in the case of aggregate matches, include the scores fired in several subsidiary matches.

(b) *Stage*—A portion of a match which consists of one or more strings fired in one position, distance, time allowance (slow or rapid fire, for example), or target.

(c) *Open Match*—A match open to anyone, except that if so stated in the program an open match may be limited to one or any combination of the following: *(a)* United States citizens; *(b)* members of the National Rifle Association of America; and/or *(c)* with respect to non-U.S. citizens, persons who are members in good standing of their respective National Shooting Federations or Associations.

(d) *NBPRP ("Leg") Matches*—The National Board for the Promotion of Rifle Practice sponsors Excellence in Competition ("Leg") Matches which are organized and conducted under the direction and rules of the NBPRP in conjunction with NRA Regional and State Championships. In addition, the NBPRP authorizes the NRA to conduct the National Trophy Matches in conjunction with the NRA National Championships. The combined events are titled "The National Matches".

All NBPRP matches are conducted in accordance with rules and regulations contained in Army Regulation 920-30; OP-NAVINST 3590.7B; AFR 50-17; and MCO P3590.13, titled "Rules and Regulations for National Matches" in its current form. They are not NRA Sanctioned Matches, and scores are not used for classification.

(e) *Restricted Match*—A match in which competition is limited to specified groups, i.e., juniors, women, police, civilians, veterans, etc.; or to specified classes, i.e., High Masters, Masters, Experts, Sharpshooters, Marksmen, etc.

(f) *Classified Match*—A match in which awards are given to the winners and to the highest competitors in several specified classes such as High Masters, Masters, Experts, Sharpshooters, Marksmen. The classification of competitors may be accomplished by the National Classification System (Sec. 19) or by other means. The program for classified matches must specify the groups or classes in which awards will be made.

(g) *Invitational Match*—A match in which participation is limited to those who have been invited to compete.

(h) *Squadded Individual Match*—A match in which each compettitior is assigned a definite relay and target by the Statistical Office. Failure to report on the proper relay or firing point forfeits the right to fire. All entries must be made before firing commences in that match, except when otherwise stated in the tournament program.

(i) *Unsquadded Individual Match*—A match in which the competi-

tor is not assigned a definite relay or target by the Statistical Office. The competitor reports to the Range Officer within the time limits specified in the program and is then assigned to a target and a relay in which to fire.

(j) *Re-Entry Match*—A match in which the competitor is permitted to fire more than one score for record; one or more of the highest scores being considered to determine the relative rank of competitors. The number of scores which may be fired, and the number of high scores to be considered in deciding the relative rank of competitors must be specified in the program. Scores fired in these matches shall not be used for classification purposes.

(k) *Squadded Team Match*—A match in which the teams are assigned a definite time to fire. Teams may be assigned one or more adjacent targets. All entries must be made before firing commences in that match. The entire team must report and fire as a unit.

(l) *Unsquadded Team Match*—A match in which the teams may report at the firing line at any time within the limits specified in the program, targets being assigned by the Range Officer. The entire team must report and fire as a unit, unless the program provides otherwise.

(m) *Aggregate Match*—An aggregate of the scores from two or more matches. This may be an aggregate of match stages, individual matches, team matches, or any combination, provided the tournament program clearly states the matches which will comprise the aggregate. Entries in aggregate matches must be made before the competitor commences firing in any of the matches making up the aggregate match.

2. ELIGIBILITY AND CATEGORIES OF COMPETITORS

Eligibility and Categories of Competitors. The conditions of a match shall prescribe the eligibility and categories of competitors, team or individuals, in accordance with Rule 1.6 and/or the definition contained in Section 2. Any limitations of eligibility to compete must be stated in the Match Program.

INDIVIDUALS

• **2.1 Members of the National Rifle Association**—Any individual member, including Benefactors, Patrons, Endowment, Life, Annual, Associate, Non-Resident and Junior members.

2.1.1 Non-U.S. Citizens—Non-U.S. Citizens who are also non-Residents, who are not members of the National Rifle Association of America, but who are members in good standing of their own National Association, and have adequate proof of such membership in hand, may compete in any NRA Sanctioned Tournament, unless further restrictions are imposed by conditions stated in the program.

2.1.2 Categories and Special Awards—If there are a sufficient number of competitors of a specific group (i.e., Women, Juniors, Service, etc.), a match sponsor may, at his discretion, establish a separate category for this group and make classification awards within this category, such as 1st Master Service, 3rd Sharpshooter Civilian, and so on. However, if there are insufficient entries of a specific group to warrant such a separation, and if the sponsor still wishes to provide recognition to this specific group, he may provide an overall Special Award such as High Woman, High Junior, etc., and all competitors in this specific group would be eligible for this one Special Award. Details concerning categories and special awards must be clearly outlined in the tournament program.

2.2 Civilian—Any civilian including all members of the Reserve Officers Training Corps (ROTC, NROTC and AFROTC), personnel of the State Security Forces (e.g., State Guard organizations having no federal recognition), retired members of each of the several services comprising the Armed Forces of the United States, and members and former members entitled to receive pay, retirement pay, retainer pay or equivalent pay, are classified as civilians except as noted in the example below. All competitors who are enrolled undergraduates of any of the service academies will be considered as civilians, and may compete in collegiate and ROTC categories.

Individuals of any Reserve or National Guard component who, *during the present calender year,* have not competed as National Guard (2.5) or Regular Service (2.6) or Reserve component (2.7) *and* have not been provided Service support for competition (in the form of firearms, ammunition, payment of travel or other expenses), wholly or in part, may fire as civilians and may be eligible to compete as Junior or Collegiate. The provision of firearms and ammunition for a specific competition (i.e., National Matches or NBPRP Regional Leg Matches), when such is available to both military and civilian competitors, is not considered Service support under this Rule.

Unless specifically authorized to do so by the tournament program, members of the regular Army, Navy, Air Force, Marine Corps, Coast Guard, members of the Reserve components on active duty, retired personnel of the several services comprising the Armed Forces of the United States on active duty, or police (2.4) are not permitted to compete as civilians.

2.2.1 Senior—A person may compete as a Senior beginning on January 1, of the calendar year in which the 60th birthday occurs.

2.3 Junior—A person may also compete as a Junior until December 31 of the calendar year in which his or her twentieth birthday occurs.

2.3.1 Intermediate Junior—A Junior may also compete as an Intermediate Junior from January 1 of the calendar year in which his or her fifteenth birthday occurs through December 31 of the calendar year in which his or her seventeenth birthday occurs.

2.3.2 Sub-Junior—A Junior may also compete as a Sub-Junior through December of the calendar year in which his or her fourteenth birthday occurs.

2.4 Police—Any regular, full time member of a regularly constituted law-enforcement agency, including the enforcement officers of the several departments of the United States Government; State, County or Municipal Police Departments; Highway Patrols; Penal Institution Guards; full time salaried Game Wardens, Deputy Game Wardens; Deputy Sheriffs and Police Firearms Instructors for Law Enforcement Agencies; regularly organized Railroad or Industrial Police Departments, Bank Guards and Armored Truck and Express Company Guards.

Special Officers, Honorary Officers, Civilian Instructors, Deputy Sheriffs, Deputy Game Wardens or Police Officers who are not on a full time, full pay basis in a single department are not eligible to compete as Police.

2.5 National Guard—Federally recognized officers or enlisted members of the Army National Guard, Air National Guard, or the Naval Militia of the several states, territories, the District of Columbia, or the Commonwealth of Puerto Rico, who are not on extended active duty.

2.6 Regular Service—Officers or enlisted members of the Regular United States Army, Navy, Air Force, Marine Corps, Coast Guard, and members of Reserve components thereof, who are on extended active duty; provided the term "Reserve Components" shall include Army National Guard and Air National Guard called into federal service and while in such status.

2.7 Reserve Components—Officers and enlisted members of any Reserve component of the Armed Forces, exclusive of the Army National Guard and the Air National Guard of the United States, not on extended active duty.

2.8 College—Regularly enrolled full-time undergraduate students who carry 12 semester hours or the equivalent, who comply with the eligibility rules of their institution, and who have not received a bachelor's degree.

2.9 School—Regularly enrolled undergraduate students of any primary or secondary school, who comply with the eligibility rules of their institutions.

TEAMS

2.10 Team Representation—No individual may be a Team Captain, Coach, firing member, or alternate firing member on more than one team in any match.

Note: Entries will not be accepted from 'Pickup' teams (teams whose members are selected without regard to club or other organization affiliation) unless the program specifically provides for such eligibility. Scores fired by pickup teams are not eligible for National Records.

2.11 Affiliated Club Teams (Art. III, Sec. 4 (c) NRA Bylaws)—All members of such teams must have been active fully-paid members of the club which the team represents, for a period of at least 30 days immediately prior to the competition; and the club must be affiliated with the NRA and in good standing. If specifically allowed by conditions of the program, a person not a club member may serve as the coach of an Affiliated Club team. (He may not be a firing member.)

2.11.1 Affiliated Other Organizations (Art. III, Sec. 4 (b) NRA Bylaws)—All members of such teams must have been fully-paid members of the organization the team represents, for a period of at least 30 days immediately prior to the competition, and the organization must be affiliated with the NRA and in good standing.

2.12 State Association Teams (Art. III, Sec. 4 (a) NRA Bylaws)—Members of such teams must be bona fide residents of the State represented, and individual members of the State Rifle and/or Pistol Association represented if such State Association provides for individual membership, or be members of a rifle and/or pistol club which is affiliated and in good standing with the State Association concerned at the time of the competition. State Association Teams permitted to enter the competition concerned by the tournament program conditions must be authorized and accredited by the State Association for that tournament. Authorization shall be signed by the

State Association President, Vice President or Secretary. Such State Associations must be affiliated and in good standing with the NRA at the time of the competition. If specifically allowed by conditions of the program, a person not a State Association member may serve as the coach of a State Association Team. (He may not be a firing member.)

Note: Teams representing State Associations, Leagues and other associations (composed of more than one club) are not club teams. Such teams may enter NRA sanctioned matches only when the program specifically authorizes such entry.

2.13 Regular Service, National Guard or Other Armed Forces Reserve Teams—Members of such teams must have been commissioned or enlisted members of their respective service for a continuous period of at least 30 days immediately preceding the day of competition. Army National Guard, Air National Guard, and Naval Militia personnel may be combined into a single team.

2.14 Police Teams—Members of such teams must have been regular, full time members of their respective organization and in active service for a continuous period of at least 30 days immediately preceding the day of competition.

2.15 Civilian Club Teams—Firing and alternate members of such teams must comply with the requirements of Rules 2.2 and 2.11.

2.16 College Teams—Firing and alternate members of such teams must comply with Rules 2.8 and 2.11.

2.17 School Teams—Firing and alternate members of such teams must comply with Rules 2.9 and 2.11.

2.18 Junior Club Teams—Firing and alternate members of such teams must comply with Rules 2.3 or 2.3.1 or 2.3.2 and 2.11.

2.20 Residence—In those matches which are limited to residents of any specified geographical area a "resident" is defined as:

(a) A person who lives within a specified area for at least 30 days immediately prior to the day of the match, whether or not his employment is at a place requiring him to commute or travel into some other area.

(b) A person who has been regularly employed within the specified area for at least 30 days immediately prior to the day of the match and who has maintained domicile in that area for the same period of time, although his permanent residence is located outside the specified area.

(c) Military, Naval and Air Force Personnel: The place of residence of members of the Military, Naval and Air Force establishments on active duty is defined as the place at which they are stationed by reason of official orders, provided they have been so stationed within the specified area for a period of at least 30 days immediately prior to the day of the match. In the case of Retired, Reserve, or National Guard personnel not on active duty, the provisions of paragraphs (a) and (b) will apply. Naval personnel assigned on sea duty qualify for a residence in the area which is the usual base or home port of the unit to which attached.

(d) Federal and State Law Enforcement Officers: The provisions of paragraph (c) will apply.

3. EQUIPMENT AND AMMUNITION

This section defines authorized equipment. Where alternative types of equipment are shown, the least restrictive conditions apply unless the tournament program sets forth limitations.

3.1 Service Rifle—U.S. Rifle, Caliber .30 M1 or caliber 7.62 mm M1, as issued by the U.S. Armed Forces, or the same type and caliber of commercially manufactured rifle, having not less than 4½ pound trigger pull, with standard type stock and standard type leather or web sling. External alterations to the stock will not be allowed. The application of synthetic coatings, which includes those containing powdered metal, to the interior of the stock to improve bedding is authorized provided the coating does not interfere with the function or operation of safety features. The front and rear sights must be United States Army design, but may vary in dimensions of rear sight aperture and front sight blade. The internal parts of the rifle may be specially fitted and include alterations which will improve the functioning and accuracy of the arm, provided such alterations in no way interfere with the proper functioning of the safety devices as manufactured. (A device consisting of a modified cartridge clip which is intended to permit single loading form the clip into the chamber during slow fire is considered an internal alteration to improve functioning and is permissible under this rule.)

3.1.1 Service Rifle—U.S. Rifle, Caliber 7.62 mm M14 as issued by the U.S. Armed Forces or the same type and caliber of commercially manufactured rifle, having not less than a 4½ pound trigger pull, with standard type stock and standard leather or web sling. The rifle must be so adjusted as to be incapable of automatic fire without removing the stock and changing parts. In all courses and in all positions the 20-round box magazine will be attached. The hinged butt plate will be used only in the folded position. The gas system must be fully operational. External alterations to the stock will not be allowed. The application of synthetic coatings, which includes those containing powdered metal, to the interior of the stock to improve bedding is authorized provided the coating does not interfere with the function or operation of safety features. The front and rear sights must be of United States Army design, but may vary in dimensions of rear sight aperture and front sight blade. The internal parts of the rifle may be specially fitted and include alterations which will improve the functioning and accuracy of the arm, provided such alterations in no way interfere with the proper functioning of the safety devices as manufactured.

3.1.2 Service Rifle—U.S. Rifle, Caliber 5.56 mm M16 series as issued by the U.S. Armed Forces, or the same type and caliber of commercially procured rifle, without bipod or grenade launcher, having not less than a 4½ pound trigger pull, with standard-type stock, pistol grip, handguard, and leather or web sling. The rifle must be so modified as to be incapable of automatic fire without removing, replacing, or altering parts. In all courses of fire and in all positions the standard 20-round or 30-round box magazine will be attached. The gas system must be fully operational. External alterations to the barrel, upper and lower receivers, stock, handguard, or pistol grip will not be allowed, except that a device may be attached to prevent selector lever movement to the auto position. The front and rear sights must be the standard design as issued by the U.S. Armed Forces on this rifle.

3.2 Any Rifle—A rifle with no restrictions on sights, ammunition or accessories, except that it must be safe to competitors and range personnel. The provisions of Rule 3.16.1 apply to this definition.

3.3 NRA Match Rifle—A center fire rifle with metallic sights and a magazine capable of holding not less than 5 rounds. The Service Rifle may be used unless otherwise specified in the program. Any Service Rifle used as an NRA Match Rifle shall conform to Rules 3.1, 3.1.1, or 3.1.2 as applies to trigger pull. Any semi-automatic rifle modified for use as an NRA Match Rifle must conform with Rule 3.14 for use in the standing position. The 20 round box magazine may only be used in the kneeling, sitting, and prone positions. Note: The use of the 20 round box magazine in the standing position is permitted with M14 rifles used as NRA Match Rifles, provided that the only modification made is replacement of the sights. Any further modifications to the exterior of the rifle, such as a different stock, barrel dimensions, or integral flash hider, require the rifle to be used without the 20 round box magazine in the standing position. A shorter box magazine may be used, provided that it conforms with Rule 3.14.

3.3.1 NRA Match Rifle-English Speaking Countries—A center fire rifle with metallic sights. This rifle must meet the requirements to be a legal Palma rifle in the participant's home country, and may only be used by someone who is a foreign national, and can provide evidence thereof. It may be used in all matches where a rifle under Rule 3.3 would be legal. (It would be wise for a foreign competitor to have a copy of his own country's rifle rule, or letter of certification from his National Association with him when competing under this rule.)

3.4 Sporting Rifle—A center fire rifle of any caliber, not equipped with palm rest or Schuetzen type buttplate, weighing not over 9.5 pounds excluding sling and including sights.

3.5 Automatic Rifle—No rifle is permitted unless it is incapable of automatic fire without the replacement or alteration of parts.

3.7 Sights

(a) Metallic—

(1) Non-corrective:
Any sighting system constructed of metal or equivalent which provides a method of aiming by aligning 2 separate but visible sights or reference points, mounted on the rifle, including tube sights and non-magnifying color filters.

(2) Corrective: (Applies to rear sight, only)
Same as (1), except that a lens or system of lenses, not containing an aiming reference or reticle at the focal plane of any such lens or system of lenses, may be included in such system.

(b) Telescopic—Any sighting system which includes a lens or system of lenses and an aiming reference or reticle at the focal plane of a lens or system of lenses.

(c) Any—Any sight without restriction as to material or construction.

Any sighting device programmed to activate the firing mechanism is prohibited.

3.8 Spotting Scope—The use of a telescope to spot shots is permitted. It may be positioned forward of the shooter's forward shoulder.

3.9 Shooting Kits—The shooting kit and/or shooting stool may not be placed forward of the shooter's forward shoulder on the firing line. (Use of a rifle rest forward of the forward shoulder is prohibited except in the prone position for resting the rifle between shots.)

3.10 Ground Cloth or Ground Pad—A ground cloth or ground pad may be used provided it is not constructed or used in a manner to provide artificial rest or support.

3.11 Gloves—Gloves may be worn which do not form an artificial support.

3.12 Padding—Shoulder pads, sling pads and elbow pads may be worn provided they are constructed so as not to provide artificial support. A button, hook or strap may be placed on the sleeve of the shooting coat to support the sling loop that is placed on the upper arm.

3.13 Slings—A sling may be a strap or straps made of leather, webbing, or synthetic material, and hooks, buckles, and keepers as necessary for attachment to the rifle and adjustment to the shooter. Unless otherwise specified in match conditions or position descriptions (Rule 5.12), the sling may be used in connection with one arm to steady the rifle.

3.14 Palm Rest—Any attachment or extension which aids the normal hand grip and support of the rifle by the forward hand that extends to a depth of more than 3¼ inches below the centerline of the bore IS A PALM REST. A palm rest may be used only in the standing position in "Any Rifle" matches. The standard box magazines of Service Rifles are not considered palm rests.

3.15 Schuetzen Type Buttplate—A butt or buttplate having a curved rear surface in which the depth of the curve exceeds ½-inch when measured from a straight line drawn from the top to the bottom of the buttplate; or any buttplate having a hook or stud engaging in a hole or receptacle in the shoulder of the shooting coat or shirt; or any buttplate having a knob or prong extending rearward more than ½-inch from the heel or toe of the butt. *May be used only in those matches where it is specifically permitted by the program.*

3.16 Release Triggers—Triggers which function on release are prohibited.

3.16.1 Compensators and Muzzle Brakes—The use of compensators and muzzle brakes is prohibited.

3.17 Ammunition—
(a) *Service*—Ammunition manufactured for or by the Government and issued for use in service arms. The use of armor-piercing ammunition may be prohibited by local range or match regulations. Use of tracer or incendiary ammunition is prohibited.
(b) *Any*—Ammunition of any description that may be fired without danger to competitors or range personnel. Tracer or incendiary ammunition is prohibited. The use of armor-piercing or any other type ammunition may be prohibited by local range or match regulations.

3.18 General—All devices or equipment which may facilitate shooting and which are not mentioned in these Rules, or which are contrary to the spirit of these Rules and Regulations, are forbidden.

The Official Referee, Jury or Match Director shall have the right to examine a shooter's equipment or apparel. The responsibility shall be upon the competitor to submit questionable equipment and apparel for official inspection and approval in sufficient time prior to the beginning of a match so that it will not inconvenience either the competitor or the official.

3.19 Eye Protection—All competitors and other personnel in the immediate vicinity of the range complex are urged to wear eye protection devices or similar eye protection.

3.20 Ear Protection—All competitors and other personnel in the immediate vicinity of the range complex are urged to wear hearing protection devices or similar ear protection.

4. TARGETS

• **4.1 Official Targets**—In NRA Sanctioned competition, only targets printed by NRA Licensed Manufacturers, bearing the Official Competition target seal, or military targets issued by the Armed Services, without modification except as authorized by NRA, will be used.

Note: The military target for 200 and 300 yards is known as "Target, Rifle, Competition, Short Range" and the target for 500 and 600 yards is known as "Target, Rifle, Competition, Mid-Range." These definitions are abbreviated as "SR" and "MR" respectively in the descriptions which follow for the reduced targets. Military targets, SR, MR and LR should all be ordered from the Director of Civilian Marksmanship.

OFFICIAL TARGET DIMENSIONS

All Highpower rifle targets have single bullseyes.

4.2 100 Yard Targets

a. N.R.A.—No. SR-1—Reduction of the SR Target for use at 100 yards to simulate the 200-yard stages of the National Match Course.

Aiming Black	(inches)	Rings in White	(inches)
X ring	1.35	8 ring	9.35
10 ring	3.35	7 ring	12.35
9 ring	6.35	6 ring	15.35
		5 ring	18.35

b. N.R.A.—No. SR-21—Reduction of the SR-3 target to simulate the 300-yard stage of the National Match Course at 100 yards.

Aiming Black	(inches)	Rings in White	(inches)
X ring	0.79	7 ring	8.12
10 ring	2.12	6 ring	10.12
9 ring	4.12	5 ring	12.12
8 ring	6.12		

c. N.R.A.—No. MR-31—Reduction of the MR-1 target to simulate the 600-yard stage of the National Match Course at 100 yards.

Aiming Black	(inches)	Rings in White	(inches)
X ring	0.75	6 ring	7.75
10 ring	1.75	5 ring	9.75
9 ring	2.75		
8 ring	3.75		
7 ring	5.75		

4.3 200 Yard Targets

a. No. SR—Military "Target, Rifle, Competition, Short Range."

Aiming Black	(inches)	Rings in White	(inches)
X ring	3.00	8 ring	19.00
10 ring	7.00	7 ring	25.00
9 ring	13.00	6 ring	31.00
		5 ring	37.00

b. N.R.A.—No. SR-42—Reduction of the SR-3 target to simulate the 300-yard stage of the National Match Course at 200 yards.

Aiming Black	(inches)	Rings in White	(inches)
X ring	1.90	7 ring	16.56
10 ring	4.56	6 ring	20.56
9 ring	8.56	5 ring	24.56
8 ring	12.56		

c. N.R.A.—No. MR-52—Reduction of the MR-1 target to simulate the 600-yard stage of the National Match Course at 200 yards.

Aiming Black	(inches)	Rings in White	(inches)
X ring	1.79	6 ring	˙15.79
10 ring	3.79	5 ring	19.79
9 ring	5.79		
8 ring	7.79		
7 ring	11.79		

d. N.R.A.—No. SR-5—Same scoring ring dimensions as No. SR—Military with scoring rings through 7 only; paper size 28 × 28 inches. For use at 200 yards on ranges with small target frames.

4.4 300 Yard Targets

a. N.R.A.—No. SR-3—Enlarged aiming black for use in 300-yard rapid fire matches only. Scoring rings the same as the SR target, with the 8-ring in the aiming black.

Aiming Black	(inches)	Rings in White	(inches)
X ring	3.00	7 ring	25.00
10 ring	7.00	6 ring	31.00
9 ring	13.00	5 ring	37.00
8 ring	19.00		

b. N.R.A.—No. MR-63—Reduction of the MR-1 target for use at 300 yards to simulate the 600-yard stage of the National Match Course.

Aiming Black	(inches)	Rings in White	(inches)
X ring	2.85	6 ring	23.85
10 ring	5.85	5 ring	29.85
9 ring	8.85		
8 ring	11.85		
7 ring	17.85		

4.5 500 Yard Target

No. MR—"Target, Rifle, Competition Mid-Range." Used in 500-yard matches only.

Aiming Black	(inches)	Rings in White	(inches)
X ring	6.00	7 ring	36.00
10 ring	12.00	6 ring	48.00
9 ring	18.00	5 ring	60.00
8 ring	24.00		

4.6 600 Yard Target

MR-1 target—Enlarged aiming black for use in 600-yard matches only.

Aiming Black	(inches)	Rings in White	(inches)
X ring	6.00	6 ring	48.00
10 ring	12.00	5 ring	60.00
9 ring	18.00		
8 ring	24.00		
7 ring	36.00		

4.7 800, 900, and 1000 Yard Target

N.R.A.—No. LR

Aiming Black	(inches)	Rings in White	(inches)
X ring	10.00	7 ring	60.00
10 ring	20.00	6 area	72×72
9 ring	30.00		square
8 ring	44.00		

N.R.A.—No. LR Center—Paper size is approximately 45 × 45 inches. Same scoring ring dimension as NRA No. LR, through 8 ring (may have arcs of 7 rings on corners of the paper). For use with NRA No. LR; or may be used to provide the equivalent of No. LR by superimposing on the Military MR Target with MR 5 ring becoming the LR 7 ring; or on the Military B Target with B 3 ring becoming the LR 7 ring. In these uses the area outside the 7 ring is the 6 area.

5. POSITIONS

Positions—The positions for use in a match shall be stated in the program under conditions of the match and shall be in accord with the definitions of positions prescribed in this section.

5.1 The Ground—All references to "the ground" in the following position Rules are to be construed as applying to the surface of the firing point, floor, or shooting mats, and platforms as are customarily used on shooting ranges.

5.2 Artificial Support—Any supporting surface except the ground not specifically authorized for use in the Rules for the position prescribed. Digging of elbow or heel holes at the firing points which form artificial support for the elbows, arms, or legs is prohibited. Use of artificial support is prohibited except as individually authorized for a physically handicapped shooter.

5.3 Position of Rifle Butt—In all positions, the butt of the rifle must be held against the front of the shoulder on the outside of the shooting coat or shirt and must not touch the ground.

5.4 Rifle Magazine—The magazine of the rifle may touch the person or clothing of the shooter, but may not touch the ground or be used to provide artificial support.

5.5 Physically Handicapped Shooters—A shooter who because of a physical handicap cannot fire from one or more of the prescribed shooting positions outlined in these Rules, or who must use special equipment when firing, is privileged to petition the NRA Protest Committee for permission to assume a special position or to use modified equipment, or both. This petition will be in the form of a written request from the person concerned to the Committee outlining in detail the reasons why the special position must be assumed or the special equipment must be used. The petition will be accompanied by pictures of the shooter in the position he desires approved and, if special equipment is required, the picture will show how this equipment is used. The petition and all pictures must be furnished in exact duplicate. The petition must be accompanied by a medical doctor's statement if the physical handicap is not completely evident in the pictures submitted.

(a) Each petition will be reviewed by the NRA Protest Committee. The Committee may require additional or supplementary statements or pictures. If approved, the NRA Secretary will issue a special authorization certificate to the individual concerned. Such certificates will have necessary pictures attached.

(b) Shooters who have received special authorization certificates are required to present them when requested by officials of the competition or by NRA Official Referees or Supervisors.

(c) In the event of a protest involving the position or the equipment used by such a shooter, the Official Referee, Jury or Supervisor will compare the questioned position or equipment with the certificate and photographs presented by the shooter. If the shooter's position or equipment does not in the opinion of the officials, conform to that authorized by the NRA Secretary (or if the shooter has no authorized certificate or pictures), the protest shall be allowed and the shooter will be required to change immediately to the position or equipment which has been approved or to an otherwise legal position or equipment.

(d) Should a protest be carried beyond the Official Referee, Jury or Supervisor, the original protest will be endorsed by the Referee, Jury Chairman or Supervisor to show the action he has taken and will be forwarded to the National Rifle Association.

(e) National Records may not be established by use of scores fired in special positions or with special equipment as may be authorized according to this Rule.

(f) Two types of authorizations are issued; temporary and permanent. Permanent authorizations are issued to competitors who are permanently handicapped.

Illustrations indicate some approved positions.

5.6 Prone—Body extended on the ground, head toward the target. The rifle will be supported by both hands and one shoulder only. No portion of the arms below the elbows shall rest upon the ground or any artificial support nor may any portion of the rifle or body rest against any artificial support.

5.8 Kneeling—Buttocks clear of the ground, but may rest on one foot. The rifle will be supported by both hands and one shoulder only. The arm supporting the rifle rests on the knee or leg. The elbow of the trigger arm will be free from all support. One knee must be touching the ground.

5.10 Sitting—Weight of the body supported on the buttocks and the feet or ankles, no other portion of the body touching the ground. The rifle will be supported by both hands and one shoulder only. Arms may rest on the legs at any point above the ankles.

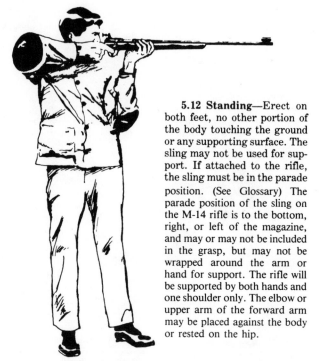

5.12 Standing—Erect on both feet, no other portion of the body touching the ground or any supporting surface. The sling may not be used for support. If attached to the rifle, the sling must be in the parade position. (See Glossary) The parade position of the sling on the M-14 rifle is to the bottom, right, or left of the magazine, and may or may not be included in the grasp, but may not be wrapped around the arm or hand for support. The rifle will be supported by both hands and one shoulder only. The elbow or upper arm of the forward arm may be placed against the body or rested on the hip.

5.13 Any—Any position in which the rifle is supported only by the body, assisted if desired by the sling, with no artificial support, and by which no competitors or range personnel are endangered. National Records may not be established by competitors using Rule 5.13.

6. RANGE STANDARDS

6.1 Firing Line—The firing line is immediately in front of the several firing points. All ranges are measured from this firing line to the face of the targets when targets are hung in their proper position in front of the backstop.

6.2 Firing Point—That part of the range provided for the competitor immediately in the rear of the firing line from which firing takes place. Each firing point is numbered to correspond with the target frames. Each firing point should have a minimum width of 6 feet.

6.3 Shelter—The firing points may be protected with a roof but may not be wholly or partly enclosed. Competitors must be exposed to prevailing winds. This does not preclude the construction of ranges within areas surrounded or partially surrounded by safety walls or structures designed for the suppression of sound. Umbrellas or other types of temporary individual shelters are not to be used.

6.4 Distances—Matches are commonly fired at ranges of 100, 200, 300, 500, 600, 800, 900 and 1000 yards.

6.5 Illumination—Artificial illumination of ranges is authorized.

6.6 Target Numbers—Target frames will be numbered on backgrounds of alternating contrasting colors. The numbers will be large enough to be identified under ordinary conditions with normal vision. Numbers must correspond with firing point numbers. Target numbers will be fixed in position so as to remain visible when targets are exposed and when concealed.

6.9 Display Red Flag—A red flag visible from the firing line will be constantly exposed at one or both ends of the butts whenever firing is in progress. Wind flags may be displayed at various distances between the firing line and the targets, (Recommended size of range flags is 5 ft, 93/8 in. at the hoist, 18 feet in length and tapered the full length of the lower edge to be 3 feet wide at the fly end and made of red cotton flag bunting.

6.10 Communication—Communication will be maintained between the target pit and firing line whenever personnel are in the pits.

7. COURSES OF FIRE

The following courses and types of fire are most commonly found in NRA-sanctioned Highpower rifle competition, fired on standard targets described in Rule 4. See Rule 8 for time allowances, Rule 17.5 for courses of fire for which National Records are recognized, and Rule 19.5 for courses of fire used for classification.

Other courses of fire, other time limits, or the use of other targets, may be scheduled by sponsors provided the conditions are clearly stated in the program.

STANDARD SINGLE-STAGE MATCH COURSES OF FIRE:
(An asterisk (*) indicates a reduced targets and distance course)

	Course Position	No. of Shots	Type of Fire	Distance	Target
7.1	*Standing	10 or 20	slow	100 yds.	SR-1
7.2	*Sitting or Kneeling from standing	10 or 20	rapid	100 yds.	SR-1
7.3	*Prone from standing	10 or 20	rapid	100 yds.	SR-21
7.4	*Prone	10 or 20	slow	100 yds.	MR-31
7.5	Standing	10 or 20	slow	200 yds.	SR
7.6	Sitting or Kneeling from standing	10 or 20	rapid	200 yds.	SR
7.7	*Prone from standing	10 or 20	rapid	200 yds.	SR-42
7.8	*Prone	10 or 20	slow	200 yds.	MR-52
7.9	Prone from standing	10 or 20	rapid	300 yds.	SR-3
7.10	*Prone	10 or 20	slow	300 yds.	MR-63
7.11	Prone	10 or 20	slow	500 yds.	MR
7.12	Prone	10 or 20	slow	600 yds.	MR-1
7.13	Prone	10 or 20	slow	1000 yds.	LR

STANDARD MULTIPLE STAGE OR AGGREGATE MATCH COURSES OF FIRE:

7.14 National Match Course (50 shots):

Standing Sitting or Kneeling from	10	slow	100 or 200 yds.	SR-1 or SR
standing Prone from	10	rapid	100 or 200 yds.	SR-1 or SR
standing	10	rapid	100, 200 or 300 yds.	SR-21, SR-42, or SR-3
Prone	20	slow	100, 200, 300, 500 or 600 yds.	MR-31, MR-52 MR-63, MR, or MR-1

7.15 80 Shot Regional Course:

Standing Sitting or Kneeling from	20	slow	100 or 200 yds.	SR-1 or SR
standing Prone from	20	rapid	100 or 200 yds.	SR-1 or SR
standing	20	rapid	100, 200, or 300 yds.	SR-21, SR-42, or SR-3
Prone	20	slow	100, 200, 300, 500, or 600 yds.	MR-31, MR-52, MR-63, MR, or MR-1

7.16 100 Shot Regional Course:

Standing Sitting or Kneeling from	20	slow	100 or 200 yds.	SR-1 or SR
Standing Prone from	20	rapid	100 or 200 yds.	SR-1 or SR
standing	20	rapid	100, 200, or 300 yds.	SR-21, SR-42, or SR-3
Prone	20	slow	100, 200, 300, 500, or 600 yds.	MR-31, MR-52, MR-63, MR, or MR-1

Prone (the 600 yd. stage is repeated to make up the 100 shots)

7.17 National Long Range Course (60 shots):

Standing Sitting or Kneeling from	10	slow	200 yds.	SR
standing Prone from	10	rapid	200 yds.	SR
standing	10	rapid	300 yds.	SR-3
Prone	10	slow	600 yds.	MR-1
Prone	20	slow	1000 yds.	LR

7.18 Palma Course (45 shots)

Prone	15	slow	800 yds.	LR
Prone	15	slow	900 yds.	LR
Prone	15	slow	1000 yds.	LR

8. TIME LIMITS

8.1 Computing Time—Time is not checked on each shot. In slow fire the time allowance is computed for a complete stage (including sighting shots when specified) on the basis of the specified number of shots multiplied by the allowance per shot. The Chief Range Officer may terminate any slow fire relay before completion of the full time allowance, if all competitors in that relay have completed firing. In rapid fire the time allowance is specified for the complete string. Targets must be fully exposed for the full time specified for that rapid fire string. Time allowed but not used does not carry over to another string or stage.

Note: To time rapid fire strings, start the stopwatch when targets are fully exposed (at the top of the travel of the target carrier) and stop the stopwatch when targets start to move to be withdrawn into the pits.

8.2 Time Allowances:

(a) *Slow Fire*—The time allowance is one minute per shot, except that at ranges over 600 yards it may be up to 1½ minutes per shot if so specified in the program. At distances of 1000 yards, where unlimited practice shots are allowed, all record firing and practice firing must be complete within the time limit of 30 minutes for a 20 shot match. This is computed at 1½ minutes per shot for each record shot.

(b) *Rapid Fire*—In rapid fire, the competitor is to be standing when the command "COMMENCE FIRING" is given.

When the sitting or kneeling position is to be used, the time limits for 10 shots will be 60 seconds.

When the prone position is to be used the time limits for 10 shots will be 70 seconds.

8.3 Team Time—Team time will be allowed as follows:

(a) For slow fire stages or matches, a team will be allowed a total team time equal to the time allowed in an individual stage or match of the same type, times the number of shooters required to fire on each target, plus 3 minutes for each change of shooter or pairs of shooters required per target.

(b) For rapid fire strings or matches team time as such is not provided. Each firing member is separately allowed the same time as for an individual string or match of the same type and number of shots.

8.4 Passage of Time—Range Officers will not voluntarily warn competitors of the passage of time. Competitors, and Team Captains in team matches, may inquire of Range Officers as to the time remaining before expiration of the time limit. The request and the response shall be given in a tone which will not disturb other competitors.

14. SCORING AND MARKING

14.1 When to Score—

(a) Before scoring any target, examine it and count the hits to determine whether there are hits of uncertain value requiring gauging (Rule 14.3), possible ricochet hits (Rule 14.8), or conditions possibly requiring application of Rules 14.9 through 14.13. Only a Pit Officer (Range Officer if targets are scored on the frames without pits, or Statistical Officer if scored in the Statistical Office) may decide the scoring when any of these Rules apply. If they do not, or if they do and their applicable procedures have been completed, then proceed as in paragraphs *(b)* or *(c)* below for each shot credited to the competitor.

(b) When targets are scored in the pits:
1. In slow fire, spot and signal each shot when fired.
2. In rapid fire, spot and signal all shots after completion of each string.

(c) When targets are scored on the frames without pits, or are scored in the Statistical Office, score at the end of each target or string.

14.2 Where to Score—Targets may be scored in the Statistical Office, in the pits or on the frame in view of competitors and spectators.

14.3 How to Score—A shot hole, the leaded edge of which comes in contact with the outside of the X ring or other scoring rings of a target is given the higher value (including keyhole or tipped shots even though the hole is elongated to the bullet's length rather than being a circle of the bullet's diameter). X's must be scored. The higher value will be allowed in those cases where the flange on the gauge touches the scoring ring. The .30 caliber gauge will be used to score all targets and calibers.

Caliber	*Flange Diameter*
.30/7.62mm	.308″ ± .001″

Devices other than scoring gauges may be used to assist in establishing the correct value of hits. These devices are not to be inserted into the bullet hole and do not constitute a scoring gauge.

Correct method of scoring.
The shot on the left bullseye counts nine,
the one on the right ten.

14.3.1 Authorized Use of Plug Type Scoring Gauges—Use of the plug type gauge will be restricted to range operating personnel who may include Range Officers, Block Officers, Pit Officers, Match Supervisor, Statistical Officer, and/or Referee or Jury as appropriate to the tournament. The tournament program should state by whom and under what circumstances plug type scoring gauges may be used.

14.4 Misses—Hits outside the scoring rings or scoring areas defined in Section 4 are scored as misses. If the competitor fires fewer than the prescribed number of shots through his own fault, or fires on the wrong target, he is scored a miss for each unfired shot or each shot fired on a wrong target.

14.5 Early or Late Shots—In matches with pit operated targets any sighting shots or record shots fired prior to the signal to "Commence Firing" shall be considered "record shots" and be scored as misses.

In slow fire matches the competitor will be penalized by being scored a miss for his first record shot. In rapid fire, he will be penalized by being scored a miss for the hit on the target of highest value.

In matches fired at stationary targets any sighting shots or record shots fired prior to the signal to "commence firing" or after the signal to "cease fire" will be penalized by being scored a miss for the hit of the highest value on the target in both rapid fire and slow fire.

14.6 All Shots Count—All shots fired by a competitor after he has taken his position at the firing point will be counted in his score even if the rifle may be accidentally discharged.

14.7 Hits on Wrong Target—Hits on the wrong target are scored as misses.

14.8 Ricochets—A hole made by a ricochet bullet does not count as a hit and will be scored as a miss. It must be noted that the bullet which keyholes is not necessarily a ricochet. If there is doubt in the mind of the target marker as to whether a hole is caused by a ricochet bullet, the Pit Officer (Chief Range Officer or Statistical Officer if pits are not used), must be called and his decision obtained before the value of the hit is signaled or scored.

14.9 Visible Hits and Close Groups—As a general rule only those hits which are visible will be scored. An exception will be made in the case where the grouping of three or more shots is so close that it is possible for a required shot or shots to have gone through the enlarged hole without leaving a mark, and there has been no evidence that a shot or shots have gone elsewhere than through the assigned target. In such case, the shooter will be given the benefit of the doubt and scored hits for the non-visible shots, on the assumption they passed through the enlarged hole. If such assumption could place a non-visible hit in either of two scoring rings, it shall be scored in the higher-valued ring.

14.10 Excessive hits—Excessive hits are defined as hits in excess of the prescribed number of shots, or in excess of the number of shots the competitor has fired. A competitor will not be credited with more shots than he has fired. If excessive hits are found, any hit which the Pit Officer (Range Officer or Statistical Officer if targets are not scored in the pit) can distinguish as having been fired by some other competitor or in some other string shall be pasted and not scored or spotted. This distinction may be by type or caliber of bullet hole, backing target (if used), or other means. If excessive hits remain indistinguishable the following procedures apply:

> (*a*) In any string, if all hits are of equal value, score the number of shots the competitor fired, assigning a miss for each required shot he failed to fire.
>
> (*b*) In slow fire:
>
> > (*1*) When targets are scored in the pit, if more than one hit appears when the assigned competitor fires, put spotters

in all hits, score the hit of highest value, and make no record of the other hit(s).

(2) When targets are not scored in the pit, a Range Officer shall notify the competitor if there are excessive hits, and the score corresponding to the number of shots he has fired of lowest value. The competitor has the option of accepting that score or of refiring a string of the same number of shots. He must select his option immediately upon being informed of the excessive hit situation. If he elects to refire, this is not chargeable under Rule 9.27.

(3) If more than one hit appears on a competitor's target while he is firing sighting shots, these hits will be spotted but not scored. A Range Officer will inform the competitor and allow him an additional sighting shot and time.

(c) In rapid fire:

(1) When targets are scored in the pit, hold any target in the pit which has excessive hits and is not covered by paragraph (a) above, until the Pit Officer directs further actions according to paragraphs (2) or (3) following. No spotters will be inserted until the Pit Officer's decision is made.

(2) If the competitor fired fewer than the required number of shots through his own fault, and more hits than he fired appear on the target, he shall be given the score corresponding to the number of shots he fired, of highest value, and scored a miss for each shot which he did not fire. (See also Rule 14.12.)

(3) If the competitor fired the required number of shots, he has the option of accepting the score for that number of shots of lowest value, or of refiring the string. He must select his option immediately upon being informed of the situation. If he elects to refire this is not chargeable under Rule 9.27.

(4) If the competitor fired fewer than the required number of shots through no fault of his own (see Rule 9.24) and more hits than he fired appear on the target, he has the option of accepting the score for the number of shots which he fired, of lowest value, or of refiring the string. If he elects to refire, this is not chargeable under Rule 9.27.

(5) A competitor who fires more than the required number of rounds shall have his score for that match disallowed. See Rule 9.42 (b).

14.11 Non-Visible Hits—All in the 9 and/or 10 Ring—In a rapid fire string where a competitor fires a complete 10 shot string in the required time, and where only nine hits are visible in the 9 and/or 10 ring, and where there is no evidence that a shot went elsewhere than through the assigned target, and where there are no excessive hits one or two targets to the left or right of the assigned target, and where Rule 14.9 does not apply, the competitor may:

(a) Accept the score as fired.

(b) Challenge the score:

(1) Before refiring an additional string, or

(2) Before accepting the score as fired.

(c) Fire an additional 10 shot string.

Scoring procedure: The value of the nine hits on the competitor's target will be recorded on the front of the score card. (If the problem occurs on the first string of a two string match or stage, it shall be recorded as the first string even though it is incomplete. The next string fired will be recorded as the second string.) The refire string will be fired on the alibi relay, and recorded on the back of the score card. The shot or saved round of lowest value of the refire string will be transferred to the front of the score card to complete the score. If the refire string results in a non-visible hit as specified above, the refire string will be disregarded and another string fired.

14.11.1 Non-Visible Hits—Late Shots—In a rapid fire string, if the scorer observes a late shot, he will immediately notify a Range Officer. If the score results in insufficient hits, a refire string will not be allowed.

14.11.2 Non-visible hits—NOT All in the 9 and/or 10 ring—In a rapid fire string where a competitor fires a complete 10 shot string in the required time, and where there has been no evidence that a shot went elsewhere than through the assigned target, that is, one or two targets to the right or left of the assigned target, and where fewer than 10 hits are visible on the target, the competitor may challenge, or accept the score of the shots visible.

14.12 Insufficient Hits—If a competitor fires fewer than the required number of shots through his own fault, he shall be given the score corresponding to the number of shots he fired, and scored a miss for each unfired shot.

14.12.1 Misses Scored—In any string the competitor must be scored the required number of shots, assigning a miss for each required shot which he failed to fire.

14.13 Notification of Competitor—In all cases where Rules 14.9, 14.10, 14.11, 14.11.1, 14.11.2, 14.12, or 14.12.1 apply, the competitor will be notified at once of the fact that there is a problem with his target in the following manner: If there are excessive shots on his target, the value spotter will be placed in the upper right hand corner of the target. The score of the ten hits of the lowest value will be written on the rapid fire scoring board and the target will immediately be placed at half mast to expose only the scoring disk and the top of the scoring board.

If there are insufficient hits on the target, the value spotter will be placed in the top center of the target and the number of hits written on the top of the rapid fire score board. If there are nine apparent hits on the target and they are all in the 9 or 10 ring, the word "yes" will be written under the figure 9 and if all the apparent hits are not in the 9 or 10 ring, the word "no" will be written under the figure 9. If Rules 14.11 through 14.12.1 apply, the competitor will also be notified if there are any excessive hits one or two targets to the left or right of the assigned target.

14.15 Score Cards—Score cards must be prepared by the Statistical Office and delivered to the competitor or to the Range Officers who will check the target assignments of each competitor as he reports at the firing point, then give the score cards to the Scorer. At the conclusion of each relay Range Officers will take up the score cards and deliver them to the Statistical Office.

14.16 Erasures on Score Cards—A Scorer is not permitted to make any erasures, corrections or changes on the score card. If correcting is necessary, it must be made and initialed by the Range Officer. To make a correction, the Range Officer draws a line, or lines, through the incorrect score and places correct score above, adding his initials opposite the correct score. When targets are scored in the pits, the recorded value of any shot will not be changed (except when re-disked or re-marked) unless some special message with reference to it is received by the Range Officer from one of the Pit Officers.

14.17 Use of Shot Hole Spotters—When targets are operated from a pit, shot hole spotters are used to show the location of hits, white spotters for hits in the aiming black and black spotters for hits elsewhere (including hits scored as misses). See Rule 14.1. In slow fire a spotter is placed in the first hit, the target exposed and the value signaled, and the target is left exposed for the next shot. As each succeeding shot is fired the target is withdrawn, the spotter moved to the new hit, the previous shot hole covered with a target paster and the target is re-exposed and the new hit value signaled. In rapid fire, spotters are placed in all hits of the string, or as many as feasible, before exposing the target to signal the values. After signaling all hits the target is withdrawn, spotters removed and holes pasted before the next string. In the case of excessive or insufficient hits in rapid fire, spotters shall not be inserted in the target until directed by the Pit Officer. The same size spotter will be utilized on all targets for each stage of fire. The following spotters will be used:

(a) A 3 inch spotter for slow fire, 200 yards through 600 yards.
(b) A 5 inch spotter for slow fire for all ranges in excess of 600 yards.
(c) 1½ inch or smaller spotters are to be used for all rapid fire matches.

14.18 Signal Systems for Scoring Targets—The visual signaling system described below will be used in all Highpower Tournaments:

(a) Slow Fire: Value spotters are placed as indicated on the target frame, all of a highly visible color such as fluorescent orange:
    X—Bottom left corner
    10—Bottom center
    9—Bottom right corner
    8—Center of right side
    7—Top right corner
    6—Top left corner
    5—Center of left side
    Miss—Top center
(b) Rapid Fire: A narrow vertical chalk board is hung on the left side of the target frame (during scoring phase only), with the successive scoring values painted on it. Opposite each value is chalked the total number of hits of that value scored in the string.

15. DECISION OF TIES

Note: All tie (same numerical score) ranking Rules shall be applied in the order listed below.

15.1 Match—The term "Match" as used in this section refers to all individual, team, and aggregate matches.

15.2 Value of "X"—In all matches an X is a hit of highest value.

15.4 In all matches ties will be decided as follows:

(a) By the greatest number of X's over the course.

(b) Any tie not decided by the above will be decided:
  (1) By the highest total numerical score at the longest range or simulated longest range.
  (2) By the greatest number of X's at the longest range or simulated longest range.
  (3) By the highest total numerical score at the next longest range or simulated longest range.
  (4) By the greatest number of X's at the next longest range or simulated longest range.
(c) In the event the tie is not broken, the scores at each range, in the above order will be ranked:
  (1) By the fewest misses.
  (2) By the fewest hits of lowest value.
  (3) By the fewest hits of next lowest value, etc.
  (4) In slow fire individual stages, by the value of the hits in inverse order, counting singly from last to first (X's being hits of highest value).
  (5) In rapid fire individual stages at one range and one position, by the value of strings in inverse order.

15.7 Slow and Rapid Fire at One Range—Ties will be ranked by considering first rapid fire scores and then the slow fire scores, in the order prescribed in 15.4.

15.8 Matches Including Both Rifle and Pistol—In matches which include both rifle and pistol stages, ties will be ranked:
(a) By the highest ranking score at the pistol stage.
(b) By the highest ranking score at the rifle stage.

15.9 Ties, Team Matches—Team match scores will be ranked by applying the preceding Rules of this section to the total team score for each range and stage, as applicable. If ties still exist they will be ranked:
(a) By the highest individual aggregate score.
(b) By the second highest individual aggregate score, etc.
(c) By the highest individual score, second highest individual score, etc., at each stage considered in the order they are listed in 15.4 above.

15.11 In Re-Entry Matches—Ties will be ranked:
(a) By considering as a unit the total score fired on all targets constituting the score for record as provided in the program and applying there the provisions of paragraphs 15.2 to 15.7 inclusive.
(b) By outranking the competitor with the lowest score on any one target of those constituting the score for record.
(c) If still a tie, by combing all cash prizes to which those tied are entitled and dividing such cash equally among those tied. Lost will be cast for merchandise prizes or medals or other trophies.

15.12 Ties, League—In League competition in which team standings are determined by the number of matches won and lost, ties will be decided by a shoot-off over the same course of fire as that used during the League season.

15.13 Unbreakable Ties—In any case where a tie cannot be ranked under the foregoing provisions of this section, the Match Director will direct that the tie be decided and prizes awarded under one of the following plans as appears necessary or advisable:
(a) By firing of a complete or partial score under the original match conditions or at longest range of the match.
(b) By drawing of lots for merchandise, medal or trophy awards,

and combining any cash awards to which those tied may be entitled and equal division of such cash among those tied.

17. NATIONAL RECORDS

17.1 Where Scores for National Records Can Be Fired—Scores to be recognized as National Records must be fired in NRA Registered competition as defined in Rule 1.6, paragraphs *(c)*, *(d)*, *(e)*, and *(f)*. National Records must be approved by the NRA before being declared official. National Records may not be established during re-entry matches.

17.2 Scores to be Used—Scores must be complete scores for an entire scheduled match. Stage scores or scores for only part of a match will not be used for Records.

17.3 Scores for National Individual Records—Such scores must be fired in individual matches. No scores fired in a team match will be considered for recognition as an Individual Record. For recognition as special group Records ("Open," "Civilian," "Police," "Service," "Women," "Juniors") scores may be fired in either open or restricted matches. See Rules 9.14 and 9.18.

17.4 Scores for National Team Records—Such scores must be fired in matches where teams fire as a unit and no combination of individual match scores will be considered for recognition as a Team Record. For recognition as special group Records ("Open," "Civilian," "Police," "Service," "Women," "Juniors") all members of the team must be members of the special group concerned (Rule 1.3). Teams must be bona fide teams as outlined in Rules 2.10 to 2.19. National Records will not be recognized for "pickup" teams (teams made up of shooters who do not represent one of the groups outlined in Rules 2.10 to 2.19).

- **17.5 Courses of Fire for which National Records Are Recognized**—
  Note: National Highpower Rifle Records are maintained for scores fired over the following courses for "Open," "Police," "Service," "Civilian," "Women," and "Junior" categories fired on the targets indicated and for metallic sights only unless specified otherwise. The "Service" category includes Regular Service, Reserve Components, and National Guard.

  In order for records to be recognized promptly, National Record Reporting forms must be submitted to NRA by the Statistical Officer of the tournament in which they were fired, after being certified by the Jury or Referee. National Record Reporting forms are mailed to sponsors of NRA Registered Tournaments by NRA Headquarters.

  Unlimited practice shots shall be fired and recorded in courses of fire described in Rule 17.5 *(l)* and *(m)*. Two sighters will be optional in course of fire *(q)*, and two sighters shall be fired and recorded in each stage of all other listed courses of fire.

Range	Target	Total Shots	Course
(a) 100 yds.	SR-1	50	National Match Course
	SR-21		10 shots, Slow Fire, Standing (SR-1)
	MR-31		10 shots, Rapid Fire, Sitting or Kneeling from Standing (SR-1)

	Range	Target	Total Shots	Course
				10 shots, Rapid Fire, Prone from Standing, (SR-21) 20 shots, Slow Fire, Prone, (MR-31)
(b)	200 yds.	SR	20	20 shots, Slow Fire, Standing
(c)	200 yds.	SR	20	20 shots, Rapid Fire, Sitting or Kneeling from Standing
(d)	200 yds.	SR SR-42 MR-52	50	National Match Course 10 shots, Slow Fire, Standing (SR); 10 shots, Rapid Fire, Sitting or Kneeling from Standing (SR); 10 shots, Rapid Fire, Prone from Standing, (SR-42); 20 shots, Slow Fire, Prone, (MR-52);
(e)	300 yds.	SR-3	20	20 shots, Prone from Standing, Rapid Fire
(f)	200 yds. 300 yds.	SR SR-3 MR-63	50	National Match Course 10 shots, Slow Fire, Standing at 200 yds. (SR); 10 shots, Rapid Fire, Sitting or Kneeling from Standing at 200 yds. (SR); 10 shots, Rapid Fire, Prone from Standing at 300 yds. (SR-3); 20 shots, Slow Fire, Prone at 300 yds. (MR-63)
(g)	500 yds.	MR	20	20 shots, Slow Fire, Prone
(h)	600 yds.	MR-1	20	20 shots, Slow Fire, Prone
(i)	200 yds. 300 yds. 600 yds. (500) yds.	SR SR-3 MR-1 MR	80	Regional Course 20 shots, Slow Fire, Standing at 200 yds. (SR); 20 shots, Rapid Fire, Sitting or Kneeling from Standing at 200 yds. (SR); 20 shots, Rapid Fire, Prone from Standing at 300 yds. (SR-3); 20 shots, Slow Fire, Prone at 600 yds. (MR-1) (500) yds. (MR)
(j)	200 yds. 300 yds. 600 yds. (500) yds.	SR SR-3 MR-1 MR	100	Regional Course 20 shots, Slow Fire, Standing at 200 yds. (SR); 20 shots, Rapid Fire, Sitting or Kneeling from Standing at 200 yds. (SR); 20 shots, Rapid Fire, Prone from Standing at 300 yds. (SR-3); 40 shots, Slow Fire, Prone at 600 yds. (MR-1) (500) yds. (MR)
(k)	200 yds. 300 yds. 600 yds.	SR SR-3 MR-1	50	National Match Course 10 shots, Slow Fire, Standing at 200 yds. (SR);

Range	Target	Total Shots	Course
(500) yds.	MR only		10 shots, Rapid Fire, Sitting or Kneeling from Standing at 200 yds. (SR); 10 shots, Rapid Fire, Prone from Standing at 300 yds. (SR-3); 20 shots, Slow Fire, Prone at 600 yds. (MR-1) (500) yds. (MR)
(l) 1000 yds.	LR	20	20 shots, Slow Fire, Prone, Metallic Sights
(m) 1000 yds.	LR ·	20	20 shots, Slow Fire, Prone (Any Sights)
(n) 200 yds.	SR	60	National Long Range Course
300 yds.	SR-3		10 shots, Slow Fire, Standing at 200
600 yds.	MR-1		yds. (SR);
1000 yds.	LR		10 shots, Rapid Fire, Sitting or Knee ling from Standing at 200
(500) yds.	MR only		yds. (SR); 10 shots, Rapid Fire, Prone from Standing at 300 yds. (SR-3); 10 shots, Slow Fire, Prone at 600 yds. (MR-1) (500) yds. (MR); 20 shots, Slow Fire, Prone at 1000 yds. (LR)

(o)   The current National Championship Aggregate Course.

(p)   Palma Course of Fire—
   800 yds. LR 15 shots Slow Fire, Prone, Metallic Sights
   900 yds. LR 15 shots Slow Fire, Prone, Metallic Sights
   1000 yds. LR 15 shots Slow Fire, Prone, Metallic Sights
   (National Records in the Palma Course can only be established with the Service Rifle, Rules 3.1, 3.1.1, or the NRA Match Rifle, Rule 3.3 chambered for the unmodified 308/7.62mm NATO or 30-06 cartridges.)

(q)   Team Matches—Four man team matches fired over the courses described in items *(d)*, *(f)*, *(i)*, *(j)*, *(k)*, *(l)*, *(m)*, and *(n)*.

17.6 Co-holder Records—Tie breaking Rules beyond the use of numerical scores including X count will not be employed when establishing National Records. Co-holder status will be accorded to individuals or teams when their score equals a National Record.

18. COMPETITORS' DUTIES AND RESPONSIBILITIES

Note: The following competitors' duties are in addition to those specified elsewhere throughout these Rules.

18.1 Discipline—It is the duty of each competitor to sincerely cooperate with tournament officials in the effort to conduct a safe efficient tournament. Competitors are expected promptly to call the attention of proper officials to any infraction of rules of safety or good sportsmanship. Failure of a competitor to cooperate in such matters or to give testimony when called upon to do so in any case arising out of infractions of these Rules may result in said competitor being considered as an accessory to the offense.

18.2 Knowledge of Program—It is the competitor's responsibility to be familiar with the program. Officials cannot be held responsible for a competitor's failure to obtain and familiarize himself with the program.

18.3 Eligibility—It is the competitor's duty to enter only those events for which he is eligible and to enter himself in the proper classification.

18.4 Classification—It is the competitor's duty to have his current Classification Card in his possession when competing in competition using a classification system. Unclassified competitors must obtain their Score Record Book from the Official Referee, Supervisor, or Tournament Officials.

18.5 Individual Entries—In individual matches it is the duty of the competitor to make his own entries on the forms and in the manner prescribed for that tournament. Errors due to illegibility or improper filling out of forms are solely the competitor's responsibility. The Statistical Office is not required to accept correction after entry closing time.

18.6 Squadding Tickets—It is the competitor's duty to secure his squadding ticket for each match (or to consult the squadding bulletin) in ample time to permit reporting at the proper time and place to fire each match. It is not the duty of Officials to page competitors in order to get them on the firing line. Competitors upon receipt of squadding tickets should inspect them for correctness of competitor's number and non-interference in squadding assignments. Errors should be reported immediately to Statistical Officer.

18.7 Reporting at Firing Point—Competitors must report at their assigned firing point immediately when the relay is called by the Range Officer. The proper rifle and ammunition for that particular match must be ready and in safe firing condition. Time will not be allowed for rifle repairs, sight blacking, sight adjustments or search for missing equipment after a relay as been called to the firing line.

18.8 Timing—Time for the firing of a string (within the official time limit) is the competitor's responsibility. Range Officers will not announce the time during the firing, but if requested will give the competitor information as to remaining time.

18.9 Loading—No competitor will load a rifle, except at the firing point and after command has been given by the Range Officer.

18.10 Cease Firing—All rifles will be unloaded and detachable magazines removed immediately upon the command, "CEASE FIRE." Actions will remain open.

18.11 Checking Scores—It is the duty of competitors to check their scores as written on the score card and to sign the score card at the conclusion of the match. When scoring is done in the Statistical Office competitors must promptly check the Preliminary Bulletin and call attention to errors within the time specified at that tournament. Failure to check scores within the time limit forfeits the right to challenge.

18.12 Clearing the Firing Point—It is the competitor's duty to leave the firing point promptly at the conclusion of his relay. When leaving the firing point, rifles must be unloaded.

18.13 Checking Bulletin Board—It is the duty of all individual competitors and Team Captains to check the Bulletin Board between each match. The Statistical Officer must be immediately notified of apparent errors. Official Bulletins must be checked and the Statistical

Officer notified of any discrepancies between the Preliminary and Official Bulletins. Official Notices on the Bulletin Board have the same effect as conditions printed in the program. It is the duty of competitors to familiarize themselves with all such Official Notices.

18.14 Score Cards Must Be Signed—When targets are scored in the pits or on frames, after the score card is signed by the Scorer (Rule 9.42) the competitor (Team Captain in team matches) checks the values of shots and the totals as recorded, and signs the card. If he leaves the firing line without so signing he is allowed no challenge or protest for that match. If he wishes to protest he writes "protested" on the score card above his signature. (For procedure when targets are scored in the Statistical Office see Rule 18.11.)

18.15 Responsibility—It shall be the competitor's responsibility:

(a) That all equipment meets all Rules and match specifications in any match in which that equipment is to be used.

(b) That competitor's position conforms to the Rules.

(c) That competitor has full knowledge of the Rules under which the match is fired.

(d) That after due warning on any infraction of existing Rules, that competitor shall understand a repetition thereof shall be the subject of disqualification for that match or tournament.

(e) Any competitor who fails to perform his squadded assignment for scoring and/or pulling targets may be disqualified from the entire tournament.

(f) When targets are framed by the competitor it is the competitor's responsibility that the correct target is framed for the range and event being fired.

(g) To insure that his target is not altered intentionally or with special marks which benefit him in any way. Scores fired on such targets will not be scored.

19. NATIONAL HIGHPOWER RIFLE CLASSIFICATION

19.1 Classified Competitors—Classified competitors are all individuals who are officially classified by the NRA for Highpower Rifle competition, or who have a record of scores fired over courses of fire used for classification (See Rule 19.4) which have been recorded in a Score Record Book.

19.2 Unclassified Competitor—An unclassified competitor is a competitor who does not have a current NRA Highpower Rifle classification, either regular or temporary by Score Record Book (Rule 19.14), nor an "Assigned Classification" (Rule 19.6). Such competitor shall compete in the Master Class.

19.4 Scores Used for Individual Classification—Scores used for Highpower Rifle classification or reclassification include all scores fired in NRA-sanctioned individual and team competitions of the types defined in Rule 1.6 subparagraphs *(c)* through *(h)* inclusive, over the courses of fire listed in Rule 19.5 fired with metallic sights, at ranges 100 through 600 yards inclusive. Scores from sanctioned League competitions may be used in Score Record Books if applicable (Rule 19.14) during the League season, but will not be entered in the official classification or reclassification procedure until completion of the League season.

19.4.1 Expanded Classification System for Juniors (Rule 2.3 only) —A match sponsor may use an expanded or a different classification for Junior shooters. Within that system, coaching may be allowed by the sponsor. However, the scores fired in classes that allow coaching will not be used for National Records or National standings, but shall be reported for NRA classification purposes.

19.5 Courses of Fire Used for Highpower Rifle Classification—
100 Yards:
  Target: SR-1; 10 or 20 shots standing, slow fire, 10 or 20 shots rapid fire, sitting or kneeling.
  Target: SR-21; 10 or 20 shots rapid fire standing to prone.
  Target: MR-31; 10 or 20 shots slow fire, prone.
200 Yards:
  Target: SR; 10 or 20 shots standing, slow fire, or 10 or 20 shots rapid fire standing to sitting or kneeling.
  Target: SR-42; 10 or 20 shots rapid fire, standing to prone.
  Target: MR-52; 10 or 20 shots slow fire, prone.
300 Yards:
  Target: SR-3; 10 or 20 shots rapid fire, standing to prone.
  Target: MR-63; 10 or 20 shots slow fire, prone.
500 Yards:
  Target: MR (only); 10 or 20 shots slow fire, prone.
600 Yards:
  Target: MR-1; 10 or 20 shots slow fire, prone.

19.6 Assigned Classification—A competitor who has no NRA Highpower Rifle classification, either regular or temporary by Score Record Book (Rule 19.14), but who has an NRA classification in one or more of the Smallbore or International Rifle categories, will be given an "Assigned Classification" corresponding to his highest in those categories. This "Assigned Classification" will apply until superseded by a temporary or regular classification.

19.7 Lack of Classification Evidence—It is the competitor's responsibility to have his NRA Official Classification Card or Score Record Book with required scores for temporary classification (see Rules 19.1 and 19.14) and to present such classification evidence when required. Any competitor who cannot present such evidence will fire in the Master Class. A competitor's classification will not change during a tournament. A competitor will enter a tournament under his correct classification and fire the entire tournament in that class. Should it be discovered during a tournament, that a competitor has entered in a classification lower than his current rating, the tournament records will be corrected to show the correct classification for the entire tournament.

19.8 Competing in a Higher Class—Any individual or team may elect, before firing, to compete in a higher classification than the one in which classified. Such individual or team must fire in the higher class throughout that tournament.

When there are insufficient entries in any class to warrant an award in that class according to the match program conditions, the individual or team concerned may be moved by the Tournament Match Director to a higher class provided this change is made prior to the individual or team concerned having commenced firing in the tournament.

19.9 Obsolete Classifications and Scores—All classifications and scores (including temporary, Rule 19.14) except Master, shall become obsolete if the competitor does not fire in NRA competition at least once during three successive calendar years. **Master classifications and scores** shall become obsolete if the competitor does not fire in NRA competition at least once during five successive calendar years. Lifetime Master classifications will not become obsolete.

19.10 Appeals—Any competitor having reason to believe that he is improperly classified may file an appeal with the NRA stating all essential facts. Such appeals will be reviewed by the NRA Protest Committee.

19.11 Protests—Any person who believes that another competitor has been improperly classified may file a protest with the NRA stating all essential facts. Such protests will be reviewed by the NRA Protest Committee.

19.12 Team Classification—Teams are classified by computing the "team average" based on the classification of each firing member of the team. To compute this "team average" the key in Table No. I for the different classes will be used, and the team total divided by the number of firing members of the team. Any fractional figure in the team average of one half or more will place team in next higher class. The "team average" will establish classification of the team as a unit but will not affect in any way the individual classification of the team members.

TABLE NO. I
TEAM

Class	Key	Class	Key
High Master	5	Sharpshooter	2
Master	4	Marksman	1
Expert	3		

19.13 Reporting Scores—NRA competition (see Rule 1.6) sponsors will report to the NRA all individual and fired team match scores fired over the courses stated in Rule 19.5. Scores fired in individual matches will be reported as aggregate totals, and scores from fired team matches will be reported as a separate aggregate total. Scores from all tournaments and sanctioned leagues will be reported by each sponsor no more than 30 days following completion of the tournament firing schedule.

19.14 Score Record Book—*(Temporary Classification)*—A competitor who does not have a regular NRA Highpower Rifle classification will obtain an NRA "Score Record Book" from the Official Referee, Supervisor, or Tournament Statistical Office, or from the Secretary of a Sanctioned League, in which he will enter all his Highpower Rifle scores fired in NRA-sanctioned individual and team competition of the types defined in Rule 1.6 subparagraphs *(c)* through *(h)* inclusive. The total of all scores so recorded, divided by the number of 10-shot strings represented, will be the competitor's average for temporary classification in accordance with Table II below. Scores from at least one complete tournament (Rule 1.1) or League Match (Rule 1.6(h)) are required in order to establish an initial temporary classification. The Score Record Book and any such temporary classification are superseded when the competitor's regular classification becomes effective.

19.15 Individual Class Averages—Competitors classified or reclassified on the basis of scores fired under the conditions specified in Rule 19.4, reduced to 10 shot averages, those averages leading to classifications as shown in Table II below:

TABLE NO. II
INDIVIDUAL

High Master	97.00 and above	Sharpshooter ..	84.00 to 88.99
Master	94.00 to 96.99	Marksman	Below 84.00
Expert	89.00 to 93.99		

19.16 Establishing Classification—A competitor will be classified when his scores for not less than 120 shots have been reported as prescribed, except that classification will not include tournament or league scores until after all scores for the tournament or league concerned have been reported. When his classification is assigned he will be furnished an Official Classification Card showing the effective date.

19.17 Reclassification—A competitor who has been classified by the NRA will be reclassified as follows:

(a) NRA Headquarters will record all scores which qualify for classification purposes according to Rule 19.4.

(b) A competitor will be considered for reclassification upward when his scores for not less than 240 shots, fired subsequent to his last previous consideration for classification or reclassification, have been recorded as prescribed, except that such consideration will not include tournament or league scores until after all scores for the tournament or league competition concerned have been recorded. If his average score so justifies, he will be reclassified upward accordingly.

(c) A competitor will be reclassified downward only upon request by him to the NRA, and only on the basis of at least 320 shots recorded as prescribed, fired subsequent to his last previous classification or reclassification. If his average on this basis so justifies he will be reclassified downward accordingly.

(d) If after reclassification downward a competitor regains the classification thus vacated, he will not again be reclassified below the latter.

(e) A reclassified competitor will be provided a new Classification Card showing the effective date.

19.21 Lifetime Master—Competitors who have been certified as Lifetime Masters will retain their Lifetime Master Cards and enter competitions in the Master Class, except that:

(a) Lifetime Masters will be reclassified to a higher class, according to the provisions of Rule 19.17(b) and must enter competitions in the higher class.

(b) Lifetime Masters may petition NRA to revoke a Lifetime Master Card and be reclassified downward according to the provisions of Rule 19.17(c).

(c) No new Lifetime Masters will be certified.

NATIONAL RIFLE ASSOCIATION
Rules for Pistol and Revolver Matches

These Rules establish uniform standards for NRA Sanctioned International Pistol Competition. Where alternatives are shown, the least restrictive conditions apply unless the tournament program sets forth limitations. They apply only to International Shooting Union (UIT) type competition. They supersede the January 1, 1985 NRA International Pistol Rules. These Rules will remain in effect until specifically superseded.

Tournament sponsors may not alter these Rules. If sponsors require additional rules for special conditions, the additions must be fully set forth in the program for the competition concerned. Forward such proposed special rules to the NRA with tournament application.

The arrangement and Rule numbering systems are such that corresponding Rules for other types of NRA competition are correspondingly located and numbered in the Rule Books for those competitions. Gaps in the sequence of Rule numbers result from there being a Rule in one or more of the other Rule Books which does not apply in this Book.

Note: Rules in which major changes have been made since publication of the previous Rule Book are marked thus: (•1.1) All revised wording is underlined.

1. NRA COMPETITION

1.0 NRA Competition—is Competition which is authorized in advance of firing by the NRA. The program, range facilities and officials must comply with standards established by the NRA.

1.1 Sanctioned Tournament—A series of matches covered by an Official Program. Such matches may be all individual matches, all team matches, or a combination of both which must be conducted by an NRA Affiliated Club or organization. They may be all fired matches or a combination of fired and aggregate matches. A tournament may be conducted on one day, on successive days, or may provide for intervening days between portions of the tournament, such as tournaments programmed to be conducted over more than one weekend.

1.2 Authorization—Before being publicized in programs or otherwise, the sponsoring organization of each type of competition mentioned in Rule 1.6 shall have agreed to comply with the current regulations for such competition and shall have received notice from the NRA that the competition applied for has been authorized.

1.3 Rules—The local sponsor of each type of competition must agree to conduct the authorized competition according to NRA Rules, except as these Rules have been modified by the NRA in the General Regulations, for that type of competition.

1.4 General Regulations—The local sponsor of each type of competition must agree to comply with the General Regulations published by the NRA for the competition concerned.

1.5 Refusal or Withdrawal of NRA Authorization—The NRA may refuse to authorize or may withdraw its authorization for any competition which cannot, or does not comply, with the requirements for that competition.

1.6 Types of Tournaments—The types of tournaments listed below are those which are Sanctioned by NRA in its Competitive shooting program.

    (a) International Matches—Arranged by the NRA with the recognized national shooting organization(s) of the countries concerned. The officials thereof are appointed by the NRA.

    (b) International Team Tryouts—Are U.S. tournaments conducted under UIT or NRA International Rules organized or authorized by the NRA as Final Tryouts for the selection of Interna-

tional Team members. The officials thereof to be appointed or approved by the NRA.

- (c) *Preliminary Tryouts (PTO)*—These matches will be used to provide qualifying scores for entry in higher level competitions. Only Registered Tournaments including matches over full courses of fire qualify as acceptable for PTO's. The words "Preliminary Tryout" must appear in tournament name.
- (d) *National Championships*—Organized by the NRA and, in some cases, in conjunction with the National Board for the Promotion of Rifle Practice, Department of the Army to form the National Matches. The officials thereof are appointed by the NRA, in some circumstances in cooperation with the NBPRP. These tournaments will be Registered.
- (e) *Sectional Championships*—Arranged between the NRA and a local sponsoring organization.
- (f) *State Championships*—Annual tournaments conducted by State Rifle and/or Pistol Associations affiliated with the NRA. Such State Associations may, if desired, authorize local organizations to sponsor and conduct State Championships. In states where there is no NRA affiliated State Association the NRA may authorize a local organization to sponsor and conduct the State Championship. State Championships will be Registered Tournaments.
- (g) *Registered Tournaments*—May be authorized by the NRA after application has been filed by the local NRA affiliated member organization which will act as the sponsor. Application forms are available from NRA on request. National Records may only be established in Registered Tournaments. (see Rule 17.1) All competitors in Registered Tournaments must be individual members of NRA, except for Juniors (Rules 2.3, 2.3.1 and 2.3.2) who may be either members of NRA Affiliated Junior Clubs or individual members of NRA. Match sponsors may require all competitors to be NRA members if specified in the program.
- (h) *Approved Tournaments*—May be authorized by the NRA after application has been filed by the local NRA affiliated member organization that will act as the sponsor. Application forms are available from NRA on request.
- (i) *Sanctioned Leagues*--(shoulder-to-shoulder or postal)—May be authorized by the NRA after application has been filed by the local group or organization. Application forms are available from NRA on request. Sanctioned League scores are used for classification.
- (j) *Postal Matches*—Organized by the NRA and publicized to groups concerned through the AMERICAN RIFLEMAN and THE AMERICAN MARKSMAN, announcements and/or special mailings.

1.7 Types of Matches

- (a) *Match*—A complete event as indicated in the program for the awarding of certain specific prizes. A match may consist of one or of several stages. It may, in the case of aggregate matches, include the scores fired in several subsidiary matches.
- (b) *Stage*—A portion of a match which consists of one or more strings fired in one position, distance, time allowance (slow or rapid fire, for example), or target.
- (c) *Open Match*—A match open to anyone, except that if so stated in the program an open match may be limited to one or any combination of the following: *(a)* United States citizens; *(b)* members of the National Rifle Association of America; and/or *(c)* with respect to non-U.S. citizens, persons who are

members in good standing of their respective National Shooting Federations or Associations. (Rule 2.1.1)

(d) *Restricted Match*—A match in which competition is limited to specified groups, i.e., juniors, women, police, civilians, veterans, etc.; or to specified classes, i.e., Masters, Experts, Sharpshooters, Marksmen, etc.

(e) *Classified Match*—A match in which awards are given to the winners and to the highest competitors in several specified classes such as Masters, Experts, Sharpshooters, Marksmen. The classification of competitors may be accomplished by the National Classification System (Sec. 19) or by other means. The program for classified matches must specify the groups or classes in which awards will be made.

(f) *Invitational Match*—A match in which participation is limited to those who have been invited to compete.

(g) *Squadded Individual Match*— A match in which each competitor is assigned a definite relay and target by the Statistical Office. Failure to report on the proper relay or firing point forfeits the right to fire. All entries must be made before firing commences in that match, except when otherwise stated in the tournament program.

(h) *Unsquadded Individual Match*—A match in which the competitor is not assigned a definite relay and target by the Statistical Office. The competitor reports to the Range Officer within the time limits specified in the program and is then assigned to a target and a relay in which to fire.

(i) *Re-Entry Match*—A match in which the competitor is permitted to fire more than one score for record; one or more of the highest scores being considered to determine the relative rank of competitors. The number of scores which may be fired, and the number of high scores to be considered in deciding the relative rank of competitors must be specified in the program. Scores fired in these matches shall not be used for classification purposes.

(j) *Squadded Team Match*—A match in which the teams are assigned a definite time to fire. Teams may be assigned one or more adjacent targets. All entries must be made before firing commences in that match. The entire team must report and fire as a unit.

(k) *Unsquadded Team Match*—A match in which the teams may report at the firing line at any time within the limits specified in the program, targets being assigned by the Range Officer. The entire team must report and fire as a unit, unless the program provides otherwise.

(l) *Aggregate Match*—An aggregate of scores from two or more matches. This may be an aggregate of match stages, individual matches, team matches, or any combination, provided the tournament program clearly states the matches which will comprise the aggregate. Entries in aggregate matches must be made before the competitor commences firing in any of the matches making up the aggregate match.

2. ELIGIBILITY OF COMPETITORS

Eligibility of Competitors—*The conditions of a match shall prescribe the eligibility of competitors, team or individuals, in accordance with Rule 1.6 and/or the definitions contained in Section 2. Any limitation of eligibility to compete must be stated in the Match Program.*

INDIVIDUALS

• 2.1 Members of the National Rifle Association—Any individual member including Benefactors, Patrons, Endowment, Life, Annual, Associate, Non-Resident and Junior Members.

2.1.1 Non-U.S. Citizens—Non-U.S. Citizens who are also Non-Residents, who are not members of the National Rifle Association of America, but who are members in good standing of their own National Association or Federation, and have adequate proof of such membership in hand, may compete in any NRA Sanctioned Tournament, unless further restrictions are imposed by conditions stated in the program.

2.2 Civilian—Any civilian including all members of the Reserve Officers Training Corps (ROTC, NROTC and AFROTC), personnel of the State Security Forces (e.g., State Guard organizations having no federal recognition), retired members of each of the several services comprising the Armed Forces of the United States, and members and former members entitled to receive pay, retirement pay, retainer pay or equivalent pay, are classified as civilians except as noted in the example below. All competitors who are enrolled as undergraduates of any of the service academies will be considered as civilians, and may compete in collegiate and ROTC categories.

Individuals of any Reserve or National Guard component who, during the present calendar year, have not competed as National Guard (2.5) or Regular Service (2.6) or Reserve component (2.7) and have not been provided Service support for competition in the form of firearms, ammunition, payment of travel or other expenses, wholly or in part, may fire as civilians. The provision of firearms and ammunition for a specific competition (i.e., National Matches or NBPRP Regional Leg Matches), when such is available to both military and civilian competitors, is not considered Service support under this Rule.

Unless specifically authorized to do so by the tournament program, members of the regular Army, Navy, Air Force, Marine Corps, Coast Guard; members of the reserve components on active duty; retired personnel of the several services comprising the Armed Forces of the United States on active duty; or police (2.4) are not permitted to compete as civilians.

2.2.1 Senior—A person may compete as a senior beginning on January 1 of the calendar year in which the 60th birthday occurs.

2.3 Junior—A person may also compete as a Junior until December 31 of the calendar year in which his or her twentieth birthday occurs.

2.3.1 Intermediate Junior—A junior may also compete as an Intermediate Junior from January 1 of the calendar year in which his or her fifteenth birthday occurs through December 31 of the calendar year in which his or her seventeenth birthday occurs.

2.3.2 Sub-Junior—A junior may also compete as Sub-junior through December 31 of the calendar year in which his or her fourteenth birthday occurs.

• 2.4 Police—Any regular, full time member of a regularly constituted law enforcement agency including the enforcement officers of the several County or Municipal Police Departments; Highway Patrols, Penal Institution Guards; full time salaried Game Wardens, Deputy Game Wardens and Deputy Sheriffs; regularly organized Railroad or Industrial Police Departments, Bank Guards and Armored Truck and Express Company Guards.

Special Officers, Honorary Officers, Civilian Instructors, except as stated above, Deputy Sheriffs, Deputy Game Wardens or Police Officers who are not on a full time, full pay basis in a single department are not eligible to compete as police.

2.5 National Guard—Federally recognized officers or enlisted men of the Army National Guard, the Air National Guard, or the Naval Militia of the several states, territories, the District of Columbia, or the Commonwealth of Puerto Rico, who are not on extended active duty.

2.6 Regular Service—Officers or enlisted men of the Regular United States Army, Navy, Air Force, Marine Corps, Coast Guard, and members of reserve components thereof, who are on extended active duty; provided the term "reserve components" shall include Army National Guard and Air National Guard called into federal service and while in such status.

2.7 Reserve Components—Officers and enlisted men of any reserve components of the Armed Forces, exclusive of the Army National Guard and the Air National Guard of the United States, not on extended active duty.

2.8 College—Regularly enrolled full-time undergraduate students who carry 12 semester hours or the equivalent, who comply with the eligibility rules of their institution and who have not received a Bachelor's Degree.

2.9 School—Regularly enrolled undergraduate students of any primary or secondary school, who comply with the eligibility rules of their institution.

TEAMS

• All teams except Collegiate will be three member teams, Collegiate Teams will be four member teams to be eligible for National Records.

2.10 Team Representation—No competitor may fire on more than one team in any one match.
Note: Entries will not be accepted from 'Pickup' teams (teams whose members are selected without regard to club or other organizational affiliation) unless the program specifically provides for such eligibility. Pick-up teams are not eligible for National Records.

2.11 Affiliated Club Teams—All members of such teams must have been active full-paid members of the club which the team represents, for a period of at least 30 days immediately prior to the competition; and the club must be affiliated with the NRA and is in good standing. If specifically allowed by conditions of the program, a person not a club member may serve as the coach of an Affiliated Club team.

2.11.1 Affiliated Other Organizations (Art. III Sec. 4(b) NRA Bylaws)—All members of such teams must have been fully-paid members of the organization the team represents, for a period of at least 30 days immediately prior to the competition, and the organization must be affiliated with the NRA and in "good standing."

2.12 State Association Teams—Members of State Association Teams must be residents of the state represented. Members of such teams must be individual members of the State Rifle and/or Pistol Association represented, if such State Association provides for individual membership, or be members of a rifle and/or pistol club which is affiliated and in good standing with the State Association concerned at the time of the competition. State Association Teams permitted to enter the competition concerned by the tournament program conditions must be authorized and accredited by the State Association for that tournament. Authorization shall be signed by the State Association President, Vice President or Secretary. Such State Association must be affiliated and in good standing with the NRA at the time of the competition. If specifically allowed by conditions of the program, a person not a State Association member may serve as the coach of a State Association Team. (He may not be a firing member.)

Note: Teams representing State Associations, Leagues and other associations (composed of more than one club) are not club teams. Such teams may enter NRA Sanctioned Matches only when the program specifically authorizes such entry.

2.13 Regular Service, National Guard or Armed Forces Reserve Teams—Members of such teams must have been commissioned or enlisted members of their respective service for a continuous period of at least thirty days immediately preceding the day of the competition. Army National Guard, Air National Guard and Naval Militia personnel may be combined into a single team.

2.14 Police Teams—Members of such teams must have been regular full time members of their respective organization and in active service for a continuous period of at least 30 days immediately preceding the day of competition.

2.15 Civilian Club Teams—Members of such teams must comply with Rules 2.2 and 2.11.

2.16 College Teams—Members of such teams must comply with Rules 2.8 and 2.11.

2.17 School Teams—Members of such teams must comply with Rules 2.9 and 2.11.

2.18 Junior Club Teams—Member of such teams must comply with Rules 2.3 and 2.11.

2.20 Residence—In those matches which are limited to residents of any specified geographical area a "resident" is defined as:
- *(a)* A person who lives within a specified area for at least 30 days immediately prior to the day of the match, whether or not his employment is at a place requiring him to commute or travel into some other area.
- *(b)* A person who has been regularly employed within the specified area for at least 30 days immediately prior to the day of the match and who has maintained domicile in that area for the same period of time, although his permanent residence is located outside the specified area.
- *(c)* Military, Naval and Air Force Personnel: The place of residence of members of the Military, Naval and Air Force establishments on active duty is defined as the place at which they are stationed by reason of official orders, provided they have been so stationed within the specified area for a period of at least 30 days immediately prior to the day of the match. In the case of retired, Reserve, or National Guard personnel not on active duty, the provisions of paragraphs (a) and (b) will apply. Naval personnel assigned on sea duty qualify for a residence in the area which is the usual base or home port of the unit to which attached.
- *(d)* Federal and State Law Enforcement Officers: The provisions of paragraph (c) will apply.

3. FIREARMS, EQUIPMENT AND AMMUNITION

3.3 Rapid Fire Pistol—Any type of 5.6mm (.22 cal.) pistol or revolver may be used which complies with Rules 3.1 and 3.2 and the following specifications:

(a) The weight of the pistol with all accessories (including balancing weights and unloaded magazines) shall not exceed 1260 grams (2.8 lbs.).

(b) The height of the barrel including foresight and all accessories (from the breech face to the end of the muzzle, with the exception of the trigger and trigger-guard) must not exceed 40mm (1.6 in.) (see Figure 2 and 2a).

(c) Ammunition: Any 5.6mm (.22 cal.) rimfire cartridge is allowed (see Rule 3.1f).

(d) Special grips are permitted provided they remain within the overall dimensions.

(e) The overall size of the pistol is limited to those dimensions which will permit the pistol to be enclosed completely in a rectangular box having maximum inside measurements of 300mm (11.8 in.) × 150mm (5.9 in.) × 50mm (1.97 in.). A tolerance of up to 5% in ONE DIMENSION ONLY in height, width, length of the pistol OR the height of the barrel is acceptable. A manufacturing tolerance of +0.5mm −0.0mm the dimensions of the box will be permitted.

3.4 Center Fire Pistol—Any center fire pistol or revolver (with the exception of single-shot pistols), caliber 7.62mm-9.65mm (including British and American caliber, .30, .32, .35, .357, .38 Spl., and .380) which complies with Rules 3.1 and 3.2 and the following specifications may be used:

(a) The weight of the pistol with all accessories (including balancing weights and unloaded magazine) must not exceed 1400 grams (3.09 lbs.).

(b) The length of the barrel must not exceed 153mm (6 inches). (See Rule 3.2c.)

(c) Muzzle brakes or any device(s) functioning in a similar manner are not allowed.

(d) The distance between front and rear sights must not exceed 220mm (8.6 in.). (See Figures 2 and 2a.)

(e) The trigger pull must be at least 1360 grams (3 lbs.) measured with the barrel vertical. (See Figure 3.)

(f) No part of the grip or accessories may encircle the hand. The heel rest may extend at a right angle to the grip only. Upward

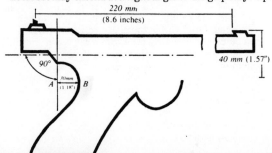

Fig. 2

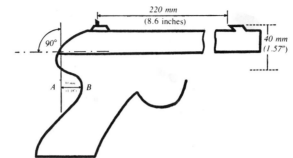

Figures 2 and 2a.   Distance between sights and
other pistol measurements

Fig.   2a

curvature of the heel and thumb rest and downward curvature of the side opposite the thumb are prohibited. (See Figure 1.) The rear part of the pistol frame or grip which rests on the top of the hand between the thumb and the forefinger must not be longer than 30mm (1.18 in.). This distance is measured at a right angle to the prolonged center-line of the barrel between points A and B of Figures 2 and 2a.

(h) Ammunition: Any 7.62-9.65 caliber center fire cartridge is allowed. (See 3.1f). (For safety reasons, "Magnum Class" ammunition is not allowed.)

3.5 Standard Pistol and Women's Sport Match Pistol—Any 5.6mm (.22 cal. rimfire pistol or revolver which complies with Rules 3.1 and 3.2 and the following specifications may be used:

(a) The weight of the pistol including balancing weights and unloaded magazine must not exceed 1400 grams (3.09 lbs.). Pistols weighing 52 oz. (3.25 lbs.) are allowed for U.S. competitions.

(b) The length of the barrel must not exceed 153mm (6 inches). (See Rule 3.2c.)

(c) The distance between front and rear sights must not exceed 220mm (8.6 in.). (See Figure 2a.)

(d) Muzzle brakes or any device(s) functioning in a similar manner are not allowed.

(e) The trigger pull must be at least 1000 grams (2.2 lbs.), measured with the barrel vertical. (See Figure 3.)

(f) No part of the grip or accessories may encircle the hand. The heel rest may extend at a right angle to the grip only. Upward curvature of the heel and thumb rest, and downward curvature of other grip projections are prohibited. (See Figure 1.) The rear part of the pistol frame or grip which rests on the top of the hand between the thumb and forefinger must not be longer than 30mm (1.18 in.). This distance is measured at a right angle to the prolonged center-line of the barrel between points A and B of Figures 2 and 2a.

(g) Ammunition: Any 5.6mm (.22 cal.) rimfire, long rifle cartridge may be used. (See Rule 3.1f.)

• **3.6 Free Pistol**—Any 5.6mm (.22 cal.) rimfire pistol or revolver which complies with Rule 3.1 and the following specifications may be used:

(a) There are no weight restrictions, however, the pistol must be capable of being held in one hand in the shooting position without support.

(b) The caliber may not exceed 5.6mm using ammunition of internationally recognized specification .22 caliber rimfire. Bullets must be of lead or similar soft material.

(c) The trigger pull is free and must be released by a finger of the hand in which the gun is held and that finger must make physical contact with the trigger.

(d) The pistol used may be equipped with a magazine. A pistol may be loaded with no more than one cartridge.

3.7 Air Pistol—Any 4.5mm (.177 cal.) type of compressed air or CO_2 pistol or revolver which complies with Rule 3.1 and the following specifications may be used:

(a) The weight of the pistol or revolver with all accessories must not exceed 1500 grams (3.3 lbs.).

(b) The trigger pull must be at least 500 grams (17.6 oz.), measured with the barrel vertical. (See Figure 3.)

(c) No part of the grip or accessories may encircle the hand. The heel rest may extend at a right angle to the grip only. Upward curvature of the heel and thumb rest, and downward curvature of other grip projections are prohibited. (See Figure 1.)

(d) The overall size of the pistol is limited to those dimensions that will permit the pistol to be enclosed completely in a rectangular box having maximum inside dimensions of 420mm × 200mm × 50mm. A manufacturing tolerance of +0.5mm −0.0mm in the dimensions of the box will be permitted.

(e) Ammunition: Any 4.5mm (.177 cal.) pellets may be used. (See Rule 3.1(f).)

3.8 Spotting Scopes—The use of a telescope with the necessary stand to visually locate shot holes on a target is permitted.

3.9 Shooting Kits—A shooting kit is allowed for the purpose of carrying the gun and accessories; however, the kit may not be so constructed or placed in or on the firing position in such a manner that it provides the shooters any advantage while firing a shot.

3.16 Release Triggers—Triggers which function on release are prohibited.

3.18 General—All devices or equipment which may facilitate shooting and which are not mentioned in these Rules, or which are contrary to the spirit of these Rules and Regulations, are forbidden.

Each competitor must have his firearms officially examined and approved prior to the competition. Examining times are fixed by the competition officials. Only firearms which have been approved for the competition concerned may be used (see Rule 9.14 and 9.35(h).)

3.20 Eye Protection—All competitors and other personnel in the immediate vicinity of the range complex are urged to wear eye protection devices or similar eye protection.

3.21 Ear Protection—All competitors and other personnel in the immediate vicinity of the range complex are urged to wear hearing protection devices or similar ear protection.

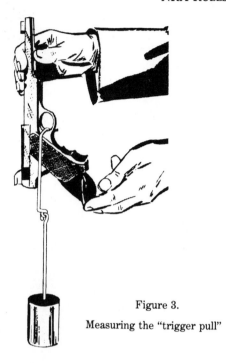

Figure 3.

Measuring the "trigger pull"

4. TARGETS

• **4.1 Official Targets**—In Registered and Approved Pistol matches, only targets bearing the words "Official National Rifle Association" and the eagle and shield insignia of the Association, official UIT targets, or military targets issued by the armed services, will be used. Targets used in National Championships will be NRA Official Targets or targets approved by the UIT for international competition.

(a) Target B-11, International 50 feet slow fire target, reduced 50 meter target for firing the Free Pistol course at 50 feet. The scoring rings 7 through 10 are black. Inner 10 ring is .15 inch.

10 ring	.45 inch
9 ring	1.05 inches
8 ring	1.65 inches
7 ring	2.25 inches
6 ring	2.85 inches
5 ring	3.45 inches
4 ring	4.05 inches
3 ring	4.65 inches
2 ring	5.25 inches
1 ring	5.85 inches

(b) Target B-17, International 50 meter slow fire target for firing the 50 meter free pistol course at 50 meters, the standard pistol, women's sport pistol and the center fire pistol, precision stage, at 25 meters. The scoring rings 7 through 10 are black. Inner 10 ring is 25mm. (See figure 5.)

```
10 ring ....................................... .50 mm
 9 ring ....................................... .100 mm
 8 ring ....................................... .150 mm
 7 ring ....................................... .200 mm
 6 ring ....................................... .250 mm
 5 ring ....................................... .300 mm
 4 ring ....................................... .350 mm
 3 ring ....................................... .400 mm
 2 ring ....................................... .450 mm
 1 ring ....................................... .500 mm
```

(c) Target B-18, International rapid fire target, used for the international rapid fire course and the duel stage of the 25 meter/25 yard center fire pistol and women's sport pistol events. The top edge of the scoring area begins at the upper midpoint in the 6 ring and ends at the lower midpoint of the 6 ring at the bottom of the target. (See fig. 4). It is divided into 5 scoring zones, (hits outside the 6 ring are scored as misses). The 10 ring is formed by two vertical lines 5cm long, 10cm apart and joined at the top and bottom by semicircles with a 5cm radius. The 10 ring is therefore 10cm wide and 15cm high. The 9 through 6 rings are similarly shaped with their widths successively increased by 10cm (5cm on each side) and their heights by 15cm (7.5cm at the top and bottom). The center of the 10 ring must be 37.5cm from the top of the target. The 10 ring is not numbered.

Figure 4

(d) Target B-19, International slow fire target, reduces the 50 meter target for firing the free pistol course at 50 yards, the standard pistol, women's sport pistol and the center fire pistol, precision stage, at 25 yards. The scoring rings 7 through 10 are black. Inner 10 ring is .88 inch.

```
10 ring ..................................... 1.78 inches
 9 ring ..................................... 3.58 inches
 8 ring ..................................... 5.38 inches
 7 ring ..................................... 7.18 inches
```

```
6 ring ...................................8.98 inches
5 ring ...................................10.78 inches
4 ring ...................................12.58 inches
3 ring ...................................14.38 inches
2 ring ...................................16.18 inches
1 ring ...................................17.98 inches
```

(e) Target B-24, International Rapid Fire target for firing the rapid fire pistol, women's sport pistol and center fire pistol events at 50 feet. Overall size 12 x 20 inches.

(f) Target B-32, International 10 meter air pistol target, for firing the air pistol course at 10 meters (33 feet). The scoring rings 7 through 10 are black. <u>Inner 10 ring is 6mm.</u>

```
10 ring .......................................12 mm
 9 ring .......................................28 mm
 8 ring .......................................44 mm
 7 ring .......................................60 mm
 6 ring .......................................76 mm
 5 ring .......................................92 mm
 4 ring ......................................108 mm
 3 ring ......................................124 mm
 2 ring ......................................140 mm
 1 ring ......................................156 mm
```

(g) Target B-33, International standard pistol target, reduced for firing the standard pistol, women's sport pistol course and center fire pistol course at 50 feet. The scoring rings 7 through 10 are black.

```
10 ring ..................................1.10 inches
 9 ring ..................................2.30 inches
 8 ring ..................................3.50 inches
 7 ring ..................................4.70 inches
 6 ring ..................................5.90 inches
 5 ring ..................................7.10 inches
 4 ring ..................................8.30 inches
 3 ring ..................................9.50 inches
 2 ring ..................................10.70 inches
 1 ring ..................................11.90 inches
```

(h) Target B-35, International 25 yard slow fire target, reduces the 50 meter target for firing the free pistol course at 25 yards.

```
10 ring ..................................0.78 inches
 9 ring ..................................1.68 inches
 8 ring ..................................2.58 inches
 7 ring ..................................3.48 inches
 6 ring ..................................4.38 inches
 5 ring ..................................5.28 inches
 4 ring ..................................6.18 inches
 3 ring ..................................7.08 inches
 2 ring ..................................7.98 inches
 1 ring ..................................8.88 inches
```

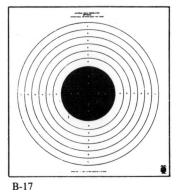

B-17

Figure 5

5. POSITIONS

Positions—The positions for use in a match shall be stated in the program under conditions of the match and shall be in accord with the definitions of positions prescribed in this section.

5.1 The Ground—All references to "the ground" in the following position Rules are to be construed as applying to surface of the firing point, floor, and such shooting platforms as are customarily used on shooting ranges.

5.2 Artificial Support—Any supporting surface except the ground not specifically authorized for use in the Rules for the position prescribed. Use of artificial support is prohibited except as individually authorized for a physically handicapped shooter.

5.3 Ready Position—In all 25m timed fire events (Rapid Fire, Center Fire Match/Women's Sport Match dueling course, and Standard Pistol 20 second and 10 second series) shooting must start from the "READY" position. In this position, the competitor waits for the appearance of the targets with his arm pointing downward at an angle of not greater than 45° from the vertical at the moment the targets begin to face (See Figure 6). Only when the targets begin to face may the competitor raise the pistol. (See Rule 9.35, for penalties).

Figure 6

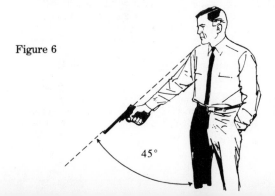

45°

5.5 Physically Handicapped Shooters—A shooter who because of physical handicap cannot fire from one or more of the prescribed shooting positions outlined in these Rules, or who must use special equipment when firing, is privileged to petition the NRA Protest Committee for permission to assume a special position or to use modified equipment, or both. This petition will be in the form of a written request from the person concerned to the Committee outlining in detail the reasons why the special position must be assumed or the special equipment must be used. The petition will be accompanied by pictures of the shooter in the position he desires approved and, if special equipment is required, the picture will show how this equipment is used. The petition and all pictures must be furnished in exact duplicate. The petition must be accompanied by a medical doctor's statement if the physical handicap is not completely evident in the pictures submitted.

(a) Each petition will be reviewed by the NRA Protest Committee. The Committee may require additional or supplementary statements or pictures. After review the NRA Secretary will be instructed by the Committee to issue a special authorization certificate to individuals who submit petitions and pictures which have been approved. Such certificates will have necessary pictures attached.

(b) Shooters who have received special authorization certificates will be required to carry them when competing in competition governed by NRA Rules, and to present the certificate when requested by officials of the competition or by NRA Official **Referees or Supervisors**.

(c) In the event of a protest involving the position or the equipment used by such a shooter, the Official Referee or Supervisor will compare the questioned position or equipment with the certificate and photographs presented by the shooter. If the shooter's position or equipment does not, in the opinion of the official, conform to that authorized by the NRA Protest Committee (or if the shooter has no authorized certificate or pictures), the protest shall be allowed and the shooter will be required to change immediately to the position or equipment which has been approved or to an otherwise legal position or equipment.

(d) Should a protest be carried beyond the Official Referee or Supervisor, the original protest will be endorsed by the Referee or Supervisor to show the action he has taken and will be forwarded to the NRA.

(e) National Records may not be established by use of scores fired in special positions or with special equipment as may be authorized according to this Rule.

(f) Two types of authorizations are issued; temporary and permanent. Permanent authorizations are issued to competitors who are permanently handicapped.

5.12 Firing Position—The competitor shall stand free, without support, completely within the space provided. The complete firearm shall be held and discharged with one hand only (with the same hand). The wrist of the hand holding the gun, the elbow, or shoulder must not be supported by the grip or any other part of the pistol, or by any other means. Bracelets, wrist watches, wrist bands, or similar things which might provide support are prohibited on the gun-hand and arm. (See Rule 5.5 for exceptions for physical handicaps.)

7. COURSES OF FIRE

7.1 Rapid Fire Pistol Match—The program is 60 competition shots. Firing will be divided into two courses each of 30 shots. Each course is subdivided into 6 series of 5 shots each, two in 8 seconds, two in 6 seconds and two in 4 seconds fired on the International Rapid Fire Pistol target. (see Figure 4). The first course must be completed by all competitors before the second course may commence. Before the beginning of each 30-shot course, the competitor may fire one sighting series of 5 shots at 8, 6 or 4 seconds at his own option.

7.2 Center Fire Pistol Match and Women's Sport Pistol Match (w/Standard Pistol)—These competitions are divided into:

(a) Precision Course—30 shots on the International Precision target (see Figure 5). The competition consists of 6 series each of 5 shots. The time limit for each series is 6 minutes. Before the course begins, a series of 5 sighting shots may be fired within a time limit of 6 minutes.

(b) Duelling Course—30 shots on the International Rapid Fire target (see Figure 4). The course consists of 6 series each of 5 shots. During each series the target appears five times, each time for 3 seconds, with a 7-second pause between each appearance. One shot will be fired during each appearance. Before the program of 30 shots begins, the competitor may shoot a sighting series of 5 shots, in the duelling course. The precision course must be completed by all competitors before the duelling course can begin.

7.3 Standard Pistol Match

(a) Comptitions are conducted in 3 consecutive courses of 20 shots each. Each course consists of four 5-shot series fired on the International Precision target (see Figure 5).

1. 4 × 5 shots in 150 seconds per 5-shot series.
2. 4 × 5 shots in 20 seconds per 5-shot series.
3. 4 × 5 shots in 10 seconds per 5-shot series.

Before the competition begins, a series of 5 sighting shots may be fired within a time limit of 150 seconds.

(b) When it is necessary to conduct the competition in two parts, a sighting series shall be fired before each part. The parts consist of:
1. 2 × 5 shots in 150 seconds per 5-shot series.
2. 2 × 5 shots in 20 seconds per 5-shot series
3. 2 × 5 shots in 10 seconds per 5-shot series.

7.4 Free Pistol Match

(a) Shooting program—60 shots Standing (Rule 5.12. Positions) *(b)* Sighting shots (unlimited in number) may only be fired before the beginning of each match. Once the first match shot has been fired, no further sighting shots are allowed unless permitted by the Jury/Referee.

(c) Target—International Precision Target

(d) If the competition is divided into two parts, then each part shall consist of 30 competition shots.

(e) Total allowable shooting time including sighting shots: Full Course—2 hours, 30 minutes; Half Course—1 hour, 20 minutes; Minimum preparation time before official start (the command, "Fire")—10 minutes.

(f) Tournament sponsors may allow a minimum of 1½ minutes per record shot. Time allowances, where less than maximum, must be specified in the program.

• **7.5 Air Pistol, 10 Meters**

(a) Shooting Program—60 shots standing <u>for Men and Junior Men</u> (40 shots for Women and <u>Junior Women</u>).

(b) Sighting shots (unlimited in number) may only be fired before the beginning of each match. Once the first match shot has been fired, no further sighting shots are allowed unless permitted by the Jury/Referee.

(c) Target—Air Pistol target for 10 meters.

(d) The placing of targets shall normally be done by the shooter himself under supervision of **Range Officials**.

(e) Total allowable shooting time including sighting shots is 2 hours, 15 minutes for <u>Men and Junior Men</u> (1 hour, 30 minutes for Women and Junior <u>Women</u>).

(f) Tournament sponsors may allow a minimum of 1½ minutes per record shot. Time allowances, where less than maximum, must be specified in the program.

14. SCORING AND MARKING

14.1 When to Score—Targets are scored after each 5 shot series or each 10 shot double series as provided in the match program.

14.2 Where to Score—Targets may be scored on the target frames, at the firing line, or in the Statistical Office as provided in the match program. The scorer must be at the target when scoring.

14.3 How to Score—A shot hole, the edge of which comes in contact with the outside of the bullseye or scoring rings of a target, is given the higher value. If a competitor fails to hit any target (shot/s outside the scoring ring) that shot will be scored as a miss (zero). A scoring gauge will be used to determine the value of close shots. The higher value will be allowed in those cases where the flange on the gauge touches the scoring ring, except that when the Air Pistol "outward" scoring plug gauge is used, the higher value is awarded when the flange fails to touch the inside edge of the next scoring ring out.

Figure 8

The Correct Method of Scoring

The shot on the left bullseye counts nine, the one on the right, ten.

No scoring gauge will be used unless the diameter of the scoring flange is within these limits:
Air Pistol, .177''-.179'' (4.5-4.55mm)
Air Pistol gauge for "outside" scoring .451''-.453''
(11.45-11.5mm)
.22 caliber, .2225''-.2240''
Center Fire, .380''-.382'' (9.65-9.70mm)
(When the Center Fire course is fired at 50 ft., the NRA plug gauge with flange corresponding to bullet diameter shall be used. .32 calibre, .310''-.314''; .38 caliber, .355''-.359'')

When the accurate use of the plug gauge is made difficult by the close proximity of another bullet hole, the shot value shall be determined by means of an engraved gauge of some flat, transparent material, to aid in reconstructing the position of a scoring ring or number of bullet holes which may overlap.

14.3.1 Use of Plug Type Scoring Gauges—Shots in dispute shall be scored with the aid of a "plug" type gauge or other instrument.

   (a) The plug gauge may be inserted only once in any bullet hole. For this reason, the use of a plug gauge shall be marked on the target by the Scoring Officials, together with their signatures.

   (b) If two Scoring Officials do not agree on the value of a shot, a decision from the Jury/Referee shall be requested immediately.

   (c) No challenge may be made against a shot value which has been decided by means of a gauge, since such a decision is final.

   (d) In Air Pistol competitions where three member scoring teams are not used to evaluate plugged shots, the competitor may challenge the score on a plugged shot and have it replugged and the challenge resolved by the Official Referee, the competition Jury or Supervisor.

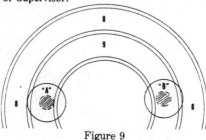

Figure 9

The "A" illustration depicts a doubtful shot hole with the "OUT-WARD" scoring gauge in place. The outside edge of the flange is not outside of the 9 ring therefore the shot would be scored 10.

The "B" illustration depicts a doubtful shot hole to the scorer. The "OUTWARD" scoring gauge shows the outside edge of the flange lying over the 9 demarcation line and into the 8 ring thereby giving a result of 9 for shothole "B."

14.4 Misses—Hits outside the scoring rings are scored as misses.

14.5 Early or Late Shots—If any shots are fired before the starting signal to commence fire or after the signal to cease fire (See Rule 10.7) the shots of highest value equal to the number fired in error will be scored as misses.

Any shots fired after the command "LOAD" has been given, but before the beginning of a competition series, shall not be counted in the competition and a penalty of two points deduction from the following series will be imposed. This penalty will not apply in the sighting series.

The beginning of a series is considered to be:

(a) The command "FIRE" or signal in Precision shooting on stationary targets (Free Pistol; Air Pistol; Center Fire Match, and Women's Sport Pistol Match).

(b) The first disappearance of the target in the timed fire courses (Duelling course of Center Fire Match and Women's Sport Pistol Match and all stages of the Standard Pistol Match). (Rules 10.9(b) 7,10.10(d))

(c) From the moment the competitor *starts* his reply "READY" in the Rapid Fire Match (Rule 10.8h)

Each shot fired after the beginning of a series will be counted in the competition.

• 14.7 Hits on Wrong Target

(a) If a competitor fires a sighting shot on the sighting target of another competitor, he shall not be allowed to repeat the shot, but he shall not be penalized.

(b) If a competitor fires a competition shot on the sighting target or competition target of another competitor, the shot will be scored as a miss (zero).

14.8 Ricochets—A hole made by a ricochet bullet does not count as a hit and will be scored as a miss. It must be noted that a bullet which keyholes is not necessarily a ricochet.

14.9 Visible Hits and Close Groups. Targets where Multiple Shots are Fired—*(This Rule will apply only in Air Pistol competition when the sponsor has specified that 5 shots are to be fired on each record target) (Rule 10.12d).*

As a general rule only those hits which are visible will be scored. An exception will be made in the case where the grouping of 3 or more shots is so close that it is possible for a required shot or shots to have gone through the enlarged hole without leaving a mark and there has been no evidence that a shot or shots have gone elsewhere than through the assigned target. In such case, the shooters will be given the benefit of the doubt, and scored hits for the nonvisible shots, on the assumption they passed through the enlarged hole. If such assumption could place a non-visible hit in either of 2 scoring rings, it shall be scored in the higher-valued ring.

14.10 Excessive or Too Few Hits

(a) In the 25 Meter events, if a competitor fires more competition shots on a target than the program calls for, or more than one shot at one appearance of the target in the duelling course, the highest valued shot or shots will be deducted from the score of that target and counted as a miss. Two points will also be deducted from the score of that series for each extra shot fired in the series or at a single appearance of the target.

(b) In the Free Pistol Match and Air Pistol Match if a competitor fires more shots on his competition target than are provided for in the program he shall not be penalized for the first two such occurrences. For the third and all succeeding such shots, he shall be penalized by the deduction of two points each time. The competitor must fire a correspondingly fewer number of shots at the succeeding target.

(c) If a competitor fires more shots in the competition than are provided for in the program, the extra shot or shots will be annulled. If the shot or shots cannot be identified, the highest valued shot or shots will be annulled on the target in question. In either case, the competitor will also be penalized by the deduction of two points for each excessive shot fired, from the score of the first series.

(d) If a competitor fires more sighting shots than provided for in the program, or approved by the Range Officer or Jury, he shall be penalized by the deduction of two points from his competition score from the first series for each excessive sighting shot fired.

(e) If a competitor wishes to disclaim a bullet hole on his target, he will report this immediately to the Range Officer.

If the Range Officer confirms that the competitor did not fire the disputed shot, he will make the necessary entry on the Range Register, and the shot will be annulled.

If the Range Officer cannot confirm beyond all reasonable doubt that the competitor did not fire the disputed shot, the shot will be credited to the competitor and will be so recorded.

The following shall be considered sufficient to justify the annulment of a shot:

1. If the Scorer confirms by his observation of the competitor and the target that the competitor did not fire the shot.
2. If a "missed shot" is reported by another competitor or Scorer at approximately the same time, and from within the neighboring two or three shooting stations.

(f) In the case of shooting in the timed fire events where target patches are used, and there are more hits on the target than the competitor fired, the Range Officer shall attempt to establish which is the earlier bullet hole that had not been patched or which had become uncovered. If this is not possible, the competitor has the option of accepting the lower valued shot, or he may repeat the series. He may not be credited with more than the five highest valued or less than the five lowest valued hits on the target/s.

NATIONAL RIFLE ASSOCIATION

Official Rules for Smallbore Rifle Matches

These Rules establish uniform standards for NRA Sanctioned Smallbore Rifle Competition. Where alternatives are shown, the least restrictive conditions apply unless the tournament program sets forth limitations. They do not apply to International Shooting Union type competition. They supersede the January 1, 1985 and all earlier editions and remain in effect until specifically superseded.

Tournament sponsors may not alter these Rules. If sponsors require additional Rules for special conditions, the additions must be fully set forth in the program for the competition concerned. Anyone wishing to submit recommendations may forward those recommendations to the Smallbore Rifle Committee in care of the National Rifle Association.

The arrangement and Rule numbering systems are such that corresponding Rules for other types of NRA competition are correspondingly located and numbered in the Rule Books for those competitions. Gaps in the sequence of Rule numbers result from there being a Rule in one or more of the other Rule Books which does not apply in this book.

NOTE: *Rules in which major changes have been made since publication of the previous Rule Book are marked thus: (• 1.1). All revised wording is underlined.*

1. NRA COMPETITION

1.0 NRA Competition—NRA Competition is a Competition which is authorized in advance of firing by the National Rifle Association. The program, range facilities and officials must comply with standards established by the NRA.

1.1 Sanctioned Tournaments—A Sanctioned Tournament is a series of matches covered by an Official Program. Such matches may be all individual matches, all team matches, or a combination of both, which must be conducted by an NRA affiliated club or organization. They may be all fired matches or a combination of fired and aggregate matches. A tournament may be conducted on one day, or successive days, or may provide for intervening days between portions of the tournament, such as tournaments programmed to be conducted over more than one weekend.

1.2 Authorization—Before being publicized in programs or otherwise, the sponsoring organization of each type of compeition mentioned in Rule 1.6 shall have agreed to comply with the current regulations for such competition and shall have received notice from the NRA that the competition applied for has been authorized.

1.3 Rules—The local sponsor of each type of competition must agree to conduct the authorized competition according to NRA Rules, except as these Rules have been modified by the NRA in the General Regulations for that type of competition.

1.4 General Regulations—The local sponsor of each type of competition must agree to comply with the General Regulations published by the NRA for the competition concerned. The General Regulations may be found in the back of this Rule Book.

1.5 Refusal or Withdrawal of NRA Authorization—The NRA may refuse to authorize or may withdraw its authorization for any competition which cannot, or does not, comply with the requirements for that competition.

1.6 Types of Tournaments—The types of tournaments listed below are those which are Sanctioned by NRA in its Competitive shooting program.

(a) *International Matches*—Arranged by the NRA with the recognized national shooting organization(s) of the countries concerned. The officials thereof are appointed by the NRA.

(b) *International Team Tryouts*—Are U.S. tournaments conducted under UIT or NRA International Rules organized or authorized by the NRA as Preliminary or Final Tryouts for the selection of International Team members. The officials thereof are appointed or approved by the NRA.

(c) *National Championships*—Organized by the NRA, and in some cases in conjunction with the National Board for the Promotion of Rifle Practice, Department of the Army, to form the National Matches. The officials thereof are appointed by the NRA, in some circumstances in cooperation with the NBPRP. (These tournaments will be Registered.)

(d) *Regional and Sectional Championships*—Arranged between the NRA and a local sponsoring organization. (These tournaments will be Registered.)

(e) *State Championships*—Annual tournaments conducted by State Rifle and/or Pistol Associations, affiliated with the NRA. Such State Associations may, if desired, authorize local organizations to sponsor and conduct State Championships. In states where there is no NRA affiliated State Association the NRA may authorize a local organization to sponsor and conduct the State Championship. State Championships will be Registered Tournaments.

(f) *Registered Tournaments*—May be authorized by the NRA after application has been filed by the local NRA affiliated member organization which will act as the sponsor. Application forms are available from NRA on request. National Records may only be established in Registered Tournaments (Rule 17.1). All competitors in Registered Tournaments must be individual members of NRA, except for Junior (Rules 2.3, 2.3.1, and 2.3.2), who may be either members of NRA Affiliated Junior Clubs or individual members of NRA. Match Sponsors may require all competitors to be NRA members if specified in the program.

(g) *Approved Tournaments*—May be authorized by the NRA after application has been filed by the local NRA affiliated member organization which will act as the sponsor. Application forms are available from NRA on request.

(h) *Sanctioned Leagues*—(shoulder-to-shoulder or postal) May be authorized by the NRA after application has been filed by a local organization. Application forms are available from NRA on request. Sanctioned League scores are used for classification.

(i) *Postal Matches*—Organized by the NRA and publicized to groups concerned through the AMERICAN RIFLEMAN and THE AMERICAN MARKSMAN announcements and special mailings.

1.7 Types of Matches—

(a) *Match*—A complete event as indicated in the program for the awarding of certain specific prizes. A match may consist of one or several stages. It may, in the case of aggregate matches, include the scores fired in several subsidiary matches.

(b) Stage—A portion of a match which consists of one or more strings fired in one position, distance, time allowance, or target.

(c) Open Match—A match open to anyone, except that if so stated in the program an open match may be limited to one or any combination of the following. (a) United States citizens; (b) members of the National Rifle Association of America; and/or (c) with respect to non-U.S. citizens, persons who are members in good standing of their respective National Shooting Federations or Associations. (see Rule 2.1.1).

(d) Restricted Match—A match in which competition is limited to specified groups, i.e., juniors, women, police, civilians, veterans, etc.; or to specified classes, i.e., Masters, Experts, Sharpshooters, Marksmen, etc.

(e) Classified Match—A match in which awards are given to winners and to the highest competitors in several specified classes such as Masters, Experts, Sharpshooters, Marksmen. The classification of competitors may be accomplished by the National Classification System (Sec. 19) or by other means. The program for classified matches must specify the groups or classes in which awards will be made.

(f) Invitational Match—A match in which participation is limited to those who have been invited to compete.

(g) Squadded Individual Match—A match in which each competitor is assigned a definite relay and target by the Statistical Office. Failure to report on the proper relay or firing point forfeits the right to fire. All entries must be made before firing commences in that match, except when otherwise stated in the tournament program.

(h) Unsquadded Individual Match—A match in which the competitor is not assigned a definite relay or target by the Statistical Office. The competitor reports to the Range Officer within the time limits specified in the program and is then assigned to a target and a relay in which to fire.

(i) Re-Entry Match—A match in which the competitor is permitted to fire more than one score for record; one or more of the highest scores being considered to decide the relative rank of competitors must be specified in the program. Scores fired in these matches shall not be used for classification purposes.

(j) Squadded Team Match—A match in which the teams are assigned a definite time to fire. Teams may be assigned one or more adjacent targets. All entries must be made before firing commences in that match. The entire team must report and fire as a unit.

(k) Unsquadded Team Match—A match in which the teams may report to the firing line at any time within the limits specified in the program, targets being assigned by the Range Officer. The entire team must report and fire as a unit, unless the program provides otherwise.

(l) Aggregate Match—An aggregate of the scores from two or more matches. This may be an aggregate of match stages, individual matches, team matches, or any combination, provided the tournament program clearly states the matches which will comprise

the aggregate. Entries in aggregate matches must be made before the competitor commences firing in any of the matches making up the aggregate match.

2. ELIGIBILITY OF COMPETITORS

Eligibility of Competitors—The conditions of a match shall prescribe the eligibility of competitors, team or individuals, in accordance with Rule 1.6 and/or the definitions contained in Section 2. Any limitation of eligibility to compete must be stated in the match program.

INDIVIDUALS

• **2.1 Members of the National Rifle Association**—Any individual member including Benefactors and Patrons, Endowment, Life, Annual, Associate, Non-Resident and Junior members.

2.1.1 Non-U.S. Citizens—Non-U.S. Citizens who are also non-Residents, who are not members of the National Rifle Association of America, but who are members in good standing of their own National Association, and have adequate proof of such membership in hand, may compete in any NRA Sanctioned Tournament, unless further restrictions are imposed by conditions stated in the program.

2.2 Civilian—Any civilian including all members of the Reserve Officer Training Corps (ROTC, NROTC and AFROTC), personnel of the State Security Forces (e.g., State Guard organizations having no federal recognition), retired members of each of the several services comprising the Armed Forces of the United States, and members and former members entitled to receive pay, retirement pay, retainer pay or equivalent pay, are classified as civilians except as noted in the example below. All competitors who are enrolled undergraduates of any of the service academies will be considered as civilians and may compete in collegiate and ROTC categories.

Individuals of any Reserve or National Guard component who, *during the present calendar year*, have not competed as National Guard (2.5) or Regular Service (2.6) or Reserve component (2.7) *and* have not been provided Service support for competition (in the form of firearms, ammunition, payment of travel or other expenses), wholly or in part, may fire as civilians and *may be eligible to compete as Junior or Collegiate.* The provision of firearms and ammunition for a specific competition (i.e., National Matches or NBPRP Regional Leg Matches), when such is available to both military and civilian competitors, is not considered Service support under this Rule.

Unless specifically authorized to do so by the tournament program, members of the regular Army, Navy, Air Force, Marine Corps, Coast Guard; members of the reserve components on active duty; retired personnel of the several services comprising the Armed Forces of the United States on active duty; or police (2.4) are not permitted to compete as civilians.

2.2.1 Senior—A person may compete as a Senior beginning on January 1, of the calendar year in which his or her 60th birthday occurs.

2.3 Junior—A person may also compete as a Junior through December 31 of the calendar year in which his or her twentieth birthday occurs.

2.3.1. Intermediate Junior—A Junior may also compete as an Intermediate Junior from January 1 of the calendar year in which his or her 15th birthday occurs through December 31 of the calendar year in which his or her seventeenth birthday occurs.

2.3.2. Sub-Junior—A Junior may also compete as a Sub-Junior through December 31 of the calendar year in which his or her fourteenth birthday occurs.

• **2.4 Police**—Any regular, full-time member of a regularly constituted law-enforcement agency, including the enforcement officers of the several departments of the United States Government: State, County or Municipal Police Departments; Highway Patrols, Penal Institution Guards; full time salaried Game Wardens, Deputy Game Wardens and Deputy Sheriffs; regularly organized Railroad or Industrial Police Departments, Bank Guards and Armored Truck and Express Company Guards.

Special Officers, Honorary Officers, Civilian Instructors (except as stated above), Deputy Sheriffs, Deputy Game Wardens or Police Officers who are not on a full time, full pay basis in a single department are not eligible to compete as police.

2.5 National Guard—Federally recognized officers or enlisted persons of the Army National Guard, the Air National Guard, or the Naval Militia of the several states, territories, the District of Columbia or the Commonwealth of Puerto Rico, who are not on extended active duty.

2.6 Regular Service—Officers or enlisted persons of the Regular United States Army, Navy, Air Force, Marine Corps, Coast Guard, and members of reserve components thereof, who are on extended active duty; provided the term "reserve components" shall include Army National Guard and Air National Guard called into federal service and while in such status.

2.7 Reserve Components—Officers and enlisted persons of any reserve components of the Armed Forces, exclusive of the Army National Guard and the Air National Guard of the United States, not on extended active duty.

2.8 College—Regularly enrolled full-time undergraduate students who carry 12 semester hours or the equivalent, who comply with the eligibility rules of their institution, and who have not received a Bachelor's Degree.

2.9 School—Regularly enrolled undergraduate students of any primary or secondary school, who comply with the eligibility rules of their institution.

TEAMS

2.10 Team Representation—No individual may be a Team Captain, Coach, firing member, or alternate firing member on more than one team in any one match.

Note: Entries will not be accepted from 'Pickup' teams (teams whose members are selected without regard to club or other organizational affiliation) unless the program specifically provides for such eligibility.

2.11 Affiliated Club Teams (Art. III, Sec. 4(c) NRA Bylaws)—All members of such teams must have been active fully-paid members of the club which the team represents, for a period of at least 30 days immediately prior to the competition; and the club must be affiliated with the NRA and in good standing. If specifically allowed by conditions of the program, a person who is not a club member may serve as the coach of an affiliated club team. (He may not be a firing member.)

2.11.1 Affiliated Other Organizations (Art. III, Sec. 4(b) NRA Bylaws)—All members of such teams must have been fully paid members of the organization the team represents for a period of at least 30 days immediately prior to the competition, and the organization must be affiliated with the NRA and in good standing.

2.12 State Association Teams (Art. III, Sec. 4(a) NRA Bylaws)—Members of such teams must be bona fide residents of the state represented, and individual members of the State Rifle and/or Pistol Association, if such State Association provides for additional membership, or be members of a rifle and/or pistol club which is affiliated and in good standing with the State Association concerned at the time of the competition. State Association Teams permitted to enter the competitions by the tournament program conditions must be authorized and accredited by the Association for that tournament. Authorization shall be signed by the Association President, Vice President or Secretary. Such State Associations must be affiliated and in good standing with the NRA at the time of the competition. If specifically allowed by conditions of the program, a person not a State Association member may serve as the Coach of a State Association team. (He may not be a firing member.)

Note: Teams representing State Associations, Leagues and other associations (composed of more than one club) are not club teams. Such teams may enter NRA Sanctioned Matches only when the program specifically authorizes such entry.

2.13 Regular Service, National Guard or Armed Forces Reserve Teams—Members of such teams must have been commissioned or enlisted members of their respective service for a continuous period of at least 30 days immediately preceding the day of the competition. Army National Guard, Air National Guard and the Naval Militia personnel may be combined into a single team.

2.14 Police Teams—Members of such teams must have been regular full time members of their respective organization and in active service for a continuous period of at least 30 days immediately preceding the day of competition. (Rule 2.4)

2.15 Civilian Club Teams—Firing and alternate members of such teams must comply with Rules 2.2 and 2.11.

2.16 College Teams—Firing and alternate members of such teams must comply with Rules 2.8 and 2.11.

2.17 School Teams—Firing and alternate members of such teams must comply with Rules 2.9 and 2.11.

2.18 Junior Club Teams—Firing and alternate members of such teams must comply with Rules 2.3 and 2.11.

2.20 Residence—In those matches which are limited to residents of any specified geographical area a "resident" is defined as:

(a) A person who lives within a specified area for at least 30 days immediately prior to the day of the match, whether or not his employment is at a place requiring him to commute or travel into some other area.

(b) A person who has been regularly employed within the specified area for at least 30 days immediately prior to the day of the match and who has maintained domicile in that area for the same period of time, although his permanent residence is located outside the specified area.

(c) Military, Naval and Air Force Personnel: The place of residence of members of the Military, Naval and Air Force establishments on active duty is defined as the place at which they are stationed by reason of official orders, provided they have been so stationed within the specified area for a period of at least 30 days immediately prior to the day of the match. In the case of Retired, Reserve, or National Guard personnel not on active duty, the provisions of Paragraphs (a) and (b) will apply. Naval personnel assigned on sea duty qualify for a residence in the area which is the usual base or home port of the unit to which attached.

(d) Federal and State Law Enforcement Officers: The provisions of Paragraph (c) will apply.

3. EQUIPMENT AND AMMUNITION

This section defines authorized equipment. Where alternative types of equipment are shown, the least restrictive conditions apply unless the tournament program sets forth limitations.

• **3.1 The Rifle**—The rifle authorized for use in smallbore rifle matches is the .22 caliber rimfire chambered for cartridges commercially catalogued as the ".22 Short," ".22 Long" or ".22 Long Rifle" cartridges. There are no restrictions on the barrel length or overall weight of the rifle and accessories. No portion of the rifle or any attachment to the rifle shall extend more than 3 inches beyond the rear of the shooter's shoulder. The trigger pull must be capable of lifting 3 pounds. The same rifle must be used throughout all stages of any one match (except aggregate) except in the case of a malfunction or disabled rifle, when the competitor may change rifles with permission of the Chief Range Officer.

• **3.2 Any Rifle**—A rifle authorized for use in smallbore rifle matches using cartridges commercially catalogued as the ".22 short", ".22 Long" or ".22 Long Rifle" cartridges. There are no restrictions on the barrel length or overall weight of the rifle and accessories. No portion of the rifle or any attachment to the rifle shall extend more than 3 inches beyond the rear of the shooter's shoulder. A butt plate conforming with NRA Rule 3.15 may be used. "Around the body," or "around the shoulder" hooks are not permitted. The same rifle must be used throughout all stages of any one match (except aggregate) except in the case of a malfunction or disabled rifle when the competitor may change rifles with permission of the Chief Range Officer. In NRA 3 Position Course shooting this Rule will govern the conduct of the match and may not be waived by the match sponsor.

3.3 Light Rifle—Any .22 caliber rimfire with not less than a 2 pound trigger pull and which weighs not more than 7½ pounds when equipped with sights.

3.4 Junior Rifle—A rifle authorized for use in Junior competitions using cartridges commercially catalogued as a rimfire ".22 Short," ".22 Long," or ".22 Long Rifle" cartridge. There shall be no restrictions on the barrel length or overall weight of the rifle. The rifle may not be equipped with thumb hole stock, Schuetzen Type Butt Plate (Rule 3.15) or palm rest (Rule 3.14.)

• **3.5 Trigger Guard**—A rifle must be equipped with an effective trigger guard. Lack of a trigger guard constitutes an unsafe rifle (See Rule 9.10).

3.7 Sights

(a) Metallic–

(1) Non-corrective:

Any sighting system, constructed of metal or equivalent, which provides a method of aiming or aligning 2 separate but visible sights, or reference points mounted on the rifle, including tube sights and non-magnifying color filters.

(2) Corrective:

Same as (1), except that a lens or system of lenses, not containing an aiming reference or reticle at the focal plane of any such lens or system of lenses, may be included in such system.

(b) Telescopic–Any sighting system which includes a lens or system of lenses and an aiming reference or reticle at the focal plane of a lens or system of lenses.

(c) Any–Any sight without restriction as to material or construction.

(d) Prohibited—Any sighting device programed to activate the firing mechanism is prohibited.

3.8 Spotting Scopes—The use of a telescope to spot shots is permitted. It may be positioned forward of the shooter's forward shoulder. (Rule 9.16).

3.9 Shooting Kits—The shooting kit may not be placed forward of the shooter's forward shoulder on the firing line, except that in the standing position a shooting kit, table, or stand may be used as a rifle rest between shots. The shooting kit, table, or stand may not be of such size and construction as to interfere with shooters on adjacent firing points or to constitute a wind break. (Rule 9.16).

3.10 Ground Cloth—Ground cloth may be used providing it is not constructed or used in a manner to provide artificial rest or support.

3.11 Gloves—Gloves may be worn which do not form an artificial support.

3.12 Padding—Shoulder pads, sling pads and elbow pads may be worn while shooting, provided they are constructed so as not to provide artificial support. A button, hook or strap may be placed on the sleeve of the shooting coat to support the sling loop that is placed on the upper arm.

3.13 Slings—Unless otherwise specified in the conditions of the match the rifle sling may be used in connection with the rifle and one arm only as an auxiliary to steady the rifle except in the standing position. Sling cuffs and sling pads are permitted. (See Rule 5.12, 5.13)

3.14 Palm Rest—A palm rest is any attachment or extension below the forearm which aids the normal hand grip and support of the piece by the forward hand and arm. . The use of a palm rest in the NRA standing position is allowed under Rules 3.1 and 3.2 and may not be prohibited by the match sponsor.

3.14.1 Kneeling Roll—A cylindrical cushion for shooting in the kneeling position; maximum dimensions will be 9.84 inches long (25 cm) and 7.08 inches in diameter (18 cm), and made of soft and flexible material.

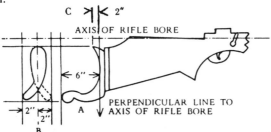

3.15 Schuetzen Type Butt Plates—A butt plate projecting more than 1 inch, but not more than 6 inches past the rear of a line which is perpendicular to a line drawn through the axis of the bore of the rifle, and which is tangent to the deepest part of the butt plate depression that normally rests against the front of the shoulder (A). The lateral curvature of the butt plate longer projection may not exceed 2 inches either to the right or left of a line drawn through the vertical axis of the (movable) butt plate (B). Adjustable curved butt plates shall not be reversed or so adjusted that they can be used as a hook to support the rifle. An upper tang exceeding 2 inches in length which might be used as a shoulder rest is prohibited (C). The use of a hook butt plate is allowed under Rules 3.1 and 3.2 and may not be prohibited by the Match Sponsor.

3.16 Release Triggers—Triggers which function on release are prohibited.

3.17 Ammunition—Rimfire cartridge commercially catalogued as the ".22 Short," ".22 Long" or ".22 Long Rifle," which have an over-all length not more than 1.1 inches and loaded with lead or alloy bullet of not larger than .22 inch diameter which weighs not more than 40 grains. Hollow point, tracer, incendiary or explosive bullets are specifically excluded from ammunition authorized for match use.

3.18 General—All devices or equipment which may facilitate shooting and which are not mentioned in these Rules, and which are contrary to the spirit of these Rules and Regulations, are forbidden. The Official Referee, Jury or Match Director shall have the right to examine a shooter's equipment or apparel. The responsibility shall be upon the competitor to submit questionable equipment and apparel for official inspection and approval in sufficient time prior to the beginning of a match so that it will not inconvenience either the competitor or the official.

3.19 Eye Protection—All competitors and other personnel in the immediate vicinity of the range complex are urged to wear eye protection devices or similar eye protection.

3.20 Ear Protection—All competitors and other personnel in the immediate vicinity of the range complex are urged to wear hearing protection devices or similar ear protection.

4. TARGETS

The dimensions given are to the outside edge of the scoring rings.

• **4.1 Official Targets**—In NRA Sanctioned competition, only targets printed by NRA Licensed Manufacturers, bearing the Official Competition target seal, or military targets issued by the Armed Services, without modifications except as authorized by NRA, will be used.

OFFICIAL TARGET DIMENSIONS

4.2 50 Foot Target. A-17—11 bullseyes (1 for sighting) for use in Conventional 4-Position competition only. 6 through 10 rings black.

10 ring	.150 Inch	7 ring	1.150 inches
9 ring	.483 inch	6 ring	1.483 inches
8 ring	.817 inch	5 ring	1.817 inches

4.3 50 Foot Target. A-36—12 bullseyes (2 for sighting) 50 meter International Smallbore Rifle target reduced for firing at 50 feet. For use in NRA 3-Position competition only. 3 through 10 rings black.

10 dot	.008 inch	5 ring	.993 inch
9 ring	.193 inch	4 ring	1.193 inches
8 ring	.393 inch	3 ring	1.393 inches
7 ring	.593 inch		
6 ring	.793 inch		

Existing supply of old A-36 targets may continue to be used until exhausted. The new A-36 target MUST be used in all Registered Tournaments.

4.4 50 Foot Light Rifle Target. A-32—6 bullseyes (1 for sighting) for use with NRA Light Rifle only. 8 through 10 rings black, with white dot in center of 10 ring.

Aiming Dot	.218 inch	8 ring	1.874 inches
10 ring	.439 inch	7 ring	2.656 inches
9 ring	1.187 inches	6 ring	3.374 inches

4.5 75 Foot Target. A7/5—5 bullseyes, and A7/10, 10 bullseyes. For use with Conventional 4-Position only. 6 through 10 rings black.

10 ring	.335 inch	7 ring	1.835 inches
9 ring	.835 inch	6 ring	2.335 inches
8 ring	1.335 inches	5 ring	2.835 inches

4.6 50 Yard Target. A-23/3—3 bullseyes, and A-23/5, 5 bullseyes. For use in Conventional 4-Position and 50 yard stage of Conventional Prone competitions only. 7 through 10 rings black.

X ring	.39 inch	7 ring	3.89 inches
10 ring	.89 inch	6 ring	4.89 inches
9 ring	1.89 inches	5 ring	5.89 inches
8 ring	2.89 inches		

4.7 50 Yard Target. A-27—5 bullseyes. 50 meter target reduced for firing at 50 yards. For use in Conventional Prone competition only. 3.89 inches diameter black.

X ring	.359 inch	7 ring	2.879 inches

10 ring	.719 inch	6 ring	3.599 inches
9 ring	1.439 inches	5 ring	4.319 inches
8 ring	2.159 inches	4 ring	5.038 inches

4.8 50 Yard Target. A-39—5 bullseyes. 50 meter UIT target reduced for firing at 50 yards. For use in NRA 3-Position and Metric Prone competition only. 4 through 10 rings black.

Aiming Dot	.016 inch	5 ring	3.424 inches
10 ring	.426 inch	4 ring	4.024 inches
9 ring	1.025 inches	3 ring	4.624 inches
8 ring	1.625 inches	2 ring	5.223 inches
7 ring	2.225 inches	1 ring	5.823 inches
6 ring	2.824 inches		

4.9 50 Meter Target. A-26—5 bullseyes, For use in Conventional Prone competiton only. 4.27 inches diameter black.

X ring	.393 inch	7 ring	3.148 inches
10 ring	.787 inch	6 ring	3.936 inches
9 ring	1.574 inches	5 ring	4.723 inches
8 ring	2.361 inches	4 ring	5.510 inches

4.10 50 Meter UIT Target. A-20/3—3 bullseyes, A-20/5—5 bullseyes. For use in NRA 3-Position and Metric Prone competition only. 4 through 10 rings black.

Aiming Dot	.039 inch	5 ring	3.768 inches
10 ring	.488 inch	4 ring	4.425 inches
9 ring	1.144 inches	3 ring	5.081 inches
8 ring	1.80 inches	2 ring	5.737 inches
7 ring	2.456 inches		
6 ring	3.113 inches		

The guard ring and bull position of this target has been changed. Old supplies may be used until exhausted.

4.11 100 Yard Target. A-25—3 bullseyes. For use in Conventional Prone competion only. 7 through 10 rings black.

X ring	1 inch	7 ring	8 inches
10 ring	2 inches	6 ring	10 inches
9 ring	4 inches	5 ring	12 inches
8 ring	6 inches		

4.12 100 Yard Target. A-33—3 bullseyes. UIT 300 meter target reduced to 100 yards. For use in Metric Prone competition only. 4 through 10 rings black.

10 ring..............	1.045 inches	5 ring..............	7.045 inches
9 ring..............	2.245 inches	4 ring..............	8.245 inches
8 ring..............	3.445 inches	3 ring..............	9.445 inches
7 ring..............	4.645 inches	2 ring..............	10.645 inches
6 ring..............	5.845 inches	1 ring..............	11.845 inches

4.13 200 Yard Target. A-21—Single bullseye. 8, 9, and 10 rings black. (A-21 C Repair Center)

X ring..............	2 inches	8 ring..............	12 inches
10 ring..............	4 inches	7 ring..............	16 inches
9 ring..............	8 inches	6 ring..............	20 inches

Note: Some stocks of targets with the old designations are still being sold. These targets are still allowable for use in NRA competition. A comparison of the old designations and new ones appears below

A-7/5 = old A-7	A-23/5 = old A-23
A-7/10 = old A-8	A-20/3 = old A-20
A-23/3 = old A-34	A-20/5 = old A-49

5. POSITIONS

Positions—The positions for use in a match shall be stated in the program under conditions of the match and shall be in accord with the definitions of positions prescribed in this section.

No portion of the shooter's body may rest upon or touch the ground in advance of the firing line.

5.1 The Ground—All references to "the ground" in the following position Rules are to be construed as applying to the surface of the firing point, floor, such shooting mats, or platforms as are customarily used on shooting ranges.

5.2 Artificial Support—Any supporting surface except the ground not specifically authorized for use in the Rules for the position prescribed. Digging or use of elbow or heel holes at the firing points or the use of depressions which form artificial support for the elbows, arms, or legs is prohibited. Use of artificial support is prohibited except as individually authorized by NRA for a physically handicapped shooter.

5.3 Position of Rifle Butt—In all positions, the butt of the rifle must be held against the front of the shoulder on the outside of the shooting coat or shirt and must not touch the ground.

5.5 Physically Handicapped Shooters—A shooter who because of physical handicap cannot fire from one or more of the prescribed shooting positions outlined in these Rules, or who must use special equipment when firing, is privileged to petition the NRA Protest Committee for permission to assume a special position or to use modified equipment, or both. This petition will be in the form of a written request from the person concerned to the Committee outlining in detail the reasons why the special position must be assumed or the special equipment must be used. The petition will be accompanied by pictures of the shooter in the position he desires approved and, if special equipment is required, the picture will show how this equipment is used. The petition and all pictures must be furnished in exact duplicate. The petition must be accompanied by a medical doctor's statement if the physical handicap is not completely evident in the pictures submitted.

(a) Each petition will be reviewed by the NRA Protest Committee. The Committee may require additional or supplementary statements or pictures. After review the NRA Secretary will be instructed by the Committee to issue a special authorization certificate to individuals who submit petitions and pictures which have been approved. Such certificates will have necessary pictures attached.

(b) Shooters who have received special authorization certificates will be required to carry them when competing in competition governed by NRA Rules, and to present the certificates when requested by officials of the competition or by NRA Official Referees or Supervisors.

(c) In the event of a protest involving the position or the equipment used by such a shooter, the Official Referee, Jury or Supervisor will compare the questioned position or equipment with the certificate and photographs presented by the shooter. If the shooter's position or equipment does not, in the opinion of the officials, conform to that authorized by the NRA Secretary (or if the shooter has not authorized certificate or pictures), the protest shall be allowed and the shooter will be required to change immediately to the position or equipment which has been approved or to an otherwise legal position or equipment.

(d) Should a protest be carried beyond the Official Referee, Jury or Supervisor, the original protest will be endorsed by the Referee, Jury Chairman or Supervisor to show the action he has taken and will be forwarded to the National Rifle Association.

(e) National Records may not be established by use of scores fired in special positions or with special equipment as may be authorized according to the Rule.

(f) Two types of authorizations are issued; temporary and permanent. Permanent authorizations are issued to competitors who are permanently handicapped.

5.5.1 Temporary Disability: Substitute Position—Any person who has a temporary physical disability which prevents him from using a specified position as defined in this Rule, may assume the next more difficult position in lieu of that position. In this manner, sitting may be used for prone, kneeling may be used for sitting, and standing may be used for kneeling. Any sibstitute position must conform to the Rule which defines it. The Match Director must be informed of the substitute, and may require that the substitute position be demonstrated so he may be certain that it meets the definition of the appropriate Rule.

Illustrations indicate some approved positions.

5.6 Prone—Body extended on the ground, head toward the target. The rifle will be supported by both hands and one shoulder only. No portion of the arms below the elbows shall rest upon the ground or any artificial support nor may any portion of the rifle or body rest against any artificial support. The forearm supporting the rifle shall form an angle with the line from the point of elbow contact, to the target of not less than 30°. (Measured through the axis of the forearm).

5.8 Sitting—Weight of the body supported on the buttocks and the feet or ankles, no other portion of the body touching the ground. The rifle will be supported by both hands and one shoulder only. Elbows may rest on the legs at any point above the ankles. (The elbow is defined as 4 inches from the point of the arm when bent.)

(Kneeling)

(Kneeling)

5.10 Kneeling—Buttocks clear of the ground, but may rest on one foot. The rifle will be supported by both hands and one shoulder only. The elbow of the arm supporting the rifle rests on the knee or leg. The elbow of the trigger arm will be free from all support. One knee must be touching the ground or shooting mat. The shooter may be all on, partially on, or all off the shooting mat. A roll as described in Rule 3.14.1 may be placed under the instep provided the foot is placed toe down at an angle not greater than 45 degrees from the vertical. (Elbow is defined in Rule 5.8.)

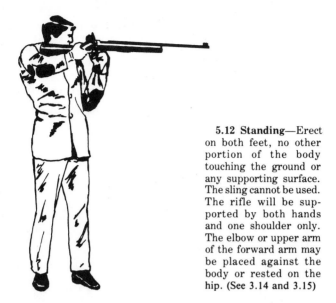

5.12 Standing—Erect on both feet, no other portion of the body touching the ground or any supporting surface. The sling cannot be used. The rifle will be supported by both hands and one shoulder only. The elbow or upper arm of the forward arm may be placed against the body or rested on the hip. (See 3.14 and 3.15)

5.13 Any—Any position in which the rifle is supported only by the body, assisted if desired by the sling, with no artificial support, and by which no competitors or range personnel are endangered.(See Rule 3.13)

5.14 Illegal—Anyone found using an illegal position shall be warned once and given an opportunity to correct his position. If the same person continues to use an illegal position or reverts to it, he shall be disqualified from that stage of the match and the corresponding score will be disallowed.

6. RANGE STANDARDS

6.1 Firing Line—The firing line is immediately in front of the several firing points. All ranges are measured from this firing line to the face of the targets when targets are hung in their proper position in front of the backstop.

6.2 Firing Point—That part of the range provided for the competitor immediately in the rear of the firing line from which firing takes place. Each firing point is numbered to correspond with the target frames. Each firing point should have a minimum width of five feet (except in gallery ranges where a minimum of four feet is permissible).

6.3 Shelter—Prone, Outdoor 4-Position and 3-Position. The firing points of outdoor ranges may be covered and enclosed on 3 sides, open toward the targets. There must be ample room for Range Officers and witnesses to move freely to the rear of the shooter. This does not preclude the construction of ranges within areas surrounded or partially surrounded by safety walls.

6.4 Distance—*(a)* Gallery rifle ranges are 50 feet or 75 feet. *(b)* Outdoor rifle ranges are 50 yards, 50 meters, 100 yards. Indoor distances may be used outdoors and outdoor distances used indoors.

6.5 Illumination—Artificial illumination of ranges is authorized.

6.6 Target Numbers—Target frames will be numbered on alternating background of contrasting color. The number will be large enough to be identified under ordinary conditions with normal vision. Numbers must correspond with firing point numbers.

6.7 Backing Targets—*(a)* At 50 feet and 75 feet backing targets must be used in Registered Tournaments. Backing targets may be used at sponsors discretion in Approved Tournaments. Distance between record target and backing target will be 3 inches.

(b) Backing targets will be used at all mid-ranges in Registered or Approved Tournaments. Target frames should be the same distance center to center as the firing points and should be carefully constructed to assure uniform spacing between record and backing targets.

Distance between record target and backing target should be as indicated in following table to give ¼'' offset in the location of the bullet holes in the target and backing cards:

Distance Between Firing Points	100 Yards	50 Yards	50 Meters
5 Ft.-0 In...................	15''	7½''	8½''
5 Ft.-6 In...................	13¾''	6''	7½''
6 Ft.-0 In...................	12½''	6¼''	6¾''

6.9 Wind Flags—*(a)* Tournament sponsors, only, may erect the desired number of flags or other devices to indicate wind direction forward of the firing line. Competitors may not change or add thereto but they may use wind indicating devices at the firing line as long as they do not interfere with other competitors or range operation.

(b) Where a firing point is enclosed (see Rule 6.3) in such a manner as to prevent competitors from being exposed to prevailing winds, the tournament sponsor shall erect a row of wind flags or other devices parallel to the targets to indicate wind direction at approximately the target line *and* midway thereto spaced between the firing lanes of at least every fourth point. Competitors may not change or add thereto but they may use wind indicating devices at the firing line as long as they do not interfere with other competitors or range operation.

7. COURSES OF FIRE

The following courses and types of fire are most commonly found in NRA Sanctioned Smallbore Rifle Competition, fired on standard NRA targets described in Section 4. See Section 8 for time allowances. Rule 17.5 for courses of fire for which National Records are recognized, and Rule 19.4 for courses of fire used for classification.

Other courses of fire, other time limits, or the use of other targets may be scheduled by sponsors provided the conditions are clearly stated in the program.

7.1 Courses of Fire—In 50 yard, 50 meter, 100 yard matches it is customary to change targets after each 20 shots. The "Time Limit" shall be the same for the first and second 20 shots, even though it is at the same distance. (See Rule 8.2 for time allowances.)

The customary number of shots on record bulls at each distance are as follows: 50 feet, 1 shot; 50 yards/meters, 5 shots; 100 yards and beyond 10 shots per bull.

The following are the courses and types of fire commonly found in competition.

7.2 Conventional Prone

Distance	Target	No. of Shots	
		Per Match	*Per Bull*
50 Yards	A-23/3, A-23/5	40	5
50 Meters	A-26	40	5
50 Yards	A-27	40	5
100 Yards	A-25	40	10
Dewar Course	A-23/5, A-25	20 each distance	5/10

7.3 Conventional 4-Position Indoor and Outdoor

Distance	Target		
50 Feet	A-17	10 or 20 in each of the four positions.	1
75 Feet	A-7/5, A-7/10	10 or 20 in each of the four positions.	2
50 Yards	A-23/3, A-23/5	10, 20, or 40 in each of the following positions: Prone, Sitting, Kneeling, Standing.	5

7.4 Metric Prone Courses of Fire—

Distance	Target		
50 Yards	A-39	40	5
50 Meters	A-20/3, A-20/5	40	5
100 Yards	A-33	40	10
Dewar Course	A-39, A-33	20 each distance	5/10

7.5 NRA 3-Position, Indoor and Outdoor Courses

Distance	Target		
50 Feet	A-36	10, 20, or 40 in each position: Prone, Kneeling, and Standing.	1
50 Yards	A-39	10, 20, or 40 in each position: Prone, Kneeling, and Standing.	5

50 Meters .... A-20/3, A-20/5   10, 20, or 40   5
in each
position: Prone,
Kneeling, and
Standing.

7.6 Long Range Conventional Prone—(200 Yards)—This event is no longer used for classification or National Records. If a sponsor desires to conduct this event Target A-21 may be used or it may be fired on high power ranges, using regulation high power targets, pit operation and scoring procedures. (Highpower Rules 9.37 thru 9.45 and 14.1 thru 14.25)

8. TIME LIMITS

8.1 Computing Time—Time is not checked on each shot. The time allowance is computed for a complete stage (including sighting shots when specified) on the basis of the specified number of shots multiplied by the allowance per shot. The Chief Range Officer may terminate any relay before completion of the full time allowed, if all competitors in that relay have completed firing. Time allowed but not used does not carry over to another string or stage.

8.2 Time Allowance:
   (a) *Indoor Conventional Type Matches* (A-17 target or its equivalent). One minute per record shot for all positions will be allowed.
   (b) *Outdoor Conventional Type Prone and Position Matches*. One minute per record shot prone and 1½ minutes per record shot for sitting, kneeling, and standing positions will be allowed.
   (c) *Indoor and Outdoor NRA 3 Position Course Matches*. One minute per record shot for prone and 1½ minutes per record shot for kneeling and 2 minutes per record shot for the standing positions will be allowed.
The competitor will be allowed a minimum of an additional 5 minutes for each position change in a stage or match. Additional time will be allowed for a target change if needed. In matches at more than one range or stage when firing must cease, to change targets or stages, time may not be accumulated at one range or stage and used at another range or stage. Time for each range or stage will be allotted separately.

8.3 Team Time—The following will apply for firing other than when pits are used.
   (a) In matches where sufficient firing points are assigned each team so all team members fire at the same time, the total "team time" will be the same as the time allowed in an individual match (or stage) of same type. (Example: 5 firers per team, 20 shots each at 50 yards, prone, total team time is 20 minutes. Same conditions except when position is sitting, kneeling or standing, total team time is 30 minutes.)

(b) In matches where sufficient firing points are assigned each team to permit all team members to fire at the same time but in which teams fire in pairs, the total "team time" will be the time allowed in an individual match (or stage) of same type multiplied by the number of pairs firing separately for each team, plus 3 minutes for each change of pairs. (Example: 4 firers (2 pairs) per team. Dewar course, time allowed each pair at 50 yards is 20 minutes plus 3 minutes for changing pairs or the total team time at 50 yards of 43 minutes. Total team time at 100 yards is also 43 minutes.)

(c) In matches where sufficient firing points are assigned each team to permit all team members to fire at the same time but in which team members fire singly, the total "team time" will be the time allowed in an individual match (or stage) of same type multiplied by the number of individuals firing separately for each team, plus 3 minutes for each change of firers. Example: 4 firers per team, 4 position match standing stage, 10 shots at 50 feet, target carriers being used. Firing time is 10 minutes per team member multiplied by 4 team members is 40 minutes, plus 3 changes of firers at 3 minutes making total team time 49 minutes.

(d) In matches where team members will fire consecutively on the same firing point, the total "team time" will be the time allowed in an individual match (or stage) of the same type, multiplied by the number of team members concerned. Example: 4 firers per team, 4 position match, kneeling stage, 10 shots per team, target carriers being used. Firing time 10 minutes per team multiplied by 4 team members is 40 minutes, plus 3 changes of firing members at 3 minutes each making total team time 49 minutes.

(e) Time is not kept on each team member individually unless firing as in (a) above, but the total time for the team is allowed and may be used by the team as a whole.

(f) In matches at more than one range, stage, or where a change of targets is required during the match and carriers are not used, time may not be accumulated at one range or stage and used at another range or stage. See Rule 8.2

8.4 Passage of Time—Range Officers will not voluntarily warn competitors of the passage of time. Competitors, and Team Captains in team matches, may inquire of Range Officers as to the time remaining before expiration of the time limit. The request for time and the response shall be given in a tone which will not disturb other competitors.

14. SCORING

14.1 When to Score—Usually targets are scored after each 10 shots in gallery matches, after each 20 shots in short and mid-range matches. Special conditions may require other than this usual procedure.

14.2 Where to Score—Targets may be scored in the Statistical Office or on the range in view of competitors and spectators. Scoring of mid-range targets on the frames, at the butts, is prohibited. Whenever targets are scored where backing cards are used the record target and backing card shall be compared.

INWARD
SCORING

The Correct method of scoring.
The shot on the left bullseye counts nine,
the one on the right ten.

OUTWARD
SCORING

The Correct method of scoring.
The shot on the left bullseye counts as a nine
as it exceeds the outside edge of the 7 ring.
The one on the right is a ten
as it does not exceed the outside edge of the 7 ring.

● **14.3 How to Score**—*(a) Shot hole*—A shot hole the leaded edge of which comes in contact with the outside of the bullseye or scoring rings of a target, is given the higher value (including keyhole or tipped shots even though the hole is elongated to the bullet's length rather than being a circle of the bullet's diameter). A scoring gauge will be used to determine the value of close hits. The higher value will be allowed in those cases where the flange on the gauge touches the scoring ring. No scoring gauge will be used unless the diameter of the scoring flange is within these limits:

1. .2225 to .2240—conventional gauge
2. .3625 to .3610—outward gauge for **A-36 10 dot only**

Devices other than scoring gauges may be used to assist in establishing the value of hits. The devices are not to be inserted into a bullet hole and do not constitute a scoring gauge.

(b) X-ring—The X-ring is the ring located inside the ten ring on targets A-23, A-25, A-26, and A-27. Any shot hole which touches the outside edge of the X-ring is counted as an X and used to break ties, rank scores and establish National Records in Outdoor Conventional Prone and 4-Position shooting.

(c) X-ring shots of higher value—Those shot holes located within the X-ring as provided in Rule 14.3(b), whose outside leaded edge, as determined with the aid of an official .22 caliber scoring gauge or overlay that does not touch the outside edge of the X-ring, are X-ring shots of higher value, and:

(1) They are scored only for the purpose of tie breaking of maximum X-ring scores (e.g. 400-40X).

(2) They are *not* used to establish National Records.

(d) Center shots—Those shot holes fired on targets without X-ring (A-7, A-17, A-20/3, A-20/5, A-32, A-33, A-36 and A-39) are

used to break ties and rank scores. Center shots are determined as follows:

(1) Indoor Conventional 50 ft. (A-17 target)—Any shot hole touching the ten ring but not touching the outside edge of the nine ring with the aid of a .22 caliber plug-type scoring gauge.

(2) Indoor Conventional 75 ft. (A-7 target)—Any shot hole within the ten ring which, with the aid of a .22 caliber plug-type scoring gauge, the leaded edge of the bullet hole does not touch the outside edge of the ten ring.

(3) Indoor, NRA 3-Position (A-36 target)—Any shot hole touching the ten dot but not touching the outside edge of the eight ring with the aid of a .22 caliber plug-type scoring gauge.

(4) Outdoor NRA 3-Position and Metric Prone (A-20/3, A-20/5, A-33, A-39 targets)—Any shot hole within the ten ring which, with the aid of a .22 caliber plug-type scoring gauge or overlay, the leaded edge of the bullet hole does not touch the outside edge of the ten ring.

(5) Light Rifle (A-32 target)—Any shot hole within the ten ring which, with the aid of a .22 caliber plug-type scoring gauge or overlay, the leaded edge of the bullet hole does not touch the outside edge of the ten ring.

(e) Center shots of higher value—All shot holes fired on the indoor conventional target (A-17 only) which, with the aid of a .22 caliber plug-type scoring gauge, obliterates the ten ring. They are used to break and rank ties of maximum center shot scores only (200-20), and will *not* be used to establish National Records.

(f) Shot groups—When scoring outdoor targets, the X, 10, and in some cases the 9 rings are sometimes partially obliterated by shot groups to such a degree that the use of a plug-type scoring gauge is not practicable. In such cases the values of the shots in the destroyed scoring ring area may be determined by authorized tournament scoring personnel, and the Referee or Jury when required, by using the NRA Smallbore Rifle Scoring Aid (plastic). The plastic Scoring Aid is not authorized for use in determining the value of single well defined shot holes. The use of this Scoring Aid supersedes any requirement for use of a plug-type gauge under the conditions described.

Note: Wherever possible targets should be scored while in a horizontal position. The plug gauge should be inserted carefully so that no pressure is exerted to any side as this may affect the final plug position in the shot hole and, therefore, the value of the hit. Never plug a shot that is not doubtful.

When scoring with a gauge or other authorized scoring aid if, in the opinion of the Scorer, Challenge Officer, Supervisor, Referee, or Jury, the value is still doubtful, the shooter will be awarded the higher hit value.

To make tie breaking easier it is suggested to score all X's, center shots, X's of higher value or center shots of higher value the first time the scoring team scores a target. Ties would be broken simply by comparing targets as opposed to re-scoring.

14.3.1 Authorized Use of Plug Type Scoring Gauges—The use of the plug type gauge will be restricted to use by range operating personnel who may include the Range Officers or Block Officers, Match Supervisors, Statistical Officer, Match Director, Jury, or Referee, as appropriate to the type of tournament concerned. The tournament program should state in match conditions by whom and under what circumstances plug type scoring gauges may be used.

14.4 Misses—Hits outside the scoring rings of the competitor's target are scored as misses.

14.5 Early or Late Shots—If any shots are fired before the starting signal to Commence Fire or after the signal to Cease Fire the shots of highest value on that target card, equal in number to those fired in error, will be scored as misses.

14.6 Blank

14.7 Hits on Wrong Target or Bullseye—

(a) If a competitor fires on a target card other than his own where backing cards are used but the total number of hits does not exceed the required number, he will be given the value of the hits on his own target card and a miss for each hit on the target card other than his own. No further penalty shall be assessed.

(b) Where backing cards are not used, hits on targets other than targets assigned to the competitor will be scored as misses, but only the required number of shots of lowest value will be scored.

(c) Hits on wrong bullseye—When more than the required number of shots are fired at one bullseye and a fewer number than required are fired at another bullseye on the same target card so that not more than the required total number of shots are fired at the target card, the competitor will be given the actual value of his score, minus a penalty of one point for each shot fired at the wrong bullseye. Penalty points shall be deducted from the shot or shots of highest value on the bullseye bearing more than the required number of hits and the net value (actual value of hits less penalty) shall be allocated to the bullseye on which there are less than the required number of hits and shall thereafter be scored as the actual value of that shot. A 10-X or a 10 so penalized becomes a 9.

14.8 Ricochets—A hole made by a ricochet bullet does not count as a hit and will not be scored.

14.9 Visible Hits and Close Groups—As a general rule only those hits which are visible will be scored. An exception will be made in the case where the grouping of 3 or more shots is so close that it is possible for a required shot or shots to have gone through the enlarged hole without leaving a mark, and there has been no evidence that a shot or shots have gone elsewhere than through the assigned target. In such case, the shooter will be given the benefit of the doubt and scored hits for the non-visible shots, on the assumption they passed through the enlarged hole. If such assumption could place a non-visible hit in either of two scoring rings, it shall be scored in the higher-value ring.

14.10 Excessive Hits

Note: The term "target card" will be interpreted as applying to all record bullseyes framed at one time.

(a) On his own target—If a competitor fires more than the required number of shots at his own target card he will be scored only the required number of hits of lowest value minus a penalty of one point for each hit in excess of the required number on the individual bullseye(s) on which the excessive hits occur.

Penalty points shall be deducted from the remaining hit or hits of highest value and the net value (actual value of hits less penalty) shall thereafter be scored as the actual value. A 10-X or a 10 so penalized becomes a 9.

(b) When one or more are on the target of another competitor—If a competitor fires more shots than the number required for one target card and one or more of the hits are on the target of another competitor, he will be scored a miss for each shot on a target card other than his own. That miss will be brought back to the corresponding bullseye on his own target card, thereafter he will be scored only the required number of hits of lowest value on that bullseye. No further penalty points will be assessed on that shot.

14.11 Scoring Altered Targets—Targets intentionally altered, or marked to benefit a shooter over other competitors, will not be scored.

15. DECISION OF TIES

15.1 Match—The term "match" as used in this section refers to all individual, team and aggregate matches.

15.2 Numbering of Bullseyes—For the purpose of ranking tie scores, the bullseye numbers printed on NRA official targets will be considered to run in consecutive sequence throughout the entire course of fire, even though all targets for an event may not be framed at one time.

15.3-6 [(Blank)] Moved to 14.3 b–e

15.7 Tie Breaking for All Matches—Competitors having the same numerical total score over the entire course will be ranked in order:

(a) By the greater number of X's over the entire course on targets with X rings or center shots on targets without X rings,

(b) By the higher numerical score at the longest range,

(c) By the greater number of X's or center shots at the longest range,

(d) By the highest ranking score in the standing position,

(e) By the greater number of X's or center shots in the standing position,

(f) By the highest ranking score on the last numbered bullseye,

(g) By the greater number of X's or center shots on the last numbered bullseye,

(h) By the highest ranking score on each bullseye applied in inverse order from last to first,

(i) By the greater number of X's or center shots on each bullseye applied in inverse order from last to first. If still a tie, apply (e) through (i) to the kneeling position, followed by the sitting position.

(j) For the 50 ft. target A-17, score the center shots of higher value and apply (a) through (i) until the tie is broken. See Rule 14.3e.

(k) For targets with X-ring, A-23, A-25, A-26 and A-27, score the X-ring shots of higher value and apply (a) through (i) until the tie is broken. See Rule 14.3c.

15.8 Team Matches—Teams having the same total numerical score for the entire course of fire will be ranked by totaling the scores fired by all team members and ranking the score as though it had been fired by an individual for the same course of fire.

15.9 Matches Which Include Both Rifle and Pistol—Competitors having the same total numerical score for the entire course of fire in matches which include both rifle and pistol stages will be ranked in order:

(a) By the highest ranking score in the pistol stage.

(b) By the highest ranking score in the rifle stage.

15.10 Re-Entry Matches—Competitors having the same numerical score will be ranked according to Rule 15.7 applied to the highest re-entry score.

15.11 League Ties—In leagues where team standing is determined by the percentage of matches won, ties will be decided as set forth in the league program.

15.12 Ties for Selection to United States Teams—(Other than Postal)—Competitors considered for selection to teams which will represent the United States having the same numerical score shall be ranked:

(a) By the greatest number of X's over the entire course of fire, when X's are scored.

(b) By a shoot-off with the course of fire determined by the Match Director.

15.13-16 [(Blank)]

15.17 Unbreakable Ties—In case a tie cannot be ranked as provided in this section the Match Director will direct the awards to be given under one of the following plans:

(a) By the firing of a complete or partial score under the original match conditions or at the longest range of the match,

(b) In a slow fire individual match by the firing of single shots at the longest range,

(c) By drawing lots for merchandise, medal or trophy awards and pooling and equally dividing award points or cash awards to which those tied may be entitled.

17. NATIONAL RECORDS

17.1 Where Scores for National Records Can Be Fired—Scores to be recognized as National Records must be fired in NRA Registered Competition as defined in Rule 1.6, paragraphs (c), (d), (e) and (f), National Records must be approved by the NRA before being declared official. National Records may not be established during re-entry matches.

17.5 *(c)* Individual Conventional Four Position (Outdoor):

(1) 10 shots in each of the four positions, Prone, Sitting, Kneeling and Standing on the A-23 target

(2) 20 shots in each of the four positions, Prone, Sitting, Kneeling and Standing on the A-23 target

(3) An aggregate of twice the 80 shot 4-Position match

(4) 20 shots sitting at 50 yards, A-23 target

(5) 20 shots kneeling at 50 yards, A-23 target

(6) 20 shots standing at 50 yards, A-23 target

(7) The Grand Aggregate of 1600 points which is a combination of the 800 point position metallic sight aggregate and the any sight 800 point position aggregate

(8) Grand aggregate of 3200 points which is a combination of the 1600 point position metallic sight aggregate and the 1600 point position any sight aggregate

17.5 *(d)* Two or Four Man Teams, Conventional Four Position:
(1) 10 shots at 50 yards in each position, prone, sitting, kneeling and standing, on The A-23 target
(2) 20 shots at 50 yards in each position, prone, sitting, kneeling and standing, on the A-23 target

17.5 *(e)* Indoor Conventional Four Position Individual:
(Course may be fired at 50 feet on the A-17 target, or at 75 feet on the A-7/5 or A-7/10 targets.)
* *(1)* 20 shots sitting
* *(2)* 20 shots kneeling
* *(3)* 20 shots standing
* *(4)* 10 shots in each of the four positions, prone, sitting, kneeling and standing.
* *(5)* The Open Sectional Aggregate Course
* *(6)* Grand Aggregate of 1600 points which is a combination of the 800 point position metallic sight aggregate and the 800 point position any sight aggregate

17.5 *(f)* Two or Four Man Teams, Conventional Indoor Four Position to be fired by each Team Member:
* *(1)* 10 shots each of the four positions, prone, sitting, kneeling and standing on the A-17, or A-7/5, A-7/10 (75 feet) targets

17.5 *(g)* Outdoor Metric Prone Courses
* *(1)* 20 shots at 50 yards, A-39 target or 50 meters, A-20 target and 20 shots 100 yards prone, A-33 target (Metric Dewar Course).
* *(2)* 40 shots at 50 yards A-39 target or 40 shots at 50 meters, A-20 target.
* *(2a)* 60 shots at 50 yards A-39 target or 60 shots at 50 meters A-20 target.
* *(3)* 40 shots at 100 yards, A-33 target.
* *(4)* Aggregate of 1200 comprised of once over matches #1, #2, #3, either iron or any sights.
* *(5)* Aggregate of 1600 comprised of twice over the Dewar Course, (#1), once over the 50 yard-50 meter course, (#2), and once over the 100 yard course, (#3), either with metallic or any sights.
* *(6)* Aggregate of 2400, combination of twice over the 1200 Course (#4), once with metallic sights and once with any sights.
* *(7)* Aggregate of 3200, combination of twice over the 1600 course, (#4), once with metallic sights and once with any sights.
* *(8)* Aggregate of 4800, combination of twice over the 2400 Course (#5), once with metallic sights and once with any sights.
* *(9)* Aggregate of 6400, combination of twice over the 3200 course, (#5), once with metallic sights and once with any sights.

17.2 Scores to be Used—Scores must be complete for an entire scheduled match. Stage scores or scores for only part of a match will not be used for Records. Scores fired over 50 feet or 75 feet will be considered for the establishment of National Records, whichever is higher. Mid-range scores must be fired outdoors and not under artificial light. Scores fired in any sight matches will be eligible for any sight records only.

17.3 Scores for National Individual Records—Such scores must be fired in individual matches. No score fired in a team match will be considered for recognition as an individual Record. For recognition as special group Records, "Open," "Civilian," "Regular Service," "Reserve components including National Guard," "Women" and "Junior" scores may be fired in either open or restricted matches.

17.4 Scores for National Team Records—Such scores must be fired in matches where teams fire as a unit and no combination of individual match scores will be considered for recognition as a team record *(except 3-position sectional teams)*. For recognition as special group Records ("Open," "Civilian," "Regular Service," "Reserve components including National Guard," "Women," and "Junior" categories) all members of the team must be members of the special group concerned (Rule 1.7(d)). Teams must be bona fide teams as outlined in Rules 2.11 to 2.18. National Records will not be recognized for "pickup" teams (teams made up of shooters who do not represent one of the groups outlined in Rule 2.11 to 2.18.)

17.5 Courses of Fire for Which National Records Are Recognized—

Note: National Smallbore Rifle Records are maintained for scores fired with Metallic and with Any Sights over the following courses for "Open," "Civilian," "Regular Service," "Reserve components including National Guard," "Women," and "Junior" categories and for courses marked * for Intermediate Junior and Sub-Junior. (See Rule 8.2 for time allowances.)

In order for Records to be recognized promptly, National Record Reporting forms must be submitted to NRA by the Statistical Officer of the tournament in which they were fired, after being certified by the Jury or Referee. National Record Reporting forms are mailed to the sponsors of NRA Registered Tournaments by NRA Headquarters.

17.5 *(a)* Individual Conventional Prone:
* * *(1)* Dewar Course, 20 shots at 50 yards (A-23); 20 shots at 100 yards (A-25)
* * *(2)* 40 shots at 50 yards (A-23)
* * *(3)* 40 shots at 50 meters (A-26) or 40 shots at 50 yards (A-27)
* * *(4)* 40 shots at 100 yards (A-25)
* * *(5)* Aggregate of the above four matches (1600)
* * *(6)* Aggregate of the combined metallic and any sight aggregates of the above four matches (3200)
* * *(7)* Aggregate of twice over the above four matches (3200)
* * *(8)* The aggregate of 6400 points comprised of four times over the 40 shot, 50 yard, 50 meter, 100 yard and Dewar Course, twice over these courses with metallic sights and twice over the same courses with any sights.

17.5 *(b)* Two or Four Man Teams, Conventional Prone, fired by each member:

(1) Dewar Course, 20 shots 50 yards, A-23 target, and
20 shots 100 yards, A-25 target

(2) 40 shots at 100 yards, A-25 target

(3) 40 shots at 50 meters, A-26 target; or 50 yards, A-27
target

17.5 *(h)* Outdoor Metric Prone Team Courses

Two and Four Man Teams—The following course to be fired by each
member:

(1) 20 shots at 50 yards prone and 20 shots at 100 yards
prone (17.5g 1)

(2) 40 shots at 100 yards prone (17.5g 3)

(3) 40 shots at 50 yards (A-39 target), or 40 shots at 50
meters (17.5g 2)

17.5 *(i)* NRA 3 Position Individual Courses

The following Records apply to NRA 3 Position Course matches with
the exception that no prone Records will be maintained indoors. Indoor
Records will be on the A-36 target, Outdoor Records on the A-20 or
A-39 targets. Each target must be fired at its stated distance.

Individual:

(1) 40 shots prone *(see note)*

* (2) 60 shots prone. May be shot as a single match or an
aggregate of No. 1 plus a 20-shot prone match.

* (3) 20 shots kneeling

* (4) 40 shots kneeling

* (5) 20 shots standing

* (6) 40 shots standing

* (7) 60 shots prone, kneeling and standing (20 shots
each)

* (8) 120 shots, may be fired as a single match, an aggregate of matches 1, 4, 6 or an aggregate of two times
match 7.

* (9) 240 shot aggregate (120 shots metallic sights, and
120 shots any sights, each may be composed as in
match 8).

*Note: 40 Shot Prone Records at 50 meters/50 yards on A-20/A-39
targets will be maintained under 17.5 (g) Outdoor Metric Prone
Course #2.*

17.5 *(j)* NRA 3 Position Team Courses

Two and Four Man Teams—The following course to be fired by each
member: *(except 3-Position Sectionals)*

(1) 30 shots prone, kneeling and standing (10 shots
each)

* (2) 60 shots prone, kneeling and standing (20 shots
each)

(3) 120 shots prone, kneeling and standing (40 shots
each)

*Note: 50 meter matches may be fired indoors on A-20 or A-39
targets. (For Record purposes scores will be considered with those fired
on A-36 targets.)*

17.6 Co-holder Records—Tie breaking Rules beyond the use of
numerical scores including X count will not be employed when establishing National Records. Co-holder status will be accorded to individuals or teams when their score equals a National Record.

19. NATIONAL SMALLBORE RIFLE CLASSIFICATION

19.1 Classified Competitors—Are all individuals who are officially classified by the NRA for smallbore competition, or who have a record of scores fired over the courses of fire used for classification (See Rule 19.4) which have been recorded in a Score Record Book.

19.2 Unclassified Competitor—Is a competitor who does not have a current NRA Smallbore Rifle Classification, either regular or temporary by Score Record Book (Rule 19.14), nor an "Assigned Classification" (Rule 19.6). Such competitor shall compete in the Master Class.

19.4 Matches Used for Individual Classifications—Scores to be used for classification and reclassification will be those fired in matches in NRA Competition as defined in Rule 1.6 (except Postal Matches) over the following courses of fire and under the indicated conditions:

Outdoor Conventional Prone Classification:
Dewar Course (50 and 100 yard) **(A-23, A-25)**
50 Yards **(A-23)**
50 Meters **(A-26 or A-27)**
100 Yards **(A-25)**
Outdoor Metric Prone Classification:
Dewar Course (50 yard or 50 meter and 100 yard) (A-39, A-20 and A-33 target)
50 yard or 50 meter **(A-39 or A-20 target)**
100 yard (A-33 target)
NRA 3-Position Course Classification:
Indoor or outdoor, prone, kneeling and standing, 50 feet or 50 yards/50 meters, A-36 target or A-39/A-20 target
4-Position Course Classification:
Indoor or outdoor, prone, sitting, kneeling and standing, 50 feet or 50 yards, A-17 target or A-23 target

Both metallic and any sight match scores will be used. Matches may be fired outdoors or indoors. Scores fired indoors over outdoor courses will not be used for outdoor classification. Scores from Sanctioned Leagues (shoulder-to-shoulder or postal) may be used during the league firing season in Score Record Books (19.14) but will only be used by NRA Headquarters at the end of the league firing season for issue of Official Classification Cards.

19.4.1 Expanded Classification System for Juniors (Rule 2.3) Only— A match sponsor may use expanded or different classification system for junior shooters. Within that system, coaching may be allowed by the sponsor. However, the scores fired in classes that allow coaching will not be used for national records or national standing, but shall be reported for NRA classification purposes.

19.5 Compilation of Scores for Classification Averages—Scores fired in complete matches over the above Outdoor Conventional Prone Courses will be combined for the "Outdoor Conventional Prone Classification." Scores fired in complete matches over the above Outdoor Position Courses will be combined for the "Outdoor Position Classification" and scores fired in complete matches over the above Indoor Courses will be combined for the "Indoor Classification." Scores fired in complete matches over the above Outdoor Metric

Prone courses will be combined for the "Outdoor Metric Prone Classification."

19.6 Assigned Classification—A competitor who has an earned classification (a classification obtained through his Score Record Book or an Official NRA Classification Card) for one type of competition in the grouping listed below will be assigned this same classification in any competition in which he does not already have an earned or assigned classification. If he has a classification in more than one type in the list below, he shall use the higher classification. After his first tournament in the new type, he will use his Score Record Book rather than his assigned classification when entering his second tournament in the new type.

Smallbore and High Power Rifle:

(a) Indoor 4-Position	*(g)* International Smallbore
(b) Outdoor 4-Position	—Rifle
(c) Indoor 3-Position	*(h)* High Power Rifle
(d) Outdoor 3-Position	*(i)* 300-Meter Rifle
(e) Outdoor Metric Prone	*(j)* Air Rifle
(f) Outdoor Conventional Prone	

19.7 Lack of Classification Evidence—It is the competitor's responsibility to have his NRA Official Classification Card or Score Record Book with required scores for temporary classification (see Rules 19.1 and 19.14) and to present such classification evidence when required. Any competitor who cannot present such evidence will fire in the Master Class. A competitor's classification will not change during a tournament. A competitor will enter a tournament under his correct classification and fire the entire tournament in that class. Should it be discovered during a tournament that a competitor has entered in a classification lower than his current rating, the tournament records will be corrected to show the correct classification for the entire tournament.

19.8 Competing In a Higher Class—Any individual or team may elect, before firing, to compete in a higher classification than the one in which classified. Such individual or team must fire in such higher class throughout the tournament and not revert to earned classification for any event in that tournament.

When there are insufficient entries in any class to warrant an award in that class according to the match program conditions, the individual or team concerned may be moved by the Tournament Match Director to a higher class provided this change is made prior to the individual or team concerned having commenced firing in the tournament.

19.9 Obsolete Classifications and Scores—All classifications and scores (including temporary, Rule 19.14) except Master, shall become obsolete if the competitor does not fire in NRA competition at least once during 3 successive calendar years. Master classifications and scores shall become obsolete if the competitor does not fire in NRA competition at least once during 5 successive calendar years. Lifetime Master classifications will not become obsolete.

19.10 Appeals—Any competitor having reason to believe that he is improperly classified may file an appeal with the NRA stating all essential facts. Such appeals will be reviewed by the NRA Protest Committee.

19.11 Protests—Any person who believes that another competitor has been improperly classified may file a protest with the NRA stating all essential facts. Such protests will be reviewed by the NRA Protest Committee.

19.12. Team Classification—Teams are classified by computing the "Team Average" based on the classification of each firing member of the team. To compute this "Team Average" the key in Table No. 1 for the different classes will be used for both outdoor and indoor competition and the team total divided by the number of firing members of the team. Any fractional figure in the Team Average of one half or more places team in next higher class. The "Team Average" will establish classification of the team as a unit but will not affect in any way the individual classification of team members.

TABLE NO. I—OUTDOOR AND INDOOR

Class	Key	Class	Key
Master	4	Sharpshooter	2
Expert	3	Marksman	1

19.13 Reporting Scores—NRA indoor and outdoor competition (see Rule 1.6) sponsors will report to the NRA all individual and fired team match scores fired over the courses stated in Rule 19.4. Scores fired in individual matches will be reported as aggregate totals, and scores from fired team matches will be reported as separate aggregate totals. Scores from all tournaments and Sanctioned Leagues will be reported by each sponsor no more than 30 days upon completion of the tournament firing schedule.

19.14 Score Record Book *(Temporary Classification)*—A Score Record Book will be obtained by each unclassified competitor from the Official Referee, Supervisor, or tournament Statistical Office at time competitor competes in his first tournament or from the Secretary of a Sanctioned League. He will record all scores fired by himself in all NRA competition (except Postal Matches) until such time as he receives his Official NRA Classification Card. Competitor will total all scores and divide that total by the number of 10 shot strings represented. The average so obtained will determine the competitor's NRA Classification at that time (see Rule 19.15 for average score for each classification).

Individual and team scores fired by the competitor during at least one tournament (Rule 1.1) or from the most recent league match (Rule 1.6) must be posted in the Score Record Book to establish a temporary classification. The Score Record Book will be presented by the holder at all NRA competitions entered until competitor's Official NRA Classification Card becomes effective.

Note: It is the competitor's responsibility to obtain the Score Record Book, enter scores and present it at each tournament until his Official NRA Classification Card becomes effective. When the NRA Classification Card becomes effective the Score Record Book becomes obsolete.

19.15 Individual Class Averages—Competitors will be classified as follows and NRA Classification Cards issued accordingly:

TABLE NO. II—INDIVIDUAL

(a) Outdoor Conventional Prone—200 shots minimum required for classification.

Master .... .99.50 and above
Expert .... .98.50 to 99.49
Sharpshooter .... .97.50 to 98.49
Marksman .... .Below 97.50

(b) Outdoor Metric Prone—200 shots minimum required for classification.

Master .... .98.00 and above
Expert .... .96.00 to 97.99
Sharpshooter .... .94.00 to 95.99
Marksman .... .Below 94.00

(c) Conventional Position—160 shots minimum required for classification.

Outdoor

Master .... .97.00 and above
Expert .... .94.00 to 96.99
Sharpshooter .... .91.00 to 93.99
Marksman .... .Below 91.00

Indoor

Master .... .98.00 and above
Expert .... .96.50 to 97.99
Sharpshooter .... .93.00 to 96.49
Marksman .... .Below 93.00

(d) NRA 3 Position—120 shots minimum required for classification.

Indoor

Master .... **95.00 and above**
Expert .... **92.00 to 94.99**
Sharpshooter .... **88.00 to 91.99**
Marksman .... **Below 88.00**

Outdoor

Master .... .92.00 and above
Expert .... .87.00 to 91.99
Sharpshooter .... .80.00 to 86.99
Marksman .... .Below 80.00

19.16 Establishing Classification—Classification or reclassification average will be based on average scores reported for 10 shot strings, computed only after the total scores for tournaments, or a league season have been posted and, therefore, the average may be based on a number of shots greater than the required minimum number as specified, When the scores for the required minimum number of shots (or more if the minimum is reached during a tournament, or league season) have been posted the average score per 10 shot string will be computed. The competitor will then be sent an Official NRA Classification Card based on the average so computed and according to the tables for the specific type of competition concerned. This classification will become effective the date shown on the card issued by NRA.

19.17 Reclassification

(a) A competitor who has been classified by the NRA will be reclassified upward when his average, as computed below, places him in a higher class. The scores used for reclassification will be his recorded NRA competition scores as maintained at NRA Headquarters, not previously used for classification purposes. The average will be computed when the scores for the minimum number of shots for reclassification (or more if the minimum is reached during the scores of any tournament or league) have been posted. The reclassified competitor shall be sent a new Classification Card which will become effective the date indicated on the card issued by the NRA.

(b) Minimum posted shots required for upward classification:

(1) Outdoor Conventional and Metric Prone

Reclassified to	Minimum Shots Required
Sharpshooter	400
Expert	400
Master	700

(See Table in Rule 19.15 for percentages)

(2) Outdoor and Indoor Conventional Position

Reclassified to	Minimum Shots Required
Sharpshooter	160
Expert	320
Master	320

(See Table in Rule 19.15 for percentages)

(3) NRA 3-Position Indoor and Outdoor

Reclassified to	Minimum Shots Required
Sharpshooter	120
Expert	240
Master	360

(See Table in Rule 19.15 for percentages)

(c) A competitor who believes his classification too high (Lifetime Master see 19.21) may file a request with the NRA Administrative Staff that his classification be lowered. Such competitor must remain in the class concerned until at least the following have been posted to his record. (These shots must be fired after the effective date of his current classification):

Outdoor Conventional or Metric Prone Reclassification—1200 Record Shots

Outdoor or Indoor Conventional Position Reclassification—960 Record Shots

NRA 3 Position Reclassification—960 Record Shots

When the average of such shots places the competitor in a lower class he will be reclassified accordingly.

(d) If a competitor thus reclassified downward, and thereafter, by scores fired in NRA competition (except NRA Postal Matches), again earns a higher classification, he shall not again be reclassified downward.

19.21 Lifetime Master—Competitors who have been certified as Lifetime Masters will retain their Lifetime Master cards and enter competitions in the Master Class, except that,

(a) No new Lifetime Masters will be certified.

(b) Lifetime Masters will be reclassified to a higher class, according to the provisions of Rule 19.17 (b) and must enter competitions in the higher class. (Does not pertain to smallbore rifle competition at this time.)

(c) Lifetime Masters may petition NRA to revoke a Lifetime Master card and be reclassified downward according to the provisions of Rule 19.17 (c).

23. PROVISIONAL LIGHT RIFLE RULES

NOTE: These Rules are provided for the conduct of Light Rifle Competition. Scores fired in this competition will be used for classification but there will be no National Records compiled.

In all cases where specific Rules are not given here, the appropriate Rules for Smallbore Rifle Competition shall be used.

In Light Rifle Competition, the goal is to achieve the highest possible score within the confines of the allowed equipment.

3.3 Light Rifle—Any rifle chambered for .22 caliber rimfire rifle cartridges only, a trigger pull of not less than two (2) pounds and weighs not more than seven and one-half (7½) pounds complete with sights, standard safety features and accessories. An adjustable butt plate placed in the center position may be used and adjustable or custom butt plates shall not extend beyond the top or bottom of the stock and shall not exceed a maximum length of six (6) inches. Barrel weights must evenly surround the barrel and not hang below. Slings (Rule 3.13), palm rests (Rule 3.14), Schuetzen type butt plates (Rule 3.15) and electric or adjustable fore-end bedding devices are not permitted. Any sights (Rule 3.7c) will be used as long as total weight of rifle and sights does not exceed seven and one-half (7½) pounds. An eye shield may be attached to the rear sight.

The same rifle must be used throughout all stages of any one match except in case of a disabled rifle (Rule 9.10) or malfunction (Rule 9.11) the competitor may change rifles with the permission of the Chief Range Officer.

NOTE: Tournament sponsors are authorized to restrict competitors to the use of only bolt action rifles if required by range regulations.

3.12 Clothing—Padding is permitted on the shoulders and elbows of the shooting coat provided no padding extends below four (4) inches from the elbow joint. The coat may be to a maximum of hip-length with no straps or other provisions for tightening or constructed with any material intended to make the shoulders or other parts more rigid. Shoes shall be a matched pair and may not be designed or altered in any way so as to provide artificial support. Competitors may shoot with or without shoes.

4.4 Targets—N.R.A. Official Targets will be used.

50 Feet A-32—Two (2) shots may be fired on each record bullseye.

50 Yard A-31x (experimental)—5 shot may be fired on each record bullseye.

Backing cards shall be used in N.R.A. Registered Competition.

5.14 Positions Authorized for Light Rifle Competition—Prone (Rule 5.6), Kneeling (Rule 5.10) and Standing (Rule 5.12). NOTE: Tournament sponsors may elect to delete the last sentence in Rule 5.12 and require that the forward hand be extended so that the forward arm will be entirely free from touching or resting against the body. If this election is made it must be so stated in the tournament program.

7.7 Light Rifle Prone, Indoor and Outdoor Courses

Distance	No. of Shots	Time
50 Feet or 50 Yards	20,30,60 or 120	1 Min. per record shot
Targets: NRA Official A-32, or A-31x.		

Aggregates as desired by the Tournament Sponsor.

Team Matches: Teams may consist of 2 or 4 firing members with 20 or 40 shots to be fired by each member.

7.8 Light Rifle 3-Position, Indoor and Outdoor Courses

Distance	No. of Shots	Time
50 Feet or 50 Yards	30 (10 each position)	1½ Min. per record shot
50 Feet or 50 Yards	60 (20 each position)	1½ Min. per record shot
50 Feet or 50 Yards	120 (40 each position)	1½ Min. per record shot

Targets: NRA Official A-32, or A-31x.

Aggregates as desired by the Tournament Sponsor.

Team Matches: Teams may consist of 2 or 4 firing members with 30 shots (10 in each position) or sixty shots (20 in each position) to be fired by each team member.

7.9 Light Rifle Standing, Indoor and Outdoor Courses:

Distance	No. of shots	Time
50 Feet or 50 Yards	20,40,60,80 or 100	1½ min. per record shot

Targets: NRA official A-32, or A-31x.

Aggregates as desired by the tournament sponsor.

Team Matches: Teams may consist of 2 or 4 firing members with 20 or 40 shots to be fired by each member.

19.4 *A. Light Rifle Prone Classification*

Scores fired either indoor or outdoor, in any course of fire listed in Rule 7.7 or any combination of these courses.

B. Light Rifle 3-Position Classification

Scores fired, either indoor or outdoor, in any course of fire listed in Rule 7.8. (Scores must include an equal number of shots in each position.)

C. Light Rifle Standing Classification

Scores fired, either indoor or outdoor, in only standing position.

19.6 *(j)* Light Rifle Prone

19.6 *(k)* Light Rifle 3-Position

19.15 *(e)* Light Rifle Prone (Indoor and outdoor combined)—90 shots minimum required for classification.

Master	98 and above
Expert	96 to 97.99
Sharpshooter	94 to 95.99
Marksman	Below 94.00

19.15 *(f)* Light Rifle 3-Position (Indoor and outdoor combined)—120 shots minimum required for classification.

Master	94.00 and above
Expert	92.00 to 93.99
Sharpshooter	87.50 to 91.99
Marksman	Below 87.50

19.15 *(g)* Light Rifle Standing (Indoor and outdoor combined)—100 shots minimum required for classification.

Master	94.00 and above
Expert	92.00 to 93.99
Sharpshooter	87.50 to 91.99
Marksman	Below 87.50

19.17b *(4)* Light Rifle— A competitor must have fired a minimum of 180 shots Prone, 200 shots Standing or 240 shots in 3-Position in NRA Approved or Registered Competition to be eligible for an advance in classification.

Index